THE WEB *OF* TRANSPORT CORRIDORS *IN* SOUTH ASIA

THE **WEB** *OF* **TRANSPORT CORRIDORS** *IN* **SOUTH ASIA**

Contents

BOXES

FIGURES

MAPS

PHOTOS

TABLES

Acknowledgments

The preparation of this report was led by Martin Melecky (World Bank), together with Arjun Goswami (ADB), Akio Okamura (JICA), and Duncan Overfield (DFID). Annette Dixon (World Bank) and Juan Miranda (ADB) played a key role in putting this partnership effort in motion. Martin Rama (World Bank) provided technical guidance throughout the process.

The World Bank core team comprised Martin Melecky, Matias Herrera Dappe, Mark Roberts, Siddharth Sharma, Muneeza Alam, Theophile Bougna, Yan (Sarah) Xu, Robin Carruthers, Hari Subhash, Ruifan Shi, Akib Khan, Nathalie Barboza, and Esther Bartl.

The ADB core team comprised Arjun Goswami, Jayant Menon, Premachandra Athukorala, Peter Warr, Archanun Kohpaiboon, Suresh Narayanan, Anna Cassandra Melendez, Victoria Corpuz, and Ruth Francisco.

The DFID core team comprised Peter Frankopan, Manish Vasistha, Roger Vickerman, Richard Bullock, and Duncan Overfield.

The JICA core team comprised Akio Okamura, Takayuki Urade, Yumi Ito, and Miwa Hiasa.

Contributors to the spotlights and boxes included Yan (Sarah) Xu, Martin Humphreys, Dominic Pasquale Patella, Daniel Sebastian Perea Rojas, Martin Melecky, Arnaud Dornel, Michel Noel, Catherine Asekenye Barasa, Stephen Muzira, Toshiaki Ono, Juan Buchenau, Panos Varangis, Mark Roberts, Vasudha Thawakar, and Roland White.

We thank for suggestions and comments Akihiko Nishio, Marianne Fay, William Maloney, Robert J. Saum, Baher El-Hifnawi, Hun Kim, Yasuyuki Sawada, Juzhong Zhuang, Ronald Butiong, Safdar Parvez, Alfredo Perdiguero, Ying Qian, Kenichi Yokoyama, Xiaohong Yang, Rana Hasan, Jong Woo Kang, Cuong Minh Nguyen, Utsav Kumar, Kavita Iyengar, Kristian Rosbach, Elizabeth Jones, Jaya Singh Verma, Arielle Dove, Koki Hirota, Naohiro Kitano, Toru Arai, Shuntaro Kawahara, Kazumasa Sanui, Akiko Sanada, Koji Yamada, Tomohide Ichiguchi, Katsuo Matsumoto, Kunihiro Nakasone, Takuro Takeuchi, Tatsuya Asami,

Charles Kunaka, Debora Revooltella, Adam Storeyard, Stephane Straub, Homi Kharas, Jean Francois Arvis, Hatem Chahbani, Uwe Deichmann, Ejaz Ghani, Somik Lall, Harris Selod, Forhad Shilpi, Luc Lecuit, Gerald Paul Ollivier, Andrew Beath, Vincent Palmade, Sanjay Srivastana, Janardan Prasad Singh, Simon Alder, Karla Gonzalez Gravajal, Ming Zhang, Catalina Marulanda, Esperanza Lasagabaster, Samuel Maimbo, and Toshiya Masuoka.

Special thanks go to the following task team leaders of transport projects, who were interviewed during the preparation of the report, for their valuable responses: Martin Humphreys, Olivier le Ber, Jacques Bure, Rodrigo Archondo-Callao, Ben Eijbergen, Simon Ellis, Diep Niguyen-Van Houtte, Martha Lawrence, Henry Des Longchamps, Jean-Francois Marteau, Graham Smith, Andreas Schliessler, and Xiaoke Zhai.

Help with logistics and organizing focus groups interviews in Bhutan, India, and Sri Lanka was provided by Rathnija Arandara, Poorna Bhattacharjee, Varsha Marathe Dayal, Shanuki Gunasekera, Anoma Kulathunga, Aphichoke Kotikula, Ugyen Lham, Nagasubramanian Kodimangalam Sundaram, Mohamed Asan Saleem, Jayati Sethi, Ashutosh Tandon, Neelam Chowdhry, and Yann Doignon.

The report benefitted from the stimulating discussion of its main messages by the panel comprising Ahsan Iqbal (Minister, Pakistan), Harsha de Silva (Deputy Minister, Sri Lanka), Yasser Rizvi (Alliance Holding, Bangladesh), and Fatema Sumar (Regional Deputy Vice President, Millennium Challenge Corporation).

The report was edited by Nancy Morrison. Barbara Koeppel edited the spotlights.

Financial support from Australia's Department of Foreign Affairs and Trade is gratefully acknowledged.

In producing this report, the World Bank emphasizes that regional cooperation and connectivity initiatives and projects shall respect the sovereignty of the countries involved, and notes that the findings and conclusions in the report may not reflect the views of individual countries concerned by these initiatives and projects.

Abbreviations

ABM	agent-based modeling
ADB	Asian Development Bank
ALM	asset-liability management
APTC	Asia Pacific Transport Consortium
ASEAN	Association of South East Asian Nations
BKIP	Batu Kawan Industrial Park
BOI	Board of Investment
BOOT	build-own-operate-transfer
BOT	build-operate-transfer
CAS	Country Assistance Strategy
CBA	cost-benefit analysis
CEO	chief executive officer
CGE	computable general equilibrium
CPEC	China-Pakistan Economic Corridor
CPIA	Country Policy and Institutional Assessment
CSO	civil society organization
CTRL	Channel Tunnel Rail Link
DBFM	design-build-finance-maintain
DFC	Dedicated Freight Corridor
DID	difference-in-difference
DPA	Dayton Peace Accord
DPO	Development Policy Operation
DSCR	debt service coverage ratio
EC	European Commission
ECER	East Coast Economic Region
EE	electronics and electrical
EIA	environmental impact assessment
EIB	European Investment Bank
EIC	East India Company
ELA	Empowerment and Livelihoods Assistance

EPU	Economic Planning Unit
ESDP	Eastern Seaboard Development Plan
ESIA	Environmental and Social Impact Assessment
ESMP	Environmental and Social Management Plan
EU	European Union
FASRB	Framework Agreement on the Sava River Basin
FBH	Federation of Bosnia and Herzegovina
FDI	foreign direct investment
FVS	financial viability support
GBV	gender-based violence
GE	general equilibrium
GIPR	Great Indian Peninsula Railway
GKC	Greater Kamunting Conurbation
GPI	Governance Performance Index
GQ	Golden Quadrilateral
GSDP	Global Supplier Development Programme
HSR	high-speed rail
IBRD	International Bank for Reconstruction and Development
ICR	Implementation Completion and Results
IDA	International Development Association
IEAT	Industrial Estate Authority of Thailand
IEG	Independent Evaluation Group
IIDF	India Infrastructure Debt Fund
IIGF	Indonesia Infrastructure Guarantee Fund
IM	Iskandar Malaysia
IOTC	International Organization of Tuna Council
IPA	Instrument for Pre-Accession
ISRBC	International Sava River Basin Commission
JFCU	Joy for Children Uganda
JICA	Japan International Cooperation Agency
KDTC	Kolkata-Dhaka transport corridor
KHTP	Kulim Hi-Tech Park
KSTP	Kedah Science and Technology Park
LCR	London Continental Railway
LPG	liquified petroleum gas
LVC	land value capture
M&E	monitoring and evaluation
MCC	Maputo Corridor Company
MCLI	Maputo Corridor Logistics Initiative
MIDA	Malaysian Industrial Development Authority
MIGA	Multilateral International Guarantee Agency
MRA	meta-regression analysis
MSME	micro, small, and medium-sized enterprise
MTR	Mass Transit Railway
NCER	Northern Corridor Economic Region
NCIA	Northern Corridor Implementation Authority
NEG	new economic geography
NEN	National Expressway Network
NHAI	National Highways Authority of India

NIIF	National Investment and Infrastructure Fund
NPA	nonperforming asset
NPDC	Nord-Pas-de-Calais
NRB	Nepal Rastra Bank
NSEW	North–South–East–West
NSS	National Sample Survey
NTSC	National Traffic Safety Committee
ODA	official development assistance
OECD	Organisation for Economic Co-operation and Development
OHR	Office of the High Representative
OLS	ordinary least squares
PE	private equity
PIP	Perlis Inland Port Project
PPA	Project Preparation Advance
PPI	Private Participation in Infrastructure
PPP	public-private partnership
PSDC	Penang Skill Development Centre
R&D	research and development
RA	research assistant
RDDBFI	Recovery of Debts Due to Banks and Financial Institutions
RF	reduced form
RGC	regional growth center
RS	Republika Srpska
SARFAESI	Securitization and Reconstruction of Financial Assets and Enforcement of Security Interests
SBI	State Bank of India
SCORE	Sarawak Corridor of Renewable Energy
SDC	Sabah Development Corridor
SDI	spatial development initiative
SIF	Strategic Investment Fund
SME	small or medium-sized enterprise
SOE	state-owned enterprise
SPSEE	Stability Pact for Southeastern Europe
SPV	special purpose vehicle
SRF	Silk Road Fund
STD	sexually transmitted disease
TFP	total factor productivity
TSDP	Transport Sector Development Project
TVET	Technical and Vocational Education Training
UNDP	United Nations Development Programme
UNRA	Uganda National Roads Authority
VAC	Violence Against Children
VAR	vector autoregression
VAT	value-added tax
VOC	vehicle operating cost
VRA	Vietnam Road Administration
WEB	wider economic benefits
WGI	Worldwide Governance Indicator
WITS	World Integrated Trade Solution

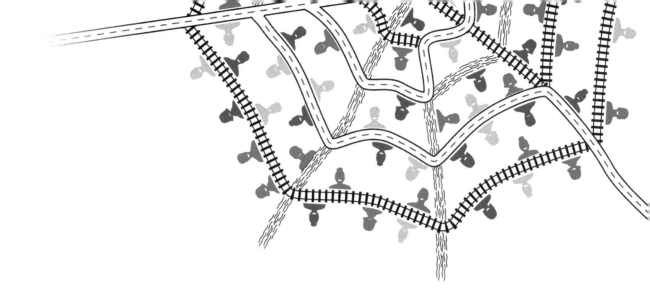

Overview

Developing large transport infrastructure projects—transport corridors—is increasingly seen as a way to stimulate regional integration and economic growth. Countries, often with the help of the international community, invest in these corridors in the hope of creating large economic surpluses that can spread throughout the economy and society. But if the corridors do not generate the expected surpluses, they can become wasteful white elephants—transport infrastructure without much traffic.

Recent international experience reveals both successes and failures. Vietnam, for instance, developed National Highway No. 5 in the 1990s to establish an effective transport corridor between the capital Hanoi and the port of Hai Phong. This investment, on the back of reforms in the business environment and investments in human capital, fostered prosperity in the populous Red River Delta region. From 1995 to 2000, the poverty rate fell by an impressive 35 percent, outpacing the national average of 27 percent (JICA 2009). In contrast, traffic volume has remained low on the multi-country Greater Mekong Subregion (GMS) corridor (ADB 2008; Srivastava and Kumar 2012).

Even when corridors generate aggregate surpluses, a relevant question is whether the net benefits are fairly distributed across the population. If they are not, corridors risk becoming inequitable investments. The end-nodes of a transport corridor may benefit more than the transit regions and countries it crosses. Along the corridor itself, people with different skill endowments may benefit differently, and farming households along the corridor may be at a disadvantage if their land tenure is not secure.

In China, for instance, the construction of the National Express Network (NEN) increased real income across its prefectures by nearly 4 percent, *on average*—but still decreased real wages in many prefectures in either the urban or rural sector (Roberts et al. 2012). Only when transport corridors share prosperity widely, not only creating winners but also not leaving behind losers, can they spur equitable growth and help reduce poverty.

Many corridor initiatives are under way or are being proposed, both in South Asia and around the world (map O.1). One ambitious proposal is to revive the Grand Trunk Road from Kabul, Afghanistan, to Chittagong, Bangladesh, connecting areas that are home to a significant share of the world's poor. Even more ambitious could be the plan for the New Silk Road Economic Belt. This very large transport corridor connects Beijing all the way to Brussels. It also branches out into South Asian countries, as is the case with the China-Pakistan Economic Corridor initiative.

The investments associated with these and other proposed initiatives could require trillions of dollars. Such an amount exceeds the financial resources available in the foreseeable future to support corridors. Moreover, it

MAP O.1   **Many large transport investments are proposed across South Asia**

a. The proposed One Road One Belt Initiative by China

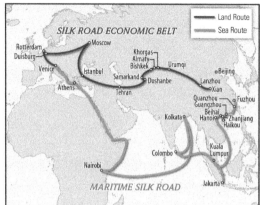

b. The possible transport corridor from Mumbai to Shanghai

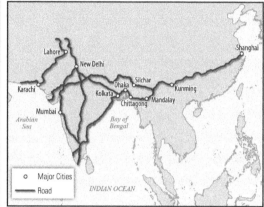

c. The 19 regional road corridors identified by JICA around Bhutan, Bangladesh, East India, Myanmar, and Nepal

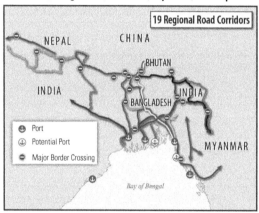

d. The 14 regional railway corridors identified by JICA around Bhutan, Bangladesh, East India, Myanmar, and Nepal

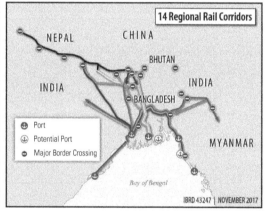

Source: Corridor Study Team.

risks crowding out other public investment in critical areas such as education, water and sanitation, or energy. By a conservative estimate, from 2014 to 2020 South Asia needs to invest at least $1.7 trillion in infrastructure (Andrés, Biller, and Herrera Dappe 2013). This is just to catch up with developing country peers, whose infrastructure may also be below "optimal" levels.

FROM TRANSPORT TO WIDER ECONOMIC BENEFITS

Given the huge resource cost and the high stakes, national governments and the international community need to think clearly about how to prioritize proposals for corridor investments, and specifically, how to select the more promising ones over the less promising or potentially wasteful ones. A clear understanding of what constitutes a transport corridor is an important first step in this direction (box O.1). Even more important is to focus on economic analysis, and not only on geopolitical considerations.

Decisions concerning transport corridors are understandably influenced by strategic aspirations, as well as by concerns about security. Various scholars offer interpretations that emphasize this geopolitical dimension. For example, according to Chatterjee and

BOX 0.1 Categorizing transport corridor connections

Transport connectivity can be categorized by the types of location that the transport infrastructure connects. Four main types of connections can be considered:

- *Urban-urban* transport corridors connect two or more urban centers or cities.
- *Urban-gateway* corridors connect urban centers with international gateways (an international port, a major land border crossing, or an airport that provides a gateway to international markets).
- *Rural-urban* transport connections link rural areas to urban centers. These types of transport connections are typically auxiliary (feeder roads, rails) linking to trunk (main) transport investments.

- *Rural-gateway* connections, in practice comprise a combination of Rural-urban and Urban-gateway connections.
- Purely *rural-rural* connections are typically not considered part of transport corridors, as they do not link to the trunk transport investments.

For some countries, most notably the landlocked ones, cross-country corridors cutting through their territory could run the risk of serving mostly as transit connections. To make the most of the cross-country connectivity, "transit" countries may need to focus on the feeder network and complementary reforms to generate and spread local socioeconomic benefits from such transit transport corridors.

MAP B0.1.1 Possible types of transport corridors (connections)

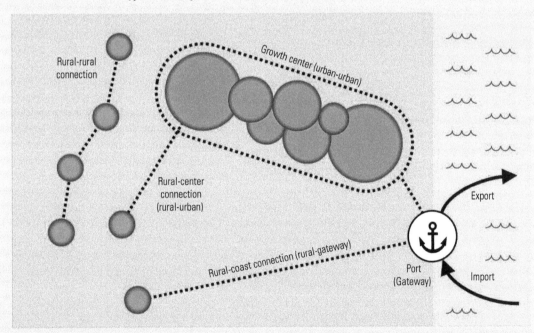

Source: Corridor Study Team.
Note: The size of the bubble corresponds to the size of the economy.

Singh (2015), India's Foreign Trade Policy for 2015–20 has highlighted the importance of the International North-South Transport Corridor in expanding India's trade and investment links with Central Asia. Ordabayev (2015, 2016) points out the competing geopolitical interests of India, China, the Russian Federation, Europe, the United States, Turkey, and Iran in Central Asia, and how they relate to decisions on transport corridor connectivity, trade, and energy. Palit (2017) discusses India's uneasy economic and strategic perceptions of China's Maritime Silk Road Initiative. And Shephard (2017) analyzes whether India and Japan have joined forces to counter China and build their own New Silk Road, in another geopolitical move.

While geopolitical considerations are certainly legitimate, they also bring risks. Some of the proposed corridors could become either white elephant investments or inequitable public investments that benefit narrow groups at the expense of national taxpayers. Risks could be even higher for smaller landlocked countries that could bear the cost of sizeable investments but see themselves become mere transit passageways. In South Asia, the landlocked countries are Afghanistan, Bhutan and Nepal. Several Central Asian countries also belong in that group.

Only when transport corridors generate wider local benefits can they be considered economic corridors.

An equally important risk is missing the "right" corridors that yield the greatest wider economic benefits (WEB) just because they do not fit the prevailing geopolitical views. Arguably, the transport corridor with the greatest economic potential is the surface link between Shanghai and Mumbai. These two cities are the economic hubs of China and India respectively, two emerging global powers. The distance between them, about 5,000 kilometers, is not much greater than the distance between New York and Los Angeles. But instead of crossing a relatively empty continent, a corridor from Shanghai to Mumbai—via Kunming, Mandalay, Dhaka,

and Kolkata—would go through some of the most densely populated and most dynamic areas in the world, stoking hopes of large economic impacts and many positive spillovers.

This report aims to balance the political economy and geopolitics of transport corridors with sound empirical analysis. Its goal is to empower key stakeholders—policy makers, economic advisors, businesses, and civil society organizations—in assessing socioeconomic benefits when considering the idea of investing in a transport corridor.

To that end, this report provides a conceptual framework to think about economic corridors and to enable a holistic appraisal of program and project proposals. The framework extends beyond the immediate effects of transport corridors—such as reducing vehicle operating costs—and focuses on the ultimate goals of having a positive impact on local economic activity, jobs, gender equality, and poverty reduction, among other desirable socioeconomic outcomes. It also helps think about negative impacts such as traffic congestion, regressive redistribution, social exclusion, environmental degradation, and other risks or unintended consequences. An important building block in this framework is to define transport corridors in an operational way (box O.2).

The framework extends to consider how well different markets—such as capital, labor, land, and product markets—function around transport corridors. In doing so, it helps determine which policy interventions might be needed to strengthen markets and maximize the potential for larger gains from transport corridors. Moreover, the framework seeks to advance the understanding of the institutions that can help the economy adjoining transport corridors evolve into prosperous and inclusive communities. It examines how incentives could be aligned to promote healthy business competition and create better jobs.

Using this framework, the report studies the conditions under which large-scale investments in transport infrastructure can generate positive spillovers on local household income, jobs, equity, and poverty reduction. It also

BOX 0.2   Defining transport corridors at the project level

For the purpose of this Report, only investments in roads, rail, or inland waterways are considered as possible transport corridor investments. In general, roads, railways, and waterways are distinctly geographically defined. They also have clearer economic spillovers along their stretches compared with, for instance, airways or maritime routes. However, the findings and recommendations of the Report could extend to air, sea, and other types of transport corridors.

At a project level, an investment is classified as a *transport corridor* if:

• The transport investment is being made on a route that is creating, upgrading, or rehabilitating at least 100 linear kilometers, or

• The value of the project at appraisal is greater than $50 million and the investment is financing a critical link in the corridor (such as a new bridge or tunnel) that connects at least two economic centers.

The transport corridor projects considered in the analyses for this Report satisfy at least one of these two criteria.

These criteria are designed to identify projects that have the potential to enhance the regional connectivity of a country or a set of countries. The projects do not need to be geographically continuous, but they need to be part of a set of road, rail, or waterway routes connecting two locations. As an example, the roads marked in red and pink in map BO.2.1 qualify as linear kilometers, but the roads marked in blue do not.

MAP BO.2.1   An illustration of linear kilometers

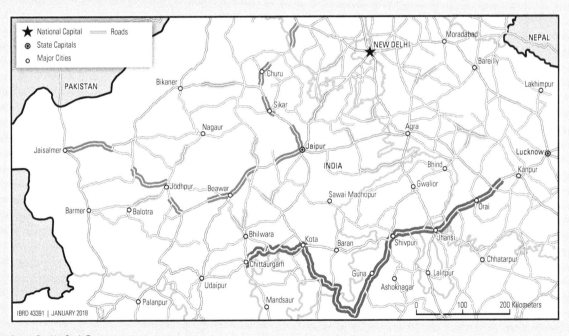

Source: Corridor Study Team.
Note: The roads marked in red and pink are linear kilometers, but the roads marked in blue are not.

studies potential trade-offs that policy makers could face and discusses how to manage them—such as increasing income at the expense of deteriorating environmental quality—using complementary policies and institutions.

To establish a comprehensive knowledge base for its recommendations, the Report includes case studies of past and recent corridor initiatives—such as Japan's Pacific Ocean Belt Initiative, Europe's High-Speed Rail Network, and Vietnam's National Highway No. 5. These are combined with a systematic review of the existing literature on the spatial impacts of corridors, and assessments of corridor investment projects supported by international development organizations.

Building on this integrative approach, and relying on spatially granular data, the Report conducts illustrative appraisals of three major transport corridors in South Asia. These are the completed Golden Quadrilateral and North-South-East-West highway systems in India; the planned China-Pakistan Economic Corridor in Pakistan; and the anticipated Kolkata-Dhaka transport corridor between India and Bangladesh.

A series of spotlights focus on selected facets of transport corridors. Some concern impacts on specific groups, such as micro, small, and medium-sized enterprises (MSMEs); women in Bhutan, India, and Sri Lanka; and groups seeking finance to take advantage of the opportunities generated by better connectivity to markets. Other spotlights discuss the challenges in engaging the private sector to co-invest in corridors at different stages of their development, or through different financial vehicles, in both South Asia and around the world. One spotlight assesses in more detail the potential of modern spatial econometrics to rigorously appraise investment proposals for transport corridors. Two other spotlights focus on the lessons learned from implementing cross-border transport corridors and on the risks that the influx of construction workers present for local women.

This Report recognizes that transport corridor interventions can generate a chain of multiple impacts beyond the travel time and vehicle operating costs that are the focus of traditional cost-benefit analyses. Transport corridor interventions have the potential to affect broader socioeconomic outcomes. Their economic impacts work through agglomeration effects, increased trade and migration, and changes in the local economic structure, among other areas. These long-term impacts ultimately yield WEB—such as the growth of income and consumption, new jobs, and greater equity.

The economic boom of 1920–29 in India provides an illustration of these WEB. By then, more than 66,000 kilometers of railway lines were in operation, carrying over 620 million passengers and 90 million tons of goods each year. Some academics have argued that the impact of the railways during this period was mixed because of the limited development of other infrastructure (Chandra 2006). But a recent study with a rigorous methodology finds that the extension of the railroad network increased real agricultural income by about 16 percent (Donaldson 2010).

Not all impacts of a transport corridors and their spillovers may be beneficial, however. While improving one development outcome (such as income), these investments could worsen another one (such as environmental quality).

An example is Japan from 1960 to 1970, at the time of the major effort to double the country's income. A key component of this initiative was the development of the Pacific Belt Zone, which increased the total shipment value of goods almost fourfold (from ¥24.7 trillion to ¥94.4 trillion, in 2005 prices). However, rapid industrialization also resulted in serious negative impacts in the form of environmental degradation and pollution (map O.2). The incidence of bronchial asthma and other diseases soared in the Pacific Belt Zone. Following several major disease outbreaks caused by water contamination, Japan was recognized worldwide as a "Paradise of Pollution." In the early 1970s, litigation favored plaintiffs for all four of the major pollution-related diseases. Since then, Japan has undertaken a full-scale effort to protect the environment.

MAP 0.2   The trade-offs generated by the Pacific Ocean Belt in Japan yield valuable lessons

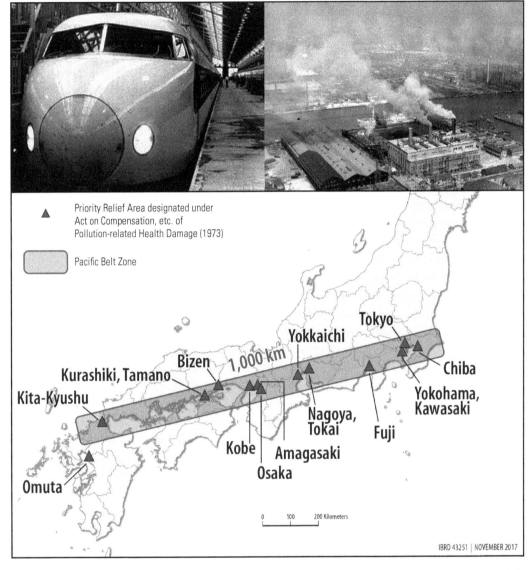

Source: Corridor Study Team. Photos by World Bank (upper left); Kanagawa Environmental Research Center, Japan (upper right). Used with permission; further permission required for reuse.

At the same time, well-designed corridor interventions can generate synergies that mitigate these potential trade-offs. For instance, by switching to more fuel-efficient and pooled transportation, income and environmental quality can improve together in some locations.

Evidence from the Golden Quadrilateral highway system in India supports this rationale.

There, the impact was different across districts depending on the educational attainment of their population. More educated districts connected to the transport corridor enjoyed both higher income growth and a lower level of air pollution (as measured by the density of aerosol particles) than their less educated counterparts (Melecky, Sharma, and Subhash, forthcoming).

Corridors may create both winners and losers, but well-designed corridor programs can help share the benefits more widely

Across locations and population groups, initial conditions can affect the predisposition to benefit from better transport connectivity. Even on a single development outcome (such as jobs), some households and some places could win, and others could lose. For instance, more educated and skilled people can migrate to obtain better jobs in growing urban areas that are benefiting from corridor connectivity, while unskilled workers may be left behind in depopulated rural areas with few economic prospects. Corridors can thus create both winners and losers.

In India, for example, farmers along the Delhi-Mumbai corridor have voiced unhappiness about the structural transformation from agriculture to manufacturing and services that is taking place along the way (map O.3). It has been argued that this transformation

has put them at a disadvantage (Kumar 2015). Benefits for this group are bound to be higher in a context where agribusiness is more developed, and farmers can connect to value-added chains boosting their income and helping them diversify their production.

Geographically, the Report focuses on South Asia—not just as one of the world's most populous and poorest regions—but prominently as a hinge between East Asia, Central Asia, the Middle East, and Europe. This focus derives from a grander vision for South Asia that also presents a challenge. South Asia has the potential to be the world's next middle-income region. Connecting it to East Asia (including through Southeast Asia) can transform it into an engine of global growth. But South Asia could also stand to lose if it were circumvented, or the "right" corridors were missed.

Assessing the potential for functioning international connectivity requires a forward-looking, holistic perspective. The future success of smaller corridors critically depends on their

MAP O.3   Some farmers along the Delhi-Mumbai Corridor fear being uprooted

a. Connectivity of India's districts to the Golden Quadrilateral highway system around 2011

b. Connectivity of India's districts to the North-South-East-West highway system around 2011

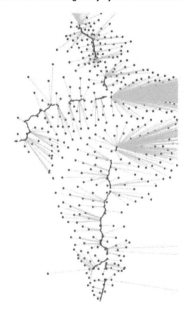

Source: Corridor Study Team for maps and calculations of connectivity.

ability to integrate into cross-border, transregional, and transcontinental corridors.

ACHIEVING WIDER ECONOMIC BENEFITS: FIT-2-DEEDS

Policy makers should aim to maximize the wider economic benefits of a proposed transport corridor investment, considering benefits net of costs. This *policy-maker's problem* can play out at different levels: local (for subnational units such as states, provinces or districts), national, and international.

The framework proposed by the Report to think through the policy-maker's problem, and guide holistic appraisals of proposed programs (projects) on transport corridors, builds on six elements. For ease of communication, these six elements are summarized in the acronym "FIT-2-Deeds." The "FIT" in this acronym refers to the Flow of expected results, the Intervention design, and the Typology of impacts. The "2" stands for two sorts of complementary public interventions, and the twin Deeds are financing and implementing the corridor.

"F": The "Flow" of expected results— The chain from corridor to benefits

Several potential transmission mechanisms and associated intermediate outcomes help predict the ultimate impact of a corridor intervention on a relevant set of final outcomes. The more favorable these outcomes are, the larger is the ratio of benefits to cost. Large WEB, net of costs, should be the *policymakers'* ultimate objective. The framework in this Report considers five categories of WEB: economic welfare, social inclusion, equity, environmental quality, and economic resilience. The potential transmission mechanisms from a corridor intervention package through intermediate outcomes to wider economic benefits can be summarized in a Flow (chain) of expected results (figure O.1.).

A corridor intervention can *directly* affect the final outcomes (WEB net of costs) given other *complementary factors* that affect many aspects of the economy at the same time. These complementary factors could comprise initial conditions in local product markets, such as the degree of business competition. They can also relate to the operation of markets for land, labor, and capital. For instance, they may refer to land-use restrictions, the availability of skilled labor, and access to credit. This direct impact can vary from beneficial to detrimental across individual outcomes, and vary considerably across locations and population groups.

A corridor intervention can also affect the final outcomes *indirectly*, by modifying the complementary factors. For instance, if the corridor reduces commuting and migration costs, it also reduces frictions in the labor market, which in turn can increase the local availability of skilled labor, overall employment, and household income. These indirect changes of complementary factors are called *intermediate outcomes*. The impact of the corridor on intermediate outcomes can also vary from beneficial to detrimental across the individual outcomes considered.

Knowledge of the direct and indirect impacts, the trade-offs they could produce, and the complementary policies that could help manage these trade-offs, can all improve the design of a corridor intervention.

"I": The "Intervention" design— Supporting a fairer distribution of greater benefits

Policy makers deliberate about corridor features such as location, length, and mode of transport infrastructure for the transport corridor project. But they may also consider complementary policies and institutions that can help amplify the expected WEB. These complementary interventions need to account for the constraints imposed by initial conditions, including geography, population density, market imperfections, and inequality of opportunity.

The chosen set of interventions can be characterized by different levels of ambition,

FIGURE O.1   **WEB are achieved through various transmission channels and intermediate outcomes**

Intermediate
outcomes

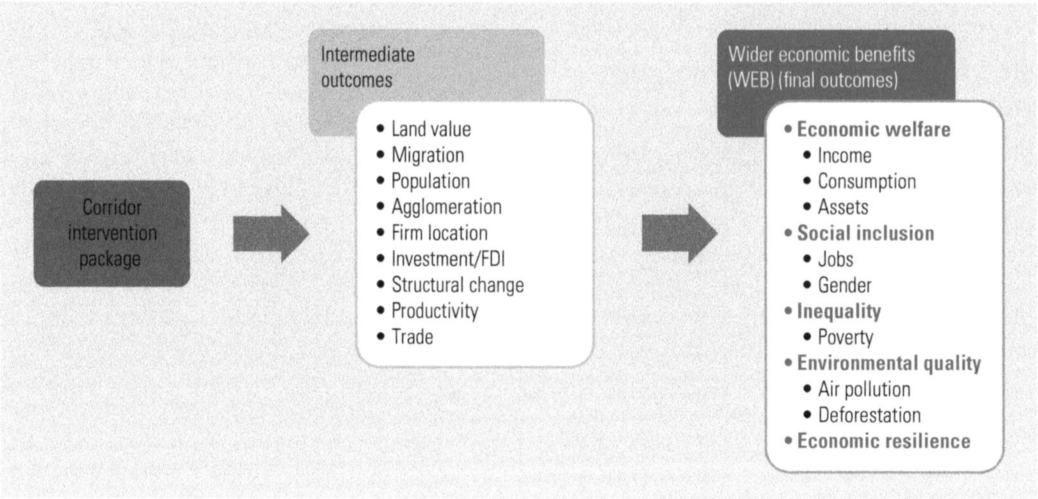

Corridor
intervention
package

- Land value
- Migration
- Population
- Agglomeration
- Firm location
- Investment/FDI
- Structural change
- Productivity
- Trade

Wider economic benefits
(WEB) (final outcomes)

- **Economic welfare**
  - Income
  - Consumption
  - Assets
- **Social inclusion**
  - Jobs
  - Gender
- **Inequality**
  - Poverty
- **Environmental quality**
  - Air pollution
  - Deforestation
- **Economic resilience**

Source: Corridor Study Team.
Note: FDI = foreign direct investment.

FIGURE O.2   **The corridor program can include trade facilitation measures, as well as soft complementary policies**

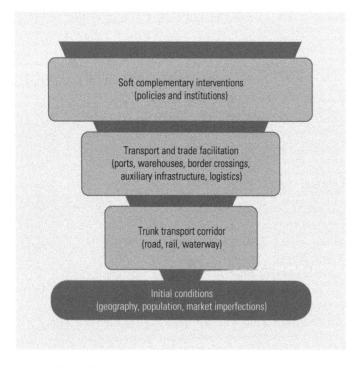

Soft complementary interventions
(policies and institutions)

Transport and trade facilitation
(ports, warehouses, border crossings,
auxiliary infrastructure, logistics)

Trunk transport corridor
(road, rail, waterway)

Initial conditions
(geography, population, market imperfections)

Source: Corridor Study Team.

from the most basic to the most comprehensive (figure O.2):

1. *Investments in trunk transport corridors.* This entails building entirely new transport infrastructure, such as roads, rail, or inland waterways. It may also involve upgrading individual links or entire segments of existing ones.

2. *Transport and trade facilitation services.* Benefits from narrow investments in a trunk transport corridor can be enhanced by simultaneous investments and reforms in enabling transport services and policies. It may also be supported by trade facilitation measures. The regulation of the trucking industry belongs in the first group; the establishment of warehouses and border crossings belongs in the second.

3. *"Soft" complementary interventions.* Benefits from improved regional connectivity can be further enhanced if the project design also addresses the most binding market imperfections and institutional failures. Policy interventions could aim to ensure efficient functioning of capital, labor, land and

product markets, or improve institutions such as public sector governance, contract enforcement, or access to social services.

Policy makers and other stakeholders may want to know which particular features of corridors and which complementary policies and institutions need to receive greater weight. The choice of the mode of transportation, or the length, location, and nodal connections of the corridor, could be its decisive characteristics. But land market reforms, improved access to finance, and regulatory improvements in product markets could also make the greatest difference. The answer is likely to depend on initial conditions, from population density to the certainty of land titling or the extent and state of any preexisting transport infrastructure.

"T": The "Typology" of impacts—Organizing multiple impacts into a hierarchy

A transport corridor intervention has potential socioeconomic impacts across multiple WEB. In some cases, these impacts may be positively correlated. For instance, the corridor could boost both incomes and job creation. In other words, the corridor intervention could create *synergies* in development impacts, producing beneficial effects for both economic welfare and social inclusion. However, in other cases, the impacts may be negatively correlated. For instance, economic welfare impacts may be beneficial, but environmental impacts may be detrimental. This leads to *trade-offs* between different outcomes.

Impacts may also be *heterogeneous*. That is, for a given outcome, they could vary significantly across different geographic areas, segments of the population, economic sectors, and the like. These varied impacts may benefit everybody, but vary in size depending on the beneficiaries' greater or lesser predisposition to gain. For instance, more educated and skilled population groups could benefit more from economic restructuring, take

better jobs, and see their incomes grow faster. Thus impacts can be *relative*. But alongside winners, corridor interventions could also produce losers in *absolute* terms. For instance, by increasing efficiency, better transport connectivity could lead to simultaneous job creation and destruction. This transformation could require massive shifts in occupations. People with more fungible skills may be able to shift more easily, but others may face a harder time.

Having clarity on the hierarchy of impacts across all these dimensions may help policy makers in achieving multiple WEB, in managing trade-offs, and in supporting possible losers from the corridor intervention (figure O.3).

"2": The "2" sorts of complementary interventions—Policies and institutions

Merging the layers of project design (the I in FIT) and the hierarchy of multiple impacts from transport corridor interventions (the T) provides a useful tool to screen the quality of project design. This tool can be illustrated in the form of a simple matrix, where the rows are the different layers of intervention design, and the columns present the overarching policy objectives (table O.1)

This simple screening tool could help ensure that the fair distribution of economic benefits from transport corridor investments remains a priority in the design of the intervention. Applying the matrix could discipline policy makers by having them answer how each layer of the design addresses the three policy objectives. For instance, cell (1,1)—that is row 1, column 1—of the matrix asks: What are the expected impacts of the trunk infrastructure on the multiple WEB? Cell (2,2) asks: Is the design of transport and trade facilitating interventions likely to generate trade-offs across individual WEB? Cell (3,3) asks: Are there likely losers (relative and absolute), and what are the most effective complementary market policies and institutions to support them?

FIGURE O.3 **A corridor intervention package triggers a hierarchy of impacts**

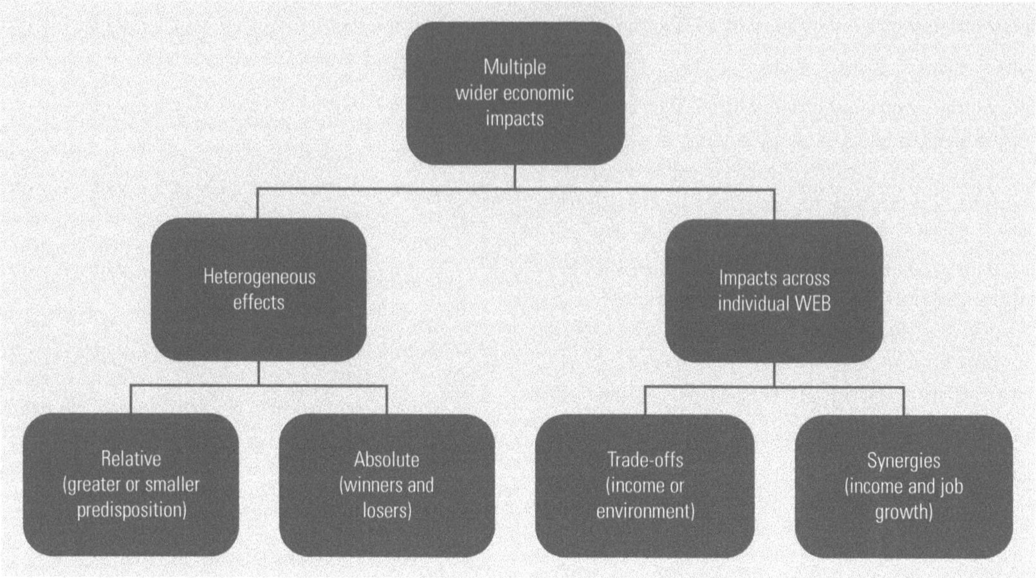

Source: Corridor Study Team.
Note: WEB = wider economic benefits.

TABLE O.1 **Combining the layers of a corridor program with the hierarchy of impacts gives a useful tool to screen for comprehensive project design**

Layers of project design	Hierarchy of multiple impacts		
	Achieve multiple WEB	Manage trade-off impacts	Support possible losers
Trunk infrastructure	?	?	?
Transport and trade facilitation	?	?	?
Complementary market policies and institutions	?	?	?

Source: Corridor Study Team.

"Deed": The "Deed" of devising a viable financing strategy for a given design

Ultimately, the cost of corridor investments is borne by taxpayers and possibly by fee-paying users of the new infrastructure. A critical decision concerns the distribution of this burden across society. The decision depends on social preferences, but also on who actually benefits from the corridor intervention. And one product of the decision is the financing strategy to fill the gaps between costs and returns over time.

Developing a viable and efficient financing strategy starts by assessing how much of the expected returns from the corridor investment could be monetized and how much could be in the form of social returns of a nonmonetary nature. The monetized portion can be recovered directly, through fees, or indirectly, through taxes. Because taxes and fees from corridor investments accrue only over time, whereas project costs must be paid during the preparation and construction phases, large corridor projects typically face a funding mismatch. The domestic or international financial systems can help bridge the gap by mobilizing resources nationally or globally.

Policy makers devising a financing strategy for a given design of corridor intervention can in principle consider the following options:

- Increasing tax revenues or reallocating public spending that is currently funded by existing tax revenues
- Increasing sovereign borrowing from concessional lenders, including multilateral and bilateral agencies, and other providers of concessional finance and grants
- Increasing sovereign borrowing from private financial institutions, or through capital markets
- Leveraging public capital to mobilize private equity and debt at the project level, or through an investment fund (special purpose vehicle).

Several of these options could include public guaranties and other explicit or implicit potential liabilities—including within public-private partnerships (PPPs). These contingent (potential) liabilities are originated with the intention of saving fiscal space—the space for the fiscal authority to further borrow and spend—by passing carefully selected risks and financing requirements onto the private sector.

However, PPPs must be devised and managed realistically and carefully (figure O.4). They require adequate capacity in the public sector—usually at the level of the central government—to assess which risks can be passed onto the private sector, which ones need to be retained, and how the retained and passed risks are interconnected. The assessment is even more complex in the case of corridor investments that cross borders.

Risk management capacity varies across countries, as it is affected by their institutional, legal, and practical contexts. When risk management capacity is low, contingent liabilities from shifted risks may ultimately shrink fiscal space. As a result, countries may be left with incomplete transport infrastructure projects, a large stock of bad loans in the domestic banking system, and additional contingent liabilities resulting from the need to recapitalize troubled systemically important or state-owned banks.

FIGURE O.4   India's market for corridor PPPs fragmented as it expanded—and quality suffered

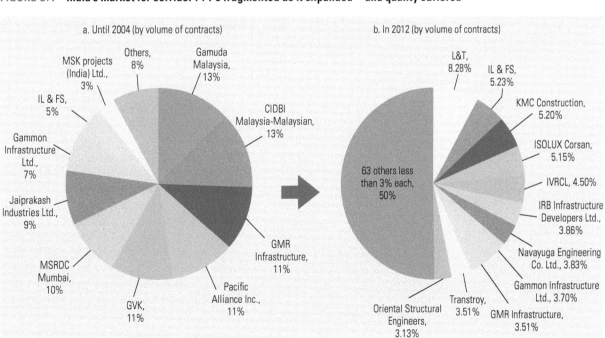

Source: Corridor Study Team of 2014 National Highways Authority of India data.

Strengthening institutional and legal frameworks, as well as well as the capacity for the public sector to carry out structured finance tailored to the projects, is thus a priority when embarking on sizeable corridor investments. Increasing the ability of the government to transfer risk using complex legal and corporate entities can be an integral part of the corridor intervention package, or be treated as a stand-alone governance reform.

"Deed": The "Deed" of successfully managing the implementation of the program

Successfully managing the implementation process presents its own set of challenges. For large cross-border corridors, four challenges stand out:

- *Integrating expertise across sectors.* To be efficient and fair, corridor interventions need to keep in mind that the WEB are the ultimate objective, and they span sectors in nature. Therefore, the expertise that needs to be mobilized for project design and implementation extends beyond transport infrastructure and its financing. A good understanding of urbanization, trade, competition and the environment, among other relevant areas, is rarely found in just a few staffers. Mobilizing such expertise and effectively integrating it could be a challenge for both the country governments and the international organizations that support corridor projects at their different stages. Governments and international organizations may want to build on the experience of other institutions that need to quickly mobilize and integrate diverse expertise, such as the U.S. space agency, NASA. This approach could lead to the identification of potential members of "Corridor Tiger Teams" to deploy well-integrated cross-sectoral expertise rapidly.
- *Boosting local delivery.* Because transport corridors concern specific locations, effective collaboration between local and central governments is needed to strengthen administration capacity and enhance the legitimacy of interventions. A key complementary action at the local level is to upgrade land administration and cadastral records, so as to protect property rights and enhance tax revenue collection. Other local interventions may include skills upgrading programs, the development of economic zones, or stronger environmental protection. This collaboration may involve temporary increases in local budgets, as well as staff transfers from the central to the local government, to boost local corridor interventions. Possible tensions involving local governments that do not directly benefit from the corridor intervention must be anticipated, and managed early on.
- *Leveraging the private sector in delivery.* Engaging the private sector in delivering commercially viable parts of complex corridor projects can help achieve WEB. However, successfully engaging the private sector during implementation requires strong governance arrangements, sufficient administration capacity, and clear knowledge of private sector preferences. Tenders must be transparent and efficient, and not be plagued by conflicts of interest. The sequencing of implementation phases must be carefully planned; announced timelines, and expectations should be adhered to; and uncertainty should be managed through effective communication, among other requirements. For the private sector to engage, a regular dialogue with the business community at all levels must be established. Without these foundations, the private sector could hold back its investments until uncertainty dissipates.
- *Managing cross-border complexity.* This challenge could be tackled by establishing effective institutions, such as supranational committees. These standing or temporary bodies need to decide how to partition the overall corridor program into "implementable" projects. In doing so, they must take into account regional

and national financing constraints, as well as agency capabilities across borders. An appropriate sequencing of subprojects must be embraced, with effective tracking of the overall program delivery, and enforceable accountability for performance. If not adequately empowered, these supranational coordination bodies could fail. Alternatively, international organizations could drive the coordination groups while playing the role of an honest broker toward all countries involved, and providing them with technical assistance.

MAIN TAKEAWAYS FOR PRACTITIONERS

When thinking about using transport corridors as an anchor investment to promote trade, regional integration, and broader socioeconomic activity, policy makers and practitioners should keep in mind four main takeaways.

1. Understand the challenge at hand before proceeding with large transport investments.

Corridors have a great potential as a development tool, but they are extremely costly—not only in terms of their direct outlays, but in terms of other forgone development opportunities, such as greater investments in education, or in water and sanitation. Because they require large funding up front, with often commensurately large borrowing, corridor investments can jeopardize fiscal sustainability and macroeconomic stability.

Risks are especially high when the WEB from corridors are highly uncertain and their contingent (potential) liabilities are badly managed. Therefore, prudence is advisable to make the most from the significant public spending on transport corridor development, and to avoid the risk of white elephant investments. Working with the private sector and the potential large users of the transport infrastructure—such as local corporations—could help mitigate these risks by ensuring enough traffic through the transport corridor.

Generating large enough economic surpluses for the country requires a smart placement of the corridors (map O.4). Policy makers can tackle this problem by prioritizing corridor placements that demonstrate gains in "centrality" from the new or upgraded connection. This is achieved through enhanced connectivity not only to important economic hubs, but also to smaller cities whose market access is highly relevant for local producers. But the "centrality" of cities along the corridor could change over time as global demand, preferences, and trade evolve. Given the long life of corridor investments, policy makers need to account for such dynamics when making placement choices.

Another problem is that economic surpluses generated by transport corridors are often unevenly distributed among the population. Realizing the WEB of a corridor is imperative not only to maximize economic returns but also to ensure the socioeconomic and political sustainability of the investments. Even if the returns from these investments are large enough to repay the incurred debts and remunerate the private investors, there can still be resistance to their implementation if the distribution of the WEB is perceived as unfair.

Corridor investments may benefit some people more than others, depending on their skills, security of land titling, access to finance, or proximity to the trunk infrastructure, among other factors. Some people may even lose in absolute terms. Failure to identify who the relative and absolute losers may be, to enhance their chances to gain from the corridor investment, and to support them as needed could instigate a political backlash against further corridor investments. Similar to the backlash against globalization in some advanced countries, this push would amount to a missed opportunity to further promote trade, economic growth, and job creation.

2. Focus on WEB in designing corridor programs right from the start.

A narrow program scope could increase risks. If the design of transport corridor programs is focused only on reducing vehicle operating

MAP O.4   Where should South Asia focus its limited resources—toward the Middle East and Europe, toward Central Asia, or toward East Asia?

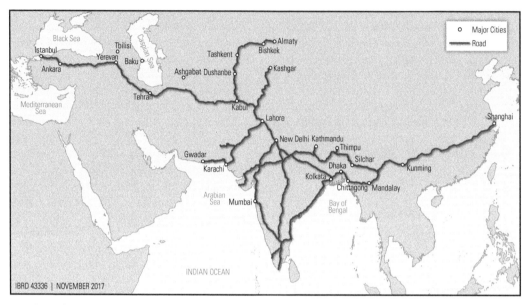

Source: Corridor Study Team.

costs or saving time, important benefits from the investment may be missed. Whichever benefits are attained may not be widely shared, and negative impacts may arise. The corridor intervention may then fail to be transformational, and could even undermine sustainable growth and social inclusion.

Corridor investments affect multiple WEB simultaneously, and can lead to trade-offs. The analyses in this Report reveal that the most likely trade-offs arising is between income growth and environmental degradation, as well as between rising incomes and worsening social inclusion (particularly lower labor force participation by women).

Policy makers should give priority to amplifying WEB, managing trade-offs, and reducing the scope for absolute and relative losers to emerge. Various policies and institutional reforms (so-called "soft" interventions) can be used to this effect, complementing the investment in "hard" (physical) infrastructure. But to identify the most promising "soft" interventions, the potential WEB, trade-offs, and losers should be identified early on. These "soft" interventions must be

integrated within a comprehensive corridor intervention package right from the start.

Across the different local contexts covered in the Report, the most promising complementary interventions appear to be upgrading skills and strengthening public sector governance around the corridors. Improving education coverage and quality, and upgrading land administration systems are examples of potentially important initiatives in this respect. Other promising complementary policies include increasing openness to foreign trade and promoting industry and trade competitiveness.

The review of literature on spatial impacts of corridors covering 78 recent studies is telling in this respect. On average across countries, impacts on economic welfare and on equity are positive and statistically significant, but impacts on the environment are negative and even more significant. The effect on social inclusion is positive, but only marginally significant. Hence, trade-offs between welfare and environmental quality are likely. But those between welfare and social inclusion may arise as well. The findings are similar for the

Golden Quadrilateral highway system in India. Comparing with control districts, GDP grew significantly faster (by about 4 percentage points) near the corridors, but so did the density of aerosol particles—a measure of air pollution (figure O.5). Impacts on equity and social inclusion measures appeared insignificant.

In a similar vein, the study of India's Golden Quadrilateral and North-South-East-West highway systems shows the importance of improving women's access to private finance. Easing their budget constraint enables them to move from farm to non-farm jobs in the districts crossed by the corridors (map O.5).

The importance of complementary interventions is also revealed by simulations for the prospective China-Pakistan Economic Corridor (CPEC) in Pakistan and the Kolkata-Dhaka corridor between Bangladesh and India. These simulations suggest that the proposed corridors could have widely diverse impacts on household expenditures, poverty, the inclusion of women in the labor market, and air pollution.

To ensure that the WEB of these investments will be fairly distributed, complementary interventions could be embedded in the corridor intervention packages. For instance, districts located in the central leg of the proposed Kolkata-Dhaka corridor

FIGURE O.5   **Corridors can increase incomes, but these gains come at the expense of environmental quality**

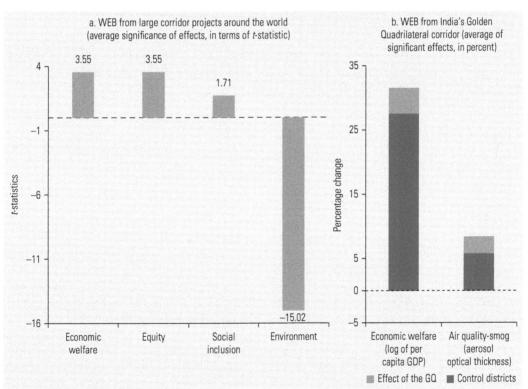

a. WEB from large corridor projects around the world (average significance of effects, in terms of *t*-statistic)

b. WEB from India's Golden Quadrilateral corridor (average of significant effects, in percent)

■ Effect of the GQ   ■ Control districts

Source: Corridor Study Team based on Bougna, Melecky, Roberts, and Xu (forthcoming), and Melecky, Sharma, and Subhash (forthcoming).
Note: In panel a, the *t*-statistic of 3.547 indicates a positive and reliable impact (at the 1 percent level) of transport infrastructure on various welfare outcomes (income, consumption, assets). The average impact on equity is not significantly different from the average impact on economic welfare. For social inclusion, the impact is smaller and/or less certain, but still, on average, marginally beneficial (*t*-statistic of 1.711). The impact of transport infrastructure on environmental quality is significantly detrimental: −15.023, on average. Panel b shows that the GQ highway increased GDP per capita growth over 2001–11 by 4 percentage points, over and above the baseline increase of 27 percent in control districts. However, the GQ highway also increased particulate pollution (measured by "aerosol optical thickness") by an extra 0.02 points relative to a baseline increase of 0.06 points, indicating a significant trade-off between economic benefits and pollution.

MAP O.5 **Spatial impacts around major South Asia corridors vary significantly**

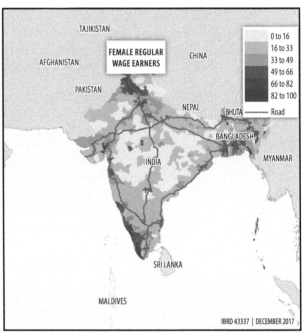

a. GDP per capita
b. Female regular wage employment

Source: GDP per capita: India: Directorate of Economics and Statistics, Planning Commission, Government of India 2011; Bangladesh: Bangladesh Bureau of Statistics 2011; Pakistan: World Bank 2017a. The GDP per capita estimation is based on calculations based on the World Development Indicators and the South Asia Spatial Database (Li et al. 2015). Female regular wage employment: India: Census of India–Primary Census Abstract (PHC–PCA), Office of the Registrar General and Census Commissioner, India; Bangladesh: Labor Force Survey 2005; Pakistan: Social and Living Standard Measurement Survey 2012–2013.
Note: Both panels display the Golden Quadrilateral highway, the North-South-East-West highway, and the anticipated Kolkata-Dhaka corridor. Panel a also includes the China-Pakistan Economic Corridor.
Disclaimer: This publication follows the World Bank's practice in references to member designations, borders, and maps. The boundaries, colors, denominations and other information shown in any map in this work do not imply any judgment on the part of The World Bank, ADB, JICA or DFID concerning the legal status of any territory or the endorsement or acceptance of such boundaries.

and the northern end of the CPEC may experience lower increases in women's employment in regular-wage jobs when there are restrictions on the use of land, limiting women's ability to move from farm to non-farm jobs. Zoning constraints could prevent the establishment of manufacturing businesses, while other land ownership restrictions could slow down the establishment of agro-processing businesses. Another factor behind the diversity of simulated effects of the CPEC and Kolkata-Dhaka corridor on household consumption is the varying share of private firms in total firms, an indicator of market contestability at the local level (map O.6).

3. Appraise the potential for WEB with spatial data and reliable econometric methods.

The available technical approaches to appraise the potential of transport corridors to yield WEB have different strengths and weaknesses.

The main trade-off is between the efficiency and reliability of an econometric approach. Efficiency (precision) in this context means that the applied econometric approach can deliver answers (estimates, predictions) with high confidence providing that the underlying problem is well understood and completely specified. Reliability (robustness), in turn, means that, even if the underlying problem is incompletely specified, the econometric approach delivers broadly correct answers or answers that point into the right direction.

Techniques that are more explicit about the economic structure and transmission mechanisms behind economic corridors can

MAP O.6 **The simulated impacts on per capita household consumption across districts along the Kolkata-Dhaka Transport Corridor (Bangladesh segment) call for complementary interventions**

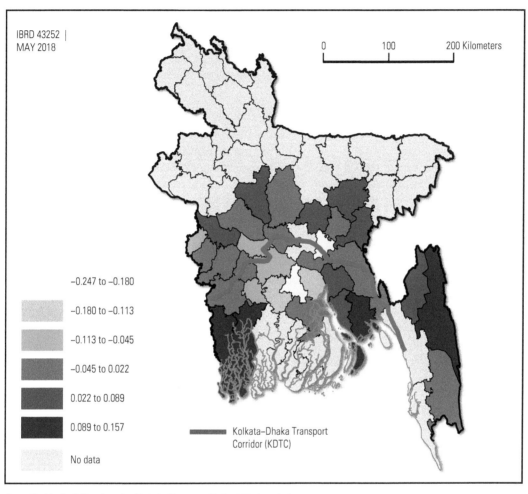

IBRD 43252 |
MAY 2018

| 0 | 100 | 200 Kilometers |

−0.247 to −0.180

−0.180 to −0.113

−0.113 to −0.045

−0.045 to 0.022

0.022 to 0.089

0.089 to 0.157

No data

Kolkata–Dhaka Transport Corridor (KDTC)

Source: Corridor Study Team based on Melecky, Sharma, and Subhash (forthcoming).
Note: The map shows the Kolkata-Dhaka Transport Corridor (KDTC) (Bangladesh segment). Units refer to average per capita household consumption expenditure, in logs. The red line indicates the highway.

produce more precise estimates, while yielding valuable insights about the transmission channels and mechanisms at play. But this is the case only if the underlying model is correctly and completely specified. If the model is even partially mis-specified, such techniques can produce misleading results.

In contrast, reduced-form econometrics are flexible and less prone to big mistakes in model specification. However, this approach struggles with the problem of endogenous placement. That is, reduced-form estimations have great difficulty distinguishing economic growth due to the corridor placement from growth that would have happened regardless,

or growth potential that could have influenced corridor placement in the first place. Reduced-form estimates are also unable to shed light on indirect effects and precise transmission mechanisms.

This trade-off between efficiency and reliability applies both to the identification of the optimal placement of a transport corridor and to the optimal intervention design to maximize its WEB (table O.2).

From a policy perspective, the most practical approach to appraise a proposed transport corridor may be to combine network analysis focusing on the centrality of corridor connections with reduced-form

TABLE O.2   The trade-offs between different econometric approaches to appraise proposed corridors give options

Technical approach	Current reliability in determining:		Econometric potential in determining:		Further research needed to attain the potential:	
	Placement	WEB	Placement	WEB	Placement	WEB
Network analysis	High	Lowest	High	Low	High	Low
Reduced-form econometrics	Low	Highest	Low	Medium	Low	Medium
Structural general equilibrium	Low	High	Medium	High	Low	High

Source: Corridor Study Team based on Melecky (forthcoming).

regressions to capture the effects of complementary interventions.

The comparative advantages of different techniques make some of them better suited for appraisals that must be done rapidly—when expertise, data, or funding are limited—and others better suited for appraisals that can be more strategic and comprehensive, but take more time. Because the process of deciding on the placement and design of a transport corridor program is dynamic, it would be advisable to utilize more reliable techniques first, before moving to more efficient but more demanding and possibly risky ones.

In practice, pre-feasibility studies and assessments could be conducted using only network analysis focused on the concept of centrality, combined with reduced-form econometrics to assess how the local context affects the expected WEB. Later on, feasibility studies and project appraisal could consider more efficient techniques such as network analysis accounting for varied responses of cities and markets on the corridor, and structural general equilibrium econometrics. This more elaborate approach would allow policymakers to think through possibly richer dynamics, and to identify direct and indirect effects of the proposed corridor intervention.

4. Engage the private sector better, considering disparities in regional development.
The success of a transport corridor intervention could depend on how well the private sector and civil society organizations are integrated into project design and implementation. The involvement of industry associations, strategic firms, private financiers, cooperatives, and grassroots organizations can increase the effectiveness of the public resources deployed. It can also pave the way for private investment. Policy makers thus need to ensure that the private sector understands the corridor program, takes ownership, and is not overwhelmed by the risks.

Private investment can happen at the level of trunk infrastructure—the main arteries of road, rail, or waterway transport systems. It can also be at the level of auxiliary infrastructure, such as feeder roads and rails, irrigation systems for agriculture, and industrial zones. However, to maximize the WEB of economic corridors, private investments at the level of individual firms are as important as direct participation in corridor-related investments.

Private investment can help increase the financial viability of corridor projects and the sustainability of public finances. More importantly, private sector confidence is vital to spur economic activity along the corridors and generate the intended positive spillovers.

However, the experience with private sector involvement in the design, co-financing, and implementation of transport corridors has been mixed. For instance, with 466 private participations in infrastructure, India may well be home to the largest public-private partnership (PPP) program in the world (World Bank 2017b). However, by 2017, the program has produced a large pool of non-performing assets and created troubles for the banking system (Singh and Brar 2016).

Further, data on a set of transport corridor projects supported by international development organizations suggests that private sector engagements have been modest in volume, while questions arise about their quality. Impact estimates using various measures of WEB indicate that so far the engagement of the private sector might not have contributed to project success, but rather the opposite (figure O.6).

FIGURE 0.6 **Private sector involvement in corridor projects has been limited, and its impact has been low**

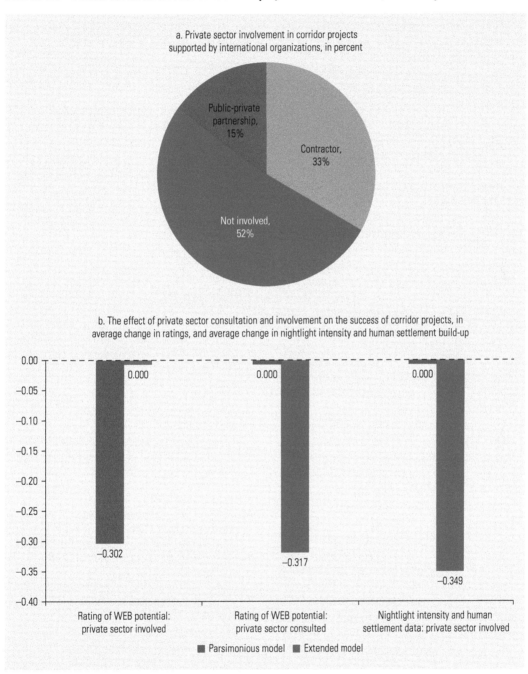

a. Private sector involvement in corridor projects supported by international organizations, in percent

Public-private partnership, 15%

Contractor, 33%

Not involved, 52%

b. The effect of private sector consultation and involvement on the success of corridor projects, in average change in ratings, and average change in nightlight intensity and human settlement build-up

Rating of WEB potential: private sector involved — 0.000, −0.302

Rating of WEB potential: private sector consulted — 0.000, −0.317

Nightlight intensity and human settlement data: private sector involved — 0.000, −0.349

■ Parsimonious model ■ Extended model

Source: Corridor Study Team based on Alam, Herrera Dappe, Khan and Melecky (forthcoming).
Note: Panel a reports the results of 60 transport corridor projects around the world. Panel b presents regression estimates using institutional ratings of "WEB potential" [1–5] and pooled nightlight intensity and human settlement data [−0.2; 4.8] along the corridor project alignments. Bars with a zero value indicate that the estimated impact is statistically insignificant. The parsimonious model groups complementary policy interventions across sectors, while the extended model disaggregates them by sector. WEB = wider economic benefits.

Private and public sector incentives in relation to the development of corridors may differ. The private sector has a relatively short investment horizon and is primarily profit-oriented, not development-oriented. Private sector actors may not enter into corridor programs by themselves because of the high risk of coordination failures, and they may be especially reluctant in the case of cross-border initiatives. It may also be difficult for them to mobilize the sizeable, long-term financial resources needed to bridge the gap between investment costs up front and monetary returns much later.

Thus, the public sector must take the lead on corridors, listening to the private sector and trying to understand the implications of its profit orientation, but keeping the development objectives in mind. One example of misaligned incentives concerns the tendering out and allocation of build-operate-transfer (BOT) contracts for transport corridors with construction firms that are interested only in the building phase of the project. Separating the building and operating stages of transport corridors can be a way to address this misalignment of incentives.

Because the private sector is profit-oriented, it will tend to cluster its investments around fast-developing growth centers on or near the corridors. Public investment may need to correct the ensuing disparities in spatial development, rebalancing the rapid growth of corridor nodes with the slow development in less productive regions.

For example, in developing the Pacific Belt Zone, the government of Japan recognized the need to address spatial divergence. Various efforts to enhance the capital of prefectures outside the Zone were promoted. Urban functions such as commerce, production, and education, were enhanced, transportation networks were improved, and support was provided for private enterprises to locate production sites outside major Belt Zone cities. Such efforts helped significantly expand local market size and increase employment opportunities in lagging regions (JICA 2009). Malaysia has also strived to correct disparities in regional development and create opportunities in previously lagging regions using public investment and support (Government of Malaysia 2006).

* * *

Transport corridor investments can be transformational and pave the way for greater economic and social welfare. But they need to be designed holistically to enhance and spread the gains while reducing the probability of negative outcomes. The examples, methodological framework, and results in this Report are presented as a guide for policy makers to maximize the WEB of transport corridors in South Asia and beyond.

REFERENCES

ADB (Asian Development Bank). 2008. *Greater Mekong Subregion: Maturing and Moving Forward*. Operations Evaluation Department, ADB.

Alam, M., M. Herrera Dappe, A. Khan, and M. Melecky. Forthcoming. "Corridor Project Design, Success Rating, and the Potential for Wider Economic Benefits." Policy Research Paper, World Bank, Washington, DC.

Andrés, L., D. Biller, and M. Herrera Dappe. 2013. *Reducing Poverty by Closing South Asia's Infrastructure Gap*. Washington, DC: World Bank and Australian Aid.

Bougna, T., M. Melecky, M. Roberts, and Y. Xu. Forthcoming. "Transport Corridors and their Wider Economic Benefits: A Critical Review of the Literature." Policy Research Paper, World Bank, Washington, DC.

Chandra, B. 2006. "Economic Nationalism and the Railway Debate, circa 1880–1905." In *Our Indian Railway. Themes in India's Railway History*, edited by R. Srinivasan, N. Tiwari, and S. Silas. Delhi: Foundation Books.

Chatterjee, B., and S. Singh. 2015. "An Opportunity for India in Central Asia: The International North-South Transport Corridor Is a Chance for India to Build Links with Central Asia and Eurasia." *The Diplomat*, May 4. https://thediplomat.com/2015/05/an -opportunity-for-india-in-central-asia/.

Donaldson, D. 2010. "Railroads of the Raj: Estimating the Impact of Transportation

Infrastructure." Working Paper 41, Asia Research Centre, Murdoch, Australia.

Government of Malaysia. 2006. Ninth Malaysia Plan, 2006–2010. Putrajaya: Economic Planning Unit.

JICA (Japan International Cooperation Agency). 2009. "Ex Post Evaluation of Japanese ODA Loan Project: National Highway No. 5 Improvement Project (I) (II)." Report prepared by Masumi Shimamura, Mitsubishi UFJ Research and Consulting Co., Ltd. https://www2.jica.go.jp/en/evaluation/pdf/2009_VNV -5_4.pdf.

Kumar, R. 2015. "Delhi Mumbai Corridor: How the World's Largest Infrastructure Project Is Uprooting Indian Farmers." *The Guardian*, September 15.

Li, Y., M. Rama, V. Galdo, and M. F. Pinto. 2015. "A Spatial Database for South Asia: Paper." World Bank, Washington, DC. http://www.worldbank.org/spatialdatabase-southasia

Melecky, M. Forthcoming. "Appraisal Econometrics for Transport Corridors: Optimal Placement, Intervention Design, and Wider Economic Benefits." MPRA Paper, University Library of Munich, Munich.

Melecky, M., S. Sharma, and H. Subhash. Forthcoming. "Wider Economic Benefits of Investments in Transport Corridors and the Role of Complementary Policies." Policy Research Paper, World Bank, Washington, DC.

Ordabayev, A. 2015. "The Geopolitics of Transport Corridors in Central Asia." Working Paper, The Institute of World Economics and Politics (IWEP). http://iwep.kz/files/attachments/article/2015-07-05/geopolitics_of_transport _corridors_in_central_asia.pdf.

———. 2016. "Transport Corridors of South Asia and Caucasus." Working Paper, The Institute of World Economics and Politics (IWEP). http://iwep.kz/files/attachments/article/2016-09-23/transport_corridors_of_south_asia_and _caucasus.pdf.

Palit, A. 2017. "India's Economic and Strategic Perceptions of China's Maritime Silk Road Initiative." *Geopolitics* 22 (2): 292–309.

Roberts, M., U. Deichmann, B. Fingleton, and T. Shi. 2012. "Evaluating China's Road to Prosperity: A New Economic Geography Approach." *Regional Science and Urban Economics* 42 (4): 580–94.

Shepard, W. 2017. "India and Japan Join Forces to Counter China and Build Their Own New Silk Road." *Forbes,* July 31. https://www.forbes.com/sites/wadeshepard/2017/07/31/india-and-japan-join-forces-to-counter-china-and-build-their-own-new-silk-road/#668bac174982.

Singh, C., and J. S. Brar, 2016. "Stressed Assets and Banking in India." IIMB-WP No. 507, Indian Institute of Management Bangladore (IIMB). https://iimb.ac.in/research/sites/default/files/WP%20No.%20507.PDF.

Srivastava, P., and U. Kumar, eds. 2012. *Trade and Trade Facilitation in the Greater Mekong Subregion.* Asian Development Bank.

World Bank. 2017a. "Growth Out of the Blue." *South Asia Economic Focus, Fall 2017.* World Bank, Washington, D.C. https://openknowledge.worldbank.org/handle/10986/28397.

———. 2017b. Private Participation in Infrastructure (PPI) database. https://ppi.worldbank.org/. Accessed June 2017.

Part I
Going Beyond Just Infrastructure

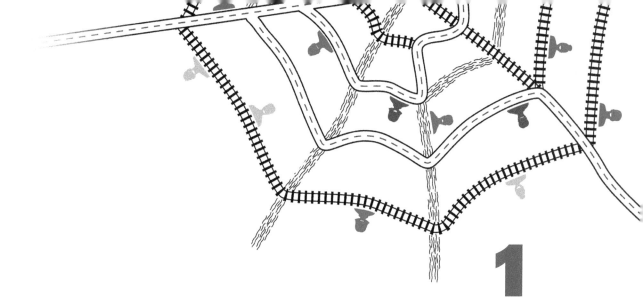

Insights into Regional Integration from Three Historical Transport Corridors in South Asia

This chapter looks at three transport corridors in South Asia that have played important roles in history. The purpose is not to explore the key reasons and drivers for change within this region and beyond it since 1600 or to shed light on the long-term development of South Asia. Rather, it is to assess the causes for three moments in time when rising exchange of goods, capital, people, and ideas, and expanding patterns of communication and trade, radically increased connectivity between regions, and to discuss the consequences.

The three corridors have been chosen to be distinct geographically, chronologically, and causally. Each has been assessed separately. Consideration has been given to the historical context under which an existing corridor was broadened or a new corridor was opened. Careful attention has been paid to the impact that each had locally, regionally, and beyond (if appropriate). The three moments chosen—1700, 1800, and 1900—are viewed not as precise points in time that are

significant in and of themselves, but rather as windows through which to explore effects of the deepening ties between two or more locations of major socioeconomic activity.

Unfortunately, attempts to build a detailed picture of the past are limited by gaps in source materials. The kinds of written materials that might be helpful to understand complex issues such as gender, literacy, and social change are not often available. Detailed data regarding topics like demographic growth, urbanization levels, infant mortality rates, and rises (or falls) in real wages are not always easy to come by. Furthermore, the analysis must rely on partial, biased, or misleading eyewitness accounts that focus on what the commentator(s) of the time thought was interesting, rather than on what observers might pick up on today. It is worth stressing the shortcomings of the evidence, for care must be taken not to overstate conclusions and not to use the gaps and problems of the material that is available to oversimplify complex issues.

It is also important to recognize that transportation corridors and the infrastructure that is put in place to establish or deepen them can change considerably over time. New means of travel and shipment of goods can have a dramatic impact over a very short period. Conversely, roads and even railway lines degrade over time because of a lack of use and/or investment. This can lead to significant change, including weakening of regional connectivity and the emergence of unforeseen challenges (Kumar 2015, 42S).

MUGHAL INDIA, CIRCA 1700: A CORRIDOR LINKING SOUTH AND CENTRAL ASIA

The first case study examines changes to South Asia in the wake of the creation of the Mughal Empire. The period of interest is not

the empire's first century, when the first Mughal emperor, Babur (1526–30), arrived in South Asia from Central Asia, and he and his heirs created and expanded a unified territory. Rather, the focus is on the 100 years that followed, until about 1700. This was a period that was broadly stable in terms of the domestic history of South Asia. It was also a time when the Mughals enjoyed peaceful relations with their neighbors in Persia as well as beyond the northern and eastern frontiers. The case looks at how domestic reforms—coupled with an expanding economy that was fueled at least in part by changes in global trading patterns—deepened connections with Central Asia.

In the 150 years after the death of Babur, South Asia went through a period of transformation and consolidation. A series of military conquests, first by Babur, and then by his heirs, created a realm that by 1650 stretched from Gujarat on the west coast of India to the Bay of Bengal in the east, from Lahore in the Punjab deep into central India, as far as the Godavari River. As new territories were brought under the control of the emperor and his court, as shown in map 1.1, administrative structures were first introduced and then streamlined to allow the single and growing polity to be managed effectively—although the pattern of change was not uniform across the region (Laroque 2004). Standardization of administrative, commercial, and judicial norms played an important role in enabling connections to deepen, and allowing for wider circulation and movements of goods, people, and services.

These changes not only streamlined exchange within the Mughal territory but also stimulated rising levels of exchange. Such outcomes are also reported in work done by modern scholars on the impact of reducing or removing the costs of trade (De 2007; Anderson and van Wincoop 2001).

The connectivity and socioeconomic vibrancy intensified following the European discovery of sea routes across the Atlantic and the nearly simultaneous successful rounding of the southern tip of Africa by Vasco da Gama, which opened up maritime links

MAP 1.1 Mughal Empire, 1690

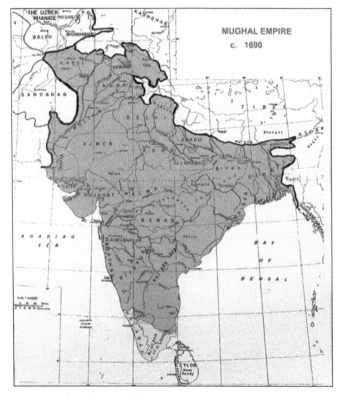

Source: Based on sheet 16A of Irfan Habib's *An Atlas of the Mughal Empire* (Habib 1982).

between Western Europe and Africa, the Arabian Gulf, the Indian Ocean, and beyond. By the early 1600s, increasing volumes of trade were beginning to move between the Americas and Asia via the Pacific Ocean, fundamentally changing global trade networks (Flynn and Girláldez 1995). Large numbers of merchants were drawn to South Asia. Levels of maritime traffic reaching ports in Bengal and in Gujarat rose sharply. The port of Surat, in particular, not only boomed as a result but also became part of an intercontinental trading network (Moosvi 1990).

By the early 1600s, the East India Company and the Dutch East Indies Company (Verenigde Oost-Indische Compagnie) had both established major footholds in Gujarat (Jha 2005). These trading companies situated themselves in key locations to supply goods, products, and commodities from South Asia—and beyond—with substantial markups in Europe as well as in Africa and the Americas. Central to these arrangements were the technological breakthroughs in shipbuilding that enabled oceangoing vessels to travel further, faster, and more safely than ever before. This, coupled with vast expropriation of silver and gold from the Americas in the sixteenth and early seventeenth centuries, fundamentally transformed global bullion flows, and had effects that were dramatic and far-ranging on China and Southeast Asia, as well as South Asia (Atwell 1982; Barrett 1990).

The influx of hard currency into South Asia had a profound impact on its domestic economy. The textile industry, in particular, grew at a staggering rate to keep up with demand. By the late 1600s, the East India Company was exporting more than 1.5 million pieces of textiles per year, and the Dutch East Indies Company almost the same amount (Prakash 2007). Rising levels of wealth flowing into the imperial court led to a golden age of building, visual arts, and calligraphy, as wealthy patrons sought out the best artisans, and gave them funds to produce their finest works. As demonstrated in European art in this period, there is a direct correlation between the quantity and quality of art that is

produced and the available number of patrons, donors, and buyers seeking to commission and acquire art. India's cultural golden age followed a similar trajectory (van der Woude 1991).

Many artistic forms had their origins in Central Asia, where the Mughal Dynasty began. Indeed, Timurid influences not only affected art but also popularized new pastimes, such as wrestling and pigeon racing (Foltz 2007).[1] Fruits and foodstuffs from this region also began to be traded in increasing volumes, with reports that fruits from "Persia, Balkh, Bukhara, and Samarkand" could be found in markets in Delhi, while the Emperor Jahangir received apples and grapes from Central Asia (Alam 1994). However, the expansion of a transport corridor running north from the Indian subcontinent owed less to the nostalgic desire to (re)connect to a former homeland than to intensification of exchange based in rising spending on one resource in particular: horses.

The interest in horses coincided with rising investment in the military. Inflows of capital from outside South Asia, alongside the rising levels of interaction and exchange across a highly sophisticated, monetized, and unified region, resulted in a greater ability to spend on the military. Spending on the army was a vital means of strengthening internal control, as well as offering the opportunity to expand the territory still further, if and when the opportunity arose. It also, of course, provided an important means of defense against opportunistic or ambitious rivals. A considerable amount of money was spent buying horses for the military. As many as 100,000 were bought each year by the start of the eighteenth century (Gommans 1991).

The most desirable horses were bred in Central Asia. They were more robust, stronger, and bigger than those reared in South Asia, which were "by nature so small that, when a man is upon them, his feet nearly touch the ground" (Gommans 2002, 112–13). With the economy in South Asia booming, vast profits could be made from selling the best steeds, as a surge in demand outstripped supply. So great were the potential returns on horse sales in South Asia that Europeans not only became actively involved in equestrian trade but also began to innovate in ship designs, in an attempt to maximize margins by bringing in stallions from Arabia and Persia (Jardine and Brotton 2005).

The corridor running north from northern India was not new. Often referred to as the Grand Trunk Road, it formed part of an ancient network that connected Kabul to Peshawar and Lahore, via Delhi through Bengal, as far as Chittagong in what is now Bangladesh. Improvements had been made in the early sixteenth century, thanks to Emperor Sher Shah Suri (1530–45),[2] who not only oversaw a major expansion of this (as well as other routes) but also set in place an ambitious program to develop and ensure its long-term future by setting up hostels where travelers could rest on their journeys along the new arteries (Singh 1991, 173–203). By the late 1600s, the scale of the horse trade prompted major investment into infrastructure. Bridges were built, caravansaries (inns that could accommodate caravans) were upgraded, and the security of the roads running north was improved (Dale 1994).

One result of the increasing levels of exchange, both within what is now northern India and the Punjab and regions lying beyond, was the surge in civic buildings in many of the major urban centers along the transport corridor running north—and in some cases, even of the foundation of entirely new cities. Gateway cities that were well located to host markets, and particularly horse markets, flourished, with the prestige and power of their governors and rulers rising accordingly (Gommans 2002). Cities like Delhi and Kabul benefited

substantially and grew rapidly in the decades before 1700. Lahore flourished as grand new monuments were built and open spaces and gardens were created to adorn the city (Westcoat, Brand, and Mir 1993).

Other locations like Jaipur, Jodhpur, and Udaipur grew exponentially, fueled by similar migratory patterns that were the hallmark of labor force movements in western India in this period (Washbrook 1993). Rapid urbanization along the corridor put pressure on water and food supplies. India's unpredictable monsoon climate, and therefore its harvests, exacerbated the difficulties posed by a period of rapid urban growth and the relationship between towns and their hinterlands (Kolff 1991). Although the agricultural landscape was transformed as a result of demographic change, what happened in urban settlements affected what was grown and where—rather than the other way round (Habib 1969).

Social structures in the Mughal-controlled territory in South Asia underwent considerable change as connections deepened and economic interaction accelerated, with a rapidly expanding class of city merchants, traders, shopkeepers, and moneylenders swelling alongside the small groups of rich elites who had previously dominated (Mukerjee 1968). The elites, traditional or otherwise, played a central role in shaping the cities, as well as the trade routes of the empire (Naqvi 1968). Improved communication networks enabled faster transmissions of information to the political center, which resulted in a greater ability if not to rule the empire, then at least to receive more accurate news in a timely manner, consolidating the power of elites (Mehta 1979, 303–4).

It is difficult to accurately assess the impact of high levels of mobility, given the records and historical material available. However, it is worth noting that competition for labor and skills was intense between traders and merchants, whether foreign or otherwise. The rising investment in cities, and the prospects and opportunities that they offered, had a significant effect on social structures. Goods, skills, and properties could be bought and

Even the earliest corridor studied was clearly linked to global trading patterns and to rhythms of supply and demand hundreds, if not thousands, of miles away.

sold by an increasing number of people, which meant that housing, farmland, and assets that were better located and closer to marketplaces became more and more valuable, in turn increasing commercialization and promoting further growth. The result, inevitably, was to create surges that increased regional imbalances rather than correcting them (Washbook 2007).

The transport corridor that linked South and Central Asia did not peter out and come to an end. Like all corridors, as well as carrying traders and merchants, it could also enable those with less benign intentions to spread easily. In the 1730s, the Persian ruler Nader Shah used the route linking Afghanistan and Central Asia with Delhi to strike at the very heart of the Mughal Empire. The attack provides a useful reminder of the fact that corridors can sometimes prove to be conduits for unexpected problems and troubles (Daryaee and Aghaie 2012).

The threat to the routes running north in the eighteenth century put urban life under pressure, as did power shifts within the Mughal world and the rise of urban centers elsewhere in South Asia. According to eyewitnesses, some towns and elites fell on hard times, with the result that artisans, traders, and craftsmen moved away in search of opportunities elsewhere (Bayly 1983, 112–13). Then and now, labor forces, especially collective groups of skilled workers, can exercise considerable autonomy when it comes to relocating to more fertile pastures (Lucassen 2006).

Nevertheless, another burst of life for the corridor was not long in coming. In the first half of the nineteenth century, major investments went into road building, which was overseen first by the East India Company and then by British imperial officials across South Asia, including the first corridor under consideration here. "As a consequence," noted the *Morning Chronicle*, "the map of India began to shrink." Communities, towns—and India itself—were becoming more closely connected than ever before. Then, as now, investment in infrastructure often yields long-paying dividends.

BENGAL AND THE EAST INDIA COMPANY, 1745–1813: THE TRIANGULAR TRADE BETWEEN BRITAIN, INDIA, AND CHINA

The second case assessed analyzes the routes emanating from the booming city of Calcutta (now Kolkata) from the middle of the eighteenth century onward. The corridor resulted from the efforts of the London-based East India Company (EIC) to establish and intensify connections across the Bay of Bengal throughout the 1700s to create a dominant mercantile and political position in South Asia.

From 1745 to 1813, the EIC reached full maturation, faced numerous crises, and morphed into a colonial state in all but name. The city of Calcutta was integral to the rise and continuing prosperity of the EIC in Bengal and throughout South Asia.[3] The city's pivotal role in international trade and its imperial might stemmed from its sophisticated inland and maritime connectivity across regions. Calcutta became the wealthiest and most important center of the EICs' activities by the early eighteenth century. As a result, heavy fortifications were built to protect commercial interests (Lawson 1993, 46–48).

The subject of continued fascination across the globe, the EIC is remembered as a formidable organization, at once respected, feared, and loathed. An English and later a British joint-stock company, formed to pursue trade with the East Indies, the company rose to account for half the world's trade in commodities, ranging from cotton, silk, indigo dye, and salt to saltpeter, tea, and opium (Roy 2012).

The EIC's interests turned from trade to territory during the eighteenth century, as the Mughal Empire declined in power and the EIC struggled with its French counterpart, the French East India Company (Compagnie Française des Indes Orientales) during the Carnatic Wars of the 1740s and 1750s. The British defeat of the Indian power at the Battle of Plassey and Battle of Buxar—led by Robert Clive—left the EIC in control of Bengal and a major military and political power in India. In the decades that followed, it gradually increased the extent of the territories under its control, ruling either directly or indirectly via local puppet rulers under the threat of force by the armies of its three presidencies, much of which were composed of Indian privates (*sepoys*) (Heathcote 1995). The EIC offered its own services in the Indian "military bazaar" (Bayly 1988, 48).

The EIC eventually came to rule large areas of India with its own private armies, exercising military power and assuming administrative functions. Company rule in India effectively began in 1757 and lasted until 1858, when—following the Indian Rebellion of 1857—the British Parliament passed the Government of India Act 1858. The British Crown assumed direct control of India in the form of the new British Raj. Maps 1.2 and 1.3 highlight this expansion of British rule on the subcontinent.

The EIC was undoubtedly extractive, but it also brought Britain and India into close connection before the development of the British Empire in Asia, in ways that empowered both British and local Indian interests—from channeling financial capital into

MAP 1.2   **Territories of the British East India Company, 1765 and 1805**

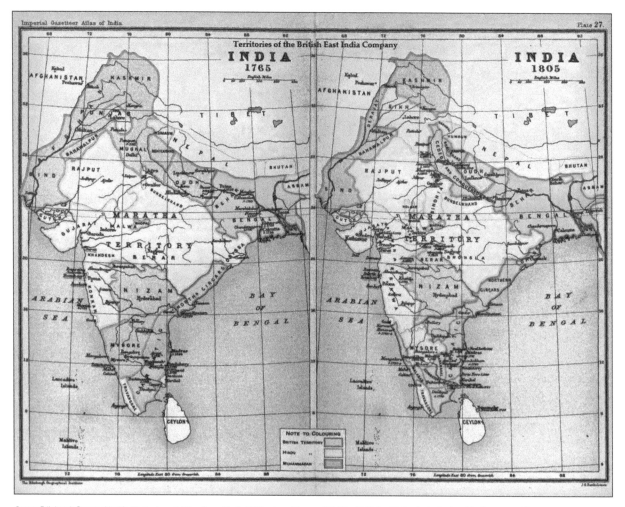

Source: Edinburgh Geographical Institute, *Imperial Gazetteer of India*, 1907, volume 26, page 190, Atlas Published Under the Authority of the Secretary of State for India in Council by Oxford University Press (https://en.wikipedia.org/wiki/Company_rule_in_India#/media/File:India1765and1805b.jpg).

MAP 1.3 Hindustan, 1864

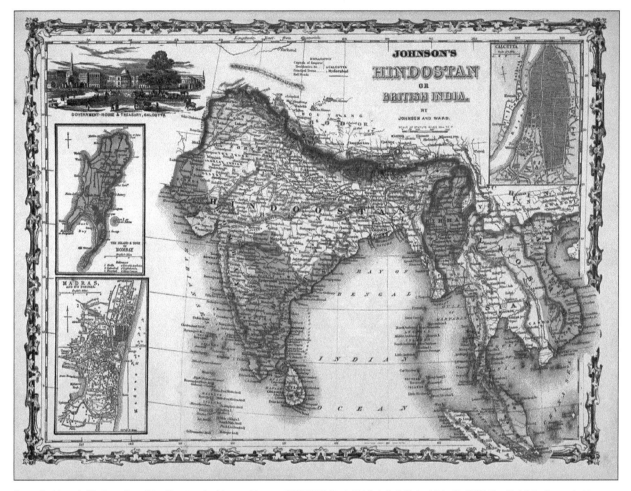

Source: A. Johnson's "Hindostan" map (http://westerncivguides.umwblogs.org/2013/12/06/the-british-in-india/). First published in 1860 in New York (http://www.davidrumsey.com/luna/servlet/detail/RUMSEY~8~1~2540~320020:Hindostan-Or-British-India-).

domestic investment within India to the construction of infrastructure projects that expanded connections across the subcontinent to shaping processes of state formation and the realms of social and cultural life. Nevertheless, the role played by the EIC is highly controversial, and one that is not always easy to assess objectively.

This international connectivity was made possible not only by the EIC's technological development and exploratory endeavor in global maritime travel but also by its private investment in creating and expanding vital new ports to augment trade and ensure company dominance. An important example of this was the EIC's instrumental role in developing Calcutta in the region of Bengal from the 1690s onward. Over the next century, the city was transformed not only into a commercial hub that linked regional, interregional, and even global trade but also into an outstanding center of learning and a contact zone between different people, faiths, languages, and ideas (Raj 2011).

With a network of inland and coastal transport corridors cultivated around them, port cities like Bombay (Mumbai), Madras (Chennai), and Calcutta (Kolkata) acted as transport hubs for the regions that the EIC dominated. The economic importance of Calcutta came to dictate the geography and timing of transport regionally, nationally, and internationally.

By 1760, Bengal had an Indian ruler backed by the EIC. In 1764, the British defeated the Mughal emperor and his ally, the Nawab of Oudh, at Buxar (Dyson 2002, 8). The British used this victory to gain considerable political leverage over Bengal. The EIC, under the guidance of Robert Clive, obtained the *diwani*—the rights to collect revenues—in Bengal, Bihar, and Orissa (Odisha). In the guise of extracting a "dividend" for its services, the EIC now effectively taxed the local authorities, as well as all traded goods. It never denied the authority of the Mughal emperor, but began to manage the administration of these three regions—acting like other independent "successor states."[4] Thus by 1765, the EIC was the de facto sovereign in Bengal and collected territorial revenues estimated to be worth £2–4 million per year in the provinces of Bengal, Bihar, and Orissa (Bowen 1989, 187).

The EIC benefited from this time of flux and opportunity. As the volume of textiles in the triangular trade between Britain, China, and India increased greatly, Bengal, and specifically Calcutta, became extremely important to British interests (Bayly 1988). The lines between the interests of the EIC, its shareholders, its officers, and the British government in controlling Bengal (and other parts of India) were often blurred—no doubt sometimes deliberately (Marshall 1987).

After the *diwani* were introduced in Bengal, the scope and scale of regulatory actions were unprecedented. All major groups of insiders—shareholders, directors, and employees—increasingly found key decisions subject to Parliamentary fiat. From 1784, the EIC's political imperatives largely overshadowed the profit motive. The *diwani* of Bengal were therefore a fundamental moment

in the lifespan of the EIC. Robert Clive, originally sent to reform the company's civil and military services, to end wars, and to return the company to a stable footing, had instead opened a Pandora's Box by accepting and promulgating the *diwani*.

News of the *diwani* and their value circulated through printed media, and Clive's boasting brought immediate public scrutiny to the conduct of the EIC's servants (overseas employees) in India and the behavior of directors and shareholders at home. Upon hearing the news, and against the directors' advice, the EIC's shareholders voted to increase the dividend on their investments from 6 percent to 10 percent. This was collected by raising the taxes imposed on traded goods across Bengal and elsewhere. The move precipitated Parliament's investigation into the EIC's affairs. In London, the possibility that shareholders—passive members of the public—might benefit from the spoils of Indian territories while excluding government spawned deep resentment. Parliament imposed new rules on the election of directors, levied a fine of £400,000 per year on the company, and regulated the size of the dividend (15 percent of gross sales in 1767/68). Thus the benefits of the *diwani* remained speculative, while the costs for the company were tangible.

After 1773, the EIC's commercial ethos came under increased scrutiny and pressure in South Asia. This followed a catastrophic and devastating famine in Bengal—which was directly linked to the EIC's misadministration, the greed of its officers, and its grotesque incompetence—led to the death through starvation of millions in Bengal (Arnold 1999). The EIC's officials in Bengal continued to devote greater attention to revenue administration than to acquiring piece goods, raw silk, or saltpeter. Particular attention was paid by the company and its officers to rationalizing and simplifying taxation, both on the value of land and on transactions in towns and markets across Bengal and beyond (Travers 2004).

The creation of a new government department, the Board of Control, under William Pitt's India Act (1784) deepened and institutionalized the ministerial oversight that had begun after the *diwani* were introduced. The act required servants (the EIC's overseas employees) returning to Britain to account for the source of their fortunes. The company had greatly inflated salaries across all ranks of servants, even as it continued to add to its workforce. Profiteering from private trade was no longer essential for recruiting and keeping young men in the covenanted service, with the attraction of good salaries and high status proving sufficiently attractive to swell the ranks. Between 1784 and the passage of the Charter Act of 1813, which ended the EIC's monopoly of trade to India,[5] the company became a company in name only. But did this shift in authority alter the network of transport corridors emanating from Calcutta? What lessons can be extrapolated from the case of the late-eighteenth-century Bengal?

The growth of Bengal's textile industry was accompanied by new procurement patterns and labor force and legal arrangements

Bengal's inland trade routes facilitated the growth of its textile industry. With the ascendancy of the *diwani* system and the EIC's shift to combine politics and business, the textile industry in Bengal changed greatly. Before political interests emerged, Bengal was a major textile-producing region on the subcontinent, alongside Gujarat and the Coromandel Coast, specializing in the production of luxury cotton, silk, and mixed textiles and therefore dominating textile exports to the European market. At the turn of the eighteenth century, as much as 40 percent of the total cargo exported to Europe from Asia by the Dutch as well as the EIC originated in Bengal, and consisted largely of textiles and raw silk (Prakash 1998).

Procurement of cotton textiles was therefore the crucial export underpinning the EIC's venture into Bengal. This venture was made possible by the thousands of weavers dispersed across the countryside. By the 1750s, textiles accounted for more than 80 percent of the value of EIC's exports from Bengal. Cotton products, in turn, constituted more than 88 percent of the value of textile products (Chaudhury 1995, 182, 192). Before the *diwani* period, Bengal thrived in the export of cotton textiles—that is to say, in the sale of finished products, as opposed to the raw material itself, which came mainly from the Deccan Plateau (at least in the eighteenth century).

> **The mobility of the labor force has been a clear factor in the ability not only to carry out infrastructure projects but also in the expansion of cities and the development of interconnected economies.**

The EIC primarily procured these textiles using the Agency System. The EIC hired local employees—agents—to transact with weavers. Typical agreements with weavers specified a loan for working capital, the quality and quantity of cloth to be produced, and prices contingent on quality. But the system did not work so well. It was fraught with "corruption"—or opportunistic behavior—by the agents, the weavers, and EIC officials. Agents often did not uphold payment agreements and cheated the weavers, and weavers often sold output to other buyers and thereby did not repay their debts to the EIC (Kranton and Swamy 2008).[6]

From the outset, there were unrealistic expectations of what taxes the local populations would be able to pay, as well as the speed and efficacy of plans put in place to transform the agrarian society and better extract surpluses. Although the limitations were recognized by some at the time, a strong cavalier, get-rich-quick attitude prevailed. It took time for this attitude to change (Travers 2005).

It was no coincidence, therefore, that as the regional and interregional exchange of goods accelerated, so did the services and ideas needed to move forward. This process of rationalization occurred not only in Bengal but also in other towns, locations, and territories where the EIC had interests.

Nowhere was this clearer than with the spread of English law and even of the law courts themselves. By the early nineteenth century, Hindu and Sikh merchants who felt that they had not been served fairly or justly in the courts in India brought their cases all the way to Westminster and even the Privy Council. The expansion of the transport corridor may not have been responsible for justice being delivered to all, but it opened new possibilities for those seeking to resolve disputes (Fraas 2014). This shift also occurred in urban centers, including Calcutta, where the increasing velocity of transactions led to rising levels of disputes over tax collecting (Sengupta 2015).

The political intrusion into mercantile practice hampered the growth of the textile industry in Bengal. However, overseas political involvement was not altogether disastrous. The volume and value of the textile trade carried on by the Europeans from Bengal in the second half of the eighteenth century was much larger than the first half, thanks to the substantial increase in the textile trade carried on by the EIC and private English traders in the wake of its Dutch and French competitors.

Furthermore, Indian merchants continued to control the bulk of the textile trade between Bengal and other parts of the subcontinent and Asia. Large quantities of cotton were being carried from the Deccan Plateau to Bengal, partly for use as raw material in the textile sector in the province. Interregional corridors were maintained, while international maritime routes helped connect consumers in Europe, Africa, and even North America. The picture of a ruined textile industry in Bengal during this period that is portrayed in some of the literature does not quite conform to the evidence available (Prakash 2007). It was only in the second half of the nineteenth century that the impact of the British cotton textile industry was felt in full force by the Indian handloom sector.

However, shifting characteristics along these inland corridors over the period immediately before and after the *diwani* era provide interesting insights about the far-reaching effects of international trade on regional networks. The EIC set up many trading outposts, employed a massive army of Indian agents and dealers, and advanced money to producers through these channels (Dasgupta 2000). The EIC oversaw the creation of a supply chain dependent on the British.

Indian agents, dealers, and intermediaries therefore played a major role in spreading, first, the EIC's economic power and, then, its political power through their extensive network in both urban and rural areas. The inland corridors of Bengal and beyond paved the way for the establishment of colonial rule. Some scholars have suggested that with its acquisition of political power in Bengal, the EIC did away with the services of these intermediaries, who were ruined in the process (Bagchi 1981). However, more recent critiques argue that the company considered the services of these intermediary merchants indispensable (Chakrabarti, 1994, 1).

Although the relationship between the EIC and the Indian merchants was essentially one of collaboration, it was often marked by competition and conflict. The Indian merchants stubbornly resisted all attempts by the EIC to ensure subordination solely on its own terms. The traders of eastern India after the Battle of Plassey were very different from the medieval maritime merchants who had once dominated the coastal port towns of India in Surat, Calicut, Masulipatnam, and Hughli (Das Gupta 1967).

During the period after *diwani*, the merchant princes—such as Khemchand and Chintaman Shah in Balasore—disappeared from the scene, but they were replaced by a new mercantile order constituted of men from disparate social groups. The disappearance of merchant princes did not necessarily mean a decline in the fortune of Bengal's merchants. The flourishing foreign trade had provided an excellent opportunity for the indigenous intermediary merchants to amass wealth and lay the foundations of the commercial aristocracy in Calcutta. Further, the demand created by European traders lured large numbers of rural workers—whose traditional caste occupations were different—to the new opportunities (Chaudhury 1995, 4).

Consider the impact on employment of five major manufacturing industries in Bengal during early colonial rule: silk textiles, cotton textiles, salt manufacturing, ship-building, and indigo dye. Tracing the precolonial roots of each, Ray (2011) assessed the roles of market forces and state policies on their performance. The data on employment are shown in table 1.1.

Table 1.1 shows that far from being deindustrialized, Bengal enjoyed industrial prosperity from 1795 to 1829. The level of employment in the five major industries increased overall by almost 1 million people. This was due to the prosperity of the precolonial industries like cotton and silk textiles as well as salt manufacturing on the one hand, and the emergence of new industries like shipbuilding and indigo dye on the other.

Therefore, while Bengal's industrial decline started in the early 1830s and continued in the decades that followed, the transport routes created during the EIC's life as a private firm continued to play a role during the early colonial period. Textiles remained a major export to the European market. The industry's cross-caste opportunities to connect weavers with the EIC were expanded to indigenous intermediary merchants, and the Bengal economy was propped up by the introduction of new industry.

Consequently, while Calcutta and its transport arteries inland and overseas were monopolized by the EIC, stifling international trade for the French and Dutch colonial economies in South Asia, the institutionalized ministerial oversight brought about by the *diwani* and Board of Control under Pitt's India Act provided opportunities for those left out under the rule of market forces. Industrial decline is traditionally thought as being a consequence of the EIC's turn from business to politics. But this conclusion is ill-founded. In some cases, market forces instead initiated and perpetuated the event. Nevertheless, the transition in mind-set and priorities that came with the EIC's mutation were both aided and driven by the continued use of transport corridors throughout Calcutta and Bengal.

TABLE 1.1   The five major industries in Bengal created almost one million jobs from 1795 to 1829, thanks to growth in both precolonial and new industries

Number of jobs

Year range	Silk	Cotton[a]	Salt	Shipbuilding	Indigo	Total employment	Change in employment
1795–99	88,775	179,905	88,020	928	460,080	817,708	—
1800–04	84,040	198,931	90,303	4,508	522,478	900,260	+82,552
1805–09	97,255	141,798	108,567	2,400	833,419	1,183,439	+283,179
1810–14	155,536	126,745	113,639	5,400	868,826	1,270,146	+86,707
1815–19	158,109	210,218	114,655	5,589	994,757	1,483,238	+213,092
1820–24	202,242	145,589	123,785	2,341	1,040,878	1,514,835	+31,597
1825–29	219,267	56,856	121,212	1,429	1,364,060	1,762,824	+599,068
1830–34	188,460	−21,616	149,887	1,074	1,230,295	1,584,100	−565,803
1835–39	237,786	−53,537	93,947	1,626	1,146,199	1,425,985	−122,115

Source: Ray 2011.
a. Cotton figures represent changes in employment opportunities.

RAILROADS OF THE BRITISH RAJ, 1853–1929: CHANGING THE TECHNOLOGY OF TRADING ON THE SUBCONTINENT

The introduction and expansion of railways was a key determinant in the development of India leading up to and following 1900. From drastically altering the distribution of the food supply to accentuating social differences, the railroad network designed and built by the British Raj brought dramatic change to the technology of trading on the subcontinent. The transport corridors of this network are the focus of this section.

Before the railroad age, bullocks carried most of India's commodity trade on their backs, traveling no more than 30 kilometers (km) per day along India's sparse network of dirt roads (Deloche 1994). By contrast, railroads could transport these same commodities 600 km in a day, and at much lower per-unit distance freight rates. Therefore, as rail penetrated inland districts, local administrative regions were brought out of near-autarky, and previously isolated provinces were connected to the rest of India and the world.

To give a brief overview of the expansion of rail in India over this period, it is critical to trace the roots of rail. The impetus was arguably a major failure of the cotton crop in America in 1846. Following this disruption, textile merchants in Manchester, England, and Glasgow, Scotland, had to seek alternative markets. It was then that traders in the United Kingdom turned their attention to the cotton crop in India—a British colony rich in cotton. However, cotton was produced in various parts of the Indian subcontinent. It took days to bring it to the nearest port to transport it to England by ship. A link was needed from the hinterlands to India's major ports to speed the transport of cotton and other goods as demand soared. This need impelled the British to introduce a railway in India, alongside the belief that rail could help the British organize and disperse the growing Indian population and more rapidly deploy troops.

The appealing prospect of railroad transportation in India was discussed as early as 1832 (Sanyal 1930), though it was not until 1853 that the first track was laid between Bombay and Thane—the start of what would form the Great Indian Peninsula Railway (GIPR). The importance of the inauguration can be gauged by the fact that Bombay's government declared it a public holiday.

With the East Indian Railway Company, the Carnatic Railway Company, and the Great Southern India Railway Company (later the South Indian Railway Company) established between 1845 and 1864, tracks started to spread from the larger cities on the subcontinent. These included links from the Madras Presidency in 1859, the 80-km link from Trichinopoly to Negapatam in 1861, and the Madras-Arakkonam-Kancheepuram line in 1865. However, the most influential day in the history of Indian rail was arguably March 7, 1870. On this date, the Great Indian Peninsula Railway and the East Indian Railway were linked at Jubbulpore (now Jabalpur). This 2,127-km railway line connecting Kolkata and Mumbai via Allahabad is now known as the Howrah–Al–Mumbai line. It resulted in a combined network of 6,400 km (4,000 miles), allowing goods and passengers to travel directly from Bombay in the west to Calcutta in the east via Allahabad in the northeast (where the Ganges, Yamuna, and "invisible" Saraswati rivers meet).[7] This connectivity over such a grand scale was unprecedented, providing the inspiration for French writer Jules Verne's book, *Around the World in Eighty Days*.

A year later, the lines from Bombay and Madras met at Raichur in Karnataka, as shown in map 1.4. By 1875, British companies had invested about £95 million in rail in India. By 1880 the network extended about 14,500 km (9,000 miles), mostly radiating inward from the three major port cities of Bombay, Madras, and Calcutta. By 1895, India had started building its own locomotives. In 1896, it began sending engineers and locomotives to help build the Uganda railways. At the start of the twentieth century, the Great Indian Peninsula Railway had become a government-owned company. The network spread to the modern-day states of Assam and Rajputhana. Soon, various autonomous kingdoms began to have their own rail systems.

The expansion of Indian rail from 1905 to 1929 can be followed through a string of key moments. In 1905, an early Railway Board was constituted, serving under the Department of Commerce and Industry. This was partly a result of the railways finally becoming commercially viable; until the turn of the twentieth century, the railways were unable to pay interest charges on the capital that had been invested in their construction. The fact that they eventually turned a net profit was not just symbolically important but also a key reason to justify further investment (Chandra 2006). The first electric locomotive appeared in 1908. The milestone of reaching 30,000 miles of track occurred in 1910, just behind Germany and Russia,[8] as can be seen in map 1.5. By 1920, the network had expanded to 38,040 miles (61,220 km).

With the arrival of World War I, the railways were used to meet the needs of the British outside India. Rail transported troops and grain to the ports of Bombay and Karachi en route to Britain, Mesopotamia, and East Africa. With shipments of equipment and parts from Britain curtailed, maintenance became much more difficult. Critical workers entered the army, workshops were converted to making artillery, and some locomotives and cars were shipped to the Middle East. The railways could barely keep up with the increased demand. By the end of the war, the railways had deteriorated badly. In 1923, both the Great Indian Peninsula Railway and East Indian Railway Company were nationalized.

The period between 1920 and 1929 was an era of economic boom. Some 41,000 miles (66,000 km) of railway lines served the country, carrying over 620 million passengers and approximately 90 million tons of goods each year. The capital value of the

MAP 1.4   Completed and planned railway lines in India, 1871

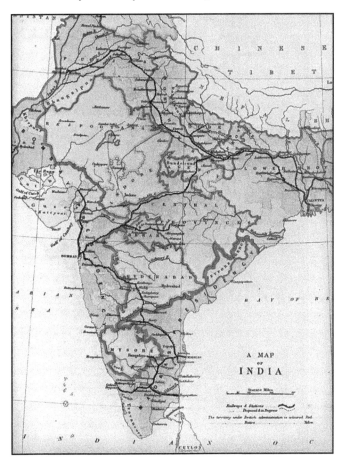

Source: Wikipedia.org.

railways was estimated at £687 million. This decade of prosperity was brought to an abrupt end with the onset of the Great Depression in 1929. For the next ten years, the railways suffered economically, and were later crippled by the onset of the Second World War.

Railroads had limited impacts on overall productivity and sectoral composition

The construction of railways in India was closely linked to the idea of improving British control, boosting production—and galvanizing economic and social change. As Lord Dalhousie, governor-general in the mid–nineteenth century put it, railways "would encourage enterprise, multiply

MAP 1.5   Rail in India, 1909

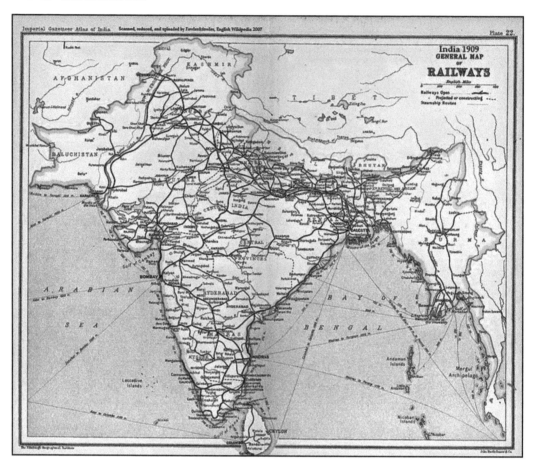

Source: Wikipedia.org.

production, facilitate the discovery of latent resources, increase national wealth and encourage progress in social improvement" (Kerr 2007, 18). This rosy view was born from seeing the impact that railways had had in other parts of the world—including in Britain itself. The railways, wrote Dalhousie, "will lead to similar progress in social improvement that has marked the introduction of improved communication in various Kingdoms of the Western World" (Headrick 1988, 64)

Assessing to what extent these aspirations were fulfilled is helped by the fact that detailed historical national accounts were compiled during the period of British Raj rule after 1871.[9] This body of data can be used to put the impact of rail on the Indian economy into context. Per capita income grew slowly during the late nineteenth century, but stagnated during the first half of the twentieth century, Gupta (2012) finds. The Indian economy grew by about 1 percent per year from 1880 to 1920, while the population also grew by 1 percent (Tomlinson 1996, 5). As a result, India did not enjoy a long-term change in income levels during this period. Agriculture was still dominant, with most peasants farming at the subsistence level. Extensive irrigation systems were built, providing an impetus for growing cash crops for export and for raw materials for Indian industry, especially jute, cotton, sugarcane, coffee, and tea (Tomlinson 1975). Agricultural income had the strongest effect on GDP. Agriculture grew by expanding the land frontier between 1860 and 1914. The price of cultivable land rose sharply after 1914 (Baten 2016, 255).

Using output and employment data from historical national accounts, Broadberry and Gupta (2016) calculate indexes of Indian labor productivity by major sector. They show that labor productivity grew fastest in industry, as modern industry developed in India, and slowest in services, despite the modernization of the transport network. During both the first and second halves of the twentieth century, although labor productivity grew respectably in industry and services, labor productivity growth in the economy as a whole was held back by slow productivity growth in agriculture.

However, to fully understand the contribution of the three main sectors to comparative productivity performance, it is necessary to track their shares in economic activity as well as their comparative productivity levels. Table 1.2 shows the changing sectoral distribution of employment in India from 1875 to 2000.

The most striking finding is the dominance of agriculture as an employer of labor. For the century after 1870, agriculture's share of the labor force was around 75 percent. Even by the end of the twentieth century, agriculture still accounted for nearly 65 percent of Indian employment. Given this commitment of resources to a sector with inherently low value added, and the poor productivity performance within that sector,

it is not difficult to understand India's disappointing overall productivity performance during this period.

The role of rail can then be factored in to these national economic patterns. Recently, Bogart and Chaudhary (2015) analyzed these national accounts and discovered that Indian railways experienced high labor and capital productivity growth from the 1880s to the 1910s, but fueled lower productivity growth in many sectors, notably agriculture. A composite productivity measure, known as total factor productivity (TFP), provides a key metric of economic performance. Bogart and Chaudhary (2015) estimate the TFP for the period before 1913 and find a healthy growth rate of 2.3 percent per year. This is in stark contrast to the rest of the Indian economy, such as agriculture, which had virtually no productivity growth in the late nineteenth century. India's TFP growth rate in railways also exceeded that of Britain in the nineteenth century. Even more remarkably, only a small part of the TFP growth was due to capacity utilization, such as running trains more frequently. It seems that Indian railways successfully adopted new technologies.

Less is known about the causes of the productivity slowdown after World War I. The collapse of world trade in the 1920s is probably the most immediate explanation. The productivity of railway tracks closely aligns with demand, which dropped substantially as international markets went through turbulent times.

The sharp price convergence in British Indian wheat and rice markets between 1861 and 1920 has been attributed to the introduction of rail. However, recent authors have countered this assumption. Andrabi and Kuehlwein (2008) carried out tests examining relative price differences between individual districts, and found that while the expansion of the rail network clearly mattered, other factors were more important. In fact, their analysis showed that the extension of railway lines, the opening up of new agricultural areas, and

TABLE 1.2 Agriculture continued to dominate the economy, despite the huge investment in rail

Indian labor force, by sector, 1875–2000 (percentage of total employment)

Years	Agriculture	Industry	Services
1875	73.4	14.5	12.1
1910/11	75.5	10.3	14.2
1929/30	76.1	9.1	14.8
1950/51	73.6	10.2	16.2
1970/71	73.8	11.1	15.1
1999/2000	64.2	13.9	21.9

Source: Broadberry and Gupta 2010.

the capabilities to deliver produce to towns and cities were less significant than climate, types of soil, and indeed wider changes in pricing patterns—locally, regionally, and even internationally.

Prices were converging during this time almost as rapidly between those districts without railways as those with railways. Andrabi and Kuehlwein's fixed-effect estimation, using yearly dummies, points out that the pattern of price convergence between a given district pair was no different before they got railways than after. One reason may be that India was already a well-established, partially integrated economy at the time railroads were being expanded. Some lines were built along existing trade routes where commerce between districts was already significant. The impact of railroads on districts not obviously linked by trade was about five times larger than the impact on districts that were previously well linked, Andrabi and Kuehlwein (2008) find.

The railways of the British Raj brought mixed economic benefits and questionable social benefits to India

This analysis highlights several issues surrounding the introduction of a rail corridor. When a rail corridor is built along an already-well-trodden trade route, the increased capacity may not lead to marked intensification of trade along the route. Importantly, in terms of economic development and poverty reduction, the largest benefactors of the introduction of rail may be those areas that had little or no previous trading ties.

However, using a new panel of district-level data collected from archival sources, Donaldson (2010) finds stronger evidence that railroads caused an increase in the level of real incomes in India. Specifically, the study concludes that railroads reduced the cost of trading, reduced interregional price gaps, and increased trade volumes. When the railroad network was extended, real agricultural income rose by approximately 16 percent.[10]

However, the analysis does not examine the volatility of real incomes over time. As in much of the developing world today, colonial India's precarious monsoon rains and its rain-fed agricultural technologies made real income volatility extremely high. Famines were a perennial concern. An important question for future research concerns the extent to which transportation infrastructure systems, like India's railroad network, can help regions smooth the effects of local weather extremes on local well-being.

Railways may have reduced the severity of famines, as argued by McAlpin (1983) and more recently by Burgess and Donaldson (2010). However, the ability of railways, as infrastructure, to curb famine pales in comparison to that of irrigation. There were several reasons for this. For example, one prominent critic of railway expansion noted that railways were used to justify higher land payments, which meant that while the prices of grain and wheat rose, growers saw little—if any—of the benefits (Sweeney 2008, 148).

Meanwhile, railways received a disproportionate share of the colonial budget. For example, the year-to-year allocation of expenditures within the Famine Insurance Fund varied between famine relief, protective railways, protective irrigation works, and programs to reduce debt.[11] Irrigation never accounted for a large share of the budget; protective irrigation works averaged 5 percent of the Famine Relief and Insurance Fund between 1893/94 and 1903/04.[12]

Overall, while the government of India was active in developing railways, irrigation was shortchanged. Railway expenditures reached 23 percent of the overall colonial budget in 1894, declining to 15 percent in 1935. During this time, no reallocation of that money was made to irrigation. Of the total expenditures on railways and irrigation works that were expected to cover the borrowing costs ("productive works"), more than 85 percent was devoted to railways between 1894 and 1919.

Some argue that this disproportionate colonial emphasis on railways was socially inefficient because of the strong link between irrigation and economic development.[13] According to this view, railways better served the strategic interests of the Raj; the differential expenditures were yet another example of colonial exploitation. However, when considering governmental investments in infrastructure in the twentieth century, it is worth remembering that the Raj was a conservative state; it did not tax much, due to political concerns, and it did not spend much. The Raj was not an active development state, either in agriculture or elsewhere.

However, the exploitative nature of the East India Company and later colonial rule is evident in the patterns of employment and procurement during the expansion of rail in India. Until the 1930s, both the Raj lines and the private companies hired only European supervisors, civil engineers, and even operating personnel, such as locomotive engineers (Headrick 1988, 8–82). The Stores Policy of the British Crown required that bids on railway contracts be made to the India Office in London, shutting out most Indian firms. The railway companies purchased most of their hardware and parts in Britain. While railway maintenance workshops operated in India, they were rarely allowed to manufacture or repair locomotives. The domestic steel supplier, TISCO Steel (Tata Iron and Steel Company), could not obtain orders for rails until the 1920s. Little was invested or reinvested in the local populations affected by rail.

Setting aside the questionable economic benefits of the railroads to the British Raj, other scholars debate the social and cultural advantages of the expansion of rail in India. For example, Marian Aguiar (2011) draws upon a rich archive of colonial correspondence, travel narratives, and striking illustrations to unpack the colonial rhetoric surrounding the railway space. She finds that not only were railway lines seen as a powerful technology with which to exert control over the Indian colony, but colonial rhetoric also imagined the shared traveling space of the railway as a leveler of social differences between Indians. As the author rightfully points out, this was a marvelous contradiction. Although the train made traveling a possibility for more people, it also accentuated social differences because passengers were separated by the kinds of tickets they could afford to purchase, as well as the whims of railway officials. For instance, in 1891, toilet facilities were introduced in first class, adding to the huge gap in "comforts and conveniences" between first- and lower-class passengers (Vaidyanathan 2002, 21). Decades later, Mahatma Gandhi would take up the lower-class passengers' cause.

The social benefits the British investment in rails brought to the Indian population were questionable, at best. Economic benefits were mixed. And the investments were accompanied by a partisan belief that investment in rail would prove to be a more efficient counter to famine than investment in irrigation. Nevertheless, the main burden on the Indian economy during this period was low productivity in agriculture. It may be unrealistic to expect railways to compensate for the poor performance of agriculture.

THE THREE HISTORICAL CASES SHARE COMMONALITIES WITH ONE ANOTHER AND WITH MODERN TRANSPORT CORRIDORS

The three transport corridors that have been assessed are entirely different from one another in terms of how and when they took shape, who and what they affected, and what their consequences were over the short, medium, and long terms.

Nevertheless, they share some notable features. The acceleration of commercial exchange had a direct and obvious impact on urban centers, socioeconomic change, and change to the physical landscape. The investment in transport corridors—whether through physical expenditures on roads, bridges, and train lines; on administrative measures that widen, improve, and expand tax collection and central spending; or on rationalizing judicial proceedings and the resolution of disputes—all served to further strengthen connections that had already began to take shape.

As each of the three corridors shows, the causes and consequences of the deepening of networks cannot simply be seen in a local or even a regional context. Indeed, even the earliest corridor under investigation was clearly linked to global trading patterns and to rhythms of supply and demand hundreds, if not thousands, of miles away.

In the context of transport corridors in the twenty-first century, it is striking to note that the mobility of the labor force has been a clear factor in the ability not only to carry out infrastructure projects but also in the expansion of cities and the development of interconnected economies.

Although top-down investment was key for immensely expensive infrastructure projects in the past—such as train lines and roads—and will doubtless remain so in the future, important by-products included the expansion of small-scale business, the galvanization of intermediaries, and the growth of the middle class. As modern scholarship has clearly demonstrated, increasing levels of commercial exchange and economic activity have not only promoted regional integration but have also reduced poverty.

Summing up and moving to the next chapter

This chapter has mapped three past transport corridors that spanned South Asia and has assessed their impacts in three eras: circa 1700, 1800, and 1900. The three transport corridors differed considerably in their emergence, life cycle, and impacts, but even the earliest corridor was clearly linked to global trading patterns and to rhythms of supply and demand hundreds, if not thousands, of miles away. Not only has labor mobility determined the ability to execute infrastructure projects, but it has also affected the dynamism with which cities have expanded and interconnected economies have developed. The investments in transport corridors (roads, bridges, and train lines) and their complementary interventions (improving tax collection and central spending; rationalizing judicial proceedings and resolution of disputes) all enabled economic connections that were already emerging. Nevertheless, the chapter notes that, at times, corridors were also conduits for unexpected problems and troubles. For instance, in the 1730s, the Persian ruler Nader Shah used the route linking Afghanistan and Central Asia with Delhi to strike at the very heart of the Mughal Empire.

Fast forwarding to more recent times, chapter 2 takes East Asia as one possible role model for South Asia and discusses the mixed successes with using transport corridors to spur regional development in Vietnam and Malaysia. The first case study describes the impacts of Vietnam's National Highway No. 5 (NH-5) on the development of private industrial zones and their significant local spillovers. The second case study examines Malaysia's experience with integrating rural areas and industrialized trade hubs in the northern part of Peninsular Malaysia.

NOTES

1. The Timurid Empire, a Sunni Muslim dynasty or clan of Turco-Mongol lineage, descended from the warlord Timur, Babur's great-great-great grandfather. It comprised modern-day Iran, the Caucasus, Mesopotamia, Afghanistan, and much of Central Asia, as well as parts of contemporary Pakistan, Syria, and Turkey (Marozzi 2004).
2. Emperor Sher Shah Suri, a Pathan from Bihar, founded the Suri Empire in northern India. He was contemporaneous with the Mughals.
3. "Bengal" spans the regions that eventually became Bangladesh and three states in independent India—West Bengal, Bihar, and Orissa.
4. A successor state is a totally new state. It is distinct from the previous state but maintains the same legal personality and possesses all the existing rights and obligations of the previous state.
5. Except for the tea trade and the trade with China.
6. Kranton and Swamy (2008) build a model of this procurement system and highlight the

problems they observe throughout the historical record.

7. In the twenty-first century, this route would comprise part of the Golden Quadrilateral that connects Delhi (North), Chennai (South), Kolkata (East), and Mumbai (West)—a highway system examined in chapter 6.

8. The United States, however, was far ahead in terms of miles of laid rack. Railway density is perhaps more important than length. Density was lower in India than in the United States and Europe, but higher than in South America, Africa, the rest of Asia, Canada, Russia, and Australia (Prakash 1998, 165).

9. See, for example, Heston (1983) and Sivasubramonian (2000).

10. While it is possible that railroads were deliberately allocated to districts on the basis of time-varying characteristics unobservable to researchers today, Donaldson (2010) finds little evidence for this potential source of bias with respect to the results in three separate placebo checks.

11. The Famine Insurance Fund was established by the Government of India in the 1880s after a devastating famine in Bengal, Orissa, Madras, and Bombay (Chaturvedi, Kumar, and Singh 2005, 444).

12. Calculations are based on Statistical Abstracts, India, 1905.

13. See, for example, Sweeney (2008).

REFERENCES

Aguiar, M. 2011. *Tracking Modernity: India's Railway and the Culture of Mobility*. Minneapolis: University of Minnesota Press. http://www.jstor.org/stable/10.5749/j.ctttsw7t.

Alam, M. 1994. "Trade, State Policy and Regional Change: Aspects of Mughal-Uzbek Commercial Relations, c. 1550–1750." *Journal of the Economic and Social History of the Orient* 37 (3): 202–27.

Anderson, J., and E. van Wincoop. 2001. "Borders, Trade and Welfare." In *Brookings Trade Forum*, edited by S. Collins and D. Rodrik. Washington, DC: Brookings Institution.

Andrabi, T., and M. Kuehlwein. 2008. "Railways and Price Convergence in British India." *Journal of Economic History* 70 (2): 351–77.

Arnold, D. 1999. "Hunger in the Garden of Plenty: The Bengal Aminre of 1770." In *Dreadful Visitations: Confronting Natural Catastrophe in the Age of Enlightenment*, edited by A. Johns. New York: Routledge.

Atwell, W. 1982. "International Bullion Flows and the Chinese Economy circa 1530-1650." *Past and Present* 95 (1982): 68–90.

Bagchi, A. 1981. "Merchants and Colonialism." Occasional Paper 38, Centre for Studies in Social Sciences, Calcutta.

Barrett, W. 1990. "World Bullion Flows, 1450–1800." In *The Rise of Merchant Empires: Long-Distance Trade in the Early Modern Worlds, 1350–1750*, edited by J. Tracy. Cambridge: Cambridge University Press.

Baten, J. 2016. *A History of the Global Economy from 1500 to the Present*. Cambridge: Cambridge University Press.

Bayly, C. 1983. *Rulers, Townsmen and Bazaars. North Indian Society in the Age of British Expansion, 1770–1870*. Cambridge: Cambridge University Press.

———. 1988. *Indian Society and the Making of the British Empire (The New Cambridge History of India)*. Cambridge: Cambridge University Press.

Bogart, D., and L. Chaudhary. 2015. "Off the Rails: Is State Ownership Bad for Productivity?" *Journal of Comparative Economics* 43 (4): 997–1013.

Bowen, H. V. 1989. "Investment and Empire in the Late Eighteenth Century: East India Stockholding." *Economic History Review* 42 (2): 186–206.

Broadberry, S., and B. Gupta. 2010. "The Historical Roots of India's Service-Led Development: A Sectoral Analysis of Anglo-Indian Productivity Differences, 1870–2000." *Explorations in Economic History* 47 (3): 264–78.

———. 2016. "Indian Economic Performance and Living Standards: 1600-2000." Chapter 2 in *A New Economic History of Colonial India*, 15–32. New York: Routledge.

Brunner, H.-P. 2013. "What Is Economic Corridor Development and What Can It Achieve in Asia's Subregions?" Working Paper 117, Series on Regional Economic Integration, Asian Development Bank, Manila, Philippines.

Burgess, R., and D. Donaldson. 2010. "Can Openness Mitigate the Effects of Weather Shocks? Evidence from India's Famine Era." *American Economic Review* 100 (2): 449–53.

Chakrabarti, S. 1994. "Collaboration and Resistance: Bengal Merchants and the English East India Company, 1757-1833." *Studies in History* 10 (1): 105–29.

Chandra, B. 2006. "Economic Nationalism and the Railway Debate, circa 1880–1905." In *Our Indian Railway. Themes in India's Railway History*, edited by R. Srinivasan, N. Tiwari, and S. Silas. Delhi: Foundation Books.

Chaturvedi, H., D. Kumar, and R. Singh. 2005. *India Insurance Report, Series I*. New Delhi: Allied Publishers Pvt. Ltd.

Chaudhury, S. 1995. *From Prosperity to Decline: Eighteenth Century Bengal*. Delhi: Manohar.

Dale, S. 1994. *Indian Merchants and Eurasian Trade, 1600–1750*. Cambridge: Cambridge University Press.

Daryaee, T., and K. Aghaie. 2012. *The Afghan Interlude and the Zand and Afshar Dynasties (1722–95)*. Oxford: Oxford University Press.

Das Gupta, A. 1967. *Malabar in Asian Trade*. Cambridge: Cambridge University Press.

Dasgupta, B. 2000. "Trade in Pre-Colonial Bengal." *Social Scientist* 28 (May–June): 47–76.

De, P. 2007. "Impact of Trade Costs on Trade: Empirical Evidence from Asian Countries." Working Paper 2707, Asia-Pacific Research and Training Network on Trade.

Deloche, J. 1994. *Land Transport*. Vol. 1 in *Transport and Communications in India Prior to Steam Locomotion*. Oxford: Oxford University Press.

Donaldson, D. 2010. "Railroads of the Raj: Estimating the Impact of Transportation Infrastructure." Working Paper 41, Asia Research Centre, Murdoch, Australia.

Dyson, K. K. 2002 (reprint of 1978 work). *A Various Universe: A Study of the Journals and Memoirs of British Men and Women in the Indian Subcontinent, 1765–1856*. New Delhi: Oxford University Press.

Flynn, D., and A. Giráldez. 1995. "Born with a 'Silver Spoon': The Origin of World Trade in 1571." *Journal of World History* 6 (2): 201–21.

Foltz, R. 2007. "Cultural Contacts between Central Asia and Mughal India." In *India and Central Asia*, edited by S. Levi. New Delhi: Oxford University Press.

Fraas, M. 2014. "Making Claims: Indian Litigants and the Expansion of the English Legal World in the Eighteenth Century." *Journal of Colonialism and Colonial History* 15 (1). doi: 10.1353/cch.2014.0006.

Gommans, J. 1991. "Mughal India and Central Asia in the Eighteenth Century: An Introduction to a Wider Perspective." *Itinerario* 15 (1): 51–70.

———. 2002. *Mughal Warfare: Indian Frontiers and High Roads to Empire, 1500–1700*. London: Routledge.

Habib, I. 1969. "Potentialities of Capitalistic Development in the Economy of Mughal India." *Journal of Economic History* 29 (1): 32–78.

———. 1982. *An Atlas of the Mughal Empire*. Delhi: Oxford University Press.

Headrick, D. R. 1988. *The Tentacles of Progress: Technology Transfer in the Age of Imperialism, 1850–1940*. New York: Oxford University Press.

Heathcote, T. 1995. *The Military in British India: The Development of British Land Forces in South Asia*. Manchester: Manchester University Press.

Heston, A. W. 1983. "National Income." In *The Cambridge Economic History of India, Volume II, c. 1757–c. 1970*, edited by M. Kumar and M. Desai, 463–532. Cambridge: Cambridge University Press.

Jardine, L., and J. Brotton. 2000. *Global Interests: Renaissance Art between East and West*. London: Reaktion.

Jha, M. 2005. "The Mughals, Merchants and the European Companies in 17th-Century Surat." *Asia Europe Journal* 3 (2): 269–83.

Kerr, I. 2007. *Engines of Change: The Railways That Made India*. Westport, CT: Praeger Publishers.

Kolff, D. 1991. *Naukar, Rajput and Sepoy: The Ethno-History of the Military Labour Market in Hindustan, 1450–1850*. Cambridge: Cambridge University Press.

Kranton, R., and A. Swamy. 2008. "Contracts, Hold-Up, and Exports: Textiles and Opium in Colonial India." *American Economic Review* 98 (3): 967–89.

Kumar, N. 2015. "Potential and Prospects of Strengthening Transport Connectivity for Regional Economic Integration in Southern Asia." *South Asia Economic Journal* 16 (2-Supplement): 39S–54S.

Laroque, B. 2004. "Trade, State, and Religion in Early Modern India: Devotionalism and the Market Economy in the Mughal Empire." PhD thesis, University of Wisconsin at Madison.

Lawson, P. 1993. *The East India Company: A History*. London: Routledge.

Lucassen, J. 2006. "Brickmakers in Western Europe (1700–1900) and Northern India (1800–2000)." In *Global Labour History. A State of the Art*, edited by J. Lucassen. Bern: Peter Lang.

Marozzi, J. 2004. *Tamerlane: Sword of Islam, Conqueror of the World*. London: Da Capo Press.

Marshall, P. 1987. "Private British Trade in the Indian Ocean before 1800." In *India and the Indian Ocean, 1500–1800*, edited by A. Das Gupta and M. Pearson. Calcutta: Oxford University Press.

McAlpin, M. 1983. *Subject to Famine: Food Crises and Economic Change in Western India, 1860–1920*. Princeton, NJ: Princeton University Press.

Mehta, J. 1979. *Advanced Study in the History of Medieval India*. Delhi: Sterling.

Moosvi, S. 1990. "Mughal Shipping at Surat in the First Half of the Seventeenth Century." *Proceedings of the Indian History Congress* 51 (1990): 308–20.

Mukerjee, R. 1968. *The Economic History of India*. London: Longmore.

Naqvi, H. 1968. *Urban Centres and Industries in Upper India, 1556–1803*. London: Asia Publishing House.

Prakash, O. 1998. "European Commercial Enterprise in Pre-Colonial India." Chapter 4 in Volume II.5 of *The New Cambridge History of India*. Cambridge: Cambridge University Press.

———. 2007. "From Negotiation to Coercion: Textile Manufacturing in India in the Eighteenth Century." *Modern Asian Studies* 41 (6): 1331–68.

Raj, K. 2011. "The Historical Anatomy of a Contact Zone." *Indian Economic and Social History Review* 48 (1): 55–82.

Ray, I. 2011. *Bengal Industries and the British Industrial Revolution (1757–1857)*. London: Routledge.

Roy, T. 2012. *The East India Company: The World's Most Powerful Corporation*. Delhi: Allen Lane.

Sanyal, N. 1930. "The Development of Indian Railways." Calcutta: University of Calcutta. https://archive.org/details/Development OfIndianRailways.

Sengupta, K. 2015. "Bazaars, Landlords and the Company Government in Late Eighteenth-Century Calcutta." *Indian Economic and Social History Review* 52 (2): 121–46.

Singh, C. 1991. *Region and Empire: Punjab in the Seventeenth Century*. Delhi: Oxford University Press.

Sivasubramonian, S. 2000. *The National Income of India in the Twentieth Century*. Delhi: Oxford University Press.

Sweeney, S. 2008. "Indian Railways and Famine 1875–1914: Magic Wheels and Empty Stomachs." *Essays in Economic and Business History* 26 (2008): 147–58.

Tomlinson, B. R. 1975. "India and the British Empire, 1880–1935." *Indian Economic and Social History Review* 12 (4): 337–80.

———. 1996. *The Economy of Modern India, 1860–1970*. Cambridge: Cambridge University Press.

Travers, T. 2004. "'The Real Value of the Lands: The Nawab, the British and the Land Tax in Eighteenth-Century Bengal." *Modern Asian Studies* 38 (3): 517–58.

———. 2005. "Ideology and British Expansion in Bengal, 1757–72." *Journal of Imperial and Commonwealth History* 33 (1): 7–27.

Vaidyanathan, K. 2002. *150 Glorious Years of Indian Railways*. Mumbai: English Edition Publishers and Distributors.

Van der Woude, A. 1991. "The Volume and Value of Paintings in Holland at the Time of the Dutch Republic." In *Art in History. History in Art: Studies in Seventeenth Century Dutch Culture*, edited by J. de Vried and D. Freedberg. Santa Monica, CA: Getty Center for the History of Art and the Humanities.

Washbrook, D. 1993. "Land and Labour in Late Eighteenth-Century South India: The Golden Age of the Pariah?" In *Dalit Movements and the Meanings of Labour in India*, edited by P. Robb. Delhi: Oxford University Press.

———. 2007. "India in the Early Modern World Economy: Modes of Production, Reproduction and Exchange." *Journal of Global History* 2 (1): 87–111.

Westcoat, J., M. Brand, and N. Mir. 1993. "The Shedara Gardens of Lahore: Site Documentation and Spatial Analysis." *Pakistan Archaeology* 25: 333–66.

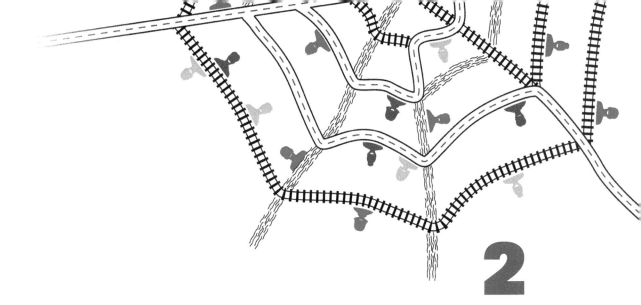

2

Insights into Regional Integration from Two Contemporary Transport Corridors in East Asia

Shifting from the eras of South Asia's historical corridors to recent times, this chapter discusses the somewhat mixed successes that large transport infrastructure investment in Vietnam and Malaysia have had in boosting regional integration and generating wider economic benefits.

The Vietnam case study focuses on the developments around National Highway No. 5 and the anchor infrastructure investment that aimed to connect the capital city of Hanoi with the port of Hai Phong, an international gateway for exports. The anchoring transport investment followed earlier probusiness reforms and the policy of increasing openness to trade. These policy interventions were nationwide and not geographically specific to the envisaged corridor. The investment aimed to substantially upgrade one of the national highway arteries and—along with the probusiness environment, educated labor force, and better connectivity to the world—attract foreign direct investment (FDI). Such an infusion of foreign investment was sought to create geographic hot spots around National Highway No. 5 that local business

could build upon in forming local supply chains. The ultimate ambition was to take advantage of the global flows of FDI and, over time, introduce local companies to and integrate them in global trade and global supply chains. Much of that ambition has been achieved—but not without trade-offs in terms of negative impacts to the environment and safety, among other areas. Some of these trade-offs occurred immediately, and others have been more gradual.

The Malaysia case study reviews efforts by the national government to integrate lagging regions with well-industrialized hubs and boost development that is more spatially (geographically) equitable. Because of the large amounts of investment and number of projects, Malaysia opted for a top-down approach by establishing a dedicated coordinating institution, along with an investment fund to back up its recommendations with adequate funding. Although it is too early to assess the impact of the Malaysia's initiative, this case study points to some interesting challenges. While the public sector can help resolve the failure of private sector stakeholders to coordinate their investments and to build needed large-scale infrastructure themselves, it can face coordination challenges of its own. Notably, the challenges could arise because coordination between the central and the local governments is needed in the case of investments that are geographically specific, and the existing institutional frameworks may not always facilitate such coordination effectively.

MAP 2.1   Vietnam's National Highway No. 5 connects Hanoi to the port of Hai Phong

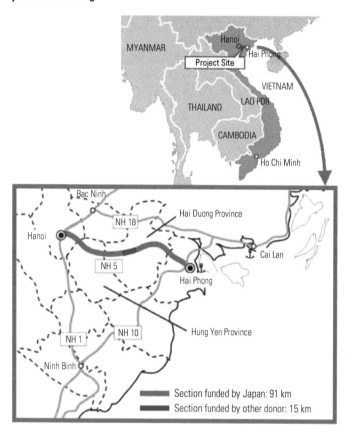

Source: JICA.
Note: Official World Bank country names are used.

Greater transport capacity attracted significant foreign direct investment. The presence of global brands—including Canon, Honda, and Panasonic—has accelerated industrial concentration and economic growth in northeastern Vietnam.

VIETNAM'S NATIONAL HIGHWAY NO. 5, INDUSTRIAL ANCHORS, AND LOCAL SPILLOVERS

National Highway No. 5 (NH-5), a 106–kilometer (km)–long national road connecting Hanoi with the international port of Hai Phong, is an important socioeconomic artery for the northern part of Vietnam (map 2.1). It was upgraded in the mid-1990s, when traffic for both freight and passengers was expected to increase dramatically, along with Vietnam's rapid economic growth stemming from its open reform policies (figure 2.1).

The corridor intervention was backed by complementary policies

Developing NH-5 was part of the effort to improve the overall transport network. Supported by Japanese official development assistance (ODA) in the mid-1990s, the development aimed to strengthen trade and industry, as well as improve living standards in the northern part of Vietnam. For that to happen, the transport capacity needed to be expanded to become much more efficient. To develop NH-5, Japan extended ODA loans totaling $187 million in three phases over 10 years (see table 2A.1 in annex 2A).

As a result of the project, the transport time between Hanoi and Hai Phong has been cut from 5 hours to 2 hours, while the average speed of the vehicles has almost doubled, from 24–30 km per hour to 50–60 km per hour, according to Ministry of Transport officials and field interviews conducted with highway users. Traffic has become much smoother, except in a few bottlenecks, such as central Hanoi and the port area in Hai Phong, ex post evaluations show. Widening roads, separating regular and light vehicles, upgrading intersections with other trunk roads, and making traffic management more efficient resulted in vast improvements compared to the prior chaos, when pedestrians and varying types of vehicles jostled in only one or two lanes.

In addition to improving NH-5 as the core physical infrastructure, institutional reforms complemented this trunk road investment

FIGURE 2.1   In the early 1990s, Vietnam needed a set of complementary efforts to promote industrialization and exports, improve transport, and upgrade labor

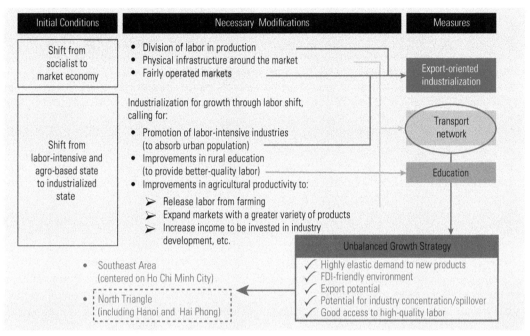

Source: JICA.
Note: FDI = foreign direct investment.

FIGURE 2.2   Foreign direct investment around Hai Phong Harbor has soared

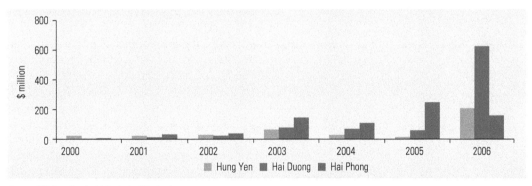

Source: JICA from Provincial Statistical Yearbook.

and played an important role in Vietnam's industrial development. Prime examples include the Amended Law on Foreign Investment (2000), the U.S.-Vietnam Bilateral Trade Agreement (2001), and the Company Law (2002) to ensure a smoother flow of goods and capital, as well as underpinning the legal status of private sector companies,

making it easier to collaborate with foreign partners.

The project attracted considerable FDI, which has grown almost exponentially (figure 2.2). The region was blessed with a good-quality but relatively low-wage workforce and was already exposed to global competition, having already attracted FDI.

Meanwhile, the national consensus to reduce poverty was building. These initial conditions were strengthened by later interventions, such as industrial zones, incentives to attract FDI, and vocational training.

The road linked four existing industrial parks (one in Hanoi and three in Hai Phong). In addition, eight new parks have been developed (three in Hung Yen Province and five in Hai Duong Province). Several industrial clusters have emerged along NH-5, centered on the garment, food processing, machinery, and electronics industries. Japanese companies contributed substantially to the development of industrial parks and clusters. By 2016, 652 Japanese companies were operating in Hanoi, Hung Yen, Hai Duong, and Hai Phong.

FIGURE 2.3   Vietnam's growth model centered on "anchor tenants" and associated firms jointly developing local supply chains

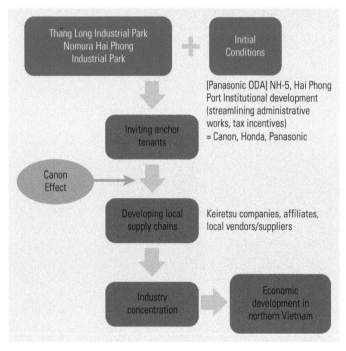

Source: JICA.
Note: ODA = official development assistance.

The areas surrounding the highway underwent a rapid and vast structural change, from the agricultural to the industrial sector.

One of the central features of Vietnam's industrial development in Vietnam was a model in which "anchor tenants" were invited to locate in the industrial parks. To establish local supply chains, these major firms have been encouraged to invite "keiretsu" companies, affiliates, and local vendors/suppliers, linked by cross-shareholdings to form a robust corporate structure. This model, named after the company that initiated it (Canon, the Japanese manufacturer of imaging and optical products) is called the Canon Effect (figure 2.3). Vietnam has been successful in creating this kind of virtuous cycle. The presence of global brands—including not only Canon, but also Honda and Panasonic—has accelerated industrial concentration and economic growth in the northeastern part of the country.

Not only core cities such as Hanoi and Hai Phong expanded, but so did production sites along the corridor (map 2.2). The surrounding provinces (Hung Yen, Hai Duong, and Hai Phong) and the port city have developed industrial parks hosting numerous foreign firms. New urban areas were also created, and local roads were built in Hai Phong near NH-5 to connect to villages that had been established before the highway was constructed (JICA 2008).

While the development of NH-5 and surrounding areas has brought about outstanding ripple effects economically as reviewed above, there still remains a view, especially from the viewpoint of foreign companies thinking about expanding local operations, that the supporting industries are not well developed, with local companies not fully capable of supplying quality products. In 2003, Vietnam and Japan started a joint effort ("Vietnam-Japan Joint Initiative") with the aim of improving the investment climate, in which various measures for fostering supporting industries are examined and put into practice.

On the Vietnamese side, the government has introduced a policy package for supporting industry development (Decree 12, February 2012), while Japanese side has been supporting the policy formation, human resource development, SME finance, etc.

MAP 2.2   Industrial parks have flourished along NH-5

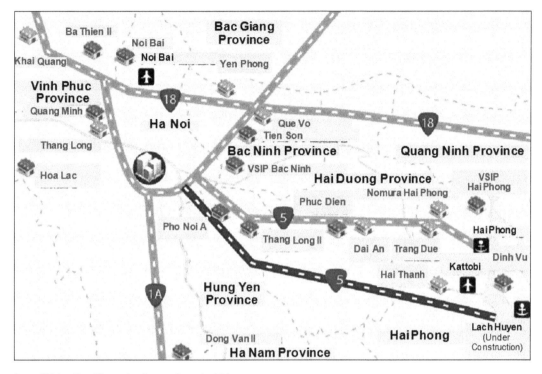

Source: JICA from Forval Corporation, Overseas Expansion Advisors.

Through these efforts, the share of local procurement by Japanese companies has seen a drastic increase from 22.4 percent in 2010 to 34.2 percent in 2016. On the other hand, the share of local suppliers in local procurement (41.1 percent) is still lower than those in India (73.4 percent), China (59.4 percent), and Indonesia (47.2 percent). (JETRO 2016). From this aspect as well, further development of local players is expected to extract WEB.

The area near the highway underwent far-reaching economic and structural change

With better connectivity, the number of enterprises has surged in the two nodal cities and the provinces along NH-5 (figure 2.4). From 2000 to 2004, after the project was completed, the number of firms in these areas grew faster than the national average (117 percent). The biggest growth occurred in Hanoi, where the number of enterprises

soared by 221 percent, while in the other nodal city, Hai Phong, the number of firms increased by 141 percent. The connected provinces of Hung Yen and Hai Duong also grew substantially (figure 2.4). The main reason that many of the firms chose to locate in all three provinces was good accessibility via NH-5, according to the beneficiary survey (JICA 2009). Hanoi became a center of gravity for firms, accounting for 16 percent of the total number of firms nationwide in 2004—up from 11 percent in 2000. While the expansion in the number of firms was impressive for Hai Phong and the other two provinces, it matched the growth in the rest of the country along major highways. Thus, these areas did not move up the ranks for the share of local firms in all firms in Vietnam.

The nodal cities and connected provinces all enjoyed double-digit economic growth from 2003 to 2006—much higher than the national average of 7.9 percent. The fastest growth in production occurred in the industrial sector (figure 2.5), ranging from 13.3 percent in Hai Duong to 20.5 percent in Hung Yen. The service sector also grew by double digits during this three-year period. In contrast, the agriculture sector declined in Hanoi and grew by only single digits in other areas around NH-5. Overall, the areas surrounding the highway underwent a vast structural change, from the agricultural to the industrial sector, from 2003 to 2006.

This structural change affected the production structure of the entire country. The shares of "commerce" and "factory" in total national production increased more than other sectors (figure 2.6). In contrast,

agricultural and livestock production declined from 65 percent to 46 percent of total GDP between 1997 and 2002.

Transport impacts

In line with the structural change and production boom, traffic volume increased during the same period. Freight volume almost tripled between 1994 and 2005, while passenger traffic increased from 400 million to 1.1 billion (figure 2.7, panel a). By 2006, passenger car units per day for NH-5 for all four major types of vehicles—cars, vans, buses, and trucks—outpaced the targeted value for 2008 (figure 2.7, panel b).

Wider economic impacts

The accelerating growth of industry in the areas along NH-5 has been reflected in the growth of overall income. The wider economic impacts of the development of NH-5 have been very beneficial, particularly for rural farmers. The improved transport corridor provided farmers with bigger and more lucrative local markets (both larger existing markets and higher value-added markets), thanks to income and population growth in the area. It also provided opportunities for nonfarming businesses, thanks to easier access to the major cities. This transformation has been further stimulated by complementary interventions, such as the development of a feeder road network and provision of public transport services.

The newly opened factories along NH-5 drew a large-scale labor force from the local farmer population and from migrants flowing into the cities along NH-5. In 2006 alone, 83,453 workers and 134,846 workers, respectively, were employed in Hung Yen (in the manufacturing sector) and Hai Duong provinces, accounting for 14 percent and 19 percent of the total working populations of these provinces.

This efficient shift in the labor force was made possible by the growing population of young people and the high quality of education in Vietnam. Education is mandatory through the lower secondary level. The completion rate for lower secondary studies for the whole country was 96 percent as of 2004. Furthermore, the upper secondary completion

FIGURE 2.4 The number of enterprises surged along NH-5 from 2000 to 2004, especially in Hanoi

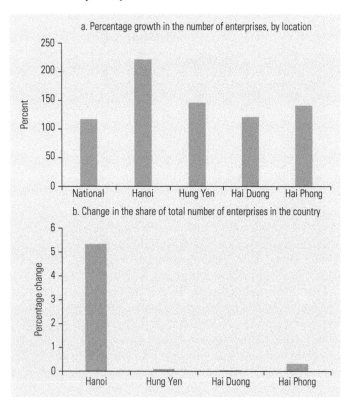

a. Percentage growth in the number of enterprises, by location

b. Change in the share of total number of enterprises in the country

Source: JICA.

The highway improvements increased production and trade, generated factory jobs, expanded supporting businesses, and activated the procurement of local inputs.

FIGURE 2.5 Production along NH-5 grew significantly more than the national average from 2003 to 2006

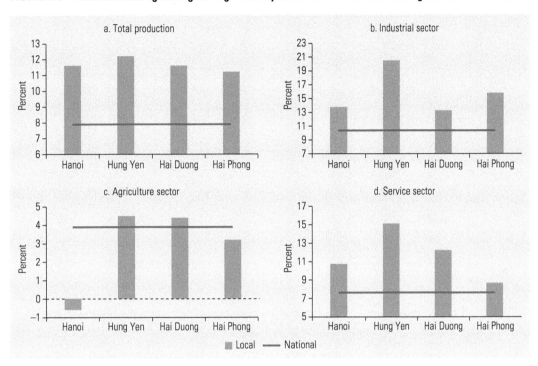

Source: JICA.
Note: The growth of production is measured by the growth of the respective city, province, and sectoral GDP. "Growth" is annualized real GDP growth from 2003 to 2006. NH-5 = National Highway No. 5.

FIGURE 2.6 The Vietnamese economy underwent a vast structural transformation from 1997 to 2002

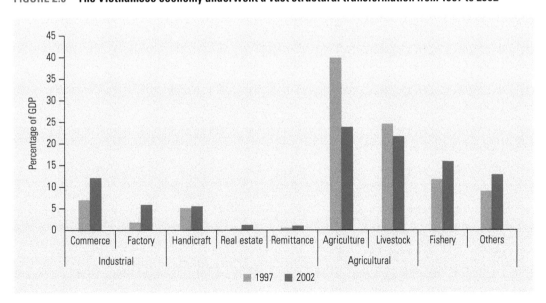

Source: JICA.

FIGURE 2.7 Traffic volume has soared in Vietnam on NH-5

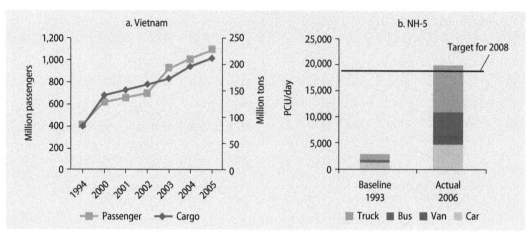

Source: JICA.

Source: JICA.
Note: NH-5 = National Highway No. 5; PCU/day = passenger car units per day.

FIGURE 2.8 The NH-5 upgrade generated significantly wider economic benefits for income and poverty

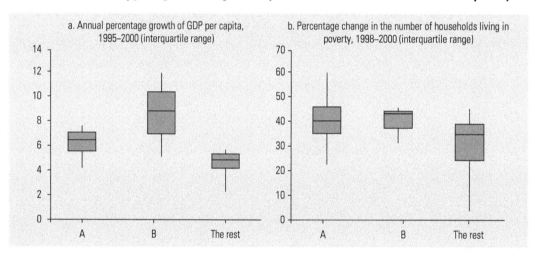

Source: JICA.
Note: In panel a, the maximum and minimum numbers are the reported numbers. The quartile numbers were calculated using the Excel command "quartile. inc." Area "A" (near NH-5) includes Hanoi, Hai Phong, Hai Duong, and Hung Yen. Area "B" (further from NH-5) includes Bac Ninh, Vinh Phuc, and Quang Ninh. "The rest" includes Ha Tinh, Ha Nam, Nam Dinh, Thai Binh, Ninh Binh, Thai Nguyen, Phu Tho, Bac Giang. GDP = gross domestic product; NH5 = National Highway No. 5.

rate for the four provinces along NH-5 was about 97–100 percent, which is much higher than the country average (90.5 percent) as of 2004.[1] Tertiary education started to be rolled out in Vietnam in the 1990s. The gross enrollment rate grew from 2.3 percent in 1990 to 9.4 percent in 2000 to 18.4 percent in 2007.[2] In 2012, Vietnam joined the Programme for

International Student Assessment (PISA), a worldwide assessment of educational attainment conducted by the Organisation for Economic Co-operation and Development (OECD). In its first year of testing, Vietnam's PISA ranking exceeded the OECD average in all three categories (reading, math literacy, and scientific literacy).[3] High-quality education has increased the quality of labor, and allowed Vietnam to take full advantage of the corridor as a driver of growth.

Among the provinces in the Red River Delta region,[4] those along NH-5 have ranked higher in the pace of income increase and poverty reduction (figure 2.8). From 1995 to 2000, GDP per capita grew by 6.1 percent in the Red River Delta region, compared with the national average of 5.7 percent. The number of households living in poverty dropped by an impressive 35 percent. The cities closer and further away from NH-5 (marked "A" and "B" in figure 2.8) both experienced higher income growth per capita as well as faster reduction in the poverty than "the rest" of the country. The country as a whole lowered its poverty rate by 27 percent during this period, thanks to broader positive spillovers from NH-5 to other regions.

The wider impacts also included unintended negative consequences. Traffic accidents soared. The highway has become more dangerous for light vehicles and pedestrians as wider roads have allowed the highway to carry larger and heavier motor vehicles, as well as a greater volume of traffic traveling at higher speeds. The lack of feeder roads has increased traffic jams around the industrial parks. And the highway has generated negative environmental impacts such as dust, noise, and vibrations.

In the 2000–06 period, traffic accidents were more frequent on NH-5 than other national highways (figure 2.9). Excessive speed accounted for nearly all (93 percent) of the traffic accidents along NH-5, according to the Ministry of Transport's Vietnam Road Administration (VRA). This share is substantially higher than the average of 60–70 percent for other highways. This high percentage of accidents can partly be attributed to the fact that residents have been slow to adapt to the huge increase in traffic volumes that accompanied the improvements in NH-5.

In recent years, the National Traffic Safety Committee (NTSC) has spearheaded various policy measures, including safety campaigns and legislation requiring all motorcycle riders to wear helmets. Bilateral donors and private sector companies have supported activities to

FIGURE 2.9 Traffic accidents have soared on NH-5, greatly outpacing the national trend as well as those of other national highways

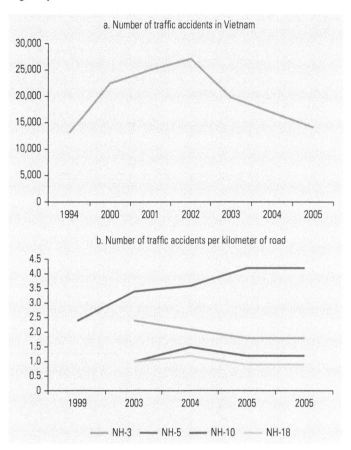

Source: JBIC 2003 and National Traffic Safety Committee (NTSC).
Note: NH-3 = National Highway No. 3; NH-5 = National Highway No. 5; NH-10 = National Highway No. 10; NH-18 = National Highway No. 18.

promote traffic safety, including the Study on National Road Traffic Safety Master Plan (2008, JICA), the Northern Vietnam National Roads Safety Improvement Project (2008–13, JICA), the Traffic Education Center (1999–present, Honda), and the Safety Driving Program (2014–present, Toyota).

As for environmental issues, NH-5 was developed before Vietnam's Environmental Impact Assessment (EIA) system was implemented. Thus, at the time the highway was upgraded, the feasibility study did not go through the EIA process. Environmental concerns were raised only later. To deal with these issues, policy measures (such as planting trees, and locating new schools and hospitals away from NH-5) have been taken. The negative environmental impacts have been gradually mitigated, although not totally removed.

Lessons learned

For a corridor intervention to be designed and implemented in a holistic fashion, policy makers must think through the potential chain (sequencing) of results originating from a particular design. They need to appraise the initial conditions, suitable policy measures, various expected outcomes, potential unintended consequences, and additional measures needed to address them (figure 2.10). Further, the design can more effectively achieve its primary goals—such as encouraging the clustering of industries—when policy makers duly consider interactions between specific policy measures and expected outcomes.

Initial conditions, including geographical advantages and constraints (such as distance from the major cities and ports, landlocked regions, surrounding countries, and markets) and demography (size, age, and the gender make-up of the labor force and population) must inform the choice of the geographical location for corridors.

Merely providing transport infrastructure for the corridor area does not automatically trigger the wider economic impacts. For positive spillovers to materialize from industrial concentration, economic and structural change must be supported by complementary policy measures—such as steps to provide an appropriate incentive structure, a legal framework to reduce operational costs for the

FIGURE 2.10 **The NH-5 Corridor generated many expected and unexpected wider economic impacts**

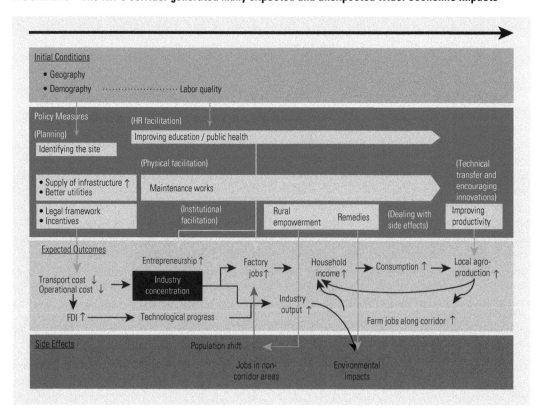

Source: JICA.
Note: NH-5 = National Highway No. 5.

companies, high-quality education to supply enough entrepreneurs and factory workers, and ensuring the quality of public health to maintain the labor supply for factories.

Policy makers must also consider some of the spillover effects from the clustering of core industries on nonindustrial sectors—such as the potential increase in local income that can help support local production. As local production rises, it can further boost the income of local suppliers and continue to strengthen local demand in a virtuous cycle. In the case of NH-5, the increasing consumption of higher-value-added commercial crops in urbanized areas motivated farmers to change their production portfolio from traditional to high-value crops.

During the process of industrialization along NH-5, the farming population and the amount of farm land have decreased. But in parallel, agricultural production and thus productivity have increased to a sustainable level. This increased productivity has been associated with booming sales of farm products to the food processing industry, as well as in exports by land and sea (see chapter 6 for a detailed analysis of such economic restructuring in India).

The original rationale for NH-5 to connect Hanoi as a regional economic center with the sea gateway delivered more than expected. As industry concentration accelerated along the corridor, there were robust spillovers to rural areas surrounding it—mostly through greater local demand stimulated by rising local income. The inflow of FDI played an important role in establishing an "ecosystem" in the regional economy, not only producing local spillovers but also integrating the NH-5 corridor into greater regional and global supply chains.

MALAYSIA'S EXPERIENCE WITH INTEGRATING RURAL AREAS AND INDUSTRIALIZED TRADE HUBS

As part of its national development strategy to redress regional economic disparities and narrow the divide between rural and urban areas, the Malaysian government is in the process of implementing five programs to create corridors of broader economic activity spurred by transport connectivity.

Malaysia is widely considered a development success story. This multiethnic nation has achieved rapid growth while reducing poverty and improving equality through affirmative action policies. Since achieving its independence in 1957, Malaysia has leapfrogged from low-income to upper-middle-income status. Economic growth has been accompanied by rising living standards and improvements in the distribution of income, ameliorating the twin problems of poverty and racial imbalances (Snodgrass 1980; Athukorala and Menon 1999; Lucas and Verry 2001; Faaland, Parkinson, and Saniman 2003; Lim 2011).

However, since about the late 1990s, Malaysian policy makers have been concerned about the widening of income disparities among urban and rural areas and among ethnic groups. Had rapid growth been accompanied by a more equitable income distribution, domestic demand would have had a far more important role in fueling growth and would have reduced the economy's reliance on exports as the engine of growth (Ariff 2012). These concerns have propelled Malaysian policy makers to focus on policies to redress the widening divide between rural and urban areas and different states in the country.

The idea of corridor development as a vehicle for achieving balanced growth was first mooted in the Ninth Malaysia Plan, 2006–10, launched in 2006. It proposed developing "new regional growth centres (RGCs) and growth corridors .... together by the Government and the private sector to promote investment, create jobs and encourage rapid development in the areas concerned" (Government of Malaysia 2006, 28). But in the Mid-Term Review of the Ninth Plan (Government of Malaysia 2008), five corridors were identified, each with an established or growing city as its core:

1. The Northern Corridor Economic Region (NCER) in northern Peninsular Malaysia, with Georgetown as its center.
2. Iskandar Malaysia (IM) in the south, with Johor Bahru as its center.

3. East Coast Economic Region (ECER) on the east coast of the peninsula, with Kuantan as its center.
4. Sarawak Corridor of Renewable Energy (SCORE), with Kuching as its center.
5. Sabah Development Corridor (SDC), with Kota Kinabalu as its center.

The proposed five corridors cover almost 70 percent of the country's landmass.

The rationale for the model of interstate corridors with interlinked economic activities is the belief that states could forgo the benefits of joint and complementary growth if they pursue their individual interests, concentrating on their own growth. By providing connections, both physical and economic, to potential or growing economic nodes or hubs within the corridor, and eventually through global economic integration, the corridor will help boost the economic potential of areas that are lagging.

The Northern Corridor Economic Region in the northern part of Peninsular Malaysia is an interesting and ambitious effort to develop a corridor that extends across several states. The four member states of the corridor form a natural bloc for economic cooperation, given their many complementarities. Kedah, Perak, and Perlis are predominantly agricultural, hinterland states, endowed with abundant land and rich natural resources that remain to be fully exploited. Penang (with its port and airport) functions as the gateway to the other three states.

Compared with the other four corridors, the NCER is at a relatively advanced stage in implementing the development program at the subregional level. It provides an interesting case study of how a corridor of broader economic activity can link an agricultural hinterland with a "modern" sector of the economy. Thus the rest of this section focuses on the NCER, with a specific analysis of the role of Penang.

The northern corridor economic region links four Malaysian states

The NCER's ultimate aims are to strengthen the country's overall competitiveness and distribute prosperity more equitably among the four states. The proximity of the region to Thailand and access to the Strait of Malacca are viewed as added advantages of the NCER in a regional context. The four states are within the Indonesia-Malaysia-Thailand Growth Triangle (IMT-GT) (ADB 2012).[5]

Several road projects have been proposed to connect northern Malaysia and southern Thailand. The Songkhla–Penang–Medan corridor is one of the five corridors identified under the IMT-GT implementation blueprint (2012–16). It aims to rejuvenate the long-standing trade routes centered on Penang that are important for bulk shipping of goods within the region and for providing outward shipping services to East Asia and Europe. The Songkhla-to-Penang subcorridor is very important for Thai exports, particularly rubber and related products, wood products, and agro products.

The NCER was officially launched by the fifth prime minister of Malaysia, Ahmad Badawi, at Kedah and Perlis on July 30, 2007, and in Penang and Perak on July 31, 2007. As originally envisaged, the NCER encompassed the northern states of Perlis, Kedah, and Penang, and five districts of northern Perak. The geographical coverage was expanded in 2016 to include the remaining districts of Perak, and thus to include the entire state. The region now spans more than 32,500 square km.

The NCER's economic profile varies greatly

The four NCER states account for about 16 percent of Malaysia's total national output. Penang contributes the largest share (6.6 percent in 2010–15), followed by Perak (5.4 percent), Kedah (3.3 percent), and Perlis (0.5 percent). Kedah is the poorest. Penang's per capita income is about 16 percent higher than the national average, while Kedah's is only about 47 percent of the national average. Penang has the lowest incidence of poverty in the NCER region and nationally. Poverty rates in the other states range from 3.5 percent to 6.0 percent.

Penang is the most industrialized of the four NCER states, with manufacturing directly contributing to over 46 percent of GDP, compared to the NCER average of 31.6 percent and the national average of 23.2 percent during 2010–15. Kedah, Perak, and Perlis are predominantly agricultural, with abundant land and rich natural resources with ample prospects for further development (Spinanger 1986; Faaland, Parkinson, and Saniman 2003).

Penang has a much more diversified manufacturing base than the other three states. Electronics, electrical goods, and related products account for a larger share of manufacturing in Penang, whereas processed food and other resource-based products are more important in the other three states.

Penang's manufacturing sector accounts for about one-third of manufacturing employment in the NCER. Penang's labor productivity of manufacturing is much higher than the other three states. This suggests that Penang has a relatively well-developed skill base, which the NCER can potentially draw on for regional development. The wage per worker in Penang is also much higher, indicating that there is room for the spread of relatively more labor-intensive production processes away from Penang to other parts of the NCER, provided that other preconditions (such as logistics, infrastructure, and skill development) are met.

The potential for subregional development is strong

Harmonious links between the private sector and government agencies already prevail in the NCER (Narayanan 1999). The NCER can leverage three other core strengths to bridge the development divide between Penang and the other three states: physical connectivity, a mature business ecosystem, and a skilled and industry-ready workforce (Sime Darby 2007).

Connectivity is strong in penang and promising for the other three states

Sea cargo. Penang's port is situated along the Strait of Malacca, which runs between Indonesia, Malaysia, and Singapore. Long the major gateway for trade to and from Asia, the Strait is one of the world's busiest shipping lanes. The port is well placed to act as the logistic hub for the NCER and southern Thailand. It is already the third-biggest seaport in Malaysia (based on total throughput).

Air cargo. The international airport at Bayan Lepas, Penang, is the second-largest airport for air cargo in Malaysia (after Kuala Lumpur), and the third-busiest passenger airport after Kuala Lumpur and Kota Kinabalu. Penang airport enhances Penang's role as a major production center within global production networks. Over the past four decades, it has served as a major outlet for high-value-to-weight electric and electrical goods from the surrounding Free Trade Zone industrial areas and high-value-to-weight electronic components from Kulim High-Tech Park in Kedah, which is 44 km away. Over 80 percent of the electronics and electrical goods exported from Penang are shipped by air.

Land cargo. The Padang Besar Inland Depot in the northern part of Perlis on the border with Songkhla Province is the entry point for land cargo destined to Penang's port from southern Thailand. It has the potential to be developed further to serve as an integrated logistics center for handling bulk products exported from the region through Penang's port from the NCER's agricultural hinterland as well as from southern Thailand.

The business ecosystem is mature

Penang is a mature manufacturing export hub that has grown, widened, and deepened over the past four decades (Narayanan 1999; Gill and Kharas 2007; Athukorala 2014, 2017). There are now over 200 branch plants of multinational enterprises (MNEs), employing over 250,000 workers, operating in Penang. They include major global players such as Intel, Motorola, AMD, Osram, and Hitachi. The partnership between MNEs and local firms has strengthened over time, resulting in the growth of a large pool of local tooling and equipment manufacturing firms. By 2005, 1,956 local firms were operating in Penang, of which 144 had graduated to "large-firm" status.

Ancillary industries that evolved around the major electronics and auto firms have expanded rapidly, enhancing the network's cohesion. Some Penang firms have become suppliers to other high-technology firms, operating both locally and overseas, in addition to supplying their MNE partners. After starting as small backyard workshops, many local vendors and some of these firms have achieved the status of full-fledged service providers with substantial research and development (R&D) and design capabilities. Others have become global players with production bases in other countries.

In 2005, exports made up over 40 percent of the total gross output of large local firms. Local firms accounted for one-third of manufacturing output and over half of total employment in the manufacturing sector in Penang.

With wages and rental costs increasing rapidly, and available space limited in Penang, there is potential for expanding the manufacturing base to neighboring states by further developing infrastructure and the workforce.

The talent pool is large and deep

More than four decades of growth of manufacturing and related activities in Penang have created a ready pool of talent (box 2.1). A broad range of engineering-based expertise has developed to support the expansion of new growth sectors in the region, such as LEDs, automotive, aerospace, machinery/automation, medical devices, and biotechnology. Many of the businesses in Penang can meet the world-class delivery standards that MNEs demand. Furthermore, the continuous engagement between industry and academia, along with the setting up of centers of excellence, ensures the availability of a workforce with relevant skills to meet the demands of the various sectors in the region.

The NCER accounts for about 20 percent of the nation's workforce, of which 68 percent are working age. In 2013, an estimated 50,000 graduates and 25,000 workers with technical and vocational education and training (TVET) were available in the region. TVET trainees are projected to increase to 187,000 between 2014 and 2020 (Hasri 2016).

BOX 2.1 Meeting the manpower requirements of an export hub through a public-private partnership: The Penang Skill Development Centre

By the late 1980s, when skill shortages began to hamper expansion of the electronics industry in Penang, the Penang Development Corporation joined with multinational enterprises (MNEs) to establish the Penang Skill Development Centre (PSDC). Its first training program began in July 1989. PSDC has since played a pivotal role in meeting the manpower requirements of the export hub. It has attracted worldwide attention as an example of a successful public-private partnership in human capital development (UNIDO 2009). PSDC officials have visited many developing countries to provide expertise on how to establish similar organizations.

Initially, the PSDC training programs focused on creating a large pool of technicians to meet the immediate needs of rapidly expanding electronics firms, particularly just-in-time measurement and precision engineering skills. Over the years, the scope and breath of the organization have expanded, influenced by technological advances and the changing operational environment. PSDC has been successfully conducting a vendor development program, known as the Global Supplier Development Programme (GSDP), to help local companies become world-class global suppliers by developing their capabilities through training and by forging linkages with MNEs. The training is divided into two streams: manufacturing and services. Once a small or medium-sized enterprise (SME) has been through basic training, it is selected to enter an MNE coaching and mentoring program. After an agreed-on period of coaching and mentoring, the MNE decides whether to accept the SME as part of its supply chain (Ruffing 2006).

To coordinate activities across the four states, an interstate authority was established

The task of achieving coordination between the planning agencies of four states can be formidable. When one or more states within the corridor have different interests or priorities, the challenges to achieving a consensus are magnified further. Malaysia therefore established a formal coordination mechanism, the Northern Corridor Implementation Authority (NCIA), to support collective decision making and implementation.

The NCIA is supervised by the NCIA Council, which is headed by the prime minister. Members include the chief ministers of the four states, as well as the deputy prime minister, the chief secretary to the federal government, and other individuals appointed by the federal government. The NCIA's chief executive serves as secretary to the council. Apart from the chief ministers of the four states, all other members are from the federal government or are federal appointees (including the NCIA chief executive). The NCIA operates under the Economic Planning Unit (EPU) of the Prime Minister's Department, which is the coordinating/monitoring body for all five corridor programs.

The NCIA is tasked with fostering the corridor's growth as a whole, while minimizing the tendency of member states to prioritize their needs over the needs of the region, and fostering private sector engagement in implementing the NCER's programs. It receives both financial resources and infrastructural support from the federal government and federal agencies.

The NCIA draws its authority from an act of Parliament, the NCIA Act 2008 (Act 687). Under the act, the NCIA has the power to require/obtain particulars and information as may be specified by the authority from all government entities, companies, and corporations, and other bodies and persons operating within the NCER. It also can make recommendations to state and local authorities on local government functions and services, including local planning, control, and

regulation, as well as the approval and control of all buildings and building operations. The NCIA also assists/facilitates investments by assisting investors in meeting investment requirements and acquiring the necessary approvals. Additionally, it acts as the principal coordinating agent monitoring the progress of such projects.

A public-private partnership unit (UKAS) was created in the Prime Minister's Department to encourage private sector participation as prime movers in the implementation of the program. UKAS is the core agency that has been given the responsibility to coordinate the privatization and PPP projects that are eligible for funding from a facilitation fund operated by UKAS. The NCIA, for its part, helps identify such companies or projects and assists them in gaining access to these funds.

The NCER blueprint guides the interstate authority (NCIA)

The NCIA is broadly guided by a blueprint prepared for the region by a government-linked conglomerate, Sime Darby Berhad, which has interests in multiple sectors, including plantation agriculture and the automotive and health care industries. It was charged to recommend "commercially sustainable measures and programs."

The Northern Corridor Economic Region's *Socioeconomic Blueprint,* which was prepared by Sime Darby, was released in July 2007 (Sime Darby 2007). It covers an 18-year period from 2007 to 2025. It initially focused on three main economic areas—agriculture, manufacturing, and services—to transform the region into a "world-class region by 2025." "Services" was later subdivided into tourism and logistics.[6] These four areas are to be developed largely by leveraging the existing strengths in the NCER and by developing potential areas of strength.

Sime Darby eventually withdrew as the major sponsor of the project, though its representative serves on the NCIA Council. The *Blueprint* now functions as the basic guide to the NCIA, though the agency has departed from the *Blueprint* as and when it was felt necessary.

The implementation of the NCIA program has been compressed into two phases
Implementation of the *Blueprint* was initially divided into three phases. The first phase (2007–12) aimed to lay the foundation by constructing "priority infrastructure" and securing anchor investors. The second (2013–15) was devoted to broadening and deepening private sector involvement in the region and fostering foreign and domestic business network and linkages. The third phase (2016–25) aims at achieving regional market leadership through sustainable market-led growth. Given the time lag involved in initiating and implementing large projects, the NCIA has combined the first and second phases into a single phase.

Phase I (2007–14): Securing Anchor Investors and Constructing "Priority Infrastructure"
During this period, the Second Penang Bridge was built, linking the emerging industrial area of Batu Kawan in Seberang Perai on the mainland portion of Penang state with Batu Maung on Penang Island, close to the airport. The 24 km–long bridge is the longest bridge in Malaysia and southeast Asia. It helped encourage the expansion of the Batu Kawan Industrial Park (BKIP) by providing direct access to the firms located there to the Penang airport and facilitating the movement of manpower between the two parts of the state. Because the 1,500-acre area of BKIP is now fully occupied, the state government is planning to develop a second industrial nearby.

The first Penang Bridge was also widened. The international airport in Penang was upgraded. The railway line that runs through the four NCER states was electrified. The NCIA supported private sector investments, including firms in the growing medical devices industry and the more mature electronics and electrical (EE) sector in Penang. More recently, a small but growing aerospace industry has begun developing. These companies draw their workforce from the universities in the north and rely on service-based industries in Penang.

Phase II (2015–25): Broadening and Deepening Private Sector Involvement in the Region
The focus in the second (current) phase is on the predominantly Malay states of Perlis and Kedah and the newly added regions of Perak. Despite budgetary cuts, the allocation for corridor development in the recently launched Eleventh Malaysia Plan, 2016–20 (Government of Malaysia 2016) remains substantial. Included are the following major investment initiatives.

1. *Kedah Rubber City Project.* The Rubber City project aims to elevate the global competitive position of the Malaysian rubber industry. It is based in the heart of the natural rubber belt that lies close to the Malaysia-Thai border in Padang Terap, in Kedah. This massive investment—the construction of an entirely new city—is a federal government initiative, implemented by Kedah state, and backed by the NCIA. When fully operational in 2025, the 1,500-acre (607-hectare) city hopes to attract RM10 billion in investment and generate between 15,000 and 20,000 jobs directly, while increasing the earnings of rubber smallholders and rubber tappers. Incentive packages for investors are being prepared, including corporate tax exemptions, waivers of the import duty on machinery, and a subsidy for the training of workers.

Malaysia's well-established base in rubber product manufacturing is expected to give the Rubber City a head start and an eventual niche in the upstream, midstream, and downstream activities of the rubber industry. Local innovation capabilities related to rubber and rubber products are also envisioned.

2. *The Kedah Science & Technology Park.* In the face of shortages of land and rising rental costs, several MNE subsidiaries that had long operated in Penang relocated some of their operations to the Kulim Hi-Tech Park (KHTP) in Kedah. This paved the way for new investors to come directly to Kulim. Since 2002, the park has reportedly attracted nearly RM32 billion in investment and generated over 30,000 high-income jobs.[7]

A second industrial park, the Kedah Science & Technology Park (KSTP), reserved for industries with advanced technologies, is planned for a 1,950-acre site in Bukit Kayu Hitam. Plans include well-equipped, high-end research laboratories; business incubation centers; and technology business incubators. The emphasis will be on collaboration between academia, government, and industry to lead research and commercialization projects. It is anticipated that the park will create 23,244 jobs by 2030 and have "an economic impact of RM57.4 billion" (Hasri 2016).[8]

3. *Chuping Valley Development Area.* The Chuping Valley Development Area is in Padang Besar, Perlis, the northernmost state on the peninsula. Encompassing 2,482 acres, it will promote three clusters—solar energy generation; green materials or technologies in manufacturing; and halal industries—to transform the area into a "Green Valley." The effort is expected to generate 12,674 jobs and contribute around RM2.58 billion to gross national income by 2025.

4. *Perlis Inland Port.* Another major project in the Chuping Valley and alongside the three industrial clusters is the Perlis Inland Port Project (PIP), which was envisioned to supplement Padang Besar Cargo Terminal, which is struggling to cope with current cargo loads and facing further increases in volume. Once completed, the PIP is expected to become the largest and busiest inland (dry) port on the peninsula, serving not only in Perlis but also Kedah and its Rubber City.

The PIP, spanning 200 hectares, is a RM1.5 billion project that includes railway lines and roads linked to the Chuping Valley area. It will feature a large-capacity container yard, extensive warehouse facilities, and a Web-based computer system. To increase its connectivity to the rest of the peninsula, a designated highway from the border to the port and a railway extension track linking it to the existing double-track rail network are also in the pipeline.

5. *Greater Kamunting Conurbation.* The Greater Kamunting Conurbation (GKC) in Perak is aimed at transforming and strengthening economic sectors such as tourism, manufacturing, and agriculture in Kamunting and Taiping, leveraging the pivotal position of GKC within the NCER. New infrastructure will be provided, along with initiatives to train and educate the workforce. The projects are projected to create 90,263 jobs by 2030.

6. *South Perak Development Region.* This is made up of new areas added to the NCER. It covers 449,252 hectares and had a population of 424,700 in 2010. It is expected that the area will attract public and private investments totaling RM30.5 billion by 2030 and generate 109,000 jobs.

It is difficult to separate the achievements of the corridor from general progress in the region

Of the RM307 billion committed by the federal government to implement the five corridors, only 57 percent has been utilized (table 2.1). The NCIA is the only one of the five corridor authorities to fully utilize all the funds allocated to it. The NCER has accounted for 63,500 of the 427,000 jobs created within the five corridors.

The first phase has attracted investment worth about RM113 billion (including RM71.63 billion in federal funds). This includes individual efforts by the NCIA and efforts made in cooperation with state and federal agencies (Hasri 2016). According to the NCIA's chief executive, from its launch in 2008 through the end of 2016, the NCIA attracted RM79.92 billion in public and private investment to the NCER and created 103,600 jobs. The combined GDP of the four states grew at an average annual rate of 5.8 percent between 2010 and 2014, much faster than the 3.5 percent average during the 2005–09 period.[9] Income distribution improved considerably. The poverty rate declined from 2.83 percent in 2007 to 0.45 percent in 2014, while the median monthly household income increased from RM2,112 to RM3,797 (Hasri 2016).

TABLE 2.1   Investment and employment in Malaysia's five corridors, 2011–14

Corridor	Investment (RM billion)		Jobs created
	Committed[a]	Realized	
1. Northern Corridor Economic Region (NCER)	51.7	51.7	63,500
2. Iskandar Malaysia	90.4	47.1	320,100
3. East Coast Economic Region (ECER)	55.4	22.9	23,000
4. Sarawak Corridor of Renewable Energy (SCORE)	12.9	8.3	5,300
5. Sabah Development Corridor (SDR)	96.7	44.5	15,200
Total	307.1	174.5	427,100

Source: Economic Planning Unit (2016), Eleventh Malaysia Plan, 2016–2020 (based on data provided by Regional Corridor Authorities).
a. The data relate to private investment supported by the NCER.

These figures, while impressive, are not adequate for assessing the growth and equity outcome of the NCER programs. Without detailed project-level data, it is not possible to separate the impact of NCER projects from the general process of economic/industrial development in the region. Moreover, the NCIA does not maintain investment and employment data at the state level, even though the prime objective of this corridor project is to narrow growth and income disparities among the four constituent states. More important, the available data do not permit an assessment of whether NCER programs have contributed to narrowing the divide between rural and urban regions and between the four states.

The impact of NCER projects is not yet discernible in the state-level national accounts data for 2010–15. The collective share of the four NCER states in total national GDP (15.7 percent) remained virtually unchanged during this period, as did the shares of each of the four states in national GDP and their per capita income relative to the national average. Data relating to the sectoral composition of GDP for the four states also do not indicate any structural changes in their economies. This persistence over a relatively short period may reflect the fact that it often takes a long time to achieve the expected gains from long-term investment projects.

Limitations in efforts to date point to new directions

The NCER initiatives have so far focused mainly on heavy infrastructure. Actions related to the other two components—logistics reforms, and business/entrepreneurial development with private sector involvement—will presumably follow in the subsequent phases.

Meanwhile, cross-border logistics issues with Thailand are impeding the potential to increase trade with Thailand. The volume of shipments from southern Thailand has not been fully exploited because of the failure to combine the development of Penang's port and railways to the Thai border with initiatives to improve customs clearance procedures at the entry point at Buki Kayu Hitam on the Perlis-Thai border. Thai producers have been diverting shipments from Penang to the Bangkok and Songkhla ports in Thailand to avoid the border tax of the 0.005 cent per kilogram on canned seafood shipments from Thailand that Malaysia recently imposed. These cross-border logistical issues are also directly relevant to the operation of the dry port currently under construction in Perlis. Admittedly, this is a bilateral trade issue, which is outside the purview of the NCIA, but the NCIA can play a useful advocacy role in highlighting the urgency of resolving it.

The business/entrepreneurial development initiatives thus far have not directly addressed the rural/urban divide—particularly the goal to raise the living standards of people living in rural agricultural areas. The programs implemented so far, as well as those proposed for the second stage, seem to have been driven by the traditional view that agriculture needs to take a backseat in the process of economic development because real income levels can be lifted only by moving rural workers to modern sectors.

The only proposed initiative in the NCER program that has direct implications for raising rural income levels relates to promoting halal food. There is potential to expand the halal food industry in Malaysia, but halal food products account for only a small share of world trade in processed food. Attention should shift to processed food in general, including food falling under the halal category.

Processed food offers great potential
The emergence of processed foods in world trade is a structural (rather than a "passing") phenomenon that is deeply embodied in the ongoing process of global economic integration. The new export opportunities in processed food offer several advantages for countries rich in agricultural resources, like Malaysia. First, the final stages of food processing are labor intensive. Second, processed food appears superior to conventional manufactured exports in terms of potential net export earnings and thus the impact on national income (GNP). Third, the processed food industry naturally has a strong rural base. Based on these considerations, the expansion of processed food exports is a powerful vehicle for linking the rural economy in a positive way with the ongoing process of economic globalization.

Neighboring Thailand is one of the main success stories of processed food exports in the developing world. Processed food accounts for more than one-fifth of Thailand's merchandise exports (Athukorala and Jayasuriya 2003, 1401). Given the similarities in terms of agricultural resource endowment and climatic conditions, the agricultural hinterland of the NCER seems to have significant potential for emulating the Thai experience.[10]

Processed food production is a class of economic activity in agriculture that closely resembles manufacturing. It requires capabilities to keep products fresh and deliver them from farm to processing plants and then to shop shelves with proper packaging and labeling, while meeting international food safety standards. Export success with these products has become increasingly challenging in recent years because of formal food safety standards and the quality requirements of demanding buyers (Fujita 2008; Page 2012).

All four NCER states have unexploited potential for expanding seafood processing, in addition to agro-based, high-value products. The International Organization of Tuna Council (IOTC) has approved Penang's port as an outlet for tuna exports. However, exports of tuna still account for only a small share of products exported from Penang's port. According to a Penang port official, trawlers from China and nearby islands, fish tuna in the surrounding seas. Their catch is exported in canned form because it is so costly to refrigerate fresh fish during the long voyage. The NCER states have potential to develop a fish processing industry. They could also use "mining ponds" (abandoned tin mines filled with water) in Perak for fish farming, transforming them from their common use as illegal land-fill sites.

The kehah rubber city project faces strong competition from Thailand
The Kedah Rubber City project is a massive investment project, largely driven by the availability of natural rubber as an input for rubber-based products. There is no evidence to suggest that the role of entrepreneurship and market links, and potential competition from Thailand, have been considered in designing the project. In resource-based industries, the availability of a strong raw material base is not the sole determinant of the development of downstream industries. In this era of falling shipping costs, raw materials can be transported to production locations elsewhere that meet the other preconditions required for competitive industrial production.

Thailand has a well-established rubber-based manufacturing industry making tires, gloves, condoms, rubber-based apparel, and rubberwood furniture. Drawing on these existing capacities, Thailand began work on its own Rubber City in southern Thailand. The first phase is expected to be fully operational in 2017. The project has already attracted Michelin, while investors from China have also expressed interest in the Rubber City. While Thai laws prohibit foreigners from owning land in their own name, the Rubber City is an exception.[11] There is little reason to expect that Thai businesses will be drawn to Kedah when similar facilities are available in southern Thailand.

Institutional coordination challenges hamper the corridor

The corridors have a top-down coordination structure. They are federal government initiatives, and the statutory bodies and implementation authorities created to oversee their development are also federal creations. This is understandable in the Malaysian federal system,[12] where the most important powers remain concentrated in the hands of the federal government.[13] Nevertheless, further engagement with state-level officials could be helpful given that the NCER cuts across four states and that these states retain sole jurisdiction over land matters within their boundaries. This is a powerful tool when determining the location of investments and other infrastructure development.[14] This may also help when priorities across states regarding projects for the corridor may differ.

The original *Blueprint* was designed with Penang as the NCER's regional integrated logistic hub (Sime Darby 2007; Lim 2007). About half the federal funds allocated to the NCIA (RM71.62 billion) during 2009–15 was channeled to Penang, while the rest was divided among the other three states. Since then, the emphasis has shifted to development projects in the other three states. Some of the infrastructure projects that were part of the original plan to develop Penang as the logistic hub of the NCER have been postponed.

The justification for the emphasis on increased investment in the other three states is that Penang is already well developed in terms of industrial maturity and physical connectivity, while the other three states are not and therefore deserve more attention. While this may be

true, it would be important to foster dialogue to fully explore possible long-term ramifications for Penang, including the proposed Kulim International Airport, which is likely to affect the status of Penang Airport.

The way forward

The four member states of the NCER form a natural bloc for economic cooperation, given their many complementarities. Kedah, Perak, and Perlis are predominantly agricultural hinterland states, endowed with abundant land and rich natural resources that remain to be fully exploited. Given its strategic location and high global economic integration, Penang can perform the role of the gateway and knowledge hub for the NCER to bridge the development gaps across the constituent states.

While it is too early to assess the full outcome of the NCER initiative, a potential problem looms in the future. The NCIA, which is charged with implementing projects in the NCER, has no formal positions allotted to planning officials from the member states. This will not pose problems in implementing projects that are in broad alignment with the interest of the states. Conflicts may arise, however, when the states' and the NCIA's views on projects differ.

The goals of the plan can be met only through consultations and coordination with the states and the private sector, as originally envisioned. This concern is of national importance because the corridor program is here to stay. It was a key theme in the past three five-year development plans. The latest (eleventh) plan has considerably increased the commitments of federal funding to the corridors, even in the face of budgetary constraints.

Moving forward, representatives from key state implementation agencies from all member states could be included in discussing, planning, and implementing NCIA projects. A transparent and nonpartisan stance should be adapted, as has been done by some other agencies established by the federal government. For instance, the Malaysian Industrial Development Authority (MIDA) has an economy-wide focus based on the comparative advantage and complementarity of various states in promoting and approving foreign direct investment nationwide and in its regions.

Summing up and moving to the next chapter

Chapter 2 has presented two case studies of government programs to develop transport corridors with positive spillover to wider economy and regional integration. In Vietnam, greater transport capacity has attracted significant foreign direct investment. As a result, the areas surrounding Vietnam's National Highway No. 5 have undergone a rapid and vast structural change from the agricultural to the industrial sector. The presence of global brands—including Canon, Honda, and Panasonic—helped establish a booming "ecosystem" in the local economy, not only producing local spillovers but also integrating the NH-5 corridor into regional and global supply chains. But these positive developments were not without trade-offs. Accidents per km of highway significantly outpaced all other national highways from 2000 to 2006. Environmental problems gradually surfaced and were mitigated only later by additional measures.

In Peninsular Malaysia, the development of the Northern Corridor Economic Region (NCER) has been less successful so far, partly because of a greater bias toward pure infrastructure investment compared to the original blueprint for the initiative. The involvement of the private sector, as originally envisioned, failed to fully materialize. An uneven presence of local representatives in central planning bodies—namely, the Northern Corridor Implementation Authority (NCIA)—resulted in diversion of some investments toward other subregions in Malaysia. The chapter suggests reforming the NCIA to help the NCER meet the original goals. A transparent and nonpartisan stance could be adopted, such as the model used by the Malaysian Industrial Development Authority (MIDA), which has also an economy-wide focus.

Turning to transport projects supported by international development organizations, chapter 3 employs a quantitative approach to analyze which features could boost a corridor project's potential for generating wider economic benefits. It takes advantage of a unique new data set based on a survey of large transport infrastructure (corridor) projects supported by the Asian Development Bank (ADB), the Japan International Cooperation Agency (JICA), and the World Bank Group, and summarizes the results of an extensive meta-analysis.

NOTES

1. *Statistical Yearbook of Vietnam 2005.*
2. World Bank, World Development Indicators.
3. The Red River Delta region, home to over 17 million people, is Vietnam's most densely populated area. It has many large industrial zones, including those in Hanoi and Hai Phong, and accounts for one-fifth of the country's rice crop.
4. The Indonesia-Malaysia-Thailand Growth Triangle (IMT-GT) subregional program aims to stimulate economic development in 32 of these three countries' less-developed states and provinces, which are home to over 54 million people (Asian Development Bank, https://www.adb.org/countries/subregional -programs/imt-gt.)
5. See, for example, http://www.mycorridor .malaysia.gov.my/IC/NCER/Pages/default .aspx.
6. See http://www.kulimhitechpark.com/kedah -to-set-up-more-technology-parks/.
7. It is unclear what is meant by "economic impact."
8. *Malaysian Digest*, January 25, 2017. See http:// www.malaysiandigest.com/frontpage /29-4-tile/655159-ncia-to-achieve-accumulated -investment-of-rm87-3-bln-by-end-2017.html.
9. Whether the existing land tenure system is a constraint on promoting the production of high-value food production is an important issue that is beyond the scope of this study. For an authoritative analysis of the tenure system in Malaysia, see appendix A in Faaland et al. 2003.
10. *Star Online*, January 30, 2016. See http://www .thestar.com.my/business/business-news /2016/01/30/thai-govt-seeks-investors-for

-rubber-city/ and http://globalrubbermarkets
.com/40439/malaysia-thailand-in-friendly-com
petition-for-rubber-city-fdi.html.

11. See Hutchinson (2014) for a succinct back-ground on Malaysia's federal system.

12. These include the power to collect all major taxes, determine the allocation of develop-ment funds to states, and provide defense, security, and transport infrastructure. Only the federal government has the power to borrow funds from external sources.

13. The states also retain powers over matters pertaining to Islamic religious matters. Sabah and Sarawak have additional powers to control immigration and the issuance of work permits in their respective states.

REFERENCES

ADB (Asian Development Bank). 2012. *Indonesia-Malaysia-Thailand Growth Triangle (IMT-GT): Implementation Blue Print*. Manila: ADB.

Ariff, M. 2012. "Development Strategy under Scrutiny." Preface to *Malaysia's Development Challenges: Graduating from the Middle*, edited by H. Hill, T. S. Yean, and R. H. M. Zin, xvii– xxiii. London: Routledge.

Athukorala, P. 2014. "Growing with Global Production Sharing: The Tale of Penang Export Hub, Malaysia." *Competition & Change* 18 (3): 221–45.

———. 2017. "Global Productions Sharing and Local Entrepreneurship in Developing Countries: Evidence from Penang Export Hub, Malaysia." *Asia & the Pacific Policy Studies*. doi: 10.1002/app5.171.

Athukorala, P., and S. Jayasuriya. 2003. "Food Safety Issues, Trade and WTO Rules: A Developing Country Perspective." *World Economy* 26 (9): 1395–1416.

Athukorala, P., and J. Menon. 1999. "Outward Orientation and Economic Development in Malaysia." *World Economy* 22 (8): 1119–39.

Athukorala, P., and S. Narayanan. 2017. "Economic Corridors and Regional Development: The Malaysian Experience."

Faaland, J., J. Parkinson, and R. Saniman. 2003. *Growth and Ethnic Inequality: Malaysia's New Economic Policy*, 2nd edition. Kuala Lumpur: Utusan Publications & Distribution Sdn Bhd.

Fujita, M. 2008. "Spurring Economic Development by Capitalising Brand Agriculture: Turning Development Strategy on Its Head." In *Annual World Bank Conference on Development Economics: Rethinking Infrastructure for Development,* edited by F. Bourguignon and B. Pleskovic, 205–30. Washington, DC: World Bank.

Gill, I., and H. Kharas. 2007. *An East Asian Renaissance: Ideas for Economic Growth.* Washington, DC: World Bank.

Hasri, H. 2016. "Economic Corridor Development for Competitive and Inclusive Asia: The Experience of Northern Corridor Economic Region" (PowerPoint presentation). Northern Corridor Implementation Authority, Penang.

Hutchinson, F. E. 2014. "Malaysia's Federal System: Overt and Covert Centralisation." *Journal of Contemporary Asia* 44 (3): 422–42.

JBIC (Japanese Bank for International Cooperation), with International Development Center of Japan. 2003. "Impact Assessment of Transport Infrastructurse Projects in the Northern Vietnam." Final Report, July. https://www.jica.go.jp/english/our_work/evaluation/oda_loan/post/2003/pdf/1-03_full.pdf.

JETRO (Japan External Trade Organization). 2016. "2016 JETRO Survey on Business Conditions of Japanese Companies in Asia and Oceania." JETRO.

JICA (Japan International Cooperation Agency). 2008. "National Highway No. 5 Improvement Project." Vietnam-Japan Joint Evaluation Team 2007. https://www.jica.go.jp/english/our_work/evaluation/oda_loan/post/2008/pdf/e_project29_full.pdf.

———. 2009. "Ex Post Evaluation of Japanese ODA Loan Project: National Highway No. 5 Improvement Project (I) (II)." Report prepared by Masumi Shimamura, Mitsubishi UFJ Research and Consulting Co., Ltd. https://www2.jica.go.jp/en/evaluation/pdf/2009_VNV-5_4.pdf.

Lim, W. S. 2007. "Penang as an Integrated Logistics and Transportation Hub under Northern Corridor Economic Region." *Penang Economic Monthly* 9 (8): 1–11.

Lim, D. 2011. "Economic Development: A Historical Survey." In Malaysia: Policies and Issues in Economic Development, edited by H. Hill, 1–38. Kuala Lumpur: Institute of Strategic and International Studies.

Lucas, R., and D. Verry. 2001. *Restructuring the Malaysian Economy: Development and Human Resources.* New York: Macmillan.

Malaysia, Government of. 2006. *Ninth Malaysia Plan, 2006–2010.* Putrajaya: Economic Planning Unit.

———. 2008. *Mid-Term Review of the Ninth Plan, 2006–2010.* Putrajaya: Economic Planning Unit.

———. 2016. *Eleventh Malaysia Plan, 2016–2020.* Putrajaya: Economic Planning Unit.

Narayanan, S. 1999. "Factors Favouring Technology Transfer to Supporting Firms in Electronics: Empirical Data from Malaysia." *Asia Pacific Development Journal* 6 (1): 55–72.

Page, J. 2012. "Can Africa Industrialise?" *Journal of African Economics* 21 (Supplement 2): ii86–ii125.

Ruffing, L. 2006. "Deepening Development through Business Linkages." United Nations Conference on Trade and Development (UNCTAD). http://unctad.org/en/Docs/iteteb20067_en.pdf.

Sime Darby. 2007. *Northern Corridor Economic Region Socioeconomic Blueprint, 2007–2025.* Kuala Lumpur: Sime Darby Berhad.

Snodgrass, D. R. 1980. *Inequality and Economic Development in Malaysia.* Kuala Lumpur: Oxford University Press.

Spinanger, D. 1986. *Industrialization Policy and Regional Economic Development in Malaysia.* Singapore: Oxford University Press.

UNIDO (United Nations Industrial Development Organization). 2009. *Industrial Development Report 2009.* Vienna: UNIDO.

Part II
Framework and Analytics

3

Can Transport Corridor Projects Produce Wider Economic Benefits? Evidence from International Development Organizations

Interest in studying the wider economic benefits (WEB) (economic welfare, social inclusion, reduction in inequality, environmental benefits, and economic resilience) of large infrastructure projects is growing (Behrens, Brown, and Lonla 2016; Redding and Turner 2015).[1] Attention is turning to economic benefits that go beyond trade and efficiency gains at the aggregate level to consider benefits that reach not only large national and international economic actors (corporations, foreign traders) but also smaller and more localized ones (micro, small, and medium-sized enterprises), as well as poorer people. This interest has been propelled in part by the increasing number of proposals for transport corridors, as well as uncertainties about their gains for regional integration and the wider population that lives and works along these corridors. There is a risk that some corridors will fail to attract the expected traffic, and thus justify the investment, while others will simply become fare-throughs, and fail to generate

any positive spillovers to the wider economy. In assessing these risks, and designing better transport corridors with wider economic benefits, there is much to learn from the design and implementation of transport investment projects and from practitioners. Such a knowledge base could complement the rich academic literature, which typically assumes a uniform project design and implementation in its investigations.

This chapter assesses which characteristics of transport corridor project design and implementation are correlated with wider economic benefits of transport corridor projects. To accomplish this, a survey tool was developed and used to collect and catalog investments in large transport projects supported by three international development organization: the Asian Development Bank (ADB), the Japan International Cooperation Agency (JICA), and the World Bank. The data were used to analyze the characteristics of project design and approaches to implementation over time, across countries, and across the three organizations. Further, the data were used to run meta-regressions of project performance as it relates to project design characteristics and implementation approaches.

The project survey tool has six modules: (1) screening for eligible corridor projects, (2) cataloging basic project characteristics, (3) surveying project designs, (4) reviewing economic analyses of projects, (5) summarizing project monitoring and evaluations, and (6) assessing project performance using institutional indicators as well as expert opinions. The data collected cover 60 projects in 23 countries approved from 1984 to 2011. The data set covers 13 ADB projects, 22 JICA projects, and 25 World Bank projects, totaling US$16.6 billion (in 2016 dollars). The meta-regressions investigate which project attributes in modules 2 through 4 (basic project characteristics, project design, and economic analyses of projects) are most significant in explaining the project performance measures considered.

The analysis focuses on answering several main questions. What country characteristics are associated with WEB? Which design and implementation characteristics of large transport projects are associated with WEB? Which complementary policies and institutions (such as reforms to improve government effectiveness and development policy) are associated with WEB?[2] Practitioners consider the Maputo corridor in Southern Africa (see box 3.1) to be an example of a corridor that produced WEB. Is the Maputo corridor an exception, or one of many successful corridors that have produced WEB?

BOX 3.1   The uncertain wider economic impacts of the Maputo Corridor in Southern Africa

In the mid-1990s, after the peace agreement in Mozambique and the collapse of apartheid in South Africa, both countries embarked on rehabilitating the Maputo corridor, which connects the Gauteng, Limpopo, and Mpumalanga provinces of South Africa with Maputo, which is a port and the capital of Mozambique.[a] The corridor had been severely damaged during Mozambique's civil war. Before Mozambique's independence, around 40 percent of South Africa's industrial exports were transported along the Maputo corridor. The corridor traverses a vast cross-border region with high potential for industry, trade, agriculture, tourism, and mining. The goal of Mozambique and South Africa was to unlock the economic potential of the region through private-sector–led investments in transport infrastructure and economically viable anchor projects. To do that, the governments of Mozambique and South Africa made the political and economic environment favorable to attract private sector investments.

The government of South Africa developed a spatial development initiative (SDI) strategy in the mid-1990s, which was later scaled up to the whole of Southern Africa. The strategy's rationale is that private sector investments are the key to unlock unrealized economic potential. The first step is to remove the bottlenecks that are hindering investments. The most common bottlenecks in the region covered by the SDI are transport and logistics. The second step is to identify strategic investment opportunities in agribusiness, industry, tourism, and other sectors with high demand for transport and logistics services that can trigger additional upstream or downstream development.

The Maputo corridor was the first regional spatial development initiative. Restoring the Maputo corridor as a credible route for regional trade required a combination of reforms and investments in the transport system. Investments in the EN4/N4 highway, the Ressano Garcia railway, the Lebombo-Ressano Garcia border post, and the Port of Maputo

(box continued next page)

BOX 3.1   The uncertain wider economic impacts of the Maputo Corridor in Southern Africa *(continued)*

became a prerequisite for reviving the corridor. The anchor investment projects underpinning the Maputo SDI included the mega-projects of MOZAL (the second largest aluminum smelter in Africa), the Beluluane Industrial Park, the Pande and Temane gas fields, and a petrochemical cluster. A pipeline and a power line were also built to support these investments.

Key aspects of the design of the Maputo corridor were the upstream work, and the role of the public and private sectors. As part of the SDI, the development potential and infrastructure needs along the corridor were scoped out and mapped. This created the foundation for a holistic approach to revive the corridor. Soon after the agreement between the governments of South Africa and Mozambique, the Maputo Corridor Company (MCC), a public-private body to facilitate investments on the corridor, was created. MCC was dominated by South African public agencies, with limited involvement from Mozambique and the private sector. In the early 2000s, MCC ceased to exist, and the Maputo Corridor Logistics Initiative (MCLI) was created. MCLI is a nonprofit organization consisting of infrastructure investors, service providers, and stakeholders from Mozambique, South Africa, and Swaziland focused on promoting and further developing the Maputo corridor as the region's primary logistics transportation route.

Private sector involvement was key in improving the transport components of the Maputo corridor.

After the civil war in Mozambique, repairing and rebuilding the transport infrastructure required major capital investments, which the country could not afford with its own public resources. The best alternatives were concessional financing from international development organizations and private sector involvement. At the same time, the trend in Africa and other developing regions was to promote the involvement of the private sector in the provision and management of transport infrastructure and services. However, the demand that would make the private sector investments viable was uncertain. The anchor projects, which were all transport-intensive, played the additional role of supporting the viability of private sector involvement in improving road, rail, and port services.

The Maputo corridor seems to be a successful corridor in many aspects, even though no robust analysis of the wider economic benefits of the corridor exists. Rehabilitating the corridor not only improved the connectivity between South Africa and Mozambique, as demonstrated by increases in road and rail traffic, but also boosted transit trade flows and bilateral trade between the two countries. The increase in road traffic has been mainly in passenger traffic—and thus an increase in people-to-people interactions. The Maputo corridor led to more than US$5 billion worth of investments, and 15,000 direct jobs in the construction and operation of transport, logistics, energy, and industrial ventures along the corridor.

Source: Sequeira, Hartman, and Kunaka 2014.
a. Swaziland and Zimbabwe, both landlocked countries, also rely on the corridor for access to the sea.

To our knowledge, this study is the first attempt to analyze transport corridor projects supported by international development organizations since 1980, and link the project investments to project performance using meta-analysis. Various studies have analyzed macro and micro determinants of World Bank project performance (Denizer, Kaufman, and Kraay 2013), and have offered explanations for the success of ADB projects and programs (Feeny and Vuong 2017). Other studies have analyzed the

determinants of success for selected projects of other international development organizations, such as the African Development Bank (Mubila, Lufumpa, and Kayizzi-Mugerwa 2000). However, these studies do not focus on the investments in transport corridors and their particular challenges, such as geographic specificity and the net economic benefits in their vicinity as well as further away. This study thus aims to contribute to the existing literature by highlighting the aspects of project design and implementation that could matter the most for the success of large transport corridor investments.

> This study highlights the aspects of designing and implementing corridor projects that could matter the most for the success of transport corridor programs.

CONCEPTUAL FRAMEWORK

Trunk transport corridors play a crucial role in connecting people with goods and services and fostering regional connectivity. The academic literature links improved transport infrastructure to wider economic benefits through four key mechanisms: reducing transport and production costs; expanding productive capacity; improving access to markets and basic services like health care and education; and reducing the prices of final goods and services. These benefits depend on supportive conditions in other sectors, such as access to credit, functioning land markets,

low trade barriers, and accessible and quality health care and education.

As globalization and innovation change the way people and goods move around the world, regional connectivity is becoming increasingly fluid and disruptive. Historically, developing countries have sought transport improvements to increase trade, catalyze growth, and create jobs. While better transport connectivity is necessary for regional integration, achieving widespread gains from regional integration requires more—a holistic approach to transport corridor development to maximize the wider economic benefits that accrue from building trunk corridors.

In general, three different types (levels) of transport project/program designs can enhance regional integration and generate wider economic benefits (see figure 3.1):

1. *Investments in trunk transport corridors.* This entails building entirely new transport infrastructure (roads, rail, or inland waterways) or upgrading existing links.
2. *Investments in trunk transport corridors, as well as transport and trade facilitation services.* Benefits from a trunk transport corridor investment can be enhanced if simultaneous investments are made in transport services (trucks, rail, and port services) and trade facilitation services (warehouses and border crossings).
3. *Investments in trunk transport corridors, transport and trade facilitation services, and other "soft" policies.* Benefits from improved regional connectivity can be expanded even further if the project designs also account for market conditions and simultaneously make complementary interventions in other sectors—to ensure that capital, labor, land, and product markets function smoothly.

The wider economic benefits of a trunk transport project also depend on the initial conditions. These conditions can include geography, population, development level, and market imperfections. These initial conditions can magnify or reduce the wider economic benefits of transport corridor investments for all three levels described in figure 3.1.

FIGURE 3.1 **The design of transport corridor projects respects initial conditions and can involve three levels of interventions**

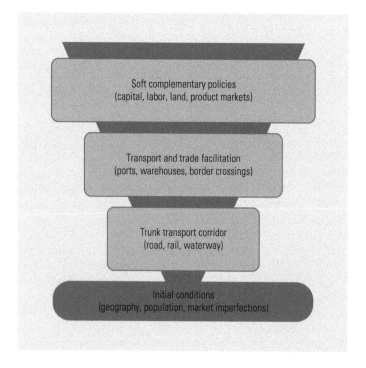

Soft complementary policies
(capital, labor, land, product markets)

Transport and trade facilitation
(ports, warehouses, border crossings)

Trunk transport corridor
(road, rail, waterway)

Initial conditions
(geography, population, market imperfections)

Therefore, any assessment of potential gains from trunk transport infrastructure and services projects should also consider the state of the initial conditions and interactions with complementary markets to identify complementary interventions that are needed to maximize the benefits that can accrue from the investment. However, the analysis of such interactions—assessing how and when transport infrastructure projects can be designed to maximize the wider economic benefits—is largely missing from the literature, leaving significant knowledge gaps across the spectrum of transportation settings.

SAMPLE SELECTION AND SUMMARY STATISTICS

The study selected a sample of 60 closed transport corridor projects from the Asian Development Bank, Japan International Cooperation Agency (JICA), and the World Bank. The study team administered a survey (comprising 68 questions) on these projects to create a database of key project characteristics, design, monitoring and evaluation, and ex post assessments. This database was created by reviewing project documents and interviewing individuals involved in the projects. The study team then performed a meta-analysis using the collected data and other spatial data sets to assess the conditions and features of corridor projects that can help produce wider economic benefits (see figure 3.2).

The sample of transport projects was limited to those involving investments in roads, rail, or inland waterways. Projects were subjected to screening criteria to assess whether they would qualify as a transport corridor. A transport *project* is classified as a *transport corridor* if:

- The transport investment is being made on a route that is creating or upgrading/rehabilitating at least 100 linear kilometers (km), or
- The loan at appraisal is greater than US$50 million and the investment is in a new bridge/tunnel connecting at least two economic centers.

These criteria were designed to identify projects that have the potential to enhance regional connectivity of a country or a set of countries. This is measured either using length (restricting the length to at least 100 linear kilometers) (see map 3.1) or by identifying investments on critical links of transport networks (large bridges and tunnels), measured using loan amounts. The analysis included those projects that satisfied at least one of these two criteria.

The screening resulted in a sample of 60 projects—13 ADB projects, 22 JICA projects, and 25 World Bank projects. For the most part, the selected projects were approved between 1984 and 2011.

The sample of selected projects consists of investments made in both domestic and international corridors. In 32 of the 60 projects, the investment is made on a route that is part of a larger regional corridor. Seven projects make an investment at the border. For 9 projects, the investment is made in landlocked countries only. While the thrust of the study is very much toward regional integration, domestic transport corridors tend to have an impact on regional connectivity as well and

FIGURE 3.2 **Overall approach of the study**

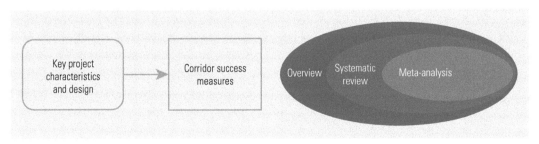

MAP 3.1   **How a linear kilometer is defined**

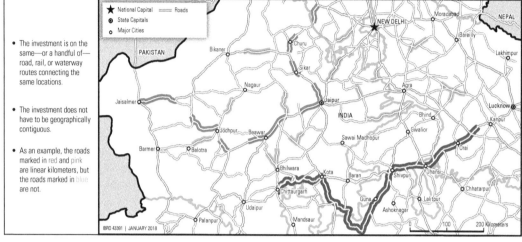

Source: Corridor Study Team.

FIGURE 3.3   **Most of the reviewed projects are in the road sector**

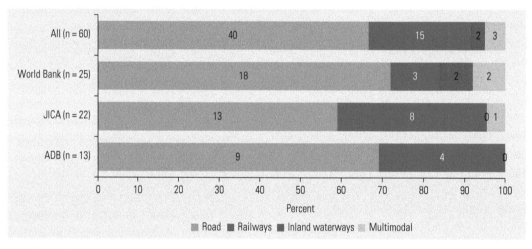

Source: Corridor Study Team.

are thus included in the sample. Much can be learned from domestic corridors in large countries (India, China, Brazil, Russian Federation). Furthermore, in landlocked countries, people usually live at the center of the country rather than at the borders. In such cases, the WEB of regional connectivity are expected to accrue where people live, rather than at the border.

As shown in figure 3.3, most the projects selected for each of the three international development organizations are based on roads. Overall, the sample spans 40 road projects, 15 rail projects, 2 inland waterways projects, and 3 multimodal projects (road and railway, and railway and port). The cumulative numbers and loan amounts of corridor projects in the sample follow similar trends (see figure 3.4).

The regional distribution of the selected projects is largely consistent with the regional portfolio of the international development organizations (see table 3.1).

The portfolios and samples of projects for ADB and JICA are largely based in Asia, while the World Bank portfolio spans five of the six regions of the world.

Figure 3.5 summarizes the geographic scope of the sample projects. Most projects appear to have an objective of improving regional connectivity within a country. Less than one-fifth of the projects have an international scope.

All projects in the sample are underpinned by a theory of change. However, the quality of that theory varies. A panel of experts assembled for this study rated the quality of the theory in 51 percent of these projects as being fairly poor or poor (see figure 3.6).

Just over one-third of the corridor projects are greenfield. Slightly more than half (55 percent) focus on rehabilitating infrastructure. The remainder (10 percent) expand the capacity of existing infrastructure.

In just over 40 percent of the projects, the private sector was either consulted or involved before, during, or after the design of the transport investment (figure 3.7). However, the level of private sector participation in the operation and management of transport infrastructure in the sampled projects remains below 50 percent. The most common mode of engagement was contractor(s), followed by public-private partnerships (PPPs) (figure 3.8).

FIGURE 3.4 **The sample of reviewed projects captures more recent projects, 1984–2011**

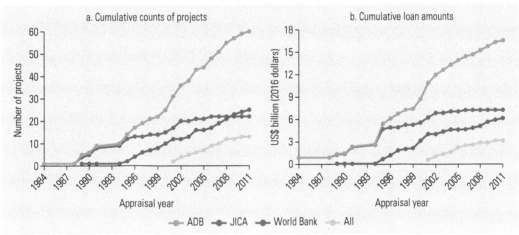

Source: Corridor Study Team.

TABLE 3.1 **Most of the projects in the sample are in Asia**

| Region | Number of projects | | | |
	ADB	JICA	World Bank	All
East Asia and the Pacific	10	17	9	36
Europe and Central Asia	1	1	4	6
South Asia	2	2	3	7
Sub-Saharan Africa	0	0	3	3
Middle East and North Africa	0	2	0	2
Latin America and the Caribbean	0	0	6	6
Total	**13**	**22**	**25**	**60**

Source: Corridor Study Team calculations.

FIGURE 3.5 **Only a small share of the projects in the sample are international**

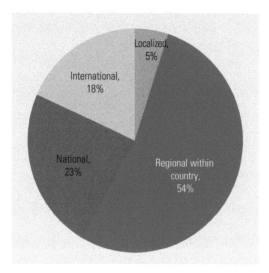

Source: Corridor Study Team.

FIGURE 3.6 **Most projects in the sample do not have a good theory of change**

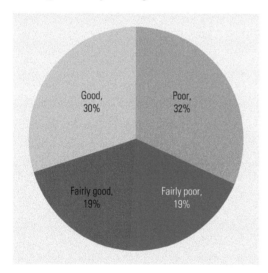

Source: Corridor Study Team.

FIGURE 3.7 **The private sector is often not involved in designing projects**

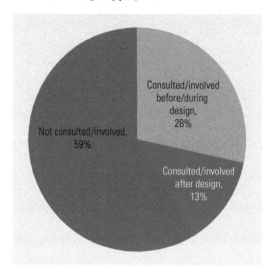

Source: Corridor Study Team.

FIGURE 3.8 **The private sector is often not involved in the operation or management of transport infrastructure**

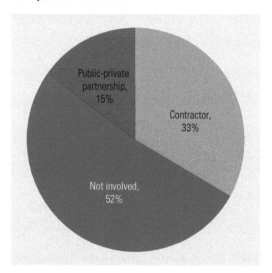

Source: Corridor Study Team.

To measure the presence or absence of complementary policies before the project started, the study ascertained whether the host country had at least one World Bank Development Policy Operation (DPO) (loan, grant, or credit)in the five years before the project was approved.[3]

Almost half the projects in the sample are in countries that had a DPO. The three most common forms of DPOs in the sample are public administration, industry-trade-services, and financial sector. Of the 29 projects with DPOs, only 8 had a DPO relating to the transport sector (figure 3.9).

FIGURE 3.9 **Only about half the projects occurred in countries that had undertaken World Bank–sponsored institutional reforms in the five years before the project was approved**

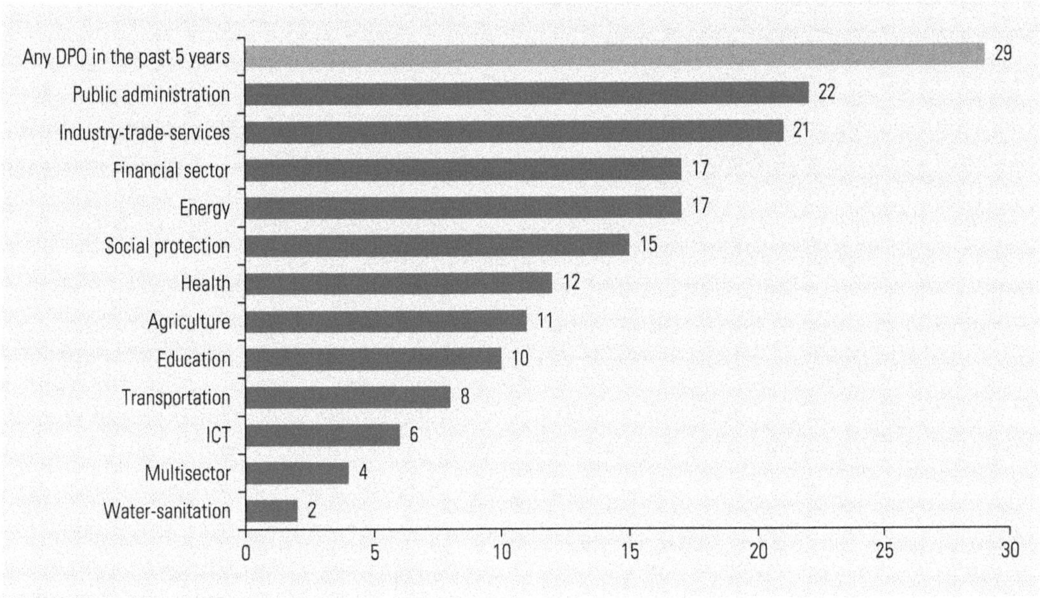

Source: Corridor Study Team.
Note: DPO = Development Policy Operation; ICT = information and communication technology.

MAXIMIZING THE WIDER ECONOMIC BENEFITS OF TRANSPORT CORRIDORS

Hypothesis and analytical framework

The analysis tested four hypotheses. Are projects more or less successful when:

- They are initiated in countries that are richer, bigger, and easier to connect (initial conditions)?
- They have a large geographic scope and include a well-thought-through theory of change (project design and characteristics)?
- They engage and/or involve the private sector (project design and characteristics)?
- They proceed against a backdrop of complementary policies and institutions (measured through openness, government effectiveness, and DPOs)?

The study tested the hypotheses by estimating multivariate regression models that use a set of project success measures as outcome variables. Explanatory variables of interest are initial conditions, project design and characteristics, and complementary policies and institutions. In addition, the analysis controlled for characteristics specific to the international development organization and the type of rating (through international development organization fixed effects and rating type fixed effects). The estimations were performed using ordinary least squares.

Four metrics of project success were used: two that capture the likelihood that a project produced WEB, and two that proxy for WEB. This allows the analysis to assess which characteristics are linked with the likelihood that the project will generate WEB and which characteristics are linked with WEB.

Both the likelihood that a project will produce WEB and the nature and extent of the WEB themselves need to be considered because the monitoring and evaluation (M&E) frameworks of projects tend to be based on concrete outputs (such as number of/km of roads built or rehabilitated, travel time, number of accidents, daily ridership, and so on) rather than focusing on outcomes, which are broader and harder to measure. It is also more difficult to determine cause and effect (attribution): how the project affects specific outcomes. All projects have monitoring and evaluation indicators that measure basic outcomes, but only some of them have indicators that capture intermediate outcomes or final outcomes (WEB).[4] In the sample, 46 percent of projects have indicators that relate only to basic outcomes, 30 percent have at least one indicator that relates to an intermediate outcome, and 24 percent have at least one indicator that relates to WEB.

Against this backdrop, measuring the success of projects based on institutional ratings or even experts' assessments can only indicate whether a project was successful in setting the conditions for WEB to arise. In other words, these measures of success are only indicative of the likelihood that a project produced WEB.

The likelihood of a corridor project producing WEB is measured using two ratings that range from 1 (lowest) to 5 (highest):

- *Official completion rating.* This is the average of the internal rating when the project is completed and the independent evaluation rating (if both ratings are available) or the rating that is available.[5]
- *Expert assessment.* Official completion ratings assess projects only according to project objectives and monitoring and evaluation measures. For this reason, this study produced a more comprehensive (although somewhat subjective) assessment that captures the extent to which the projects contributed to or established the conditions to achieve higher-level outcomes. These assessments were performed by knowledgeable experts from each organization. The assessment was based on existing data and analysis on the projects. Five objective criteria were used to create the expert assessment:
  - Rating = 1. Failure to achieve even simple objectives, such as reduced transport operating costs and travel times.

  - Rating = 2. Achievement of basic outcomes of reduced operating costs and travel times.
  - Rating = 3. In addition to the basic outcomes of (2), lower transport fares (for passengers) and/or tariffs (for freight).
  - Rating = 4. In addition to the lower-level outcomes of (3), a higher level of trade and/or economic growth than would have been achieved without the project.
  - Rating = 5. In addition to the outcomes of 4, some increase in levels of personal incomes and or reductions in poverty levels.

In the sample, the average official completion rating for projects is 4.08, while the average expert's rating is 3.53. Why were the expert ratings lower? Some projects have objectives that are very easy to achieve, while other projects that are very similar in content could have objectives that are much more difficult to achieve. Ranking projects on the extent to which they achieve their own stated objectives would run the risk of assessing a project that achieved objectives that were not very ambitious more highly than one that achieved the same lower-level objectives, but did not completely achieve its more ambitious objectives.

To measure WEB, the study uses two proxies for spatial economic activity near transport corridors: nightlights data (as a proxy for the intensity of economic development) and human settlement data (as a proxy for the density of development).[6] In both cases, the outcome variable is created using a difference-in-difference approach. The first difference compares average nightlights and human settlement levels observed in areas close to the corridor (treated areas) to areas far away from the corridor (control areas). Thus, it is a comparison across space. The second difference compares the first difference across time, subtracting the level before the project started from the level after the project was completed to ascertain the effect of the project. The outcome variable is the difference of these two differences (that is, the difference in difference itself).

For the first difference, the control group consisted of areas far away from the corridor

(90–100 km away), while the treatment group consisted of areas "on" the corridor) (0–10 km from the corridor) and "by" the corridor (0–20 km from the corridor). For the second difference, for the initial year, the study used the latest year before the project was appraised for which the data on nightlights and human settlement data were available. For the final year, the study allowed for the longest gestation period possible for WEB to emerge after the project was completed. Thus, the last year for which data were available was used: 2012 in the case of nightlights, and 2014 in the case of human settlement data. The analysis pooled the data from the two data sets (nightlights and human settlement) and pooled the data for the two treatment and control groups (0–10 km, 90–100 km) and (0–20 km, 90–100 km). Unfortunately, human settlement data were available for only 45 projects and nightlights data were available for only 34 projects. Thus the sample of projects the analysis could use to estimate WEB was much smaller than the total sample of 60 projects.

In terms of potential correlates, the analysis considers the following set of variables:

- *Initial conditions* are captured through three variables:
  ○ *Log land area.* This is the logarithm of a country's area, in 1,000 hectares.[7]
  ○ *Terrain ruggedness index.* This is measured in terms of the average difference in elevation (measured in hundreds of meters of elevation) for points 30 arc-seconds apart (that is, 926 meters on the equator or any meridian) not covered by water.
  ○ *Log GDP per capita at appraisal.* This is the log of GDP per capita at the time the project is appraised (in constant 2010 US$million).
- *Project design and characteristics* are captured through seven variables:
  ○ *Quality of theory of change.* This is an expert rating of the theory of change, with ratings of 1 (poor), 2 (fairly poor), 3 (fairly good), 4 (good), and 5 (excellent). The following objective criteria were used to create these rankings:

○ Rating = 1. Project objectives are limited to transport operating costs and times.
○ Rating = 2. The project documents mention some higher level of objectives (such as an increase in trade or economic growth), but is silent on the conditions needed to achieve these objectives (for example, competitive markets to translate reductions in transport operating costs and times into lower tariffs).
○ Rating = 3. In addition to 2, the project documents mention conditions in the transport sector needed to achieve the higher-level objectives.
○ Rating = 4. In addition to 3, the project documents mention conditions beyond the transport sector needed to achieve the higher-level objectives.
○ Rating = 5. In addition to 4, the project documents include an assessment of whether the conditions have been met, and if not, what actions will be taken to create them.
○ *Private sector consultation* [0–1]. This is a dummy that is 1 if the private sector was consulted before, during, or after the project was designed, and 0 if the private sector was not consulted.
○ *Degree of private sector involvement* [0–3]. This captures the extent of private sector involvement in the operation or management of the transport infrastructure. The variable is 0 if no private sector actor is involved; 1 if the involvement is only as a contractor; 2 if the involvement is as part of a public-private partnership; and 3 if the private sector actor is the owner:
○ *Degree of connectivity increase* [1–3]. This variable captures the degree of increase in connectivity, ranging from 1, for the highest increase in connectivity (greenfield projects), to 2 (expanding the capacity of an existing link), to 3, for the lowest increase in connectivity (rehabilitation of an existing link).
○ *Investment at border* [0–1]. This is a dummy that is 1 if the project makes

any investment at a country border, and 0 if it does not.

○ *Geographic scope* [1–4]. This variable captures the geographic scope of the investment, ranging from 1 (local), to 2 (subnational or regional within the country), to 3 (national), to 4 (international).

○ *Landlocked-ness* [0–1]. This is a dummy that is 1 if all countries involved in the project are landlocked, and 0 if they are not.

• *Complementary policies and institutions* are captured through three variables:

○ *Openness at approval.* This measure of trade openness consists of the sum of imports plus exports as share of GDP.

○ *Government effectiveness at approval.* This is the Worldwide Governance Indicator (WGI) on government effectiveness. It reflects perceptions of the quality of public services, the quality of the civil service and the degree of its independence from political pressures, the quality of policy formulation and implementation, and the credibility of the government's commitment to such policies.

It ranges from approximately –2.5 (weak) to +2.5 (strong).

○ *DPOs.* Dummies are included for whether, in the five years before the project was approved, the World Bank had any Development Policy Operations in the country. Various dummies are used in relation to DPOs. The general dummy is 1 if any DPO had been undertaken in the country in the past five years, and 0 otherwise. Similarly, separate dummies are included for DPOs in various sectors, including transport, agriculture, financial sector, and industry-trade-services.

Regression analysis: potential for WEB

The estimated regression pools data for both metrics capturing the likelihood of achieving WEB (institutional project completion ratings and expert success ratings). This pooling helps enhance the sample size for the regression model and averages the pros and cons of the two success measures. Based on this pooling, a regression analysis of 120 observations should be possible. However, because some project success ratings and some values in the explanatory variables were missing, the sample that results includes 55 projects and 107 observations. Figures 3.10 and 3.11 present the ordinary least squares estimations results. Two models were estimated: a parsimonious version that estimates only an average effect for development policy operations, and an extended version that breaks down the development policy operations by sector.

Some findings from the regression analysis are consistent across different specifications, despite the small sample size. Initial conditions do not seem to be significantly associated with the success of a project in setting the conditions for WEB. Characteristics of the project and project design process are significant (figure 3.11). In all the specifications, a well-thought-out theory of change is consistently associated with the success of projects in setting the conditions for WEB. These findings suggest that projects with a clear link between the intervention,

FIGURE 3.10   Well-thought-out theory of change can help corridor projects succeed, the expected benefits of consulting or involving the private sector have not been realized

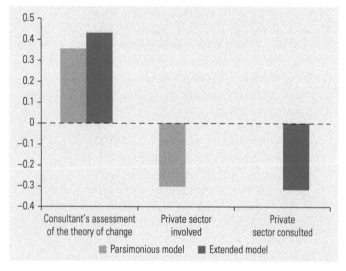

Source: Corridor Study Team.
Note: Significance level = 10 percent.

FIGURE 3.11 Complementary financial, and industrial and trade reforms undertaken before a corridor project is implemented could help the project succeed

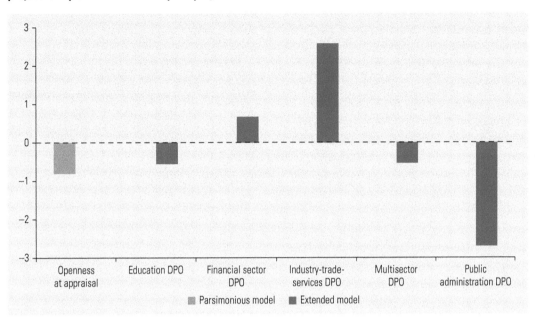

Source: Corridor Study Team.
Note: Significance level = 10 percent. DPO = Development Policy Operation.

intermediate outcomes, and WEB are more thorough in their design and more cognizant of the design features needed to be successful.[8]

The degree of private sector involvement (contractor, public-private partnership, or ownership) and consultation appear to have a somewhat negative association with project success. This could be interpreted as the need to improve the quality of engagement with the private sector, not necessarily to limit it.

Some complementary reforms implemented before a corridor project has been approved appear to alter the likelihood of a project producing WEB (figure 3.11). When using reforms supported by World Bank DPOs as proxies for sectoral complementary reforms, the analysis finds that financial, industrial, and trade reforms undertaken before a project is implemented have a positive association with project success. Projects implemented in countries where public administration reforms took place not long before the project was approved have a negative

association with project success. The World Bank supports public administration reforms through DPOs when a country has weak government capacity. Hence, this result might be picking up continuing weaknesses in the country's implementation capacity. It could also be the case that reforms of public administration are highly centralized and draw public resources away from the transport sector that is implementing the corridor projects.

Regression analysis: selected WEB (economic activity)

The estimated regression pools data across two different measures of economic activity: nightlights and human settlement. In addition, the regression pools data for two treatment groups: 0–10 km and 0–20 km away from the corridor project. These measures are aimed to capture areas both "on" and "by" the corridor to varying degrees (to varying distances). The corridor impact (treatment effect) is estimated against a control group of areas

90–100 km "away" from the corridor project. The variance of the two measures of economic activity is standardized. This double pooling helps enhance the sample size and robustness of the estimated regression, thanks to the information delivered by two complementary measures of economic activity—that is, the intensity of development (nightlights data) and the extension of development (human settlements data). The transport corridor treatment becomes a common factor for the two measures of economic activity. Thus, the estimated regression can be seen as a simple common factor model. As before, two models were estimated: a parsimonious version that estimates only an average effect for development policy operations, and an extended version that breaks down the development policy operations by sector. The results are reported in figures 3.12 to 3.14.

The estimations reveal, on average, a significant increase in economic activity in connected regions (those areas 0–10 km and 0–20 km away from the corridor), after transport corridor projects have been built, as measured by human settlement and nightlights data. This average positive change is gauged relative to the data for control regions 90–100 km away from the alignment.

It indicates that, on average, building a large transport corridor project is associated with a 0.7 standard deviation increase in economic activity (measured using nightlights and human settlement data across projects in that country). Using the sample estimated standard deviation and assuming 0.3–0.4 correlation of nightlights with GDP (based on Henderson, Storeygard, and Weil 2012), a US$100-million-plus transport corridor intervention could, on average, be associated with a GDP increase of about 0.78–1.04 percentage points near the corridor. The analysis captures a partial effect; that is, the increased economic activity near a transport corridor could just be a reallocation of economic activity from another area, instead of a newly generated activity.

Several conditional effects accompany the average change in economic activity near a given transport corridor project. The conditional effects are associated with initial conditions, project design and characteristics, and complementary policies and institutions. Four initial conditions are significantly associated with the average increase of economic activity near transport corridor projects (figure 3.12). The increase in economic activity near the corridor could be significantly greater in smaller countries. Further, economic activity

FIGURE 3.12   Initial conditions of a smaller, flatter, less developed, and coastal country could increase the likelihood for WEB

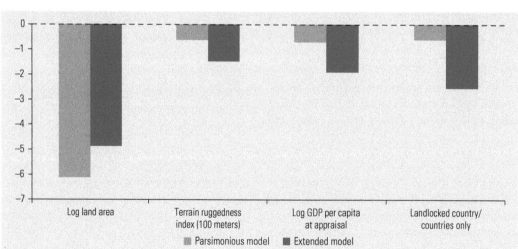

Source: Corridor Study Team.
Note: Significance level = 10 percent. GDP = gross domestic product; WEB = wider economic benefits.

FIGURE 3.13 Investing at the border and in connectivity to border crossings shows smaller increases in local economic activity: inherent complexity could be the challenge

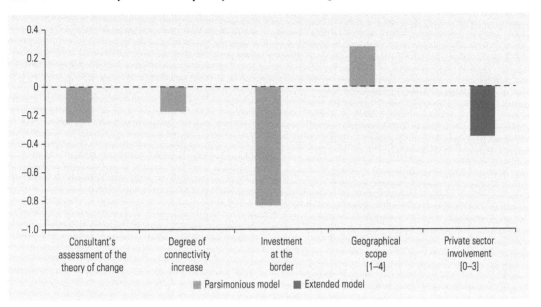

Source: Corridor Study Team.
Note: Significance level = 10 percent.

FIGURE 3.14 Policies promoting trade openness and institutions boosting governance effectiveness appear the most robust complementary interventions to help corridor investments spur local economic activity

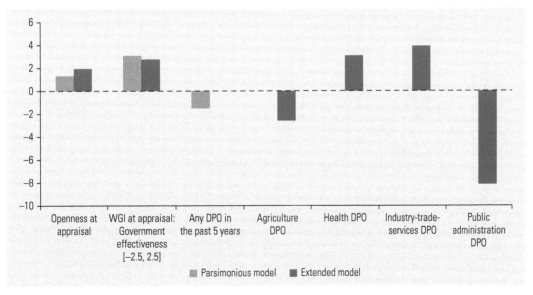

Source: Corridor Study Team.
Note: Significance level = 10 percent. DPO = Development Policy Operations; WGI = Worldwide Governance Indicators.

near a transport corridor project could increase more in countries with flatter or smoother terrain. In less developed countries (with lower per capita GDP), the increases in economic activity near the transport corridor intervention could be relatively larger—perhaps spurring the income convergence process in the connected regions. Also, when the corridor intervention happens in coastal countries, the positive association with economic activity is much greater than in landlocked ones.

Some project designs and characteristics of transport corridors are estimated to be significantly associated with changes in economic activity (figure 3.13). Adding new infrastructure or upgrading existing infrastructure is associated with a larger increase in economic activity than rehabilitating trunk infrastructure. Investment at the border and connectivity to border crossings are associated with significantly smaller changes in economic activity—perhaps because of the additional complexities that border crossing interventions entail. However, even this estimate is not robust against the inclusion of more detailed complementary policies. The estimated association of geographic scope suggests that changes in economic activity near national and international projects could be larger than near subnational or local transport infrastructure projects—perhaps because of their greater potential for regional integration. Interestingly, only the estimation accounting for detailed complementary policies picks up a possible negative association between private sector involvement in the transport corridor projects and economic activity. This finding, if confirmed by future studies, could suggest that, so far, public-private partnerships have hindered widespread economic activity rather than spurred it. One explanation could be that it is difficult to align the private sector's focus on monetary profits with society's focus on generating wider socioeconomic benefits.[9]

The cross-sectoral complementary policies and institutions, such as trade openness and governance effectiveness, have robust and positive association with the generation of economic activity around the transport corridor (figure 3.14). The estimation results suggest that increases in economic activity near corridor projects could be much greater in countries with greater trade openness. Similarly, the average increases in economic activity near transport corridor projects are associated with greater governance effectiveness. For instance, a 1-point increase in the index of governance effectiveness of a country (for example, from zero (India) to 1.0 (Malaysia) or –0.7 (Pakistan) to 0.3 (South Africa)is associated with a more than fourfold increase in economic activity.[10]

Reforms, however, could be also disruptive or take a long time to complete. In some cases, broad-based reforms—approximated by the presence of World Bank Development Policy Operations (DPOs)—undertaken before a corridor project is implemented could interact negatively with transport corridor interventions. Estimations containing greater detail on the sectoral composition of these reform programs reveal that the effect varies substantially by sector. First, on average, the effect of the DPOs becomes statistically insignificant. Second, the estimation suggests that some complementary reforms could have significantly positive associations, while others could have significantly negative associations with changes in economic activity near transport corridor projects. As expected, policy reforms that promote trade and industry competitiveness are associated with significantly higher economic activities along transport corridors. A similar positive association is delivered by health sector reforms.[11] In contrast, reforms of public administration and the agricultural sector are associated with smaller changes in economic activity. One explanation could be that reforms of public administration are highly centralized and draw policy attention and public resources to the aggregate, national level rather than leaving them freely available to support economic development along transport corridors. Further, if transport corridors aim at inducing structural transformation from agriculture to manufacturing, reforms to boost agricultural performance could pro-long the needed reallocation of resources from agriculture to manufacturing.

In sum, smaller developing countries with smoother terrain and access to the sea could experience a greater boost in economic activity near transport corridors projects if they are open to foreign trade and have effective governance. More tentatively, the quality of engagement with the private sector needs to improve for corridor projects with private participation to be associated with widespread increases in economic activity. Finally, com-plementary policies for trade and industry competitiveness, as well as better performance of the health sector, could help spread the economic benefits and increase economic activity along the transport corridors.

CONCLUSION

This study conducted a survey of large transport corridor projects supported by the Asian Development Bank, the Japanese International Cooperation Agency, and the World Bank. It used the survey data to cata-log project characteristics and relate them to success measures. To this end, the study per-formed multivariate meta-regressions link-ing project characteristics to the likelihood that a project would produce wider eco-nomic benefits (WEB) as well as achieve specific WEB (specifically, economic activ-ity). The likelihood that a project will produce WEB is measured through institu-tional ratings specific to the international development organization, along with expert assessments of project success. The achievement of WEB is measured through spatially disaggregated data on nightlights and human settlement near and further away from the project location.

It can be revealing to compare the link from the project design to broad-based insti-tutional measures of success with the link from the project design to changes in selected measures of economic activity actu-ally achieved. This exercise can indicate whether the international development organizations that design the project and

evaluate its success—typically right after the implementation stage has been completed—are "getting it right."

Improvements in economic activity near corridor projects could be greater in smaller, less-developed countries with smoother terrain and direct access to the sea.

This analysis found that initial condi-tions do not seem to be associated with the success of a corridor project in setting preconditions for WEB (with "success" rated by international development organi-zations and experts). In contrast, increases in economic activity near the corridor proj-ect are significantly associated with initial conditions, such as the country size, rug-gedness of the terrain, level of development, and geography (whether landlocked or open to the coast). Specifically, the estima-tions suggest that increases in economic activity near corridor projects tend to be larger in smaller, less-developed countries with smoother terrain and direct access to the sea.

As expected, the project design and characteristics do influence the success in setting conditions for WEB. That is, some project designs and characteristics are systematically perceived by the international development organizations as well-established preconditions for development success. For instance, international development organiza-tions are more likely to rate projects with a well-developed theory of change as successful, perhaps because these projects have clearer designs and matching monitoring and evalua-tion frameworks that better demonstrate the achievement of development objectives. Some project designs and characteristics seem to be more associated with positive effects on economic activity—such as national and international projects, as opposed to subna-tional and local projects. However, the effect is not robust and significant across different estimations. Interestingly, for both international development organization success ratings and economic activity, greater private sector involvement in the operation and management of transport infrastructure (for example, through public-private partnerships) seems to have been associated with negative effects in some cases. This tentative finding could point to a challenge of obtaining the expected benefits from the collaboration of public and private sectors in development investments.

Implementing certain complementary reforms before undertaking the corridor project could make the project more successful in setting the preconditions for WEB and actually spurring greater economic activity (a proxy for WEB). Using reform programs supported by World Bank Development Policy Operations as proxies for complementary reforms in different sectors, the analysis found that reforms promoting industrial and trade competitiveness are associated with increases in both the perceived potential for WEB and increased economic activity near the corridor.

If the corridor intervention package includes complementary reforms to increase openness to foreign trade, improve governance effectiveness, and boost industry and trade competitiveness to the levels of higher-performing developing countries, the host country could expect GDP to increase 9.3–12.4 percentage points near the new or upgraded corridor.

Summing up and moving to the next chapter

This chapter took advantage of a unique new data set based on a survey of large transport infrastructure (corridor) projects supported by the Asian Development Bank (ADB), the Japan International Cooperation Agency (JICA), and the World Bank Group. It summarized the results of an extensive meta-analysis aiming to identify which features could boost a corridor project's potential for generating WEB. Chapter 3 links the detailed project characteristics to institutional success ratings and measures of economic activity

around the corridors and thus enriches the evidence from the academic literature, which does not work with such detailed project design characteristics.

The next chapter aims to inform policy makers by summarizing the growing body of academic and policy literature on the impact of large transport investments on WEB. Chapter 4 conducts a quantitative summary by using a large new data set of studies in different country contexts and meta-regressions. It aims to integrate current knowledge and point to knowledge gaps of which policy makers must be aware when appraising the design of proposed corridor projects. Knowledge of the direct and indirect impacts, the trade-offs they could produce, and the complementary policies that could help manage these trade-offs can all help shape the optimal policy design of future corridor interventions.

NOTES

1. For a review of the literature, see Bougna et al. (forthcoming).
2. For a detailed discussion of complementary policies, see chapter 6.
3. World Bank assistance to its clients can be provided in the form of a Development Policy Operation (DPO). This could be a loan, grant, or credit that rapidly disburses financing to help a borrower address actual or anticipated development financing requirements. The World Bank's use of DPOs in a country is determined in the context of a comprehensive Country Assistance Strategy (CAS) drawn up by the government and the World Bank. The World Bank makes the funds available to the country when the country maintains an adequate macroeconomic policy framework (as determined by the World Bank, with inputs from assessments by the International Monetary Fund); the overall reform program is being implemented in a satisfactory manner; and the World Bank and the client have completed a set of critical, mutually agreed-on prior policy and institutional actions (prior actions). See http://siteresources.worldbank.org/PROJECTS/Resources/40940-124473262 5424/Q&Adplrev.pdf.

4. *Basic outcomes* include transport access, transport governance/management, road safety, and increased competitiveness in the transport sector. *Intermediate outcomes* include trade, tourism, and access to basic services such as health and education. *Final outcomes* (wider economic benefits, or WEB) include changes in economic growth, aggregate/spatial equality, social inclusion, resilience (such as food security), and environmental quality (such as deforestation and carbon dioxide emissions).

5. For the World Bank, the internal rating is the rating reported in the Implementation Completion and Results report (ICR). The independent evaluation rating is the assessment by the Independent Evaluation Group (IEG).

6. The nightlights data measure the intensity of human-made light on a scale of 0 to 63 using satellite imagery. These annual data are high resolution (they have a resolution of 0.86 square kilometer at the equator). The data correct for cloud coverage and report the average visible and stable lights. This study uses the annual nightlights data that are comparable across time and space. These data are available from 1992 to 2012. The Global Human Settlement measures the intensity of human settlements through satellite on a scale from 0 to 1. These data are available for four years: 1975, 1990, 2000, and 2014.

7. One hectare is equivalent to 10,000 square meters.

8. In addition, the regression analysis also finds that landlocked-ness, the geographical scope of the project, and the type of corridor intervention project alignment (greenfield, upgrade, or rehabilitation) do not affect the success of a project.

9. Most of the projects in the sample utilizing public-private partnerships invest in roads. In these cases, the private sector has limited or no power to increase revenue through changes in the volume or composition of traffic. The efficiency added by the private sector comes from construction and maintenance, which produce hardly any WEB.

10. Using Worldwide Governance Indicators for 2015.

11. This is perhaps because healthier people can better face risks and seize opportunities created by better connectivity to markets and jobs. For instance, greater transport connectivity helps spread diseases (Tatem, Rogers, and Hay 2011). Health sector reforms may boost the preparedness and coping mechanisms of areas near the transport corridors.

REFERENCES

Behrens, K., W. M. Brown, and T. Bougna Lonla. 2016. "The World Is Not Yet Flat: Transport Costs Matter!" Working Paper 7862, World Bank, Washington, DC.

Bougna, T., M. Melecky, M. Roberts, and Y. Xu. Forthcoming. "The Estimated Wider Economic Benefits of Transport Corridors: A Critical Review of the Literature." Policy Research Paper, World Bank, Washington, DC.

Denizer, C., D. Kaufmann, and A. Kraay. 2013. "Good Countries or Good Projects? Macro and Micro Correlates of World Bank Project Performance." *Journal of Development Economics* 105: 288–302.

Feeny, S., and V. Vuong. 2017. "Explaining Aid Project and Program Success: Findings from Asian Development Bank Interventions." *World Development* 90: 329–43.

Henderson, J. V., A. Storeygard, and D. N. Weil. 2012. "Measuring Economic Growth from Outer Space." *American Economic Review* 102 (2): 994–1028.

Mubila, M. M., C. L. Lufumpa, and S. Kayizzi-Mugerwa. 2000. "A Statistical Analysis of Determinants of Project Success: Examples from the African Development Bank." Economic Research Paper 56, African Development Bank, Abidjan, Côte d'Ivoire.

Redding, S. J., and M. A. Turner. 2015. "Transportation Costs and the Spatial Organization of Economic Activity." Chapter 20 in *Handbook of Regional and Urban Economics,* Vol. 5, edited by G. Duranton, J. Vernon Henderson, and W. C. Strange, 1339–98. Amsterdam: Elsevier.

Sequeria, S., O. Hartman, and C. Kunaka. 2014. "Reviving Trade Routes: Evidence from the Maputo Corridor." Discussion Paper 4, Sub-Saharan Africa Transport Policy Program (SSATP), Washington, DC.

Tatem, A. J., D. J. Rogers, and S. I. Hay. 2011. "Global Transport Networks and Infectious Disease Spread." https://www.ncbi.nlm.nih.gov/pmc/articles/PMC3145127/.

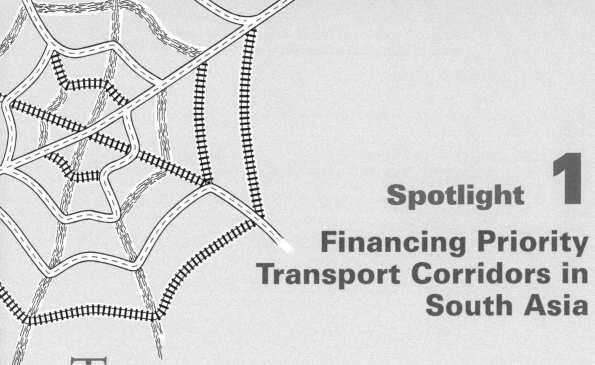

Spotlight 1

Financing Priority Transport Corridors in South Asia

Transport corridors support trade flows and economic activity along certain routes. They may be domestic (such as India's Golden Quadrangle, connecting Mumbai, Delhi, Kolkata, and Chennai) or cross-border/regional (such as the West Bengal Corridor, serving Bangladesh, the states of Sikkim and Assam in India, and landlocked Nepal and Bhutan).

The corridors involve transport links (rail, roads, and waterways on which passengers and freight travel), nodes (interconnecting transport and other services, such as ports and logistics centers), and gateways (access roads, allowing traffic to enter or exit the corridor to reach the hinterland) (World Bank 2005).

In addition, they entail large infrastructure investments and multiple assets—some already completed, and others built from scratch, called *greenfield projects*. They also involve different stakeholders, which sometimes have conflicting objectives. Because of the magnitude, externalities, and monopolistic aspects of transport corridor investments, as well as the need to coordinate across different stakeholders, governments are crucial to the planning, controlling, and funding of these projects. Given the fiscal constraints of the host or participating countries, the corridors require considerable financing on a commercial basis, not only to construct,

maintain, and operate the infrastructure but also to develop the supply chains along the routes.

WHO BENEFITS AND INVESTS IN THE CORRIDORS?

Transport corridors can produce large socioeconomic benefits, but they also carry large costs. Depending on the beneficiaries' level of income, the operators' ability to control access, and the quality of services provided, some of the costs can be recovered from users. Other important economic benefits are less direct—such as increased trade, commercial development, and job opportunities along the routes—and may be monetized only by the state, through general tax revenues.

Ultimately, the cost of corridors will be covered either by individual taxpayers, commercial taxpayers, or both. However, tax and tariff revenues accrue over time, while project costs are paid at the preparation, development, and construction stages. Small projects can be paid for from current cash resources, but large ones face a mismatch in the maturity of funding, which can be addressed by financing from the domestic or international financial system (*financial intermediation*). This could involve sovereign borrowing (from multilateral, bilateral, or other financial institutions),

TABLE S1.1   Who pays for transport corridors?

Type of funding	Individual taxpayers	Commercial taxpayers
Funding from current revenue	*Budget transfer.* Investment undertaken by the state is funded from current tax revenue. Taxpayers prefinance future infrastructure users.	*Internal accruals.* Commercial investment is funded from current tariff revenue. Current taxpayers prefinance future infrastructure users.
Funding from future revenue	*State financing.* Investment is financed by sovereign borrowing or contingent liabilities,[a] ultimately repaid from future tax revenue. Future taxpayers pay for future infrastructure users.	*Commercial financing.* Investment is financed by project equity and debt, which are ultimately remunerated and serviced from future tariff revenue. Future taxpayers pay for future infrastructure users.

Source: Corridor Study Team.
a. Potential liabilities that may occur, depending on the outcome of an uncertain future event.

or equity/debt financing on a commercial basis (*commercial financing*), where equity is remunerated and project debt are serviced from tariff revenues (see table S1.1).

PROJECTS THAT CAN BE COMMERCIALLY FINANCED

Commercial finance combines three elements: commercial investors or lenders, equity or debt finance on commercial terms, and commercial infrastructure borrowers and other *obligors* (those with contractual obligations, including payment obligations). Since the state plays such an extensive role in infrastructure, commercial finance often occurs in a hybrid rather than pure form. For example, private lenders may lend to state utilities, and state-owned financial institutions may facilitate equity and debt financing to private utilities on commercial or concessional (favorable) terms. This is especially true with transport corridors, given their socioeconomic externalities and coordination challenges. The concept of *commercial* finance does not fully overlap with *private* finance, in the sense that public sector utilities or financial institutions may operate commercially, despite their ownership by the state.

The extent and channels of cost recovery directly affect the way investments are financed. Commercial investors will only become involved in projects that can generate sufficient financial returns and produce cash flows. Arrangements for private sector participation range from management contracts (with no commercial investment), to leasing, build-operate-transfer (BOT) arrangements, concessions, and full private investment, among others. Projects in the most commercial sectors (those that allow full recovery of operating and investment cost) can be financed on a "user-pays" basis. These projects obtain revenues from retail end users (such as fares paid by train passengers or tolls paid by vehicle drivers); from anchor users by way of *off-take contracts*, in which major sponsors guarantee a minimum use of the infrastructure (with shipping companies in the case of ports, or rolling-stock operators or commodity shippers in the case of railway lines); or from dedicated taxes paid by users (surcharges on railway freight or fuel taxes allocated to road funds). Projects involving social infrastructure (such as public schools or fire stations) that generate no fee revenue, or projects involving economic infrastructure with low cost recovery that do not generate sufficient tariffs (as is often the case for water supply) can be commercially financed on a "government-pays" basis. Projects that create large economic benefits but face uncertain demand can be financed based on state *availability* payments (a payment for performance made irrespective of demand)— although these create long-term liabilities with a fiscal impact.

Transactions related to South Asian transport corridors that have been commercially financed in recent years include:

Ports and airports. These projects are preferred by commercial investors and lenders, especially if the financing is backed by long-term off-take actions (such as for ports), and access to foreign exchange revenues (such as for international airports). Transactions financed in 2016 were predominantly in India, and included the Gangavaram Port in Visakhapatnam, a project in Andhra Pradesh, and the JSW Jaigarh Port in Ratnagiri, Maharashtra.

Bridges, tunnels, and toll roads. Many of these transactions have been financed in India (and to a lesser extent, Pakistan). In view of the mixed outcomes of past transactions, investors and lenders are now wary of traffic risks, especially on greenfield projects.

Railways. A few transactions have been financed in India, but mostly in the form of annuities (where the debt service is secured by payments from Indian Railways) and a handful of *last mile* projects incorporated in international ports, with off-take from major industrial users.

When user fees do not provide full cost recovery and the state must bear part of the investment, it tends to invest in basic infrastructure (such as civil works, like ports), while private financiers invest in superstructure and logistics (like jetties and cranes for ports, rolling stock or sidings for railways, and toll plazas and operations for toll roads).

POSSIBLE FINANCING FOR CORRIDOR ASSETS

The three main ways in which infrastructure can be financed by the domestic or international financial system are public finance, corporate finance, and project finance, as well as their hybrid forms, as shown in figure S1.1. Each mode is defined by the structure of its debt financing (although equity is also required in the case of corporate and project finance).

Public finance involves borrowing by central and local governments, or by state

FIGURE S1.1   There are three main forms of infrastructure finance, plus hybrid financing

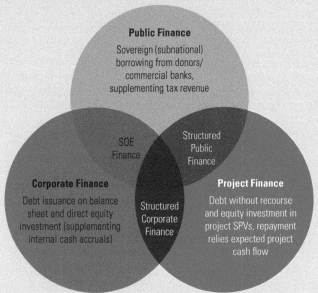

Source: Corridor Study Team.
Note: SOE = state-owned enterprise; SPV = special-purpose vehicle.

agencies or state-owned enterprises (SOEs) with sovereign guarantees. It is convenient for large infrastructure projects, and is used by default to finance assets that do not produce distinct cash flows (such as electrification, signaling, or gauge conversion, in the case of with railways), or projects for which there is no private sector interest, due to their market risk or long payback horizons. The state contribution to these projects—particularly in fragile, low-income, and lower-middle-income countries—may be supported by concessional financing from multilateral and bilateral financial institutions (*donors*). Since many countries face challenges to their fiscal space (their flexibility in spending choices), the amounts available for public finance may be limited by the need to keep the state's debt service obligations and overall indebtedness at sustainable levels, and/or by limiting government-contingent liabilities resulting from sovereign guarantees.

Corporate finance supports investments by established corporate entities, which carry both the projects as well as associated equity and loans on their balance sheets. Corporate investments may be financed by a mix of equity, quasi-equity, and/or debt issuance. In their most basic form, corporate finance loans are plain (*vanilla*), with a final maturity usually of not over five years. Lenders assess the creditworthiness of borrowers based on past financial results and available collateral. Alternately, these loans can be structured (through financial covenants, commercial undertakings, assignment of project contracts, escrow accounts and other limitations on the use of future cash flows, and the like) to allow for larger amounts, grace periods during construction, and longer repayment maturities. Smaller loans can be *bilateral* (self-standing credit facilities separately extended by each bank), while larger ones need to be *syndicated*—collectively extended by a group of banks sharing the same loan documents and security. The key metrics that determine the obligors' borrowing capacity are the debt/equity ratio (the traditional approach, more relevant for vanilla corporate loans) as well as the ratio of debt/cash flow from operations (a modern approach, especially relevant for structured corporate finance). In general, corporate finance is more suitable for well-established commercial entities that make investments of a moderate size relative to the balance sheet.

Larger commercial projects are handled on a *project finance* basis through equity and debt finance, allowing maturities up to 10–15 years, and even 20 years (depending on market conditions and the transaction's risk profile). Equity investments in ad hoc project companies (special-purpose vehicles, SPVs) are made by project developers, infrastructure private equity (PE) funds, and/or strategic investment funds (SIFs). Project finance loans are extended to project SPVs with limited (or no) recourse to the balance sheet of the project sponsors; instead, loans are expected to be repaid from a project's future cash flows. The key metric to determine a project's borrowing capacity is its projected debt service coverage ratio (DSCR), the ratio of operating cash flow generated by the

project to its debt service obligation. Project finance requires careful structuring of contracts so that risks are well identified and allocated to the parties best placed to bear them. A well-structured transaction with abundant, predictable cash flows acceptable to commercial lenders is said to be *bankable* (and *investable*, to investors). Due to its relative complexity, project finance tends to be uneconomic for deals that are less than US$50 million–US$100 million.

Hybrid financing forms include equity and/or debt finance by a state utility (SOE finance). They are a mix between public and corporate finance, depending on the extent to which the borrower derives its credit strength from its own cash flows, or from state support. If financially viable, SOEs may attract private sector equity investment (such as through a stock exchange listing) as part of privatization efforts. Hybrid project/corporate debt can be used to finance expansions, with repayment secured by a mix of existing and planned cash flow. Borrowings by public sector entities backed by commercial receivables, such as state-owned toll roads, can be viewed as *structured public finance*.

FINANCING SOURCES FOR CORRIDOR PROJECTS

Commercial infrastructure, including transport corridor projects, is financed by a mix of equity (usually 25 percent to 30 percent in the case of project finance, depending on the risk profile of the project, and 35 percent to 50 percent in the case of corporate finance) and debt.

Traditionally, project developers provide the core of equity finance in greenfield projects. However, in recent years, particularly in India, they have become increasingly stretched as their balance sheets have become highly leveraged. Thus, project cost overruns had to be funded by equity, since added debt was not forthcoming. As a result, developers in India have a limited appetite for further risk since they have already scaled back their ambitions substantially.

In recent years, PE funds have emerged as a new source of equity for infrastructure projects. For example, in India, over 15 PE infrastructure funds operate, with total assets under management of US$1.7 billion. The top three funds are Reliance Diver Power, UTI Infrastructure, and ICIC Prudential Infrastructure Fund, representing 41.8 percent of the total infrastructure PE industry.

Historically, these PE funds rarely took development risks. However, given limited project pipelines, several infrastructure PE funds have shifted focus earlier in the project life cycle and increasingly are entering at the development stage. While some funds build internal development teams, they more often invest in one or more portfolio companies that do project development and investment management work on their behalf. Portfolio companies are paid an annual retainer for their services and are entitled to a share of carried interest.

Debt financing can be sourced from the domestic financial system or from international financial institutions. With respect to domestic debt, banks remain the major source for commercial infrastructure projects in South Asia. Although the specifics of prudential regulations differ from country to country, banks may generally lend up to 20 percent of their regulatory capital to a nonstate borrower. So far, in the largest economies in South Asia (India, Pakistan, and Bangladesh, and to some extent Sri Lanka), this credit limit has been sufficient for the domestic banking sector to finance all but the largest commercial infrastructure projects. In practice, banks may decide to lend less than the amount allowed by the prudential limit, due to other considerations. But these limits do not apply to loans guaranteed by the central government.

However, in practice, the financing of corridor projects faces steep hurdles—some specific to the transaction, some related to the characteristics of the financial sector, and some contingent on the broader macroeconomic environment. These challenges translate into growing constraints on traditional bank lending to infrastructure projects in the region.

The first challenge relates to the nature of the underlying transactions. Corridor projects generate valuable socioeconomic benefits, but not necessarily high financial returns that can be captured by commercial investors and lenders. Greenfield transport corridor projects may have risk profiles (particularly related to the acquisition of rights of way, construction, coordination with other infrastructure, and traffic volume) that may require public support through various instruments, including concessional equity and partial guarantees. In India, some leading domestic banks have lent considerable amounts to toll roads and other transport projects that have not performed up to expectations. In recent years, this has meant large equity losses for investors, as well as large volumes of impaired loans for commercial lenders, which have dampened the appetite of commercial financiers for such projects.

Other challenges stem from the characteristics of the host countries' banking sectors, especially related to asset-liability management (ALM). In particular, infrastructure loans require very long maturities, but bank resources consist mainly of short-term deposits. Thus, infrastructure loans expose banks to maturity mismatches. Another issue relates to the structure of interest rates. Banks typically lend on the basis of variable rates, rather than fixed ones, since the bulk of their resources (short-term deposits) involve variable rates. Lacking a sufficiently deep market to hedge local currency interest rates, infrastructure borrowers are exposed to the risk that their debt service obligations may become unsustainably high if market rates rise in the future. In other cases, borrowers would rather obtain loans in foreign currencies to avoid paying the higher interest rates on local currency loans. Even if this does not create a currency mismatch for domestic banks (to the extent that they have access to matching foreign exchange resources), it exposes borrowers to a high foreign exchange debt service obligation in case of devaluations. While the impact of asset-liability management reaches beyond infrastructure and affects the financing of other types of investments, it is strongly preferred for infrastructure investments, including transport corridor projects, given the large amounts and long maturities.

Cross-border commercial debt financing for projects related to the South Asia corridors has mostly come from two sources: the commercial arms of multilateral donors (such as the World Bank Group's International Finance Corporation, IFC), and state policy banks (such as China Exim and China Development Bank).

IFC and similar commercial arms of international donors are well suited to finance infrastructure transactions due to their strong structuring capability and their focus on emerging markets. China has earmarked very large resources to finance infrastructure projects in South Asia under the One Belt One Road Program. In particular, with respect to Pakistan, China has committed over US$45 billion to construct infrastructure projects under the China-Pakistan Economic Corridor (CPEC) Agreement, with funding from Chinese banks and corporations focused on energy (75 percent of the total committed) and roads/ports/railways (25 percent of the total). Usually, the loans are based on a sovereign guarantee (for example, in the case of province-level transport projects); on a repayment guarantee for project loans from domestic banks with an acceptable credit rating guaranteeing the repayment of project loans; or on a repayment guarantee from a Chinese sponsor that holds majority ownership in the infrastructure project. To date, few such loans have been extended on a project finance basis.

In recent years, international corporate and investment banks have had relatively limited involvement in financing South Asia's transport corridors and related infrastructure. International banks, in principle, have a strong comparative advantage in financing infrastructure due to their very large size, and their competence and long-standing leadership in global project finance. But with countries that have sub-investment-grade credit ratings (currently the case for all South Asian

countries except for India, which is rated BBB- by Fitch and Standard & Poor's), international banks are reluctant to extend long-term infrastructure loans—except for transactions for which one of their core clients is a project sponsor and for which they are extensively covered against country risk through an export credit provided by a member country of the OECD (Organisation for Economic Co-operation and Development) with a high credit rating or a guarantee from the World Bank Group's Multilateral International Guarantee Agency (MIGA), or where debt repayment is secured by offshore revenue, as with international airports or commodity exports.

Besides bank lending, corporate bonds are another major source of infrastructure finance. India has the deepest financial investor base and largest corporate bond volume in South Asia. Bonds subscribed to by an investor such as a life insurance company have maturities extending up to 30 years for issuers with the strongest maturity profile. Most listed corporate bonds relate to infrastructure, either directly in the form of bonds issued by infrastructure utilities, or indirectly in the form of bonds issued by specialized financial institutions, such as India Railway Finance Corporation, Ltd (IRFC).

In other South Asian countries, the corporate bond market is much more limited, and in some cases, it is nonexistent (as in Afghanistan). However, in countries such as Pakistan, there is significant untapped potential. Bond issuers could include toll roads and other brownfield (existing or upgraded) commercial infrastructure assets suitable for Islamic issuances (equity-based certificates of investment, or *sukūk*). Currently, several infrastructure utilities are listed on the Pakistan Stock Exchange (PSX), including Pakistan International Container Terminal.

Beyond corporate bonds, there is also a global market for project bonds. However, in practice, such transactions mostly occur in investment-grade countries and relate to the refinancing of transactions once a project is complete and has a satisfactory track record in terms of operations and cash flow guarantees. But market interest appetite is very limited for international project bonds in non-investment–grade countries, and even more so for greenfield transport projects.

In recent years, private debt funds have emerged as a new source of long-term finance for infrastructure projects globally. New infrastructure debt funds raised US$34 billion globally from 2013 to 2016. In India, the India Infrastructure Debt Fund (IIDF), sponsored by commercial banks and non-bank financial corporations, acts as a vehicle for refinancing the existing debt of infrastructure SPVs, thus providing headroom for new lending by commercial banks, including for infrastructure.

COMMERCIAL FINANCING FOR TRANSPORT CORRIDOR PROJECTS

Beyond its necessary role as a direct investor, the state also has a key role in facilitating investment and financing from the private sector (or the commercial public sector) for priority corridor projects. Broadly, state policies need to provide an enabling environment, including macroeconomic stability (in terms of interest rates and sovereign credit rating), viable infrastructure tariffs, good governance, professional management of state utilities, transparent public-private partnership (PPP) procurement and contract enforcement, creditors' rights, capital market regulations, and equitable tax regimes.

In addition, to attract private investors to infrastructure projects, including transport corridor projects, authorities may consider specific state interventions through various instruments.

The first type of instrument aims to strengthen the project structure to make it suitable for commercial investors and lenders. Such instruments include financial viability support (FVS) schemes, which support priority projects that are economically viable but whose financial returns are not high enough or

are too uncertain to attract private sector investors. Such schemes exist in both developed and emerging markets, and are typically incorporated in the host country's PPP framework. Examples are found in Chile, India, Mexico, Peru, India, and South Africa. These schemes can take different forms, such as viability gap funds (targeting priority projects whose economic returns are good but do not attract private sector investors due to insufficient financial returns) and availability payment schemes that support projects exposed to demand risk, such as transport corridor projects, for which operating cash flows cannot be reliably predicted.

A second type of instrument involves establishing a guarantee fund for the payment obligations and other key contractual undertakings to the project company and related project financing, where the state counterparts in major contracts are not strong enough to support commercial financing. An example is the Indonesia Infrastructure Guarantee Fund (IIGF). A comparable scheme is the African Trade Insurance Agency, which was established in 2001 and is headquartered in Nairobi, which covers infrastructure investors and lenders against a variety of risks, including possible default by African member states.

Other interventions promote financial intermediation for viable infrastructure projects. State interventions in the financial sector may follow a *wholesale* or *retail* route. Wholesale development finance schemes foster lending from domestic financial institutions by providing them with long-term liquidity, sharing selected financial hedging risks, and sharing credit risks on the financing. Wholesale schemes do not require the creation of a new institution.

Wholesale financing schemes. Instruments designed to address market gaps related to long-term liquidity include *mirror* (matching) refinancing, where domestic banks (*primary* or *retail* lenders) may obtain long-term funds from a state agency (acting in a *secondary* or *wholesale* capacity) that matches the maturities of their long-term loans to eligible infrastructure obligors (borrowers). One example is the IPFF project in Bangladesh, which is managed by the central bank on behalf of the Ministry of Finance and is backed by World Bank financing. Other options include *take-out* facilities, such as those offered by the U.S. Export-Import Bank, which gives banks the option to sell (at a predetermined price) eligible long-term loans back to a state agency—thereby freeing up their balance sheets so they can finance new projects. Liquidity schemes can also share maturities, where banks finance earlier maturities, while a state agency funds the longest ones.

Besides long-term liquidity, there is also scope for state agencies to act as market makers, along with pension funds or other commercial financial institutions. They can provide hedging that mitigates the interest-rate mismatch carried by primary lenders, extending fixed-rate, long-term loans to infrastructure obligors. In practice, state agencies carry exchange rate fluctuation risk when they on-lend in local currency the foreign currency resources they obtain from international financial institutions. Exposure to either interest rate or exchange rate fluctuation risk needs to be carefully monitored and managed, given a country's macroeconomic and fiscal situation.

Another type of wholesale instrument focuses on sharing credit risk. Under such schemes, the risk participation of the secondary financial institution can be pro-rata, as in the case of partial credit guarantees, or unfunded risk participations. Alternately, the risk sharing may be in the form of long-term contingent facilities, such as those pioneered by the European Investment Bank (EIB) as part of its Project Bond Initiative, which supports the Trans–European Network–Transport (TEN–T) (see chapter 5). Under this scheme, a secondary financial institution extends a contingent credit line, which can be drawn on if the cash flows generated by the project are not sufficient to ensure senior bond debt service or to cover construction costs overruns.

Retail financing schemes. In contrast to secondary or wholesale instruments, the *primary* or *retail* approach involves direct financing of commercial infrastructure obligors. Direct intervention typically involves establishing a new financial institution dedicated to infrastructure finance. Countries where the World Bank and IFC have supported primary development finance institutions include India (with IIFCL), Colombia, and Indonesia, and an institution is planned for Pakistan. While these institutions can help kick-start market development, they may also face pitfalls such as competition with the private sector, cronyism (where financial support is exchanged for some privilege or benefit), political capture, and a lack of financial discipline or of development impact. To avoid such pitfalls, development finance institutions need to adopt good international practices, notably a clear mandate that focuses on well-identified market gaps, as well as strong management, governance, and supervision—ideally, with majority private sector ownership. Because the resources of these institutions are limited compared to the scale of infrastructure needed by host countries, their impact should be measured in terms of the total financing they facilitate, rather than the amount they provide or the size of their balance sheet.

In recent years, a number of countries have established strategic investment funds (SIFs) to serve as anchor investors for international and domestic investors in projects in key sectors of the domestic economy. SIFs are created as investment funds or corporations and are sponsored and/or fully or partly capitalized by a government, by several governments, or by government-owned global or regional finance institutions. They invest for financial as well as economic returns, according to a double-bottom-line objective. SIFs aim to attract private capital to invest in key economic sectors; operate as expert investors on behalf of their sponsors; provide long-term "patient" capital (from those who are willing to invest with no expectation of turning a quick profit), primarily as equity, and may also invest in quasi-equity or debt; and are created as investment funds or corporations (see Havard, Noel, and Tordo 2016). Over the past 15 years, at least 30 SIFs have been were created around the world. Another 12 are planned. Examples of existing SIFs are Bahrain's Mumtalakat (2006), Italy's Strategic Investment Fund (2011), Kazakhstan's Baiterek (2013), Mexico's Macquarie Mexico Infrastructure fund, Morocco's Ithmar Capital, Senegal's Fonds Sénégalais d'Investissements Stratégiques (FONSIS), and the Africa Renewable Energy Fund (2014) (see Havard, Noel, and Tordo 2016). In South Asia, India created the National Investment and Infrastructure Fund (NIIF) as an SIF in 2015, with US$3 billion of seed capital from the government of India.

The structures of SIFs vary, from the private management of public capital through hybrid funds with private and public shareholding, to fully state-owned direct investment funds. Private management of public capital occurs when the government invests in a private fund on terms that reflect policy priorities, or when a public entity shares risk as a limited partner in a hybrid fund. In this model, investment decisions are made independently by the private sector general partner that manages the fund, or by an independent investment committee that may include government representatives. The overall investment policy is set by the fund's board, which is usually controlled by limited partners. The fund manager and general partner may be required to put up some share of the total capital. In funds that are fully owned and/or operated by the government, market validation may come from limiting the ownership share in each investment, and limiting the SIF's investments to minority participation of a certain size. For these funds, management is frequently provided by a government-owned entity operating at arm's length from the government (see Havard, Noel, and Tordo 2016).

FINANCING CROSS-BORDER AND TRANS-REGIONAL TRANSPORT CORRIDORS

Cross-border infrastructure projects—such as international canals; regional ports; and integrated water management systems, including waterways, railway lines, roads, and associated border and customs logistics—are important for developing regional and transregional trade, and can wield immense benefits for beneficiary countries. But these projects face financing challenges that are even more daunting than domestic transport corridor projects.

Much of the international experience in financing cross-border infrastructure relates to either telecommunications (submarine cables, fiber-optic backbones) or energy trade, such as power generation and transmission projects in Latin America, the Mekong River Delta subregion, and Sub-Saharan Africa; and gas pipelines in Eastern Europe, Western and Central Asia, the ASEAN (Association of Southeast Asian Nations) region, and the Southern Cone of Latin America. Examples in South Asia include hydropower plants in Bhutan and Nepal, and the associated transmission lines for export to India.

The two most prominent historical examples of cross-border infrastructure projects are related to greenfield transport corridors: the Suez Canal (opened in 1869) and the Panama Canal (opened in 1914). The Suez Canal was undertaken on a commercial basis by a concession company responsible for its construction and operation. This company listed its shares on the Paris Bourse and raised debt financing through a bond issue (which ultimately ended in default). A similar approach was attempted for the Panama Canal, but failed. Eventually, construction of the Panama Canal was completed by the U.S. Army Corps of Engineers.

Cross-border transport corridor projects have involved three types of investment and financing vehicles:

National public finance. Each state is responsible for investment in its territory.

This method is the simplest and most common. However, it may lead to suboptimal outcomes (projects with a strong economic rationale that are not undertaken or are postponed, particularly where costs and benefits do not arise proportionally in the respective states—as may be the case for the Canal Seine Nord, a 107-kilometer waterway project intended to connect France, Belgium, and the Netherlands).

Public joint ventures involve the public sectors of the respective countries, as illustrated by the Oresund Link between Sweden and Denmark (see box S1.1).

Private joint ventures, which, given their very large size, tend to be structured along the lines of project finance (as was the case for Eurotunnel), rather than corporate finance.

Private joint ventures in transport corridors may be supported by a regional SIF sponsored by one or more governments in the region, with the goal of being the anchor investor for regional or international investors in infrastructure. The most prominent example of a regional corridor SIF is the Silk Road Fund (SRF), which was established by the Government of China in 2014 with US$40 billion in capital (see box S1.2).

BOX S1.1   Financing the Oresund link between Denmark and Sweden

Oresund (Øresund in Danish, Öresund in Swedish) is a 16-kilometer (km) fixed rail-road link connecting Copenhagen in Denmark and Malmö in Sweden. It also serves the Copenhagen airport, which is halfway between the two cities. The project was constructed from 1995 to 2000 and includes an 8-km two-deck bridge, an artificial island, and a 4-km tunnel, at a cost of approximately €4 billion. The infrastructure is owned and operated by a consortium formed by the Danish and Swedish states. The two national governments, along with respective local governments, separately financed the ancillary infrastructure and access roads in their countries.

To simplify the financing and reduce its cost, the project was financed by loans and bond issues guaranteed by the two governments through the Swedish National Debt Office and Denmark's National Bank, both rated AAA (the highest possible sovereign credit rating). The financing was entirely serviced from the proceeds received from automobile tolls and railway access charges and is expected to be repaid within 34 years from the date when the project was begun. The project company is exposed to a moderate level of currency fluctuation risk (loans are denominated in three currencies—euros, Swedish kronor, and Danish kroner) and interest rate fluctuation risk (parts of the loans are on a floating rate basis, and the fixed-rate bonds may vary at the time they are retired for refinancing). The project company dynamically hedges these financial market risks to optimize the risk/cost profile of its financing.

The solution of commercial financing guaranteed by the two states worked well for Denmark and Sweden, given their close relations and low likelihood of default. But it could require adjustments in countries with lower credit ratings and a higher likelihood of default, commanding different loan prices, as could be the case for transport projects across neighboring South Asian countries.

Sources: Øresundsbron website (https://www.oresundsbron.com/en/info/finance); Painvin 2009.

BOX S1.2   The Silk Road Fund: A regional transport corridor strategic investment fund

As part of its One Belt One Road Initiative (a strategic development program designed to enhance the links and cooperation among Eurasian countries), China established the Silk Road Fund Co., Ltd. (SRF) in Beijing in December 2014. The initial capitalization was US$40 billion from the State Administration of Foreign Exchange, China Investment Corporate, China Development Bank, and Export-Import Bank of China. The aim is to promote the common development and prosperity of China and other countries/regions involved in the One Belt and One Road initiative. Besides financial returns, SRF focuses on environmental and sustainable development issues, and actively works to address its social responsibilities.

SRF is a medium- to long-term development and investment fund. Through various forms of investment and financing (mainly equity investment), SRF is dedicated to supporting infrastructure, resource and energy development, industrial capacity cooperation, and financial cooperation in countries/regions involved in the One Belt One Road Initiative to ensure medium- and long-term financial sustainability and reasonable returns on investment. SRF invests in equity, debt, and other funds. It can work with international development organizations, along with domestic and overseas financial institutions, to jointly set up funds, manage assets entrusted to it, and commission others to invest.

SRF was established as an investment fund with complete corporate governance, which created a board of directors, a board of supervisors, and a management term according to the Company Law of the People's Republic of China. It has also recruited high-caliber professionals from different backgrounds and disciplines, and set up an effective, efficient corporate governance mechanism.

Source: Silk Road Fund website (http://www.silkroadfund.com.cn/enweb/23775/23767/index.html).

REFERENCES

Havard, H., M. Noel, and S. Tordo. 2016. "Strategic Investment Funds: Opportunities and Challenges." Policy Research Working Paper 7851, World Bank, Washington, DC.

Painvin, N. 2009. *Large Projects, Giant Risks? Lessons Learned: Suez Canal to Boston's Big Dig.* Fitch Rating Transportation Global Special Report (May 18).

World Bank. 2005. "Best Practices in Corridor Management." World Bank, Washington, DC.

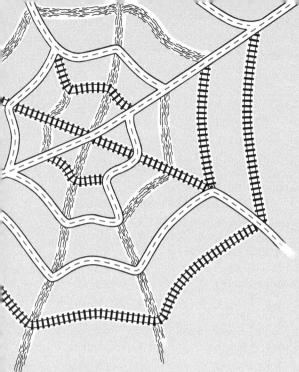

Spotlight 2

Private Investment in Corridor Infrastructure

Private sector sponsors vary in their involvement in developing transport corridors. Their role can be as minimal as helping plan these projects, or it can extend through the financing and/or operations of the infrastructure and services. The most successful schemes are usually developed as part of a public master planning exercise because the private sector cannot be expected to address issues surrounding the provision of public goods. Private sponsors' involvement cannot be understood without examining the views of the lenders and equity investors that make their participation possible. Both types of participants usually have similar views when analyzing a project's risks. However, their opinions and interests diverge about a project's upside potential. When returns on equity are higher than returns on debt, equity investors benefit, while lenders do not benefit (that is, higher profitability does not translate into higher debt repayments).

From the lenders' perspective, there are four basic requirements to support a corridor project:

1. The level of projected cash flows under a base-case scenario will cover operations and maintenance costs, concession fees, and debt

service (a debt service coverage ratio equal to or greater than 1.5 is frequently required).
2. The private sponsors have the expertise and the financial ability to implement the project and provide lenders with an adequate works' completion guarantee.
3. The host governments can regulate private sponsors' operations and, more important, can provide lenders with a creditworthy early termination guarantee as well as an appropriate security covering currency convertibility and an offshore debt repayment structure.
4. Lenders can secure political risk guarantees that are appropriate for the project's risk profile.

From the sponsors' perspective, the corridor projects' requirements are the same as those for the first and third requirements for lenders. However, sponsors' requirements differ and/or are contradictory regarding the size and duration of the guarantees they need to offer their debt providers, as well as the public service obligations, including those that imply the added upfront investment they need to provide to local communities.

Private investment projects usually create a special-purpose vehicle (SPV) that is responsible for developing, managing the finances of, constructing, and operating a project. The SPV, as the holder of the debt, caps the exposure of private sponsors to their equity contribution if, and when, it is linked to a *nonrecourse* type of project structure. If a project is not performing and the debt is not being served, the lenders' recourse to private sponsors is limited to the amount of equity invested in the SPV.

When authorities seek private sector participation to develop transport corridors, the plans must consider various *bankability* factors. Thus, public–private sector dialogue on risk allocation/mitigation must occur before project planning commences and private investors' participation is secured. This dialogue is essential to determine whether private sponsors will assume public service obligations, which can include enlarging their investments to ensure wider benefits to local communities. Dialogue is also needed to clarify if they will scale up their investments or make part of their infrastructure available to other end users to motivate them to contribute to the project.

CO-INVESTING IN CORRIDOR INFRASTRUCTURE: ATTRACTING DEBT AND EQUITY PROVIDERS

Before investing in corridor infrastructure, private sponsors must secure funding by attracting more equity holders and/or mobilizing debt from lenders. Their ability to do so will be determined by the nature and/or degree of the market's volatility. That is, will the infrastructure be competitive or noncompetitive; promoted by one or more products; serve one or more clients; and /or rely on an *off-take* agreement?[1] The key to bankability in this case is the creditworthiness of the project sponsors and the producer's competitiveness (both in cost and value) in relevant markets (specifically, if its price is among those in the lowest quartile).

While most lenders are prepared to assume the risk on large projects that rests on a single *anchor* client—especially when dealing with

greenfield projects—smaller projects can also be structured in a way that allows them to raise commercial debt through public-private partnerships. In these cases, a project's success rests on the sponsors' ability to design shared-use regimes (among themselves) to maximize revenues from multiple clients, without exposing them to local authorities' accusations about perceived or real abuses with respect to market access and/or price. This is particularly true when uncertainties exist about the interest and credit quality of prospective clients at the time a project is designed. Sponsors must then ensure that lenders and regulatory authorities have given them enough contractual and oversight flexibility to adapt to changing demand. While lenders may accept that sponsors provide access to new and unidentified clients (at the time of financial closing), they will try to maintain the right to block sponsors' decisions to expand their client pool if this weakens their debt service capacity. Indeed, sharing infrastructure investments across multiple sponsors and/or multiple clients raises lenders' perception of a project's risks. Thus, this type of public-private partnership (PPP) structure makes sense to private sponsors when their participation/investment complements investments in a corridor's backbone infrastructure made by other private or public investors.

PRIVATE INVESTMENT AND THE BUSINESS ENVIRONMENT

Corridor projects are often structured as PPPs, in which regulations are clear, that can attract private sector participation. However, private equity investment in infrastructure depends particularly on the private equity holders being offered attractive concession terms. This is critical since the legal and regulatory risks can easily exceed the tolerance of project sponsors and/or lenders due to potential losses from government actions and/or exposure to discriminatory practices regarding equal access.

Laws and regulations that foster corridor infrastructure PPPs cover the following aspects, among others:

- Responsibilities shared among public and private parties;
- Contractual guidelines for PPPs and the scope of infrastructure concession contracts;
- Contractual arrangements to accommodate multiple private parties;
- Status and ownership of assets—including when the PPP ends;
- Securities;
- Taxes and customs, setting and revising of fees, royalties, and tariffs;
- Service and performance obligations, especially regarding public services;
- Rules on terminating PPPs and dispute resolution;
- Authorizations, licenses, and rules regarding competition;
- Rules regarding labor, safety, and environmental and social commitments; and
- The nature and role of institutions involved at the various stages of the PPP (inception, conclusion/negotiations, and supervision).

For investors (sponsors and lenders), these issues can be considered either "systemic" (pertaining to all corridor PPPs in the jurisdiction) and/or "project specific."

A transparent legal framework is often a prerequisite for a PPP. Investors require clear, stable, and secure laws and institutions that support the proposed operation. These involve three sets of issues.

Host country laws. The first set of issues pertains to the host country's laws, particularly those related to corporations; securities; foreign investment and taxes; sector and PPP regulations; lease and real estate rights; procurement laws; and labor, safety, and environmental regulations.

The absence of clear laws in any of these areas can represent a significant risk. This risk can be mitigated through a contractual approach that is strongly supported by the host country and is promoted by the government's negotiating team. This contractual approach is easier to implement in common law systems or where no PPP regulations exist. The contract must be legally acceptable and have a clear precedent over any conflicting regulations.

Where laws are unclear, investors can consider the process (to define a legal regime through a contract) too long and risky. In such cases, a complete review and/or modernization of PPP laws might be warranted.

Institutional framework. The second set of issues regards the institutional framework. Establishing a PPP requires interacting with various public authorities responsible for finances, sector policies, labor and social security, and safety and the environment, as well as other authorities whose jurisdiction relates to the PPP.

To ensure predictability and stability, the private sector seeks to deal with as few actors as possible, and it assumes that the public authority has already consulted with other public institutions.

In countries where institutions are unstable, private sector stakeholders are concerned that new institutions may appear and claim the right to intervene under the PPP. To avoid this risk, the host governments should early on identify all public institutions that need to be consulted. Where this is ambiguous, they need to clarify each party's role under the PPP.

Enforcement of laws and contracts. The third set of issues pertains to how well laws and contracts are enforced. This requires appropriate laws, along with a reliable, independent, and functioning judiciary. Often, because private investors do not have enough confidence in local jurisdictions, PPP contract disputes are submitted to arbitration. Thus, it is important that the host countries see arbitration as a valid method to resolve disputes and will enforce it.

TWO CASE STUDIES

Many lessons emerge from attempts to involve the private sector in developing corridor infrastructures. Interactions among the different stakeholders are complex, and interests are diverse in projects, both with and without an *anchor* economic activity (where the major function is served by the infrastructure). Two cases are considered next.

The Maputo Corridor in Mozambique. This effort was part of a government strategy to launch PPP programs to develop transport infrastructure that had deteriorated during a period of low economic development and civil war (see box 3.1). The Maputo Corridor promised the potential to contribute to domestic and regional economic development. Since it ended at the Port of Maputo, the second-largest deepwater port in Mozambique, this made it a natural gateway to export goods from Mozambique's neighbors and domestic mines. Mining was considered an anchor activity for the corridor, which provided a critical mass for the railway and port.

The government planned the PPPs to rehabilitate the port and restore and develop the railway to connect the port with domestic and foreign customers. Although the two were structured and organized as separate projects, they were to be developed simultaneously.

The PPP's structure and financing consisted of the public sector, represented by the government (49 percent of the concession)—including Mozambique Ports and Railways (which has 33 percent of the concession)—and by a private group with interests in the region, represented by Mersey Docks Group, Skansa, and Liscont (51 percent), which united in a joint venture to form the concessionaire. The Maputo Port Development Co. (MPDC) agreed to finance, develop, and restore the port, in return for receiving the right to operate it for 15 years in a classic build-operate-transfer (BOT) structure. Fifteen years were added to the concession in 2010, with an option for another 10 years after 2033.

The concession included fixed annual payments of US$5 million indexed to the U.S. Consumer Price Index. MPDC was required to pay the Public Port Authority 10 percent of its gross income during the first five years, 12.5 percent from years 6 to 10, and 15.5 percent from years 11 to 15.

It was expected to take three years to restore the port, and cost US$67.5 million.

The financing plan consisted of US$32 million in equity, senior debt of US$27 million, and subordinated debt of US$8.5 million. Senior debt consisted of two term loans: a US$14 million 12-year term loan from the Standard Corporate and Merchant Bank, which included political and partial commercial guarantees from the Swedish International Development Agency; and a US$13 million, 10-year loan from the Development Bank of South Africa and the Netherlands Development Finance Company. Subordinated debt consisted of a 10-year loan from FinnFund and the Nordic Development Fund.

Because the port was developed simultaneously with the railway, the port concession lasted nearly two years, and was delayed until an operator chosen for the rail concession. Although the process collapsed in 2005, the rail PPP relaunched in 2006, when Mozambique Ports and Railways and Spoornet, a South African state-owned enterprise, signed a cooperation agreement.

The initial rail PPP failure did not significantly affect the port. Instead, miners used toll roads and heavy trucks to deliver products to the port. Volume increased to 11.8 million tons per year in 2011, and reached nearly full capacity in the following years.

The Maputo Port PPP is an example of a multiclient/multimodal project designed on an *unbundled* basis, where the railway (a key part of the infrastructure) was designed and executed separately. It ultimately revealed the problems attached to unbundling corridor infrastructure that shared an anchor economic activity (in this case, mining). Because different pieces of the infrastructure played integral roles in the entire supply chain, the unbundled organization and execution of each part added complexity and time, and possibly had negative impacts.

This example also shows the role international finance institutions and development finance agencies can play in bringing mining-related infrastructure PPPs to market by addressing funding gaps. Indeed, without the institutions' funding and guarantees, commercial lenders may not have considered the project bankable.

Without credit financing, it is unlikely that private sector sponsors would have been interested.

The Alice Springs–Darwin railway project in Australia. This project aimed to provide a new transport corridor linking the northern and southern coasts, offering an alternate route for goods from Australia's industrial center to Asia, and improved passenger service leading to more tourism. In this case, the project did not have an anchor activity.

In 1995, the Northern Territory and the state of South Australia signed a memorandum to establish a joint approach to create a north-south continental railway. By 1996, the regional parliaments had created the AustralAsia Railway Corporation (AARC), which was a state-owned enterprise designed to award a build-own-operate-transfer (BOOT) concession and hold the titles to the land for railway construction. The Asia Pacific Transport Consortium (APTC)—which was led by Kellogg Brown & Boot and included the John Holland Group, Barclay Mowlem, Macmahon Holdings, and the Australian Railroad Group—was awarded the concession in June 1999. The concession involved the design, construction, and operation of the railway for 50 years. Construction began in July 2001 and was completed in September 2003. Rail traffic started in 2004.

The total cost of this rail line was $A1.32 billion. APTC provided $A842 million, and AARC provided $A478 million. The financing plan consisted of equity of $A238 million, senior debt of $A491 million, subordinated debt of $A112 million, and government funding of $A478 million. Senior debt consisted of a $A150 million, five-year bullet loan;[2] a $A261 million, 12-year loan; and a $A80 million, 12-year rolling stock loan. Subordinated debt included a tier-one mezzanine loan of $A86 million and a tier-two mezzanine loan of $A26 million. Finally, government funding consisted of a $A50 million loan and $A428 million in works' contribution. The contract was very complex, with over 300 documents and 112 separate signatories.

The rail project won immediate praise for its efficient construction, for creatively resolving challenges that arose regarding land and indigenous property titles, and for resolving environmental concerns. It was projected to add billions to the GDP of the federal and regional governments and create many jobs.

However, it faced various economic issues. There were concerns about whether it could get shippers of lower value and/or less time-sensitive cargoes to switch to the faster but costlier rail alternative. Also, it was thought that even without a secured customer arrangement, it could attract domestic and international freight with mixed loads. However, the banks' financing model suggested that the project needed to capture approximately 45 percent of the market share to break even, and repay its senior debt within 12 years of commencing operations.

Unfortunately, this rail project did not attract enough customers or make an operating profit during its first three years. By October 2006, APTC could not meet the debt service on the senior debt. Thus, in December 2006, APTC entered into a nonaction agreement with senior debt holders to restructure the business or refinance the senior loans. In December 2010, the assets and business were sold to the operator-contractor, Genesee & Wyoming Inc. At this time, APTC had liabilities of nearly $A900 million, a ratio of total debt to capital of 256 percent, and interest coverage of 0.3.

The Alice Springs–Darwin rail PPP illustrates the level of complexity and risk, and relative lack of clarity, of multiuser/multimodal projects. Although the project had many benefits, and was completed on time and almost on budget, it failed because revenue projections were significantly overestimated.

NOTES

1. An off-take agreement serves as a guarantee to the lender that the client has secured the sale of a specified amount of the goods/services to be produced provided by an anchor client. The simplest case is when a corridor serves a single customer that makes a single product and the project's sponsors can rely on an off-take guarantee from the corridor's main user/anchor client that is low risk.

2. With this type of loan, interest is paid during the course of the loan and the principal is paid at the end.

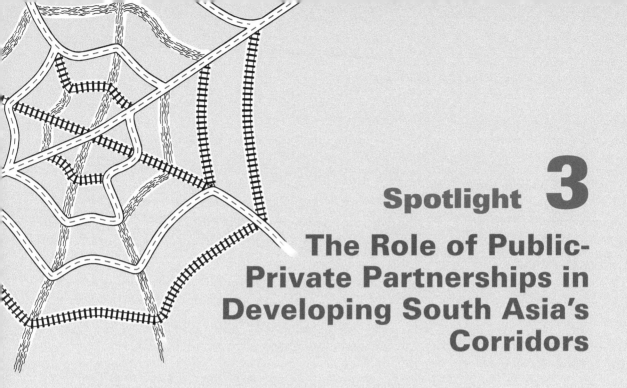

Spotlight 3

The Role of Public-Private Partnerships in Developing South Asia's Corridors

SOUTH ASIA'S EXPERIENCE WITH PPPs FOR TRANSPORT INFRASTRUCTURE

Corridors offer unique opportunities for PPPs

If corridor projects that aim for wide economic benefits are to succeed, funding and financing arrangements must serve the goals that underlie a corridor. In South Asia, where corridor projects are difficult to deliver (regardless of the financing mode), the goals of public-private partnerships (PPPs) and those for developing corridors are often misaligned. However, they could be resolved if the region's PPP models evolve in ways that meet expectations for what they can deliver.

South Asia has huge financing needs to develop its infrastructure. In 2014, the World Bank estimated that Bangladesh, India, Nepal, Pakistan, and Sri Lanka would require US$408–US$685 billion in investment at 2010 prices to bridge gaps in the transport sector alone (Andrés, Biller, and Herrera Dappe 2013). Moreover, many of the projects are complex and risky because of the political-economy environment. This is particularly true for major corridor projects. Thus, PPPs are an enormous challenge because unstable project environments can easily compromise bankability.

The experiences of general transport PPPs in South Asia are also mixed. In India, which has more PPPs than the other countries, it appears that the insolvencies of many highway PPPs are challenging the banking sector and impeding physical progress on construction. These problems have not yet been addressed, which affects both infrastructure assets and their wider economic benefits. The issues with the PPP highways are linked to a heavy reliance on public sector banks for PPP lending, combined with speculative behavior in contracts for short-term gains while the projects were being constructed. Similarly, in Nepal, PPP models have failed to deliver on major corridor projects such as the Fast Track highway, despite six attempts since 1996.

Conversely, in Pakistan, PPPs for ports and container terminals appear to have performed better. For example, Gwadar Port entered into an agreement with the Port of Singapore Authority to manage operations, and Karachi Port engaged Hutchison Port Holdings to construct and operate the Karachi Deep Water Port. It also appears that India's relatively small but important railway PPP projects are succeeding. However, the positive examples of delivering better results in the highways sector projects are limited. Generally, the ability of PPPs to consistently deliver the large-scale, complex, greenfield corridor infrastructure projects South Asia needs is still unproven, despite significant support from the international community and the region's governments.

In considering the future role of PPPs in developing South Asia's main transport corridors, it is important to explore past experiences. First, this entails examining cash flows and risk profiles of projects where investors were asked to tolerate both calculated risks and complete uncertainty. Second, this involves understanding the South Asian context, where financial sectors, construction industries, laws, and general governance are still developing. Third, it involves addressing the issue of whether private finance should be considered a primary solution or if expectations should be lowered. This last point might mean a greater focus on expanding public finance to facilitate infrastructure investment, either in support of the private sector or corporatizing public sector entities that operate on commercial principles.

South Asia's mixed experiences

To date, private participation in South Asia's transport infrastructure has mainly been in India's road subsector, according to the World Bank's Private Participation in Infrastructure (PPI) data. Table S3.1 calculates the transactions for airports, ports, railways, and roads by country. These data should be seen as indicative, rather than definitive. For example, the road project in Nepal (the Kathmandu-Kulekhani-Hetauda Tunnel Highway) has struggled to obtain financing for more than four years, and its future is still uncertain. Similarly, when analyzing the volume of investment, different sources offer different figures.

India's road PPPs are concentrated on national highways. The program is large (US$32 billion–US$47 billion), depending on whether the developer's or India's National Highway Authority calculate the total project costs. Importantly, roughly 80 percent of the debt to finance this portfolio has come from public sector banks in which the government owns more than 50 percent of capital shares. Since 2013, projects have faced mounting financial and operating challenges that have been passed on to the banks and developers supporting them and have contributed to the rising number of nonperforming assets (NPAs) in India's banking sector. The State Bank of India (SBI), which holds the greatest nominal amount of Indian highway-related debt, reported that about 20 percent of loans to ports and highways were in nonperforming status by the end of 2016, with the trend increasing in 2016 (figure S3.1). Developers, several of which are India's national construction industry champions, also show signs of stress, slowing investment growth. (This dual stress among

TABLE S3.1   Roads in India dominate the number and share of private participation in infrastructure in South Asia

Country	Airports	Ports	Railways	Roads	Total number, by country	Percentage of total, by country
India	9	48	10	399	466	95.5
Pakistan	1	13	0	0	14	2.9
Bangladesh	1	2	0	2	5	1.0
Sri Lanka	0	2	0	0	2	0.4
Nepal	0	0	0	1	1	0.2
Bhutan	0	0	0	0	0	0.0
Total	**11**	**65**	**10**	**402**	**488**	**100**
Percentage of total, by subsector	2.3	13.3	2.0	82.4	100.0	

Source: World Bank, Private Participation in Infrastructure data.

FIGURE S3.1   A growing share of the loans to ports and highways that are backed by the State Bank of India are nonperforming

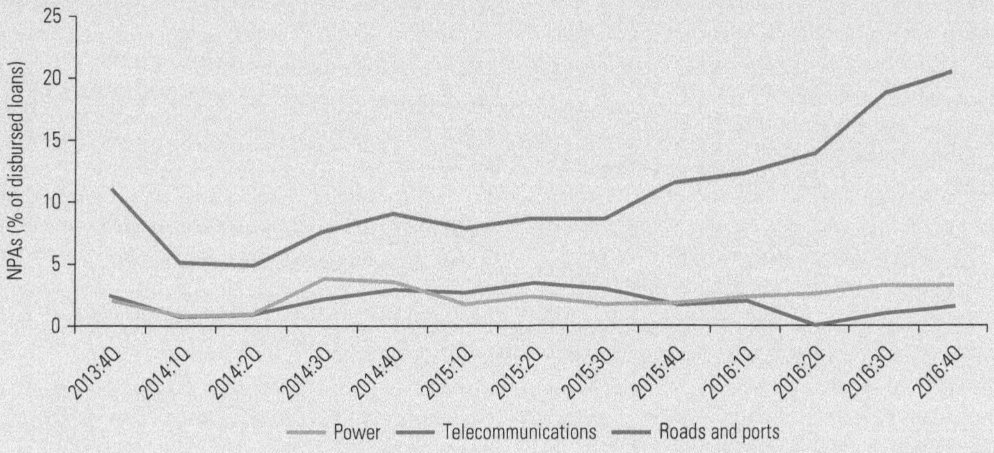

Source: Corridor Study Team analysis of Basel III disclosures.
Note: NPAs = nonperforming assets; Q = quarter.

public and private lenders and developers is called the "twin balance sheet problem.") Recapitalization of the banks and projects appears inevitable, but the government's ability to recapitalize public sector banks and ensure that the projects are completed in time has been doubtful. The announced bank recapitalization announced on October 24, 2017, could be a step in the right direction. However, many have criticized it for not addressing moral hazard issues, cooperate governance of banks, and the negative fiscal impact.[1]

Railway PPPs in India have fared better than road PPPs

India's experience with railway PPPs has been less extensive than with roads but still offers valuable lessons. These PPPs have adopted an *unbundled* approach to infrastructure and service delivery, where investment and maintenance are handled by special-purpose vehicles (SPVs), while the rolling stock and operations are handled by Indian Railways. Revenues are based on a formula that nets out the operating cost of railway services from an access charge payable to the SPV. Two variations of the model exist with respect to land acquisition. Under the first, the SPV acquires the land.

Under the second, Indian Railways handles acquisition. Regardless of the model, any land acquired for the railway may be used only for railway purposes, so broader corridor development in the PPP project is limited.

India's railway PPPs have experienced strong demand and support from off-takers or groups of them, as they have a serious stake in the service to be delivered, as well as financial stakes in the project SPV. For example, the Angul-Sukinda New Railway Line Project in Odisha benefited steel plants in the Angul region—as well as ports, mines, and aluminum smelting operations—providing them with better transport of bulk commodities. Several of these off-takers have contributed capital to the SPV and have representatives sitting on the board of Angul Sukinda Railway Ltd., wearing multiple hats as investors, customers, and governors of the railway.

The large, concentrated nature of commercial stakes in a project's railway service have created strong security for investment because the off-takers' own demand secures the debt and equity to finance the project. In addition to lenders, project sponsors also understand the importance of their demand for the services, as well as their control over it and the service. In contrast, road PPPs are usually secured against a broader revenue base, where revenues from a single road user or small group of them would be unlikely to account for most of project cash flows. Thus, demand risk in India's railway PPPs has been largely controlled by groups with strong links to the SPV. As a result, financing for the railway PPPs has been more stable than for India's roads. Several SPVs have reportedly retired debt sooner than expected, with robust project cash flows.

Two factors affect the replicability of the experiences with India's railway PPPs. First, the scope of the nine projects in this portfolio was limited and targeted to serve certain beneficiaries. Second, the scale of individual transactions was generally smaller than for road projects, ranging from US$17 million to US$300 million. The potential for expanding the model to larger corridors is limited by questions about the long-term model for India's railway services and the role of Indian Railways. The World Bank–supported Eastern Dedicated Freight Corridor (DFC) conducted a pre-feasibly analysis for using a PPP to develop the DFC lines. This exercise showed that larger projects with more complex demand and land acquisition risks, along with more complex access charges, may not simply be viable in the current context as PPPs.

Contracts and investment security are weak

The enforceability of contracts—the glue for project finance—is a key concern in South Asia. The region's context has challenged the foundations on which transport PPPs depend, specifically the use of contracts as the backing for investment. Typically, these would include a project agreement with government authorities (such as a concession agreement), as well as off-take contracts, partnership agreements, supplemental project support agreements, construction contract(s), financing agreements, credit enhancements/guarantees, supply agreements for inputs of raw materials, leases, and potentially many others. In a traditional project finance structure, security

for investment and associated repayment would derive from the cash flows that these agreements help ensure. Countries in South Asia (except for Bhutan) fall below the average among comparable country groups regarding the time needed to enforce contracts, the World Bank Group's 2016 Doing Business survey shows (see figure S3.2). For example, in Bangladesh, India, and Sri Lanka, it takes about four years to enforce a contractual claim. This uncertainty creates a challenge for investors that is difficult to meet through project-specific mechanisms that are also acceptable to governments.

PPPs are addressed in laws and precedents that relate to corporations and partnerships, competition, property rights, insolvencies, regulation of public services, safety, environmental protection, labor, sector-specific provisions, and the like. These arrangements are complex, particularly for one-off projects that may have atypical structures.

To reduce complexity and facilitate PPP projects in transport and other sectors, India has sought to standardize agreements. But it has still not addressed the consistency and time required to enforce provisions that secure investment. For example, India's laws for enforcing security are relatively developed but ineffectively applied. The way insolvencies are treated to recover nonperforming loans is particularly challenging. The 1993 Recovery of Debts Due to Banks and Financial Institutions (RDDBFI) Act created debt recovery tribunals to help collect bad debts. The 2002 Securitization and Reconstruction of Financial Assets and Enforcement of Security Interests (SARFAESI) Act strengthened the lenders' ability to collect. But the enforcement process is slow, inconsistent, and subject to outside influences. India's Supreme Court recognized this, noting, "It is a matter of serious concern that despite the pronouncements of this Court, the High Courts continue to ignore the availability of statutory remedies under the RDDBFI Act and SARFAESI Act."[2] Moreover, the Reserve Bank of India noted that large borrowers—the same ones

FIGURE S3.2   The time needed to enforce contracts varies from less than a year to more than four years in some South Asian countries

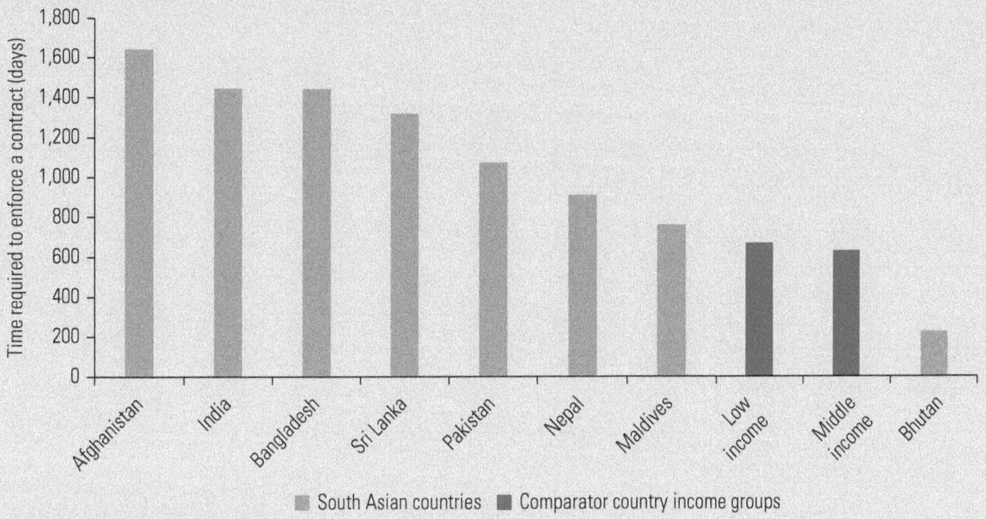

■ South Asian countries   ■ Comparator country income groups

Source: 2018 Doing Business Survey.
Note: Low- and middle-income countries are as defined by the World Bank.

entrusted to deliver on India's PPP projects—are able to manipulate the enforcement process in their favor.[3] Laws across South Asia are still underdeveloped. For example, in Bhutan and Nepal, laws regarding transportation are likely to undergo revision in the near future.

Financial markets are underdeveloped

South Asia's financial markets are at different stages of development, and governance varies from country to country. South Asian countries, except for Bangladesh, rank above average compared to their low- and middle-income peers, while the depth of credit provided by domestic sources is comparable, according to the World Bank's Country Policy and Institutional Assessment (CPIA) of financial sector governance (figure S3.3). However, the countries have limited ability to meet PPP investment needs in transport corridors. For example, India's highway PPP projects have struggled to source long-term debt. While loans up to 15 years have been made,

these have had floating interest rates with rate resets of 1 to 2 years. Such rates and limited hedging instruments expose projects to added risks due to fluctuating interest rates. Project delays, often attributed to public authorities and project companies, can exacerbate these risks—particularly during a project's early years, when debt service is often most sensitive. The rate on India's PPP debt has also been an issue, with highway-related PPP debt generally at 12 percent to 16 percent in nominal terms. Perhaps most important, these PPP programs have shown that the ability to source debt on amenable terms is based on relationships. On account of this, many projects have not stood on sound technical or financial fundamentals. Thus, financial sectors' may not be able to support such PPPs and large, high-risk projects.

The role of underdeveloped markets

The substantial size of corridor PPP projects relative to the banking sectors in South Asia makes transactions potentially unwieldy.

FIGURE S3.3 **Most countries in South Asia compare well to their low- and middle-income peers in the share of domestic credit provided by their financial sectors**

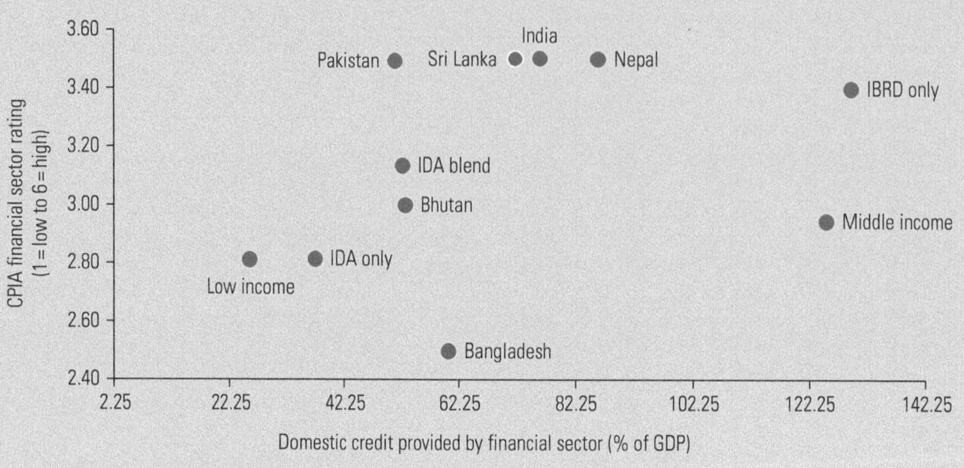

Source: World Bank, World Development Indicators.
Note: Low- and middle-income countries are as defined by the World Bank. "IBRD only" refers to countries that are eligible only for near-market-based financing from the World Bank Group's International Bank for Reconstruction and Development (IBRD). IDA blend refers to countries that are eligible for a blend of concessional financing from the World Bank Group's International Development Association (IDA) and other financing, including IBRD financing.

For example, Nepal's central bank, the Nepal Rastra Bank (NRB), reported that the total Tier I and II capitalization of the domestic banking sector was NPR 255.7 billion in January 2017 (US$2.3 billion).[4] To put that figure in context, most recent cost estimates for the Fast Track highway project, which would provide the transport backbone of a key corridor with improved trade links to India (Nepal's largest trading partner), exceed US$1.3 billion. Nepalese banks face significant risks in taking on high levels of exposure relative to their capitalization against a single high-risk project. However, while it may be possible to obtain international financing, the geopolitical implications of tapping significant levels of cross-border debt in a region with a history of instability and conflict are troubling. Whether these considerations outweigh the benefits of using PPPs to develop a corridor may raise sovereignty issues more than considerations about finance and project delivery. Similarly, political economy considerations of cross-border lending also introduce high levels of uncertainty for investors that are difficult to price.

These considerations have contributed to six unsuccessful attempts to pursue PPPs related to Nepal's Fast Track project since 1996, although these efforts have had international support from bilateral and multilateral development partners. There have been at least 10 different studies and technical assistance engagements since 1974, including from the World Bank / Public-Private Infrastructure Investment Facility, the Asian Development Bank, the United Nations Development Programme (UNDP), and the governments of Finland, Japan, Switzerland, and the United Kingdom. These efforts, along with Nepal's own actions, have been constructive despite challenges that have made delivery of the Fast Track project elusive. Major infrastructure projects are challenging—even in developed countries. However, the complexities related to Fast Track as a PPP within a difficult country context may have contributed to delays and distracted from efforts to address project fundamentals. Specifically, PPP attempts involving Fast Track seem to have led to the view that the private sector would do the engineering to prepare the project, which is a common misconception. Despite its long history of technical assistance, the Fast Track project still does not have a credible and buildable design or enough engineering due diligence to warrant the design being produced.

Finance from outside the region is low in general, and especially low for corridor PPPs

Given the constraints on domestic financial sectors, a key question is whether South Asian countries can obtain international capital for programmatic projects for corridor PPPs, if not for one-off projects. In answering this question, it is important to consider the potential of cross-border infrastructure investment relative to the overall attractiveness of foreign investment in South Asia. Data on inflows of foreign direct investment (FDI) to South Asian countries offers a mixed view (figure S3.4). Most of the countries lag peer groups in the amount of FDI inflows they capture relative to GDP.

An important consideration when seeking finance from outside each South Asian country and outside the region is whether macroprudential regulations of domestic banks could be one way to encourage foreign lending to PPP projects in South Asia. India has used central bank regulations to provide special treatment for loans to infrastructure, and this effort seems to have encouraged bank lending. For example, the Reserve Bank of India previously allowed banks to risk-weight their infrastructure loans at a level that was more favorable than for standard corporate debt. However, sector policies that target PPPs and central bank regulations of domestic banks can have both positive and negative implications for the projects. Specifically, India's experience is that the actual risk of loans, particularly in the highway subsector, was materially different than the risk-weightings allowed for capital provisioning in general. Challenges in highways have occurred along with high rates of nonperforming loans across other sectors as well. The public sector banks in India are also facing a need to increase capitals in order to meet Basel III capital requirements.

FIGURE S3.4   **Overall foreign direct investment is relatively low in South Asian countries**

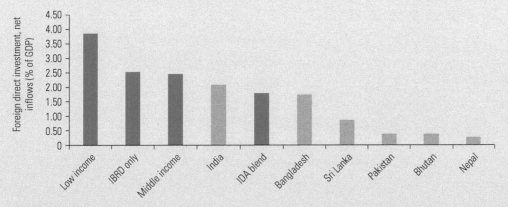

Source: World Development Indicators.
Note: Low- and middle-income countries are as defined by the World Bank. "IBRD only" refers to countries that are eligible only for near-market-based financing from the World Bank Group's International Bank for Reconstruction and Development (IBRD). IDA blend refers to countries that are eligible for a blend of concessional financing from the World Bank Group's International Development Association (IDA) and other financing, including IBRD financing.

The impact of unstable projects and programs on national champions

Except for Pakistan's PPPs for ports, developers in South Asia's corridor PPP programs have been dominated by domestic players. India's highway program, which has evolved over several years, offers a look at the deepest and most developed of such markets in the region. Two interesting observations emerge from this analysis (figure S3.5). First, as the volume of India's PPP transactions expanded during the boom years, the market for potential developers fragmented. In 2004, there were 10 major players in the developer market for India's highway PPPs. However, the number of prospective developers increased dramatically, and the market fragmented. By 2012, no single player held more than a 10 percent market share and developers with market shares of under 3 percent each held roughly half of all contracts.

Less stringent eligibility criteria and a reduced focus on bid quality helped drive market fragmentation. In the program's later years, developers were no longer required to disclose their financing plans or provide evidence that net cash accruals would not be less than 10 percent of a project's total cost (which was previously required). Eligibility criteria were also reduced, which allowed firms, regardless of their capabilities, to qualify as bidders using an associate's credentials. Changes to the qualifications removed nearly all barriers to entry for would-be developers. New market entrants included traditional contractors-turned-concessionaires, as well as financiers-turned-concessionaires. Anecdotal interviews from the World Bank's 2013/14 research noted that the market fragmentation led to particularly aggressive bidding against speculative factors. Further, new and underqualified bidders had fewer technical capabilities to implement projects.

Another important finding from the analysis is that stress in the portfolio of PPP projects seems to have contributed to financial weakness in several of India's leading

FIGURE S3.5   India's market for corridor PPPs fragmented as it expanded—and quality suffered

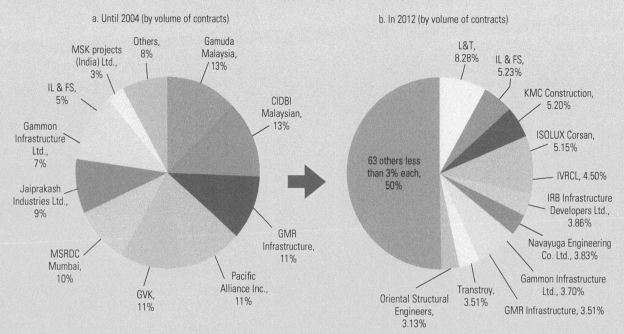

a. Until 2004 (by volume of contracts)

- Gamuda Malaysia, 13%
- Others, 8%
- MSK projects (India) Ltd., 3%
- IL & FS, 5%
- Gammon Infrastructure Ltd., 7%
- Jaiprakash Industries Ltd., 9%
- MSRDC Mumbai, 10%
- GVK, 11%
- Pacific Alliance Inc., 11%
- GMR Infrastructure, 11%
- CIDBI Malaysian, 13%

b. In 2012 (by volume of contracts)

- L&T, 8.28%
- IL & FS, 5.23%
- KMC Construction, 5.20%
- ISOLUX Corsan, 5.15%
- IVRCL, 4.50%
- IRB Infrastructure Developers Ltd., 3.86%
- Navayuga Engineering Co. Ltd., 3.83%
- Gammon Infrastructure Ltd., 3.70%
- GMR Infrastructure, 3.51%
- Transtroy, 3.51%
- Oriental Structural Engineers, 3.13%
- 63 others less than 3% each, 50%

Source: Corridor Study Team analysis of 2014 National Highways Authority of India data.

domestic construction firms. Publicly traded sponsors provide insight regarding how these factors matter. For example, while Larson & Toubro appeared to hold the largest portfolio of stressed national highways contracts in 2013/14, the total amount of these contracts was only 28 percent of the firm's total shareholder capital and reserves in the 2014 financial year. In contrast, GMR's portfolio of stressed assets was equal to 110 percent of the firm's shareholder capital and reserves, while Gammon Infrastructure's portfolio of highway assets was roughly equal to 518 percent of the firm's reported shareholder capital and reserves in the same year (figure S3.6).[5]

The accumulation of stress in India's national highway PPP program also coincided with an accumulation of debt by many (but not all) developers. Publicly traded developers provide an indication of how this occurred. The level of indebtedness for developers also believed to hold large portfolios of stressed national highway PPPs is noteworthy, given the increased risk of insolvency and illiquidity resulting from proportionately large liabilities and debt service payments. These factors are behind the buildup of nonperforming assets in the banks that lent to individual projects.

There are two views concerning developer and project stress. The first considers developer stress as the self-induced outcome of speculation in contracts for short-term gains during early construction stages of projects. This may be accurate and justified to some extent; evidence shows that developers played a short-term game when bidding for highway contracts. An opposing view is that these actions responded to risk allocation frameworks, tender strategies, and financing models that invited speculation under an unsound PPP model. Delays in land acquisition, clearances, and other public sector obligations also played a large role in further stressing the highway PPP portfolio. This fact, combined with the need for strong domestic firms that can develop India's infrastructure, may mean considering ways to relieve stress in overleveraged developers that could be financially viable in the future. It may also mean reconsidering traditional notions of PPP risk transfer, given the dilemma countries will face if they also want to prevent their domestic construction industry from being exposed to added financial risks.

MOVING FORWARD

PPPs and private finance both have a role in developing South Asia's transport corridors. However, it is unclear whether they can deliver at the scale and on the types of projects such development requires. Where PPPs may be a viable approach, it is important to also consider how best to accommodate South Asia's context. International partners working in this area may need to change their approach and adjust expectations about what PPPs can reasonably achieve.

Corporate finance modes need to be modified

South Asian countries might consider departing from the traditional project finance (non-recourse) mode for financing

FIGURE S3.6 Debt-to-equity ratios of four publicly traded developers in India varied considerably from 2010 to 2015

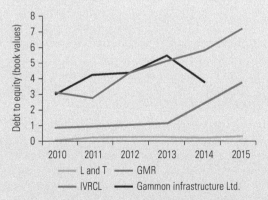

Source: Corridor Study Team analysis of publicly available audited financial statements.
Note: In 2014, Gammon Infrastructure Ltd. executed a private placement of shares to increase shareholder capital and reserves.

PPPs—particularly where lending is often recourse-based and relationship-based. Models commonly found in utility sectors could offer some possibilities. In the case of major road corridors and their tributaries, alternatives could include placing toll-supporting geographical areas under a single corporate entity, using a regulated-asset base approach, and having financing secured through that entity's balance sheet (Helm 2012). These entities would be mandated to maintain the existing network and carry out a program of incremental investment, as agreed upon with its regulator, using cash flows from tolls and any potential subsidies to meet costs and provide returns to capital. This model would be analogous to that applied to a regulated utility operating under defined tariffs and investments to meet service targets. If the model could demonstrate stability, it would simplify potential financing arrangements and allow for an incremental approach to the overall development of networks around the key corridors. A major challenge would be the governance environment of the entity managing the network assets.

Preparing projects to commoditize the role of private sector partners

It is difficult for an authority to effectively outsource what it does not understand. A key constraint on the broader use of PPPs in South Asia is the common expectation that the private sector will compensate for the public sector's failings in project preparation. In particular, the design-build elements that constitute many transport PPPs may have led authorities to underprepare projects with a view that private sector engineering or due diligence would compensate. In the Indian example, highway PPPs were created on the basis of what could be considered a prefeasibility study. With Nepal's Fast Track project, attempts to award PPP contracts proceeded with very little engineering due diligence and with a proposed preliminary design that would have created unsustainable slope cuts into unstable terrain. An alternate approach could entail extensive engineering due diligence and developing tender strategies that first focus on extracting efficiencies and commoditizing the private sector's role(s) to drive value. Enhanced preparations could then help shape project structures that would be more targeted. To be clear, these preparations should not only be aimed at PPPs, and would likely benefit both publicly financed and privately financed undertakings.

The capacity of public funding and finance needs to be expanded

A case can be made for bringing in more beneficiaries to fund corridor projects (whether or not financed under PPPs), considering the broad nature of the wider economic benefits the corridor investments ideally will produce. This expansion could take the form of incremental taxes or charges levied on wider beneficiary groups. These revenues could be sequestered for projects or programmatic approaches. India previously uses a tax on fuel to capitalize its central road fund, which has fueled the National Highways Development Program. Outside of South Asia, the funding approach to London's Crossrail project (which is not a PPP) is meeting approximately one-third of its costs with wider beneficiary contributions—notably a supplemental tax on London businesses and added taxes on land development. An important result is that it has helped the Crossrail project survive budget cuts in the United Kingdom because canceling the project would have forgone much larger investment (and revenues) than the treasury might have hoped to save (World Bank and Imperial College London, forthcoming). Efforts to adopt PPPs more widely to develop South Asia's corridors may benefit from approaches that seek to augment the funding mix using public sources derived from a wider range of beneficiaries.

Expectations should be moderated

South Asia's positive and negative experiences offer valuable lessons for the international community. Some of these lessons are technical, relating to risk allocations, the need for technical due diligence, contract management, and managing implementation challenges. Others are more strategic, relating to institutional behavior, the relationship between central authorities and states, oversight of the banking sector, and general governance. However, the main lesson may be that South Asia offers a window on how governments and the international community can approach PPPs and what they should expect from them.

There is often confusion about the difference between funding and financing infrastructure. PPPs are not a funding mechanism, in that they do not create *new* money to pay for infrastructure investments. They do not fill vast funding gaps—despite all hopes and hype that they may. Rather, they offer value for money only to the extent that they capture incremental efficiencies. The cash that supports privately financed infrastructure investments must ultimately come from one of three sources: user or other beneficiary charges; transfers from general tax revenues; or foreign donor grants. The financing that the private sector can provide is a net consumer of cash, which can just as easily destroy value as create it. When private financing is deployed on poorly prepared projects in weak institutional environments

with deficient oversight according to speculative models, the likelihood of destroying public value is high. This has often been the case when PPPs in South Asia have led to unintended negative outcomes. The international development community should consider how its actions or inactions may have contributed to such outcomes, and what adjustments to country engagements must be made to improve the chances of success in the future.

NOTES

1. See Shenoy, D. "Explained: The Great Indian Bank Recapitalisation Push." *The Wire*. https://thewire.in/190554/explained-great-indian-bank-recapitalisation-push/.
2. Supreme Court of India, *Union of India v. DRT Bar Association*, January 22, 2013.
3. Raghuram G. Rajan, Governor, Reserve Bank of India, at the Third Dr. Verghese Kurien Memorial Lecture at IRMA, Anand, November 25, 2014.
4. Nepal Rastra Bank, "Key Financial Indicators," January 2017.
5. World Bank analysis of publicly available financial reports for the companies mentioned. The end of the financial year varies between companies.

REFERENCES

Andrés, L., D. Biller, and M. Herrera Dappe. 2013. "Reducing Poverty by Closing South Asia's Infrastructure Gap." World Bank and Australian Aid.

Helm, D. 2012. "What to Do about the Roads?" September. http:/www.dieterhelm.co.uk/assets/secure/documents/What-to-do-about-the-roads.pdf.

World Bank and Imperial College London. Forthcoming. "The Operators' Story."

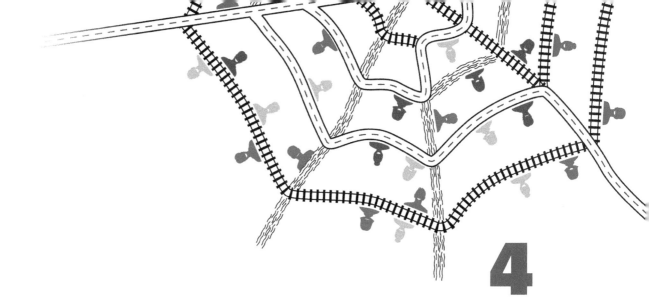

4

Learning from the Literature about the Estimated Wider Economic Benefits of Transport Corridors

Current initiatives and proposals to build transport corridors could demand trillions of dollars in the near future—much more than the capacity of public finances (Bougna et al., forthcoming). By reducing transport costs, such initiatives typically aim to unleash efficiencies in regional and transregional trade. But they also strive to generate net benefits for households and firms that extend beyond savings of travel time and vehicle operating costs. These net benefits stem from the positive spillovers and increased economic opportunities that transport corridors could generate. However, to help realize these benefits, national governments, the private sector, and the global development community need clear economic thinking about how to prioritize investment proposals for large transport projects and a proper methodology to appraise projects. Without these, there are risks of uncoordinated efforts that could result in missed opportunities, wasted public and private funds, geopolitical considerations prevailing over economic

prospects, and misunderstandings between governments and among international organizations.

> The literature offers insights into prioritizing investment proposals for large transport projects and the proper methodology to use to appraise projects.

In parallel with rising interest among policy makers in the prioritization and appraisal of transport corridors, there has been a surge of academic interest in empirically evaluating the economic, social, and environmental impacts of large transport infrastructure projects (Redding and Turner 2014; Berg et al. 2017; Laird and Venables 2017). This surge has partly been driven by improved techniques for rigorously evaluating the economic impacts of these investments and recently completed large-scale investments in transportation networks by countries such as China and India. The academic interest covers these recent investments as well as historical large-scale investments—such as the nineteenth-century investments of the United States in its railway network and the construction of the colonial Indian railway network in the nineteenth and early twentieth centuries. It also covers investments at a variety of scales, ranging from the evaluation of the impacts of individual links within a preexisting or a new system to the evaluation of entire national or even continental systems. Some of these investments may not adhere to what is today considered a transport corridor investment. Nevertheless, the large academic literature estimating the impacts of these investments could inform policy makers' thinking on corridors and help develop a comprehensive methodology to appraise corridor projects.

Knowledge of the direct and indirect impacts, the trade-offs they could produce, and the complementary policies that could help manage these trade-offs all can help shape the optimal policy design for the corridor intervention.

This chapter aims to provide a rigorous review of the empirical literature that estimates the impacts of large transport investments. In doing so, it also seeks to improve policy makers' understanding of the multiple impacts of transport corridor investments, which may have varied effects on certain economic sectors, locales, and population groups. This includes improving understanding of the potential trade-offs that the investments may give rise to, both between different development outcomes and between different groups of economic actors. The review also seeks to extend policy thinking to considering the types of complementary policies and institutions that may be needed to attain wider economic benefits. The aim is to help determine which project elements constitute an optimal *corridor intervention package*—defined as a set of interventions that extends beyond the investment in the main (trunk) transport infrastructure to include reforms and policies that amplify the net benefits of this infrastructure in the wider process of economic and social development. The optimal package then becomes the one that a benevolent social planner would choose to maximize overall *net* benefits.

In reviewing the literature and thinking about the wider economic impacts of transport corridors, this study is interested not so much in the direct benefits (immediate outcomes), such as savings of travel time and vehicle operating costs (VOC), that remain the focus of most cost-benefit analyses for transport projects.[1] Although their importance should not be dismissed and their accurate measurement remains an issue for cost-benefit analysis, these savings are unable to capture the full economic benefits of a transport project in anything other than a hypothetical world of perfectly competitive and complete markets (see, for example, Vickerman 2007 on this point).[2] Rather, this report's interest is in the wider economic impacts of large transport projects, which include impacts on development outcomes such as *economic welfare* (monetary measures of well-being, including income, wages, and consumption), *social inclusion* (jobs, gender), *equity* (poverty, inequality), *environmental quality* (pollution and deforestation), and *economic resilience* (unexpected losses from socioeconomic and other shocks).[3] Furthermore, the study is interested in the potential trade-offs that may occur between these different types of wider economic outcomes—for example, boosting income at the expense of increasing pollution or inequality—as well as the varied impacts of transport projects on a given outcome across different places and economic agents, such as economic impacts that differ across subnational regions, industries, and segments of the population. These heterogeneities are hidden by estimates of average impacts. In some cases, "winners" and "losers" may only be relative. For instance, when all subnational areas along the route of a transport project gain, some areas gain more than others. But in other cases, the losses for some areas may be absolute.

To achieve greater rigor, this chapter adopts a quantitative approach to reviewing the literature. The chapter is based on a review (a meta-analysis) of 78 papers that have been published since 1999 and that meet a series of qualifying criteria. Taken together, these papers provide 243 individual results, which constitute the sample for the quantitative analysis. This sample includes both descriptive analysis and formal econometric meta-regression analysis. The literature review covers papers published in peer-reviewed academic journals and recognized working paper series, as well as "gray" literature that has not (yet) been published through a formal outlet and that is available only for download on authors' personal websites.[4] The review excludes literature that is solely concerned with the evaluation of transport infrastructure projects within an urban area (intra-urban transport).[5] It also excludes literature in which more general transport-related variables appear in the empirical estimation, but these are either not related to evaluating the impacts of a particular large-scale transport infrastructure project and/or they appear as one of several general variables of interest.[6]

A few recent reviews of literature on the economic impacts of large-scale transport infrastructure projects have been published. The most notable are the reviews by Redding and Turner (2014) and Berg et al. (2017). In both cases, the authors present qualitative reviews of the literature. In contrast, this chapter attempts more of a quantitative review of the literature, which includes the use of formal meta-regression analysis techniques. It also considers a broader set of potential economic impacts than is considered by Redding and Turner (2014). Finally, it provides a review that connects more directly to the deliberations of policy makers. The framework for the review is designed to reflect the problem faced by the policy maker who is trying to maximize the net wider economic benefits of a proposed transport corridor (*the policy maker's problem*). This framework also helps highlight important research gaps that remain from the policy perspective.

> **There is strong evidence that transport corridors generate significant positive impacts on economic welfare, but environmental quality and possibly social inclusion could suffer in parallel.**

FRAMEWORK FOR STRUCTURING THE LITERATURE REVIEW

To provide a conceptual structure for the literature review, this chapter proposes the following simple canonical model. Policy makers try to maximize the wider economic benefits of a potential corridor, considering benefits net of costs. They deliberate about corridor features such as location, length, and mode of transport, as well as accompanying complementary policies that can help maximize the targeted wider economic benefits. The cost of the new transport corridor intervention includes trunk infrastructure (such as highways), transport and trade facilitation (such as improving border crossings and removing obstacles to foreign trade), as well as the costs associated with the design and implementation of complementary policies and institutions. This cost increases with the gap between the new set of policies and the preexisting set of policies. This policy maker's problem can play out at different levels of aggregation: local (subnational units such as districts), national, and transregional.

The final outcomes (net wider economic benefits) can be *directly* affected by a corridor intervention and its features, depending on other *complementary factors* (initial market conditions, policies, and institutions) that affect many aspects of the economy at the same time, such as initial conditions in local product markets and factor markets for land, labor, and capital. This direct impact can vary from beneficial to detrimental across individual outcomes. Furthermore, the structural factors can themselves be affected by the corridor intervention. Thus, the corridor intervention can affect the final outcomes *indirectly*. For instance, if the corridor reduces commuting and migration costs, it also reduces frictions in the labor market, which in turn can increase employment and income.

These indirect changes on structural factors are called *intermediate outcomes*. The impact of the corridor on intermediate outcomes can also vary from beneficial to detrimental across the individual outcomes. Knowledge of the direct and indirect impacts, the trade-offs they could produce, and the complementary policies that could help manage these trade-offs all can help shape the optimal policy design for the corridor intervention.

Some features of the optimal corridor package may be needed regardless of the initial conditions. Other features will work best or will be needed only under certain initial conditions—including the preexisting transport network. For instance, if land markets are functioning poorly, making it difficult or costly to acquire land for a transport corridor or harming certain groups, such as smallholders, then land market reforms may be needed to attain all the wider economic benefits and distribute them fairly. Such reforms are unlikely to be needed if land markets are functioning well. Similar considerations apply to the need for reforms in other key markets—including product, labor, and capital markets—as well as crosscutting institutions (such as public sector governance).

The corridor intervention package can be characterized by:

- Placement of the trunk infrastructure, connection type, transport mode, intermodal transport, resilience and redundancy of the system to ensure its resilience to shocks and minimize transport disruptions (backup redundancies).
- Transport and trade facilitation, including auxiliary transport network such as feeder roads or railways.
- Regulatory and institutional reforms (land market, labor market, capital market, and product market conditions, performance of crosscutting institutions).

Several potential transmission mechanisms and their associated intermediate outcomes help determine the ultimate impact of a corridor intervention on the set of final outcomes. These can be summarized in a chain of expected results (a results chain). A stylized version is shown in figure 4.1.

Policy makers and other stakeholders would like to know which particular features of corridors (mode of transportation, length, location, nodal connections, and so on) and which complementary policies (land market reforms, improved access to finance, regulatory reforms

FIGURE 4.1   The web of WEB: The final outcomes of a corridor intervention are achieved through many transmission channels and various intermediate outcomes

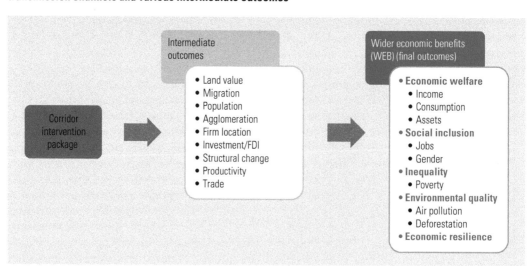

Source: Corridor Study Team.
Note: FDI = foreign direct investment.

FIGURE 4.2   **Direct and indirect impacts determine the overall impact of a corridor intervention**

Overall impact of corridor intervention on WEB	=	Direct (unconditional) impact	+	Indirect impacts (conditional on initial frictions in markets and institutions)

Source: Corridor Study Team.
Note: WEB = wider economic benefits.

in product markets, and so on) need to receive greater weight under different sets of initial conditions (unclear land titles, labor market frictions, financial market imperfections, extent and state of any pre-existing transport infrastructure, and so on).

Although an optimal policy rule to design corridor interventions might be desirable, it may not be fully attainable with current knowledge (see Bougna et al., forthcoming). Less ambitiously, this chapter thus focuses on understanding how different corridor packages affect the net wider economic benefits, considering both direct (unconditional) and indirect (conditional) effects. For instance, how does changing the types of nodes linked by a corridor, or the mode of transportation within the corridor, affect development outcomes—both directly and indirectly, by improving access to markets, land use, and migration patterns?

Figure 4.2 illustrates the relationship between the direct (unconditional) and indirect (conditional) impacts. *Direct (unconditional) impacts* captures the average impact of different aspects of a corridor intervention package on the set of final development outcomes with which a policy maker may be concerned (such as economic welfare, social inclusion, equity, environmental quality, and resilience). *Indirect (conditional) impacts* captures how aspects of a corridor intervention package might interact with different initial conditions to influence the set of final development outcomes.

A transport corridor has potential impacts across multiple outcomes. In some cases, these impacts may be positively correlated—that is, the corridor boosts both incomes and job creation. In other words, the corridor intervention creates *synergies* in development impacts, producing beneficial effects for both economic

welfare and social inclusion. However, in other cases, the impacts may be negatively correlated. For instance, economic welfare impacts may be beneficial, but environmental impacts may be detrimental. This leads to *trade-offs* between different outcomes.

Impacts may also be *heterogeneous*. That is, for a given outcome, they could vary significantly across different geographic areas, segments of the population, economic sectors, and the like. These heterogeneous impacts may be beneficial to all, but vary in size. Thus, the impact will be *relative*, depending on the beneficiaries' greater or smaller predisposition to benefit. Losses can also be *absolute*. For instance, if people migrate in search of better jobs, towns lose population and become more fragile. Certain communities with bleak prospects and poor endowments get left behind. Figure 4.3 presents a hierarchy of multiple impacts across all these dimensions.

METHODOLOGY

Selection of papers

A three-step process was used to identify papers for inclusion in the literature review. In step one, a long list of papers for possible inclusion was identified by performing a series of Google Scholar searches based on different permutations of three categories of keywords: transport-related keywords; keywords relating to variables of interest regarding outcomes, including intermediate outcomes and wider economic impacts (both beneficial and detrimental); and other keywords designed to identify empirical or econometric studies (for a full list of keywords, see table 4A.1 in annex 4A). These searches were confined to papers published since 1999.

FIGURE 4.3   **The overall balance between beneficial or detrimental impacts of a corridor intervention package depends on a hierarchy of impacts**

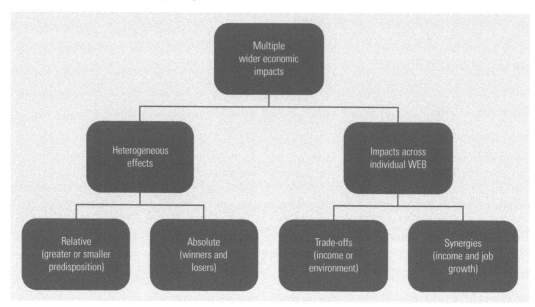

Source: Corridor Study Team.
Note: WEB = wider economic benefits.

In step two, the papers were subjected to two further screening criteria designed to narrow down the list. First, the paper must consider a "large" transport infrastructure investment. "Large" is defined two ways:

- A "large" investment could result in a significant improvement in connectivity between at least two major nodes of economic activity, such as cities or ports. This condition is designed to reflect this study's underlying interest in transport corridors.
- A "large" investment could also entail extensive improvements in last-mile connectivity, such as widespread improvements in a rural road network that connects directly to a national network of highways and primary roads. This condition is designed to capture papers that consider transport infrastructure investments that may be complementary to investments in the trunk infrastructure of corridors.

The second screening criterion requires a paper to meet an "academic standard"; that is, the paper must present the results from original applied research involving statistical or econometric methods.

The standard is indifferent as to whether a paper was published through a formal academic outlet—such as in a peer-reviewed academic journal, a recognized working paper series, or in an edited book volume—or on an author's personal website. This allows the literature review to capture unpublished literature (so-called gray literature). In formal meta-regression analysis (MRA), the inclusion of such literature is considered important to detect and avoid publication bias (see, for example, Card, Kluve, and Weber 2009).

In step three, an attempt was made to capture any relevant papers that might have been missed from the list produced by steps one and two. This was done by analyzing the references in the papers from the list, consulting with experts within the World Bank in areas where the search had found little coverage (such as on the subject of resilience), and by visiting the personal websites of authors of papers on the list in order to identify additional papers that were "works in progress." In addition, any obviously or only marginally relevant literature was weeded out.

The final sample consists of 78 papers (see annex table 4A.2 in annex 4A).

Figure 4.4 shows the breakdown of papers by mode of publication. Of the 78 papers, 9 percent are unpublished (that is, not published in a formal academic outlet). The papers yielded a total of 243 separate results.[7]

Tagging of papers

A tagging system was applied to extract relevant information for the purposes of this review. Information was collected from each paper for five basic categories of variables:

FIGURE 4.4   The literature search yielded 78 papers, of which 9 percent were unpublished

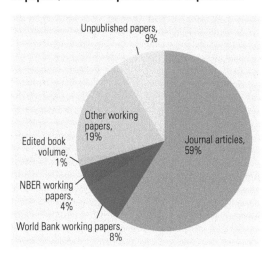

Source: Corridor Study Team.
Note: NBER = National Bureau of Economic Research.

publication details, intervention details, methodology, results, and "additional." To ensure consistency in the collection of information across papers, the value for each variable was restricted to a certain number of multiple-choice options. Annex 4.D (online) provides a detailed list of these options, as well as descriptions of the variables. The information collected was compiled in a database.

To maximize accuracy in the data collection process, the tagging system was implemented through a double-blind review system. Two appropriately trained research assistants (RAs) reviewed and independently tagged papers in batches of ten. Then the study team would meet to compare the results between the two RAs and to reconcile any differences. Sometimes, the tags chosen by both RAs would be overridden based on the chapter authors' own reading of the papers.[8] As the papers were tagged, the system for tagging was also refined to reflect the study team's evolving understanding of the literature. For a sample entry, see table 4A.3 in annex 4A.

DESCRIPTIVE STATISTICS

Publication time-trend

The trend in terms of number of papers published per year has been strongly upward, as seen in figure 4.5. While only one paper in the

FIGURE 4.5   Rigorous evaluations of the impacts of large-scale transport projects have surged recently

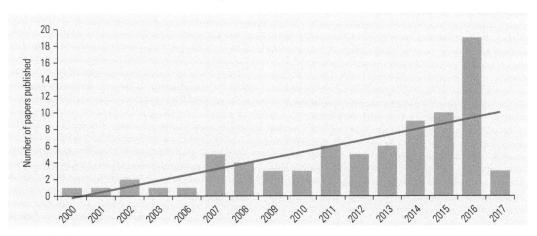

Source: Corridor Study Team.
Note: The sample consists of 78 papers with 234 tagged results (analyzed outcomes). In the case of unpublished manuscripts, the year of publication corresponds to the date on the manuscript.

sample was published in 2000, 19 papers were published in 2016 (the last full year of data). More generally, 71 percent of papers in the sample were published between 2011 and 2016. This strong upward trend reflects the growing academic focus on rigorously evaluating the impacts of major transport infrastructure projects.

Focus of the "typical" paper

Geographical focus

Of the 78 papers in the sample, 33 papers—or 42 percent—focus on transport infrastructure projects in only three countries: the United States (13 papers), India (11 papers), and China (9 papers). This overwhelming focus on these three countries reflects the number of extremely large-scale transport infrastructure projects that they have undertaken either recently or historically. Over the past two decades, both China and India have constructed major new highway networks—the National Expressway Network (NEN) in China (constructed between 1992 and 2015),[9] and the Golden Quadrilateral (GQ) network in India (constructed between 2001 and 2012) (see chapter 6).[10] In historical analyses, several papers have evaluated the impacts of extensive national railway networks constructed in both the United States in the nineteenth century and in India in the nineteenth and early twentieth centuries (Haines and Margo 2006; Donaldson 2010; Atack and Margo 2011; Herrendorf, Schmit, and Teixeira 2012; Donaldson and Hornbeck 2016). Crucially, these evaluations have been facilitated by the existence of high-quality historical data on both the networks themselves and relevant outcome variables. Other papers have examined the Interstate Highway System that the United States built in the mid–twentieth century (Chandra and Thompson 2000; Baum-Snow 2007; Michaels 2008).

Numerous papers focus on countries in either Africa (18 papers) or Latin America (13 papers). Several focus on environmental outcomes, particularly on roads' impacts on deforestation (see, for example, Pfaff et al. 2007; Weinhold and Reis 2008; Damania

and Wheeler 2015; and Dasgupta and Wheeler 2016). A number of the papers on Africa focus explicitly on transport networks that cut across national boundaries and therefore cover more than one country (for example, Buys, Deichmann, and Wheeler 2006; Jedwab and Storeygard 2016).

Intervention details

More than three-quarters (78 percent) of the 234 reported results in the sample evaluate the impacts of some sort of road transport infrastructure (figure 4.6, panel a). The only other transport mode that receives significant attention in the literature is rail (17 percent of results). The overwhelming focus on road networks partly reflects the focus on evaluating the impacts of the NEN in China and the GQ in India, as well as the impacts of the Interstate Highway System in the United States. All these systems were newly constructed networks. Accordingly, 63 percent of results in the sample focus on the evaluation of new network systems (figure 4.6, panel b). About 21 percent of results evaluate the upgrading of a preexisting transport system, while 8 percent of results assess the impacts of upgrading an individual link within a wider transportation network.

In terms of the type of connection considered, the typical paper focuses on projects that are designed to link urban centers (45 percent), although a significant proportion of the literature (22 percent) looks at the impacts of urban–rural connections. Typically, the focus is on evaluating connections between places that fall within national boundaries.[11] However, a number of studies (8 percent) focus on evaluating the impacts of connection between one or more urban centers and an international gateway (a port or an airport).[12] The preoccupation of the literature with urban–urban connections that fall wholly within national borders is, again, related to the dominance of China, India, and the United States as countries of study.

Methodology

The most frequently analyzed category of final outcomes is "economic welfare." The categories of intermediate outcomes

FIGURE 4.6   Evaluations of road projects and new systems dominate the literature
Percentage of reported results

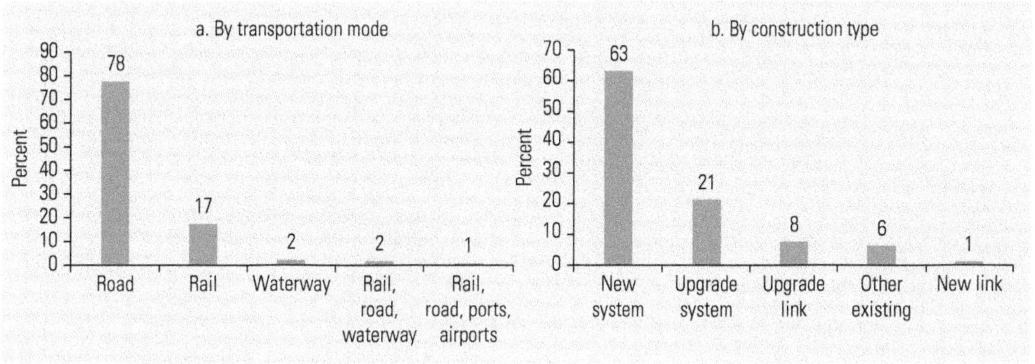

Source: Corridor Study Team.
Note: The sample consists of 78 papers with 234 tagged results (analyzed outcomes).

analyzed most often are "trade and productivity" and "population and assets" (figure 4.7). The typical paper focuses on ex post evaluation and uses subnational geographical regions—such as Indian tehsils (Khanna 2016; Alder, Roberts, and Tewari, forthcoming), Chinese counties (Banerjee, Dufo, and Qian 2012), U.S. counties (Donaldson and Hornbeck 2016), and electoral wards in the United Kingdom (Gibbons et al. 2016)—as the unit of analysis (figure 4.8).[13] In particular, 80 percent of sampled papers rely on data for subnational regions, while 15 percent of studies utilize micro data for individual households. By contrast, a mere 2 percent of papers use micro data for firms (Martincus and Blyde 2013; Gertler et al. 2014; Martincus, Carballo, and Cusolito 2014).

The typical paper is also explicitly motivated by some underlying theoret model— quite often, an economic geography model of trade—and relies on reduced-form estimation (figure 4.9).[14] Specifically, 70 percent of results employ reduced-form estimation, while 21 percent evaluate the impacts of transport infrastructure using a structural model.

Reduced-form estimation tends to rely on the use of a difference-in-difference (DID) estimator. The impacts of the treatment (for example, on the treated subnational regions) are evaluated against those of a set of comparators (untreated subnational regions)

before and after the transport infrastructure investment occurs (see chapter 6). Such estimation focuses on the identification of impacts in the immediate geographic vicinity of the investment without explicitly seeking to identify the mechanisms through which such impacts occur (see, for example, the papers by Ghani, Goswami, and Kerr 2016, 2017).

Meanwhile, papers that use a structural model focus on a particular mechanism, which is normally related to internal trade. Examples include Alder (2015) and Asturias, García-Santana, and Magdaleno (2016). Finally, 9 percent of sample results use a computable general equilibrium (CGE) model. These results are invariably from papers that undertake ex ante impact evaluation analysis (such as Arman and Izady 2015). Structural and CGE-based approaches to evaluation possess the advantage over reduced-form regressions that, in principle, they can separate out the creation of new activity from the redistribution of existing activity. However, the downside of these approaches is that they make the strong assumption that the true underlying structure of the economy is known.[15]

Finally, the typical paper pays strong attention to the fact that the locations that policy makers chose to link with transport infrastructure are not random. In principle, this can lead standard ordinary least squares (OLS)

FIGURE 4.7   **The final outcome most often evaluated is economic welfare, while the intermediate outcomes studied are split between trade/productivity and population/assets**

Percentage of reported results

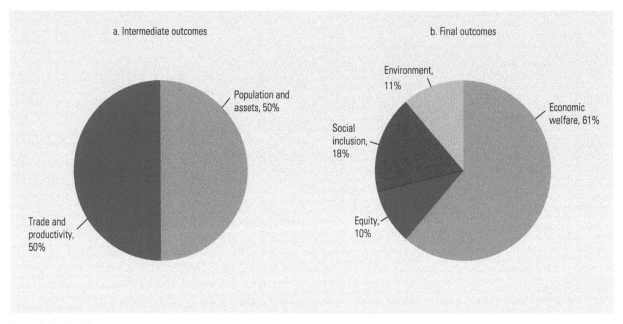

a. Intermediate outcomes

Population and assets, 50%

Trade and productivity, 50%

b. Final outcomes

Environment, 11%

Social inclusion, 18%

Economic welfare, 61%

Equity, 10%

Source: Corridor Study Team.
Note: The sample consists of 78 papers with 234 tagged results (analyzed outcomes).

FIGURE 4.8   **Studies at the subnational level and ex post evaluations predominate**

Percentage of reported results

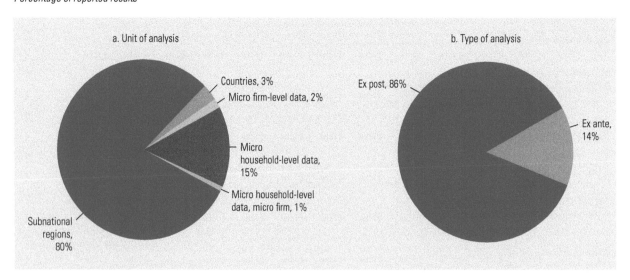

a. Unit of analysis

Countries, 3%
Micro firm-level data, 2%
Micro household-level data, 15%
Micro household-level data, micro firm, 1%
Subnational regions, 80%

b. Type of analysis

Ex post, 86%
Ex ante, 14%

Source: Corridor Study Team.
Note: The sample consists of 78 papers with 234 tagged results (analyzed outcomes).

estimation to either overestimate or underestimate the impacts of the infrastructure. For example, if the outcome variable of interest is a measure of local economic activity, overestimation is likely to occur if policy makers deliberately target the linking of locations that they expect to grow quickly. By contrast, underestimation is likely to occur if policy makers deliberately prioritize connections to lagging regions with low underlying economic potential.

It is fair to say that addressing the issue of endogenous placement has become the overwhelming empirical concern in the literature (Berg et al. 2017; Redding and Turner 2014). In an attempt to address endogeneity concerns, more than 70 percent of sample results adopt an explicit identification strategy (figure 4.10, panel a). Such identification strategies most frequently involve a strategy based on instrumental variables (IV).[16] Additional strategies have emerged in recent years—particularly, the use of a placebo, following Donaldson (2010) (figure 4.10, panel b).

A recent trend in the "strongest" papers has been to employ multiple strategies—for example, both IV and placebo strategies—to convince the reader that estimated impacts are accurately identified (see, for example, Ghani, Goswami, and Kerr 2016). The papers that focus on the economic welfare category of final outcomes are most advanced in terms of their attention to endogeneity concerns. By contrast, papers that focus on, for example, environmental outcomes tend to pay relatively little attention to employing identification strategies designed to address concerns about endogenous placement.

Descriptive analysis of results

Estimated average impacts
The analysis of the 234 tagged results reveals that the literature provides evidence of statistically significant impacts of wider economic benefits (at the 5 percent level or greater) on economic welfare, social inclusion, equity, and environmental quality

FIGURE 4.9 **Two-thirds of studies are motivated by a theoretical model, and 70 percent rely on reduced-form estimation**
Percentage of reported results

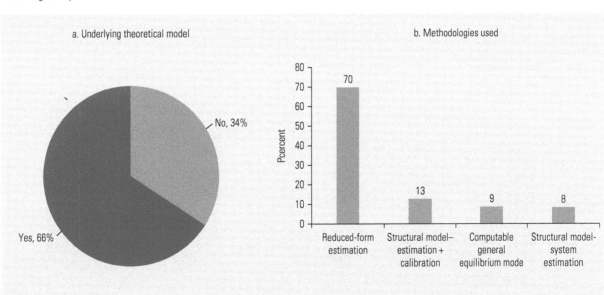

Source: Corridor Study Team.
Note: The sample consists of 78 papers with 234 tagged results (analyzed outcomes).

FIGURE 4.10   To improve reduced-form estimations, the literature employs rigorous identification strategies

Percentage of reported results

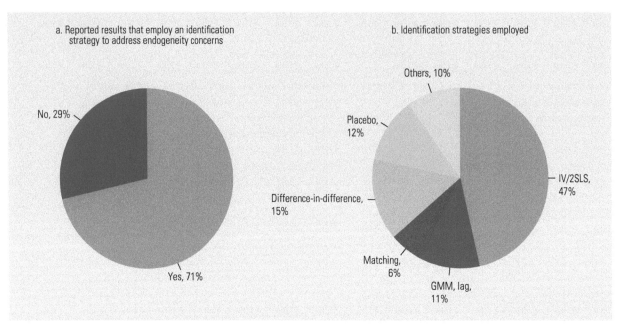

a. Reported results that employ an identification strategy to address endogeneity concerns

No, 29%

Yes, 71%

b. Identification strategies employed

Others, 10%

Placebo, 12%

Difference-in-difference, 15%

Matching, 6%

GMM, lag, 11%

IV/2SLS, 47%

Source: Corridor Study Team.
Note: The sample consists of 78 papers with 234 tagged results (analyzed outcomes). GMM = generalized method of moments; IV = instrumental variable; 2SLS = two-stage least squares.

FIGURE 4.11   The literature has focused on estimating corridor impacts on welfare, much less on the inclusion, environment, and equity

Percentage of reported results

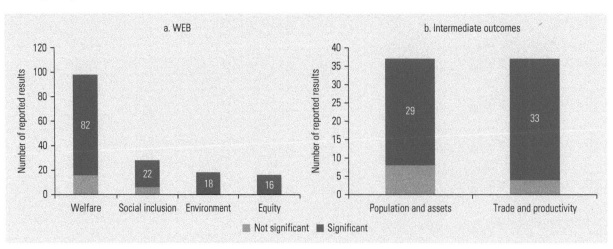

a. WEB

b. Intermediate outcomes

Number of reported results

Welfare 82, Social inclusion 22, Environment 18, Equity 16

Population and assets 29, Trade and productivity 33

■ Not significant ■ Significant

Source: Corridor Study Team.
Note: The sample consists of 78 papers with 234 tagged results (analyzed outcomes). WEB = wider economic benefits.

outcomes (figure 4.11, panel a). For a given type of outcome, the amount of confidence that can be attached to this evidence depends on both the number of results reported and the proportion of those results that are significant. In this sense, the evidence of significant impacts on economic welfare outcomes is fairly strong. Almost 100 results relate to economic welfare outcomes, and more than 80 of these results are statistically significant. For social inclusion, equity, and environmental quality outcomes, the proportion of reported impacts that are statistically significant is even greater than for economic welfare. However, in each case, the number of results is far fewer (22 for social inclusion, 16 for equity, and 18 for environmental quality outcomes). The sample contains no results for the wider economic benefit of resilience, which highlights a prominent omission in the literature. As for intermediate outcomes, there is considerable evidence that transport infrastructure has significant impacts on both population and assets (such as land values), as well as on levels of trade and productivity (figure 4.11, panel b). For population and assets, 29 out of 37 reported impacts are statistically significant, while for trade and productivity, 33 out of 37 are statistically significant.

Most reported impacts on levels of real income, poverty, consumption, and jobs are beneficial (in the sense that they can be expected to enhance social welfare).[17] However, there are some notable exceptions. *All* reported results for environmental quality outcomes are detrimental (in the sense that they can be expected to diminish social welfare). Likewise, transport infrastructure projects had significant detrimental effects on reported levels of equity among geographical units (places) and people. In about one-quarter of cases, the projects increased levels of inequality between subnational regions (spatial inequality) (figure 4.12). This implies that major transport infrastructure projects can entail trade-offs between different types of outcomes. While average impacts on economic well-being tend to be positive, this can come at the potential cost of worse outcomes for

both environmental quality and equity. The existence of such trade-offs suggests an important potential role for complementary policies.

In terms of intermediate outcomes, the evidence suggests that investment in transport infrastructure tends to reduce prices and boost levels of investment, trade, and productivity, while promoting industrial diversification and improvements in the efficiency of allocating resources. However, in some cases, reported impacts on levels of trade, population, and land values are detrimental (figure 4.13). Care should be taken in interpreting what constitutes a detrimental impact in terms of population and land values from both a welfare and productivity perspective. For example, Baum-Snow (2007) provides evidence to show that the construction of new limited-access highways in the United States between 1950 and 1990 contributed to suburbanization by inducing people to move away from central cities. However, while this study tags this impact as "detrimental" in terms of the population of a central city, it is not clear that it is detrimental from the perspective of overall social welfare.

Evidence of heterogeneous impacts
There has been a growing trend in the literature to move beyond simply estimating average impacts of transport infrastructure on the various final outcomes (WEB) and intermediate outcomes, to analyze how these impacts vary across the different units of analysis considered in a study (figure 4.14). Most papers analyze impacts across space (subnational regions) or economic sector (figure 4.15). A few studies have analyzed how impacts vary over time.[18] However, the literature provides very little evidence (in terms of number of reported results) on whether, and how, impacts may vary across different types of firms and differently endowed individuals.

The evidence of heterogeneous impacts in the literature implies that some geographic areas or groups of households or firms gain more from transport infrastructure improvements than others. In some cases, however, the losses may not be relative but absolute.

FIGURE 4.12   **Environment and equity outcomes could be suffering due to corridor placements**

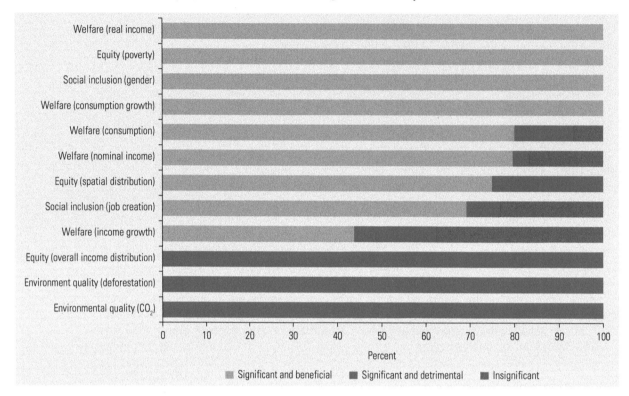

Source: Corridor Study Team.
Note: The sample consists of 78 papers with 234 tagged results (analyzed outcomes). CO_2 = carbon dioxide.

Major transport infrastructure projects can entail policy trade-offs not only between different types of WEB (such as economic welfare versus environmental quality and social inclusion) but also between different geographic areas and subgroups of the population.

A fair amount of evidence of absolute losses can be found in the subsample of results that look for evidence of heterogeneous impacts—even where overall average impacts tend to be overwhelmingly positive.

A good example is provided by a study of the impacts of the construction of the National Expressway Network (NEN) in China (Roberts et al. 2012). Although the authors find that the construction of the NEN increased real income across Chinese prefectures by slightly under 4 percent, on average, in many prefectures, the NEN had a *negative* impact on real wages in either the urban or rural sector.

To account for this type of variation in outcome, this study reports evidence of absolute losers alongside evidence of absolute winners for the final outcomes of both economic welfare and social inclusion, as well as the intermediate outcomes of population and trade (figure 4.16).[19] The conclusion to be drawn is that major transport infrastructure projects can entail policy trade-offs not only between different types of WEB (such as economic welfare versus environmental quality and social inclusion) but also between different geographic areas and subgroups for a given outcome.

Complementary policies

Complementary policies can mitigate the trade-offs between different types of WEB

FIGURE 4.13 While land values, population, and trade can increase in some areas as a result of corridor connectivity, they may decrease in other areas in parallel

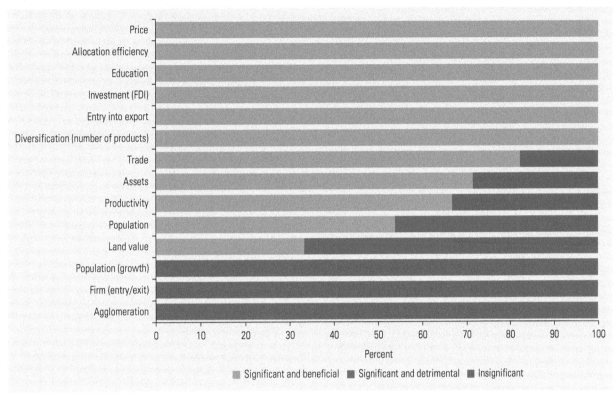

Source: Corridor Study Team.
Note: The sample consists of 78 papers with 234 tagged results (analyzed outcomes). FDI = foreign direct investment.

FIGURE 4.14 The trend to analyze heterogeneous impacts is growing, 2000–17

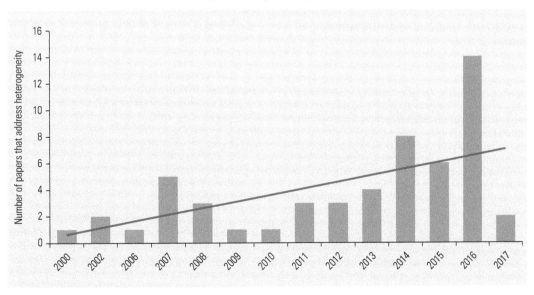

Source: Corridor Study Team.
Note: The sample consists of 78 papers with 234 tagged results (analyzed outcomes).

FIGURE 4.15 **Geographic location is the most studied aspect of heterogeneous impacts**

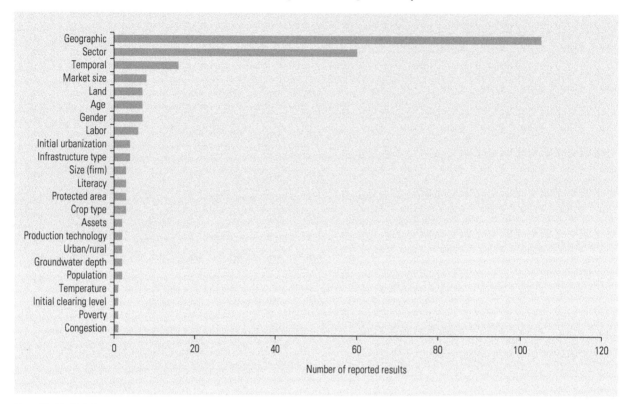

Source: Corridor Study Team.
Note: The sample consists of 78 papers with 234 tagged results (analyzed outcomes).

Spatially informed complementary policies and institutions could help mitigate policy trade-offs in transport corridor investment, but their effects require more research.

and among different subgroups for a given WEB. Unfortunately, of the 234 results analyzed, only 17 percent seek to investigate how complementary policies might influence a transport infrastructure project's impact on a given outcome (figure 4.17). This lack of analysis of the role of complementary policies may, in part, reflect the literature's preoccupation with isolating the effects of a transport infrastructure project from other, potentially "confounding," influences for the purposes of clean identification. When papers do explicitly analyze the role of potentially complementary policies, they tend to focus on labor market policies and adopt a more structural modeling approach.[20] An important exception are papers that focus on environmental outcomes, especially deforestation. Several papers consider the role of protected areas in mitigating the impacts of roads on deforestation (Cropper et al. 2001; Damania and Wheeler 2015; Dasgupta and Wheeler 2016).

One interesting example of a complementary policy that needs to be studied more by the literature is land value capture, which attempts to "capture" the rising land values around a corridor. This mechanism can help finance urban development along corridors, as well as complementary interventions to mitigate the varied effects of corridors across locales and population groups—such as those who do and those who do not own land that is appreciating in value, or those

FIGURE 4.16 **Income and population are the most studied aspects of reported evidence of absolute losers**

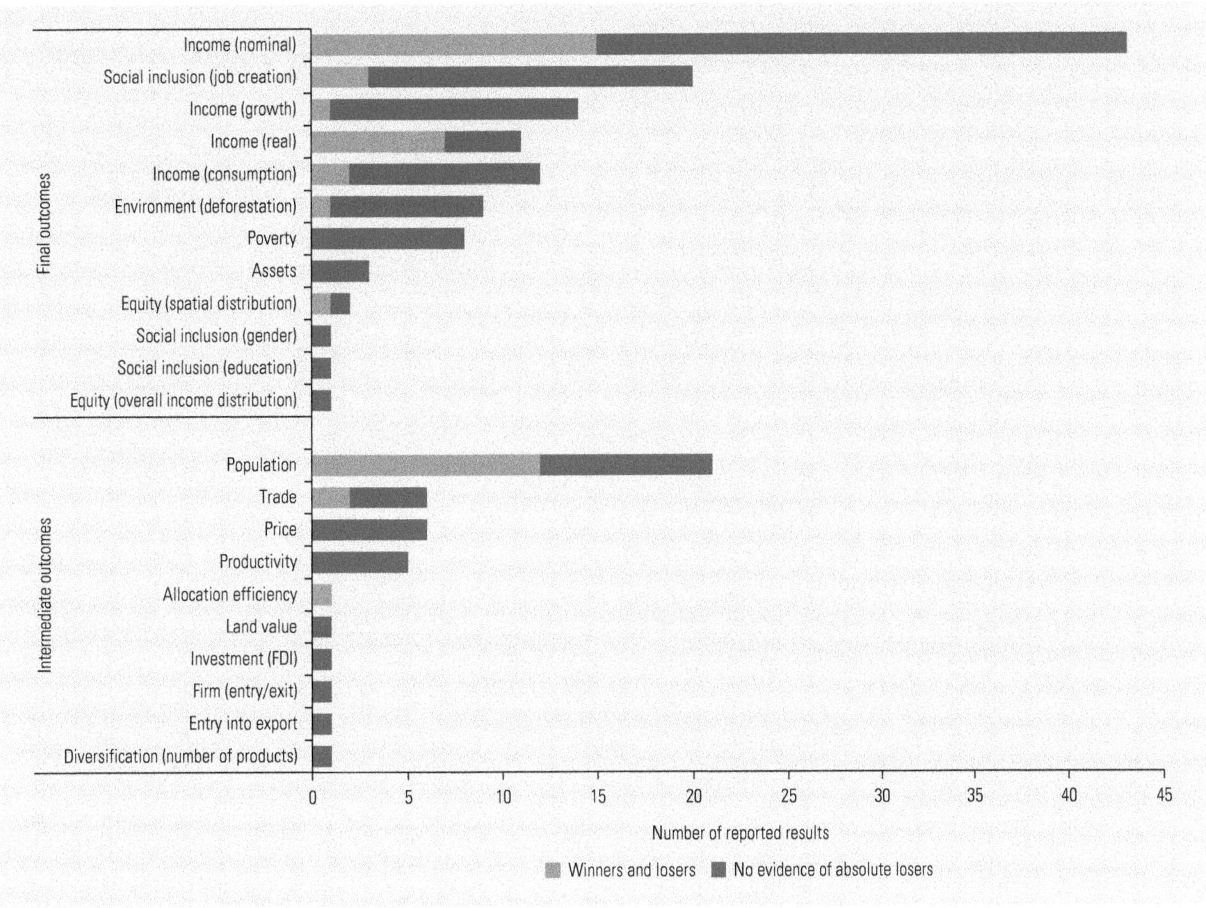

Source: Corridor Study Team.
Note: The sample consists of 78 papers with 234 tagged results (analyzed outcomes). FDI = foreign direct investment.

who have and those who lack skills to take advantage of the development. Using land value capture can thus help fully realize the wider economic benefits of transport corridors. This particular complementary policy is discussed in box 4.1.

META-REGRESSION ANALYSIS

This section presents the results of the formal meta-regression analysis (MRA) of the literature. MRA is a quantitative tool that helps synthesize findings from diverse empirical studies of a particular phenomenon. It has become a commonly used methodology in the social sciences. By combining the results

from multiple papers into a single statistical analysis, it allows primary effects to be distinguished from background variation and contaminating influences (Stanley, Doucouliagis, and Jarrell 2008).

The MRA undertaken for this chapter is intended to shed light on two questions. First, can the variations in the estimated impacts of large-scale transport infrastructure projects that are found in the literature be "explained" by variations in the characteristics of the projects themselves, and by methodological variations across papers? Second, do policy-relevant insights emerge from the literature? For example, is there evidence that certain features of projects (such as the mode of

FIGURE 4.17 **Most studies do not estimate the impacts of complementary policies**

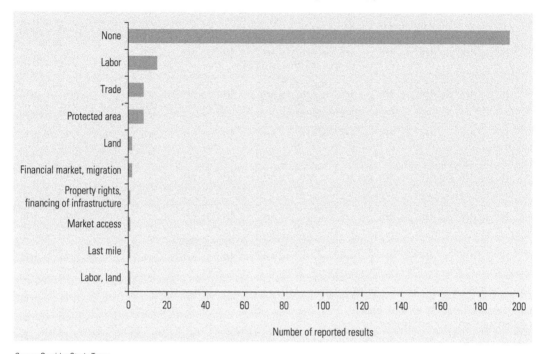

Source: Corridor Study Team.
Note: The sample consists of 78 papers with 234 tagged results (analyzed outcomes).

transportation or the type of locations they connect) are, on average, associated with better (more beneficial) outcomes?

The MRA must contend with a major problem. The impacts of interest span a wide set of outcomes and are derived from a diverse set of treatment variables for different countries based on a nonuniform set of modeling approaches. Thus, estimated coefficients on the treatment variable are not comparable across different papers. In some cases, they are not even comparable across different regression results reported *within* a paper. To overcome this issue, the MRA uses the reported *t*-statistic for the coefficient on the treatment variable as the measure of impact rather than the actual treatment coefficients themselves. This allows the analysis to standardize results across different papers and model specifications. It is important to note that a higher reported *t*-statistic can result from either a higher estimated

treatment effect of the transport infrastructure *or* a more precisely estimated (that is, a more certain) treatment effect.[21] The MRA is implemented using the sample of results for final outcomes (wider economic impacts) only, leaving formal meta-analysis of results for intermediate outcomes for future work.[22] Annex table 4B.1 in annex 4B presents the results of the MRA. The model is summarized in annex 4C.

Before turning to the estimation results, it is important to mention that the estimated impacts of large-scale transport infrastructure projects vary widely in the literature. This variation is captured in figure 4.18, which presents the distributions (kernel densities) of the estimated coefficients and the *t*-statistics. As the vertical lines (mean estimated coefficient and *t*-statistic) show, both the distributions are skewed to the right. This is consistent with the fact that the mean paper finds a positive (beneficial) and significant impact. Annex 4E (online) presents

BOX 4.1 Financing and facilitating urban development along corridors by "capturing" rising land values

While the construction of major transport corridors between cities and other nodes of economic activity is expected to provide a stimulus for accelerated urban development in locations along these corridors, such development needs to be supported by complementary investments in infrastructure, including in transport networks that feed into the corridors. Stimulating the growth of cities along the corridors through increased market access also increases demand for wider and more efficient transport systems within these cities.

The question arises of how to finance such complementary investments in urban transport and development. One particularly promising option is "land value capture" (LVC). LVC takes advantage of the fact that improvements in connectivity generated by public investments in transport systems tend to boost land values—whether along the corridor or in a network connecting urban areas that feeds into the corridor. Rather than allowing the increase in land value to be entirely captured by whoever happens to own the land—even though they have undertaken no investment to increase its value—LVC seeks to capture some of the gain to finance public investments. More generally, the purpose of LVC is to "mobilize for the benefit of the communities some or all of the land value increments (unearned income) generated by actions other than the landowner's, such as public investments in infrastructure" (Smolka 2013).

LVC instruments can be broadly classified into two groups: tax- or fee-based instruments such as land and property taxes, betterment charges, and tax increment financing; and development-based instruments such as land sale or lease, joint development of areas by government and private parties, land pooling, and urban redevelopment schemes. The implementation of development-based instruments normally involves joint action by the government and private parties. Such instruments have the advantage of providing increased resources to finance capital-intensive investments with limited fiscal distortion and public opposition. They are also able to generate sustainable revenue streams through the construction of revenue generators such as shops, leisure facilities, and parking facilities.

Successful LVC schemes have four common denominators. They return land value increases generated by public investments to communities, thereby allowing the benefits of those increases to be more widely shared; they tap the combined potential of both public and private land; they are based on sound planning principles; and they benefit from efficient coordination among governmental bodies and agencies.

An excellent example of LVC that helps recoup not only the investment costs but also covers operation and maintenance expenses is the Mass Transit Railway (MTR) in Hong Kong, China. Over half of MTR revenue comes from property development and asset management. MTR Corp. uses land lease conditions to partner with developers based on the full market value, which assumes, at the time when the rail line project is only about to start, that the new rail line is completed and in place (Murakami 2015). In Japan, the Tokyo Metropolitan Area uses land readjustment to finance transit systems in built-up and peripheral areas (Sorensen 2000). It does so through master plans at the economy, provincial, and metropolitan levels that provide a clear vision and promote polycentric regional development. The system is characterized by excellent stakeholder coordination across public and private entities. New York City has used transferable development rights to preserve landmarks and increase the density of activities in specific locations (Suzuki et al. 2015).

By facilitating the financing of complementary urban investments that are required to help fully catalyze the wider economic benefits of major transport corridors, land value capture can itself be viewed as a complementary policy. LVC also has the potential to help channel the urban development that a major transport corridor can stimulate in a well-organized and planned manner. Essential to the successful application of LVC instruments are adequate capacity and coordination among key institutions and clear earmarking of revenues for infrastructure investment.

FIGURE 4.18 **The distributions of *t*-statistics are skewed to the right, suggesting that the transport infrastructure projects yield positive and significant impacts**

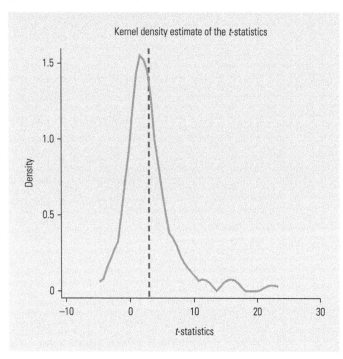

Source: Corridor Study Team.

distributions for each of the four major WEB: economic welfare, equity, social inclusion, and environmental quality.

Estimation results

For estimations, the dependent variables are transformed so that a positive value always indicates a beneficial outcome and a negative value denotes a detrimental outcome. The discussion that follows focuses on the results from the preferred specifications (for details and further results, see Bougna et al., forthcoming).

Main results

The literature finds, on average, that transport infrastructure has a significant beneficial effect on economic welfare (figure 4.19). On average, the literature estimated a *t*-statistic of 3.547 for the impacts of large transport infrastructure on economic welfare, indicating that the beneficial impact of large transport infrastructure could be reliable, especially on income. This result is statistically significant at the 1 percent level. The literature also finds, on

FIGURE 4.19 **Average net impacts of corridors on final outcomes estimated by the literature should alert policy makers**

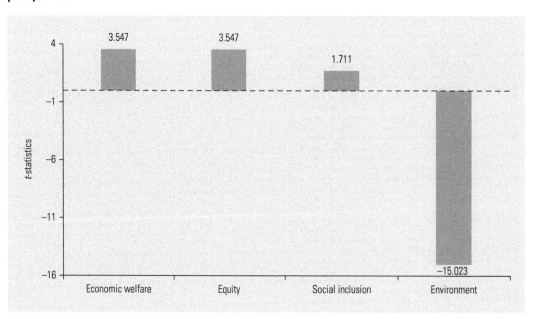

Source: Corridor Study Team.
Note: The average impact on equity is not significantly different from the average impact on economic welfare.

average, that the transport impact on equity is not significantly different from the estimated beneficial mean impact on economic welfare.

By contrast, the impacts on social inclusion and environmental quality are significantly smaller than the average impact on welfare. For social inclusion, the impacts are smaller and/or less certain, but still, on average, beneficial (the net estimated coefficient on social inclusion is 1.711 (that is, 3.547 minus 1.836). The less certain impacts on social inclusion could also indicate possible trade-offs between boosting economic welfare and social inclusion through large transport infrastructure in some contexts. The effect of transport infrastructure on environmental quality is detrimental. The net coefficient is −15.023 (that is, 3.547 minus 18.57). These findings are consistent with those reported in the descriptive analysis of the literature in the earlier section titled "Descriptive Statistics."

The results also suggest that several "policy variables" are important and could inform the design of future corridor intervention packages. First, the transport mode matters. Compared with roads and waterways, the reported impacts of investments in railways are significantly smaller and/or less certain.

Second, the type of connection also matters. The t-statistics are, on average, significantly smaller for investments that focus on connecting urban centers to international gateways such as ports, land border crossing points, and airports. This result could suggest that the ability of such connections to generate beneficial outcomes depends on other factors, such as the efficiency of port operations, tariff and nontariff trade barriers, and the functioning of markets, including those to which the gateways connect.

Third, policy makers could end up prioritizing enhanced connectivity between locations that would, in any event, be expected to yield more beneficial outcomes. This "endogenous placement" of transport corridors is a real and important issue when trying to estimate corridor development impact. Hence, the estimated coefficients for studies that do not use any identification strategy is significantly higher (more positive). More

specifically, relative to identification strategies using instrumental variables and/or difference-in-difference methods, estimations using ordinary least squares (OLS) yield a t-statistic on the treatment variable that is, on average, 3.81 higher.[23]

Fourth, a failure to consider varied impacts across geographic units and the population is not only a gap in itself; it leads to an overestimation of either the wider economic benefits of transport infrastructure and/or the level of confidence about these impacts (figure 4.20). Compared with studies that ignore varied impacts, studies that do report evidence of varied impacts along several different dimensions (such as across subnational geographic areas or across different economic sectors) also tend to report significantly smaller t-statistics.

As an additional level of analysis, this chapter examines studies that report some evidence of absolute losers alongside winners—that is, the existence of geographic units, economic sectors, or population groups that incur absolute losses of a development outcome. For instance, Chandra and Thomson (2000) studied the impact of U.S. interstate highways on economic growth. They found that interstate highways significantly increased earnings growth in services, retail, manufacturing, and transport and public utilities industries in counties through which highways run, but adjacent counties without highways experienced significantly decreased earnings in the government and retail trade sectors. This analysis found that these studies tend to report larger t-statistics. However, this result is not very robust.

To further investigate the consideration of winners and losers as an important aspect of estimating the wider economic benefits of transport corridors, an alternative method for the metaregression analysis was also employed: the ordered-probit regression. Specifically, a variable was created that takes a value of 0 when a paper reports a significantly beneficial impact; a value of 1 when a paper reports an insignificant impact (despite positive or negative estimated values); and a value of 2 when a paper reports a significantly

FIGURE 4.20 Varied impacts of corridors estimated by the literature (by the factor of variation) can inform complementary interventions to support losers from corridors

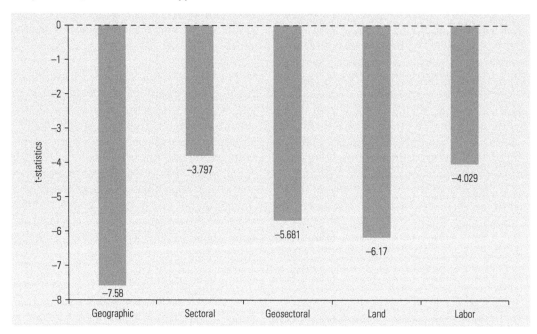

Source: Corridor Study Team calculations.

detrimental impact. This method categorically separated the significant results in the literature from the insignificant ones.

It is reassuring that most results from this alternative estimation are consistent with the baseline regression results for the t-statistics—although some results do change (for details, see Bougna et al., forthcoming).[24] Importantly, the analysis found significant results for the consideration of winners and losers in the evaluation of transport corridor impacts on wider economic benefits. Once an evaluation (study) considers the possibility of losers alongside winners, the probability of finding beneficial wider economic impacts decreases by 34.7 percentage points. Similarly, the same consideration makes the probability of finding detrimental results increase by 18.3 percentage points. Both findings are statistically significant at the 1 percent level.

It is possible that this finding on evaluation design can also apply to the design of the transport corridor intervention. That is, corridor intervention packages designed in a way

that ignores the possibility of losers alongside winners could deliver much smaller wider economic benefits and much larger wider economic costs—possibly including those for social inclusion (jobless GDP growth) or environmental quality (smog and greenhouse gas emissions).

MAIN INSIGHTS AND DIRECTIONS FOR FUTURE RESEARCH

This chapter has conducted a quantitative review and formal meta-regression analysis of studies estimating the wider economic impacts of large-scale transport infrastructure projects. Its main objective is to help policy makers chose the optimal features and design of policies and options to promote transport corridors. The core of this package of interventions are investments in the trunk transport infrastructure (roads, rails, waterways). A set of complementary policies and institutional reforms can extend and deepen the net wider economic benefits of the trunk infrastructure by boosting average impacts and mitigating trade-offs. To assist policy makers, the chapter yields three main insights.

First, when designing a transport corridor package, policy makers must account for potential trade-offs in different development outcomes and across different (sub)sets of economic actors. This follows from two key findings of the literature review:

- While for *economic welfare* and *equity*, the average estimated impacts of the wider economic outcomes tend to be beneficial, for *social inclusion* and *environmental quality*, they are often detrimental.
- Even for economic welfare and equity, while the average impacts may be beneficial, these impacts can vary considerably across locales, economic sectors, and population groups. Some locales or population groups may lose in absolute terms.

The existence and nature of these trade-offs should drive the choice of complementary interventions, such as compensation policies for the identified losers from trunk infrastructure investments.

Second, the set of complementary policies and institutions that form part of the optimal transport corridor package could depend on the nature of the transport infrastructure intervention that forms the core of this package. This follows from the finding of the metaregressions that estimated impacts depend on the type of locations being connected. Specifically, transport projects that seek to enhance connectivity between urban centers and international gateways (such as ports, land border crossings, and airports) yield significantly smaller or less certain impacts than projects that target purely domestic enhancements of connectivity (such as enhancements between two domestic cities). Realizing the full benefits of better connectivity to international gateways requires tackling such impediments as inefficient port operations or prohibitively high tariff and nontariff barriers to trade. The canonical model of the policy maker's problem developed by Bougna et al. (forthcoming) suggests that the set of complementary policies and institutions that optimize a corridor intervention package will depend on two aspects: imperfections in product, capital, labor, and land markets that existed before the intervention; and the initial endowments of different locations and economic agents that are affected by the transport intervention. This point is explored further in chapter 6.

Third, the placement and design of the transport infrastructure matter, and so does the mode of transportation. The size and certainty of estimated impacts depends on the type of locations being connected, as well as the mode of transportation. The estimated wider economic benefits of sampled rail projects are smaller/less certain than those of road projects. However, this finding should be interpreted with care because the literature mainly studies historical rail projects—such as the colonial railway network in India and the transcontinental railway network in the United States. It is possible that the impacts of modern freight and passenger railway networks—including modern high-speed railway networks, which have not been studied much—differ considerably from those of the historical networks.

Directions for further research

The literature review also highlights many important areas where further research is needed to better inform the optimal design of transport corridor packages. Five areas are most pressing:

1. *Trade-offs.* Much more research is required to clarify the nature and extent of the trade-offs in the average impact of transport corridors on various development outcomes and the varied impacts across various subsets of economic actors. While the impacts of large transport projects on measures of economic welfare have been studied extensively, the evidence of impacts on other types of outcome is more limited and less rigorous. A big omission is the impact on economic resilience—defined as the resilience of economic agents to various types of shock, rather than the resilience of the

transport infrastructure itself. This study found a lack of papers about resilience that met the criteria for inclusion in the sample.[25]

Although environmental impacts are better studied, the literature is not as advanced as the literature focusing on economic welfare in addressing possible identification issues.

A particularly useful area of research would be to study the impact of a single transport project on the outcomes of economic welfare, social inclusion, equity, and environmental quality simultaneously. This would provide more direct insight into the nature of the trade-offs between these outcomes, rather than the more indirect inference this chapter made by looking across papers. Likewise, more research is required to explore trade-offs across different segments of the population for each development outcome. Although the analysis of heterogeneous impacts and winners/losers has become more common in recent years, it is still relatively rare for papers to consider varied impacts along any dimension other than geographic location.

2. *Complementary policies.* The literature has done little to analyze the role of other policies in shaping the impacts of transport infrastructure. Hence, this chapter found virtually no evidence on the appropriate design of complementary policies in different circumstances. An important technical reason for this neglect may be that the literature has been striving to clearly identify the impacts of the transport infrastructure itself. This requires isolating the impacts of infrastructure from the impacts of other factors, including other policy changes and reforms. While this is desirable from the perspective of academic rigor, such rigor may limit the relevance of findings to policy, which is necessarily concerned with the full range of impacts from a corridor intervention package.

3. *Structural general equilibrium modeling.* In principle, a promising way to study trade-offs and the interaction of transport infrastructure investments with other policies could be through structural general equi-

librium modeling. As the review shows, the literature is dominated by reduced-form estimations. Perhaps there is some skepticism about structural general equilibrium modeling because it assumes that the model structure is correct at capturing the factual transmission mechanisms and behavioral rules of economic agents when linking policy interventions to outcomes, as well as when drawing conclusions about the multiple and second-round impacts. If the model structure is correct, the structural general equilibrium models could be the best tool to use for policy decision making. But if incorrect, it could be an inferior tool to use. By contrast, standard reduced-form, difference-in-difference estimation is purely empirical and requires little knowledge of the underlying mechanisms. Thus, reduced-form estimation is generally seen as being more flexible and reliable. But the flexibility comes at the cost of little consideration of second-round effects. Further research is required to improve the quality and accuracy of structural general equilibrium models, and the identification and comprehensiveness of reduced-form regressions (see also spotlight 6, "Appraising Proposed Transport Corridors Using Spatial Econometrics").

4. *Modern rail.* The literature has been concerned mainly with estimating the impacts of road projects. When it has evaluated rail projects, it has mainly focused on historical projects. More research is needed to evaluate modern rail projects, including both high-speed rail and freight railway corridors, such as those that India is currently constructing. More research is also required on the impacts of multimodal transport projects—especially because multimodal freight movements are likely to be critical to the design of many transport corridor projects in the future.

5. *Country coverage.* The literature surveyed covers a wide variety of countries. Nevertheless, much of the research (42 percent of papers in the sample) has focused on only three countries: China, India, and the United States. The literature

would benefit from research on other countries to gain insights into impacts in different country contexts.

Summing up and moving to the next chapter

This chapter has followed a quantitative approach—including formal meta-regression analysis techniques—to review the growing literature studying the impact of large transport investments on wider economic benefits. The review collected a large new data set of studies in different country contexts. The framework for the review is designed to reflect policy makers' objectives to maximize the net wider economic benefits of a proposed transport corridor. In addition to integrating current knowledge, this chapter has pointed to gaps in the knowledge base that policy makers must be aware of when appraising the design of proposed corridor projects.

Building on the findings from chapters 3 and 4, the next chapter starts a new section, illustrating how both qualitative and, more important, quantitative appraisals of large-scale transport investments could be performed following the methodological framework developed by the report.

NOTES

1. Savings on transport costs also form the focus of the social savings approach to assessing the impacts of transport infrastructure investments. This approach was originally pioneered by Fogel (1964) in his assessment of the benefits of the construction of the U.S. railroad system in the nineteenth century.
2. It is sometimes argued that, even when the assumptions that underpin traditional cost-benefit analyses break down, the exercise remains useful in providing a lower-bound estimate of the net benefits of a transport infrastructure project. However, this line of argument implicitly assumes that all the wider impacts not captured by a traditional cost-benefit analysis are, on net, positive. This may or may not be true.
3. This study attempted to consider *economic resilience*—defined as the resilience of economic agents to various types of large shocks (such as climate change, natural disasters, or commodity price shocks)—as a development outcome. However, virtually no examples of empirical literature that rigorously examine the impacts of transport infrastructure on economic resilience were found. Note that economic resilience is different from the resilience of the transport infrastructure itself to shocks. Literature on this topic exists (see, for example, Gapanovich et al. 2015), but it is not a direct subject of interest for this review.
4. The inclusion of such literature is important to both assessing and, at least partially, addressing possible issues of publication bias. That is, formal outlets (particularly peer-reviewed journals) are more likely to publish studies with statistically significant results (see, for example, Card, Kluve, and Weber 2009). Even if publication bias can be perfectly addressed, a serious potential issue of "writing-up" bias cannot be addressed. That is, authors may refrain from writing up results that are statistically insignificant, even in an initial, unpublished draft version of a paper.
5. For a discussion of the literature on the impacts of intraurban infrastructure, see Redding and Turner (2014).
6. Thus, the literature review excludes a large empirical New Economic Geography (NEG) literature on the relationship between market access and outcomes of either wages or GDP per capita. For a meta-analysis of this literature, see Bosker and Garretsen (2010). It further excludes a large empirical literature in macroeconomics that builds on the work of Aschauer (1989) and analyzes the relationship between a country's stock of infrastructure, including its stock of transport infrastructure, and its level of development. For a review of this literature, see Straub (2011).
7. The 78 papers reported more than 243 results. Typically, any given paper will report results from numerous regressions. This study extracted only those results from the most relevant regressions, which typically constitute the authors' preferred specification(s).
8. Before being applied formally, an initial dummy run of the double-blind tagging system was undertaken using a sample of ten papers. This dummy run was used to both help train the RAs in the system and

identify any initial obvious areas for improvement. The results from this dummy run were discarded, and the papers were reviewed again.

9. Papers that focus on the evaluation of China's National Expressway Network (NEN) include Roberts et al. (2012); Faber (2014); and Bosker, Deichmann, and Roberts (2015). China has also been building an extensive high-speed railway network, which has attracted some attention in the literature. See, for example, Wang and Wu (2015).

10. Papers that focus on India's GQ include Alder (2015); Ghani, Goswami, and Kerr (2016, 2017); and Khanna (2016).

11. With the exception of a few papers for Africa, such as Buys, Deichmann, and Wheeler (2006); and Jedwab and Storeygard (2016).

12. Examples of such studies are Cosar and Demir (2016); and Martincus and Blyde (2013).

13. A very recent innovation in the literature has been to use subnational "grid cells" of uniform area as units of analysis (Ali et al. 2015; Jedwab and Storeygard 2016).

14. Economic geography models of trade include both "new economic geography" models (Krugman 1991a, 1991b; Fujita, Krugman, and Venables 1999) and Ricardian models of internal trade of the Eaton-Kortum (2002) variety. Examples of papers that are motivated by a NEG model include Roberts et al. (2012); and Bosker, Deichmann, and Roberts (2015). Papers motivated by an Eaton-Kortum–style Ricardian trade model include Donaldson (2010); Donaldson and Hornbeck (2016); Alder (2015); and Alder, Roberts, and Tewari (forthcoming).

15. Baum-Snow et al. (2016) provide a comparison of results for the impacts of the construction of China's NEN obtained using reduced-form estimation and a structural model—specifically, the Eaton-Kortum model. In doing so, they demonstrate that "technique matters"—that the results obtained depend fundamentally on the approach adopted. They also provide evidence to show that the Eaton-Kortum model misses some quantitatively important features that are evident in the data.

16. Redding and Turner (2014) identify three main different types of IV-strategy that are employed in the literature: the "planned route IV," the "historical route IV," and the "inconsequential units approach."

17. Increases in levels of real income and jobs are considered to be beneficial, while increases in rates of poverty and inequality are considered to be detrimental.

18. A particularly interesting paper in this regard is that by Pereira, Hausman, and Pereira (2014). The authors analyze the overall impact of railroad investment on economic growth in the United States in the mid-1800s. Their methodological approach—a bivariate, dynamic time series, based on the use of a vector autoregressive (VAR) model—is very different from the cross-sectional approach used in most of the literature. This approach allows the authors to distinguish short-term, demand-side effects on economic growth from longer-term, supply-side effects.

19. Again, some care in interpretation is required here. Although a subnational region may experience a decline in population as a result of a transport project that improves its connections to other regions, it is not necessarily clear that this makes the region a "loser" from a welfare and productivity perspective. A loss in population may stimulate an overall increase in productivity and real wages for the region if, for example, it helps ease congestion forces within the region.

20. A good example is the paper by Bosker, Deichmann, and Roberts (2015), which analyzes both the national and spatial impacts of the National Expressway Network (NEN) in China on levels of real income, while simultaneously considering how these impacts have been influenced by restrictions on migration associated with the country's permanent household registration (Hukou) system.

21. Ideally, we would like to run our meta-analysis by looking only at average effects on subsets of papers with more comparable outcomes and independent variables. However, the huge heterogeneity observed in papers and interventions limits this avenue.

22. Thus, estimates of treatment effects based on CGE models are dropped from the sample because these estimates lack accompanying t-statistics.

23. This could also be attributable to a relatively greater precision of OLS estimates, especially if valid (exogenous) instruments are less relevant (weak).

24. The full results from the estimation ordered-probit model are presented in annex 4E, annex table 4E.1 (online). For comparison

with the OLS results, the signs of the estimated coefficients were flipped, and only results for the model with final outcomes and policy variables are reported.

25. Revoltella et al. (2016) provide evidence of the catalytic role that transport infrastructure plays when it comes to linking local businesses with global growth opportunities during periods of both positive and negative economic shocks. This paper was brought to the authors' attention only after the analysis on which this chapter is based had been completed.

REFERENCES

Alder, S. 2015. "Chinese Roads in India: The Effect of Transport Infrastructure on Economic Development." Working Paper, University of North Carolina, Chapel Hill.

Alder, S., M. Roberts, and M. Tewari. Forthcoming. "The Effect of Transport Infrastructure on India's Urban and Rural Development."

Ali, R., A. F. Barra, C. N. Berg, R. Damania, J. D. Nash, and J. D. Russ. 2015. "Transport Infrastructure and Welfare: An Application to Nigeria." Policy Research Working Paper 7271, World Bank, Washington, DC.

Arman, S. A., and A. T. Izady. 2015. "Design of a CGE Model to Evaluate Investment in Transport Infrastructures: An Application for Iran." *Asian Economic and Financial Review* 5 (3): 532–45.

Aschauer, D. A. 1989. "Is Public Expenditure Productive?" *Journal of Monetary Economics* 23: 177–200.

Asturias, J., M. García-Santana, and R. Ramos Magdaleno. 2016. "Competition and the Welfare Gains from Transportation Infrastructure: Evidence from the Golden Quadrilateral of India." CEPR Discussion Paper DP11283, Centre for Economic Policy Research, London.

Atack, J., and R. A. Margo. 2011. "The Impact of Access to Rail Transportation on Agricultural Improvement: The American Midwest as a Test Case, 1850–1860." *Journal of Transport and Land Use* 4 (2): 5–18.

Banerjee, A., E. Duflo, and N. Qian. 2012. "On the Road: Access to Transportation Infrastructure and Economic Growth in China." Working Paper 17897, National Bureau of Economic Research, Cambridge, MA.

Baum-Snow, N. 2007. "Did Highways Cause Suburbanization?" *Quarterly Journal of Economics* 122 (2): 775–805.

Baum-Snow, N., J. V. Henderson, M. A. Turner, Q. Zhang, and L. Brandt. 2016. "Highways, Market Access and Urban Growth in China." Working Paper C-89114-CHN-1, International Growth Centre, London School of Economics and Political Science.

Berg, C. N., U. Deichmann, Y. Liu, and H. Selod. 2017. "Transport Policies and Development." *Journal of Development Studies* 53 (4): 465–80.

Bosker, E. M., U. Deichmann, and M. Roberts. 2015. "Hukou and Highways: The Impact of China's Spatial Development Policies on Urbanization and Regional Inequality." Policy Research Working Paper 7350, World Bank, Washington, DC.

Bosker, E. M., and H. Garretsen. 2010. "Trade Costs in Empirical New Economic Geography." *Papers in Regional Science* 89 (3): 485–511.

Bougna, T., M. Melecky, M. Roberts, and Y. Xu. Forthcoming. "Transport Corridors and Their Wider Economic Benefits: A Critical Review of the Literature." Policy Research Working Paper, World Bank, Washington, DC

Buys, P., U. Deichmann, and D. Wheeler. 2006. "Road Network Upgrading and Overland Trade Expansion in Sub-Saharan Africa." Policy Research Working Paper 4097, World Bank, Washington, DC.

Card, D. E., J. Kluve, and A. M. Weber. 2009. "Active Labor Market Policy Evaluations: A Meta-Analysis." CESifo Working Paper 2570, Center for Economic Studies, Munich.

Chandra, A., and E. Thompson. 2000. "Does Public Infrastructure Affect Economic Activity? Evidence from the Rural Interstate Highway System." *Regional Science and Urban Economics* 30 (4): 457–90.

Coşar, A. K., and B. Demir. 2016. "Domestic Road Infrastructure and International Trade: Evidence from Turkey." *Journal of Development Economics* 118: 232–44.

Cropper, M., J. Puri, C. Griffiths, E. B. Barbier, and J. C. Burgess. 2001. "Predicting the Location of Deforestation: The Role of Roads and Protected Areas in North Thailand." *Land Economics* 77 (2): 172–86.

Damania, R., and D. Wheeler. 2015. "Road Improvement and Deforestation in the Congo Basin Countries." Policy Research Working Paper 7274, World Bank, Washington, DC.

Dasgupta, S., and D. Wheeler. 2016. "Minimizing Ecological Damage from Road Improvement in Tropical Forests." Policy Research Working Paper 7826, World Bank, Washington, DC.

Donaldson, D. 2010. "Railroads of the Raj: Estimating the Impact of Transportation Infrastructure." NBER Working Paper 16487, National Bureau of Economic Research, Cambridge, MA.

Donaldson, D., and R. Hornbeck. 2016. "Railroads and American Economic Growth: A 'Market Access' Approach." NBER Working Paper 19213, National Bureau of Economic Research, Cambridge, MA.

Eaton, J., and S. Kortum. 2002. "Technology, Geography, and Trade." *Econometrica* 70 (5): 1741–79.

Faber, B. 2014. "Trade Integration, Market Size, and Industrialization: Evidence from China's National Trunk Highway System." *Review of Economic Studies* 81 (3): 1046–70.

Fogel, R. W. 1964. *Railroads and American Economic Growth: Essays in Econometric History.* Baltimore: Johns Hopkins University Press.

Fujita, M., P. R. Krugman, and A. J. Venables. 1999. *The Spatial Economy: Cities, Regions and International Trade.* Cambridge, MA: MIT Press.

Gapanovich, V. A., I. B. Shubinsky, E. N. Rozenberg, and A. M. Zamyshlyaev. 2015. "System of Adaptive Management of Railway Transport Infrastructure Technical Maintenance (Urban Project)." *Reliability: Theory & Applications* 10 (2): 30–41.

Gertler, P. J., M. Gonzalez-Navarro, T. Gracner, and A. D. Rothenberg. 2014. "The Role of Road Quality Investments on Economic Activity and Welfare: Evidence from Indonesia's Highways." Unpublished.

Ghani, E., A. G. Goswami, and W. R. Kerr. 2016. "Highway to Success: The Impact of the Golden Quadrilateral Project for the Location and Performance of Indian Manufacturing." *World Bank Economic Review* 126: 317–57.

———. 2017. "Highways and Spatial Location within Cities: Evidence from India." *World Bank Economic Review* 30 (Supplement 1): S97–S108.

Gibbons, S., T. Lyytikäinen, H. Overman, and R. Sanchis-Guarner. 2016. "New Road Infrastructure: The Effects on Firms." CEPR Discussion Paper DP11239, Centre for Economic Policy Research, London School of Economics and Political Science.

Haines, M. R., and R. A. Margo. 2006. "Railroads and Local Economic Development: The United States in the 1850s." NBER Working Paper 12381, National Bureau of Economic Research, Cambridge, MA.

Herrendorf, B., J. A. Schmitz Jr., and A. Teixeira, A. 2012. "The Role of Transportation in U.S. Economic Development: 1840–1860." *International Economic Review* 53 (3): 693–716.

Jedwab, R., and A. Storeygard. 2016. "The Heterogeneous Effects of Transportation Investments: Evidence from Sub-Saharan Africa 1960–2010." Working Paper, Oxford University and London School of Economics and Political Science.

Khanna, G. 2016. "Road Oft Taken: The Route to Spatial Development." Presented at the Michigan, the Indian Statistical Institute, NEUDC (MIT), Center for Global Development.

Krugman, P. 1991a. "Increasing Returns and Economic Geography." *Journal of Political Economy* 99 (3): 483–99.

———. 1991b. *Geography and Trade.* Cambridge, MA: MIT Press.

Laird, J. J., and A. J. Venables. 2017. "Transport Investment and Economic Performance: A Framework for Project Appraisal." *Transport Policies* 56: 1–11.

Martincus, C. V., and J. Blyde. 2013. "Shaky Roads and Trembling Exports: Assessing the Trade Effects of Domestic Infrastructure Using a Natural Experiment." *Journal of International Economics* 90 (1): 148–61.

Martincus, C. V., J. Carballo, and A. Cusolito. 2014. "Routes, Exports, and Employment in Developing Countries: Following the Trace of the Inca Roads." http://econweb.umd .edu/~carballo/Routes_Incas_Exports.pdf.

Michaels, G. 2008. "The Effect of Trade on the Demand for Skill: Evidence from the Interstate Highway System." *Review of Economics and Statistics* 90 (4): 683–701.

Murakami, J., 2015. "Rail Plus Property Program, Hong Kong SAR, China." Chapter 3 in *Financing Transit-Oriented Development with Land Values: Adapting Land Value Capture in Developing Countries,* edited by H. Suzuki, J. Murakami, Y.-H. Hong, and B. Tamayose. Washington, DC: World Bank.

Pereira, R. M., W. J. Hausman, and A. M. Pereira. 2014. "Railroads and Economic Growth in the Antebellum United States." Working Paper 153, Department of Economics, College of William & Mary, Williamsburg, VA.

Pfaff, A., J. Robalino, R. Walker, S. Aldrich, M. Caldas, E. Reis, S. Perz, C. Bohrer, E. Arima, W. Laurance, and K. Kirby. 2007. "Road Investments, Spatial Spillovers, and Deforestation in the Brazilian Amazon." *Journal of Regional Science* 47 (1): 109–23.

Redding, S. J., and M. A. Turner. 2014. "Transportation Costs and the Spatial Organization of Economic Activity." NBER Working Paper 20235, National Bureau of Economic Research, Cambridge, MA.

Revoltella D., P. Brutscher, A. Tsiotras, and C. Weiss. 2016. "Linking Local Business with Global Growth Opportunities: The Role of Infrastructure." *Oxford Review of Economic Policy* 32 (3): 410–30.

Roberts, M., U. Deichmann, B. Fingleton, and T. Shi. 2012. "Evaluating China's Road to Prosperity: A New Economic Geography Approach." *Regional Science and Urban Economics* 42 (4): 580–94.

Smolka, M. O., 2013. *Implementing Value Capture in Latin America: Policies and Tools for Urban Development.* Cambridge, MA: Lincoln Institute of Land Policy.

Sorensen, A. 2000. "Land Readjustment and Metropolitan Growth: An Examination of Suburban Land Development and Urban Sprawl in the Tokyo Metropolitan Area." *Progress in Planning* 53 (4): 217–330.

Stanley, T., C. Doucouliagis, and S. B. Jarrell. 2008. "Meta-Regression Analysis as the Socioeconomics of Economics of Research." *Journal of Sociology-Economics* 37 (1): 276–92.

Straub, S. 2011. "Infrastructure and Development: A Critical Appraisal of the Macro-Level Literature." *Journal of Development Studies* 47 (5): 683–708.

Suzuki, H., J. Murakami, Y. H. Hong, and B. Tamayose. 2015. *Financing Transit-Oriented Development with Land Values: Adapting Land Value Capture in Developing Countries.* Washington, DC: World Bank.

Vickerman, R. 2007. "Cost-Benefit Analysis and Large-Scale Infrastructure Projects: State of the Art and Challenges." *Environment and Planning B: Planning and Design* 34 (4): 598–610.

Wang, Y., and B. Wu. 2015. "Railways and the Local Economy: Evidence from Qingzang Railway." *Economic Development and Cultural Change* 63 (3): 551–88.

Weinhold, D., and E. Reis. 2008. "Transportation Costs and the Spatial Distribution of Land Use in the Brazilian Amazon." *Global Environmental Change* 18 (1): 54–68.

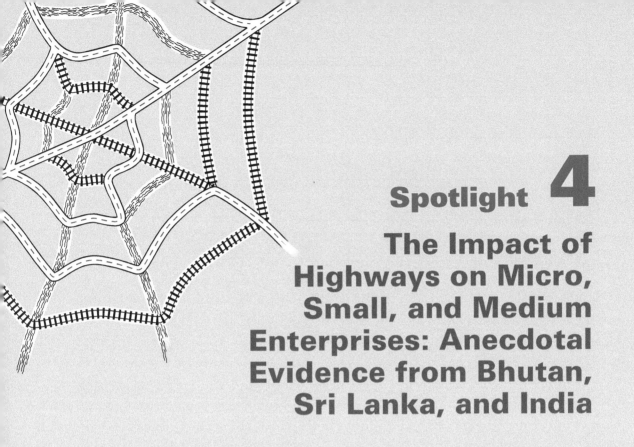

Spotlight 4

The Impact of Highways on Micro, Small, and Medium Enterprises: Anecdotal Evidence from Bhutan, Sri Lanka, and India

Upgraded or reopened highways have successfully linked major commercial centers and trade corridors, and have eased congestion in South Asia. These include the 5,800-kilometer (km) Golden Quadrilateral (GQ) highway in India, which links four major metropolitan areas; the A9 highway in Sri Lanka, which connects the Sri Lankan cities of Kandy in the south to Jaffna in the north (photo S4.1); and the Thimphu-Phuntsholing and Thimphu-Gelephu highways in Bhutan, which connect the country's capital to the Indian border.

To study the impact of these highways on micro, small, and medium-size enterprises (MSMEs), the World Bank held a series of focus group meetings and interviews. In Sri Lanka, the team travelled over 150 kilometers along the A9 route and interviewed 52 MSMEs in the towns of Dambulla, Naulla, Ipalogama, and Vavuniya. In Bhutan, it held three sessions in the towns of Hongtsho, Jemina, and Babesa, where 36 entrepreneurs took part (21 men and 15 women). In India,

the team visited the outskirts of Delhi and Mumbai and spoke with MSME owners operating along the major highways.

Participants included women and men who grow and sell fruits, vegetables, plants, and flowers, or make sweets, yogurt, and coconut oil. Others weave or sew fabrics and clothes, or make handbags, shoes, mosquito nets, furniture, and handcrafts. Some own small and medium-sized transport, construction, and food/clothing export companies.

BENEFITS

Saving time. While their stories vary, the entrepreneurs all agreed that the highways, which are now reliable, save them time in obtaining inputs and delivering final goods. With shorter travel times, business owners can also travel further and gain access to a greater variety of inputs than before. Some said the improved highways have reduced the costs of transporting inputs, and brought new customers and business opportunities.

PHOTO S4.1   Spice producers use the A9 Highway in Sri Lanka to dry spices

Source: Martin Melecky, World Bank.

The highways also shifted the geographic locations of firms to some extent—with firms often clustering along the highways.

For example, Choki Wangmo, who produces wooden bowls and cups in Hongtsho (Bhutan), noted, "Before, we hired horses and walked days to get raw materials. Now we do this in a few days with public transport." Mr. Kabir, who manages the Ongdi Wood Industry, said the upgraded highway has greatly helped businesses in Khasadrapchu (Bhutan). "We can now hire an 18-wheeler to transport raw materials as well as our end products." He also has more control over the time he spends obtaining inputs and can deliver goods just in time.

Saving fuel and vehicle maintenance costs. Better roads increase fuel efficiency. Six of the eight participants in one focus group in Hongtsho, who own their vehicles, said their private vehicles cost less to maintain and run because they have fewer problems on the road and use less fuel. Four of the eight said it now costs less to transport raw materials, although most cannot calculate their exact savings and profits.

Saving input costs. The improved transportation system also helps some entrepreneurs save on input costs. Pema Dorji, a 29-year-old Bhutanese with a graduate degree, who inherited a bronze-casting business, said, "I use the Thimphu-Phuntsholing highway to get my raw materials from India. Since I can use larger trucks and place bigger orders, I lower unit costs and at the same time meet my clients' growing demand." The owner of a flower shop in Dambulla (Sri Lanka) reported that the flower pots and flowers she ships are no longer damaged. Tashi Dorji, a carpenter from Hongtsho (Bhutan), said some of his products used to break en route to his customers; now this rarely happens.

Saving transaction costs. Some entrepreneurs have profited in unexpected ways. For example, rice growers in Vavuniya (Sri Lanka) say buyers now come directly to their farms, and their profits have increased because they can supervise the weighing of the rice—which eliminates cheating by middlemen!

Expanded variety of inputs and products. The improved highways have enabled more types of products to be brought into the local markets. For example, more varieties of seeds and textile inputs are available in Dambulla (Sri Lanka) and entrepreneurs can more easily modify and invent new products with the new inputs.

Accessing markets more easily and getting better prices. The improved roads also make it easier to access markets. One man in Ipalogama (Sri Lanka) has been producing and selling curd in his local area since 2006. Now, he uses public transport on the A9 to deliver his product as far as 60 kilometers away. As his business grew, he hired four more employees. In Bhutan, the highways have also cut marketing and distribution costs. Tashi Dorji, a carpenter in Hongtsho, reported, "I now have customers coming from the capital of Thimphu to my production site to buy their products." Equally important, the improved access from the villages to towns means some women have eliminated the middlemen and now take their vegetables directly to the market, instead of having a distributer pick them up at their farms. By arriving at the market early, they can sell when prices are the highest.

Spurring new business ventures. Business opportunities have also grown. In India, once the GQ highway was improved, new housing was constructed along the corridor. One women from the Mumbai area said that after the houses were built, her son started a business installing CCTVs (closed circuit television) in them. In Bhutan, building on local traditional craft techniques, new business lines such as bronze casting, saw mills, and furniture making started in Khasadrapchu.

Expanding financing. Some financial institutions have opened branches in the towns and helped locals start businesses. In the Vavuniya (Sri Lanka) area, one exporter of rice-based products said a new local bank helped him develop his business, lent him funds, and connected him to clients. Today, he gets inputs from 3,000 farmers, has 30 employees, has wholesale dealers who export his products to Germany, and has opened new production sites in Jaffna, Colombo, and Kandy. 'Without the financial institution moving to the area, I wouldn't have started my business," he noted.

Attracting more customers. In addition, the better roads have attracted more business. Some firms have located their shops/stalls closer to the highway, where they attract more customers in transit. As one entrepreneur in Vavuniya (Sri Lanka) reported, "the closer you are to the A9, the more prosperous your business, since people driving on the highway stop and buy your products."

Expanding the scope of business activities. The improved roads have also changed the geographic scope of various companies. An Indian bank manager said the improved GQ has attracted more economic activities to Thane, which is near Mumbai and is close to the airport and cheaper land (photo S4.2). In Bhutan, of 29 focus group participants, 7 moved their businesses closer to the highway. Dechen Zangpo, who makes religious statues in Hongtsho and who relocated closer to the highway, said, "From the time I shifted my business location, my client base has increased. Five to seven more clients place orders every week. I can't keep up with the

PHOTO S4.2 The World Bank team speaks with a textile shop owner (second from right) in Thane, India

Source: Yan (Sarah) Xu, World Bank.

demand, so I want to expand my workshop and am negotiating with the landlord for more space." He also plans to hire a few more employees from his area.

PROBLEMS AND POLICIES

Besides the positive impacts, focus group participants also described some problems.

Constraints on land. For example, since demand for land near the highway has grown, less land is available for the MSMEs' needs. Dechem M., a carpenter in Bhutan, said that because the highway increased his business, he needs more land to expand, but it is in short supply. Parking spaces are in short supply along A9 in Dambulla (Sri Lanka). Small shop owners there say that more travelers would stop to buy goods if parking was better.

Traffic congestion and environmental trade-offs. For example, in Dambulla (Sri Lanka), traffic was greater than expected and the road became quite congested. Travelers started to use another parallel highway to avoid traffic. The local shops ended up getting less transit customers than they used to have. In Bhutan, the surge in regional tourists—who, unlike high-end international tourists, do not use guides and drive their own vehicles—increased congestion.[1] Local MSMEs must spend more time travelling for their businesses, which is diminishing their productivity. Moreover, communities are raising concerns about environmental pollution due to unguided and unregulated regional tourism.

Landslides and other natural disasters. MSMEs also need the government to help them cope with natural disasters. For example, in Bhutan, landslides are still an issue. Before the highway was upgraded, the road was narrow, uneven, and full of potholes. Participants said the soil along the roads often eroded, which caused landslides (particularly in summer), blocking the roads and stranding commuters, sometimes for days. Sonam Jamtsho, who runs a mid-sized factory in Khasadrapchu (Bhutan) that makes uncoated calcium carbonate, said that in the past, landslides damaged his shipments. While he enjoys the benefits from the improved road, the issue of landslides has not yet been resolved.

Need for improvements in feeder roads. Some focus group participants say that besides the highway upgrade, more needs to be done to improve the poor conditions on rural feeder roads. One entrepreneur, who runs a wholesale fish business and employs 35 people in the Kurunegala area (Sri Lanka), says while more customers now take the A9 to reach him, fishermen who supply his shop must still use the rural roads to bring him their catch. During the rainy season, some roads are not passable. The rough conditions cause vehicles to break, which raises transport costs. Poor feeder roads make it difficult for firms to get inputs, distribute goods, and reach clients.

Need for more training. While large export firms, the government, and some private institutions offer training, the overall level of technical, management, and marketing skills among MSMEs is low and prevents some firms from expanding. For example, a producer of spice powder producer from Naulla (Sri Lanka) changed the traditional spicy paste into powder to improve its portability and taste. He designed the package himself and produced the products at home with his family's help. However, to expand the business beyond local markets, he still needed to improve his marketing skills. Some firms participate in training provided by the government and private institutions. A lady from Iplogama (Sri Lanka) who supplies plants to an export company was selected to attend a training program run by a community bank, along with 14 other people. The community bank issued a certificate to her firm after she completed the program and connected her firm to suppliers. Of the 15 trainees, 10 started plantation businesses with loans provided by the community bank. Despite the effectiveness of such training programs, they are available only to a few people. More programs are needed.

Difficulty connecting to more distant markets. While the improved roads make it easier to obtain inputs, they do not necessarily link entrepreneurs to clients in other parts of the country or world. Most focus group participants said it was still difficult to enter new markets in the major cities and supply large exporters. At the local level, many would like to have a town market where they can sell products and attract more customers. Rural MSMEs do not seem to be involved in e-commerce—which could help them find new clients and expand their businesses to markets that are further way in their own country and across borders.

Limited access to finance. Many focus group participants said that with more capital, they could buy inputs and stock inventories in larger quantities, increase production/sales, and lower unit costs. One woman who runs a tourist bus service in Sri Lanka said could increase her business if she could buy another bus to meet the demand—but lacks the credit to do so.

Increased competition. In some areas, the improved transport links have allowed new businesses to enter the local markets, which has increased competition. In the worst cases, smaller businesses have been crowded out and prices have been driven down. For example, a rice-based product exporter said that after the A9 highway reopened in Sri Lanka, more businesses competed for the local market and sold at lower prices. A caterer reported that competitors moved into the area, selling food services at a lower rate, and he has lost market share.

Need to attract foreign investment. The improved highways, by themselves, do not attract foreign investment. Governments will need to develop smarter policies to promote it. For example, when exports increase, warehouses are needed for storage and value-added services such as packaging and consolidation. State-level governments have offered incentives, such as tax credits, although such policies need to undertaken carefully.

While the MSMEs benefitted from the improved highways to some extent, complementary polices need to be pursued to help them grow. Improving the availability of land, putting in place measures to recover from natural disasters, and upgrading rural feeder roads can boost their productivity further. Warehouse receipt financing can be used as collateral so farmers can borrow to meet their business financing needs. Training, e-commerce, and town markets are crucial to help MSMEs reach more clients.

NOTE

1. See http://www.kuenselonline.com/need-to-regulate-regional-tourism/.

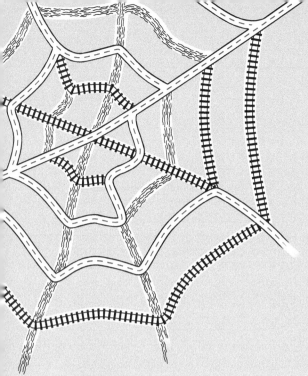

Do Highways Help Women?

Dawa Zam, who used to be an accountant for an Indian construction company at the hydropower construction site in Wangdue (Bhutan), has now moved to Gidagom and has a shop at the capital city of Thimphu. She said the upgrade of the Thimphu-Phuntsholing highway "offered new opportunity for me to earn a decent living from the grocery shop in Thimphu and grow vegetables on my mother's farmland at Kasadrapchu. I am able to save rent in Thimphu by staying at Gidagom, which is adequately linked by public transport services." She noted, "I am now able to start my own family and be independent."

Several thousand kilometers of recently opened or upgraded highways in Bhutan, Sri Lanka, and India have dramatically changed the lives of women like Dawa Zam and their families.

In Sri Lanka, the A9 highway, which was closed during the civil war, was reopened and now links towns and villages along a route from the city of Kandy in the south to Jaffna in the north.

In India, the Golden Quadrilateral (GQ), a four-to-six lane highway (with two and three lanes in each direction), now connects the country's four major metropolitan areas—Delhi, Mumbai, Chennai, and Kolkata.

In Bhutan, the Thimphu–Phuntsholing and Thimphu–Gelephu highways were upgraded and now pass through the smaller towns and villages and extend to India's northeastern border.

Before, roads were narrow, uneven, and full of potholes. Sometimes they were blocked, stranding commuters for days (in Bhutan). Public transport from the towns and villages to the larger cities was limited. Thus, most women did not travel to urban centers or commute to jobs, which limited them to work that was available nearby. If they did make the trips, travel was long and tiring, due to poor road conditions.

To study the impact of the highways, the World Bank held focus group discussions from February to May 2017 with women (many of whom are microentrepreneurs) in several communities, mainly in Bhutan and Sri Lanka.

In Bhutan, 27 women attended the groups that focused on women's issues (photo S5.1), while in Sri Lanka, 48 women attended (photo S5.2). To compare women's responses with those of men, the focus group organizers invited 12 men to participate in Bhutan. Although almost all the women interviewed were housewives, they also work in unpaid family businesses or run small shops to earn an income. The women included small farmers, weavers, dressmakers, furniture makers, vegetable sellers with stalls along the highways, and civil servants, or those who

PHOTO S5.1 **Focus group in Khasadrapchu, Bhutan**

Source: Martin Melecky, World Bank.

PHOTO S5.2 **Focus group in Naulla, Sri Lanka**

Source: Martin Melecky, World Bank.

rent space in their homes to tenants. Some of the focus group participants had no education, while others had completed either primary or secondary school.

Almost all said the improved highway had helped them significantly—although they noted some negative effects and offered suggestions for improvements to the authorities.

Most of the benefits that the women report have enriched their lives are similar in the three countries. The women said that it is easier and takes them less time to travel, conduct business, shop for food and household items, and take their children to schools and hospitals. This means they have more time to do household chores and engage in income-producing work, or to work more hours.

For example, in Bhutan, the trip from Phuntsholing to Thimphu, which used to take eight hours, now takes five, while the trip from Hongsho to Thimphu, which took nearly an hour, has been cut in half.

In Sri Lanka, some of the focus group participants live in a village that is 8 kilometers from the town of Vavuniya. The trip, which used to take 1½ hours, is now just 30 minutes. The trip from the town of Ipalogama (on the A9 highway) to Colombo was 5 hours each way and is now just 3½ hours.

The reduced travel times also mean women can leave their children with a neighbor, do errands, and return quickly; in addition, they can make the trips and return home the same day. Since these trips would have involved an overnight stay in the past, the women did not make them.

With the better road conditions, public buses and taxis run more frequently. For example, in Dambulla (Sri Lanka), buses, which formerly operated only during the day, now also run at night. Thus women travel more often, taking buses locally for jobs, obtaining social services, or riding to cities to attend school or find better-paying jobs. For example, Dema, who lives in Hongtsho village (Bhutan), says she now takes public transport to Thimpu, since buses run twice a day, when there were none before. Tshering Yangchen said the frequency of travel has greatly increased: "About 16 residents from Hongtsho travel every day to Thimphu for work and return in the evening on a city bus. Even students travel to Thimphu schools on public transport and return in the evening," because neither Hongtsho nor Kasadrapchu have schools that go beyond level 10.

The women report that they now travel to the cities for entertainment or to visit their families and friends more often, which improves the quality of their lives. They have greater access to social services, since travel to the cities is easier, and in Sri Lanka, local governments now offer some services in the smaller towns.

Safety is another plus. The roads are wider, and children can walk to school more easily. In Sri Lanka, women said their children were sometimes attacked because the roads were isolated. Now, because of the increased activity along the highways, families are more comfortable sending their children to school alone. In Dambulla (Sri Lanka), where the road was dark and empty after 6 p.m., women now feel safe traveling alone at night because of the increased traffic on the road and extended night-time bus schedules. Teachers and other government workers also benefit from the safer and faster travel. For example, female government workers from Jaffna (Sri Lanka) were reluctant to take jobs in Vavuniya due to safety concerns (with not many people on the road). Now, with the more efficient travel, female teachers not only are more willing to work there but also can get there faster and arrive on time.

In general, the women are involved in microbusinesses, such as growing and selling vegetables and fruit, or raising chickens to produce and sell eggs near the highways. The increased traffic from the highway has brought more customers to their businesses.

Although few in the focus groups own vehicles, those who do say they spend less on oil and maintenance because of the improved road conditions. Women usually do not drive themselves or drive only within the city where they live. Instead, their husbands take them to places that are farther away. Thus, while it seems that the availability and quality of public transport have improved the mobility of women more than men, given social norms, this mobility is still limited to local commutes and to public transport for longer distances.

The improved and reopened roads are also improving villagers' health and the environmental quality of the area. Previously in Vavuniya (Sri Lanka), vendors transported water to towns and villages on unpaved roads. Dirt often got into the water supply, so the government banned the transportation of the water into the area. Over time, villagers developed kidney disease from drinking the polluted water from wells. But since the A9 reopened, water has been transported on better roads and is no longer contaminated by dust or dirt. Further, with the reopening of the A9, the government now sends public health staff to the rural areas to inform residents about the importance of clean water, the effects of polluted water, and how to purify untreated water.

The improved road links have also increased some land values, particularly of property located closer to the highway. This benefits women who own land because it helps them generate rental income and increases their accessibility to credit—as they can use their property as collateral. In Bhutan, although inheritance practices vary by region, in the western part of the country, where Thimphu is located, matrilineal practice is common; thus, the oldest daughter usually inherits the agricultural land and other property (such as livestock). Several women say they own property that they or their mothers converted into apartments or commercial buildings to rent or lease.

Some benefits are unique to certain locales. For example, in Sri Lanka, private businesses and the government moved into the Vavuniya area after the road reopened, which created new jobs. One woman said this allowed her daughter to find a good job, locally.

Besides these positive effects, participants also described some negative impacts. They note that there is more traffic, more congestion, more noise, more air pollution (from exhaust) due to the big increase in vehicles, more litter caused by drivers throwing trash out their windows, and more deforestation, which has led to a general loss of wildlife habitat. In addition, Manlice, who practices traditional medicine in Naulla (Sri Lanka) and the surrounding areas, reported that since the A9 reopened, she finds that more children have respiratory problems because pollution from the traffic has increased.

People also drive more rapidly (especially truck drivers, at night) than when the roads were in poor condition and they had to be cautious. Thus, more accidents are occurring—two or three a month, mainly from heavy vehicles hitting small cars—and sometimes individuals and animals along the roads and at crossings are killed. Sonam Pelden, a resident of Hongtsho (Bhuta), says that because of the speeding, she worries about her children, who walk to school on the highway. Rinzin, who lives in Babesa (Bhutan), says there are more drunk drivers and crime at night along the highways.

Some prices have also increased. For example, Tshering Lhaden, a civil servant who rents an apartment in Babesa (Bhutan), says that because the highway has made travel between her town and the city easier, "my rent has increased twice in the past two years."

When asked what the authorities could do to resolve the new problems, the groups had various suggestions, depending on where they lived.

In Sri Lanka, to reduce speeding and accidents, the women said that speed bumps should be built into the roads to slow the traffic, especially near schools. Tshering Yangchen from Hongtsho (Bhutan) suggested that the government build sidewalks and footpaths along the highway to make it safer for pedestrians, particularly children.

To make travel even easier, one Sri Lanka focus group noted that the government should also improve local roads. Although the A9 highway is in good condition, secondary roads are still poor, which means it is difficult for women to travel to and from villages. Buses still do not travel more than 2 kilometers off the main road because of the poor surface conditions. If the feeder roads were upgraded, this would improve the quality of life and business operations, and allow people greater access to their temples, which are an important part of the culture. In Bhutan, focus group participants noted the importance of allowing drivers to make U-turns in certain spots.

Some said that to help working mothers, the government should offer child care in its offices or centers. Tshering Lham told the group "I have a 22-month old daughter, and as a working mother, it's hard to take care of my child and work at the same time. But if there were child care centers in offices or near highways, this would make the infrastructure projects more valuable, particularly for working women like me." At present, there are only a few centers, which are far from the mothers' jobs, or the children are sent home before the women finish work. Tshering Lham added that workplaces should offer flexible hours for mothers, which would encourage more to join the workforce.

Often, women in both countries said they would like to be trained with more skills. For example, many sew garments while caring for their children at home. However, few acquire technical or marketing skills, and thus cannot sell to exporters. Although most of the housewives want to increase their income-producing activities, they do not have the skills needed to expand their businesses, nor do they know how to obtain them. The government and private institutions such as banks are providing such training in Sri Lanka, but it is available to only a limited number of women.

Finally, on the basis of the focus group responses, it appears that despite the economic improvements and gains in quality of life generated by the highway upgrades or reopening, the women in Sri Lanka and Bhutan, in general, are not more socially empowered.

Part III
Appraising Corridor Projects

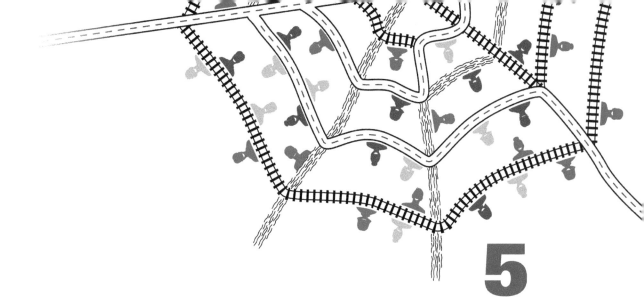

Appraising Transport Corridors in Japan, Europe, and Thailand

Drawing on the framework that this report proposes, chapter 5 appraises the impact of three transport infrastructure programs in Japan, Europe, and Thailand on wider economic benefits (WEB). It does so by means of a narrative supported by anecdotal evidence and selected data.

The case study on Japan reviews the Pacific Belt Zone Initiative proposed by the government as an engine of industrialization to double Japan's national income between 1960 and 1970 in an equitable way. The case study on Europe reviews three selected high-speed rail corridors of the Trans-European Network–Transport (TEN-T), and the diverse ways in which spillovers from these corridors helped—or did not help—generate WEB in their vicinity. The final case study on Thailand appraises the role that investments in large-scale transport infrastructure played in helping develop a booming automotive industry on the back of several complementary reforms.

The appraisal of Japan's Pacific Belt Zone Initiative illustrates the importance of focusing on an equitable diffusion of benefits from large-scale investment right from the beginning. The positive effects of these large infrastructure investment do not automatically trickle down to the more disadvantaged locales and groups of the population. Complementary investments and reforms must be implemented in tandem with these investments to ensure that economic benefits are spread most widely.

Along with examining the challenges of financing and implementing cross-border rail corridors, the appraisal of Europe's three rail corridors reveals that the placement of rail corridors and their alignment with important and relevant population and productive centers could be a major determinant of their wider economic impacts. These impacts take more than 10 years to realize. Again, transport infrastructure alone does not deliver WEB unless it is part of a comprehensive package of measures to support wider economic and social development.

> **Transport infrastructure alone does not deliver wider economic benefits unless it is part of a comprehensive package of measures to support wider economic and social development.**

The appraisal of Thailand' success in developing a booming automotive industry portrays infrastructure investments as the centerpiece of a broader set of proactive measures to diversify overly concentrated production near Bangkok. A new deep-sea port, an energy production complex, and public utilities were part of the anchor infrastructure investment. But it was only the investment incentives and the government's flexible policy stance on access to finance and foreign direct investment that provided the sufficient conditions for the shift to heavy, automotive industry. Environmental trade-offs again surfaced and were dealt with only after the infrastructure was put in place.

> **Investments in transport infrastructure—including high-speed rail, roads, and ports—were part of a policy package ranging from power to health care and education.**

MAP 5.1   The Pacific Belt Zone runs through Japan's industrial core

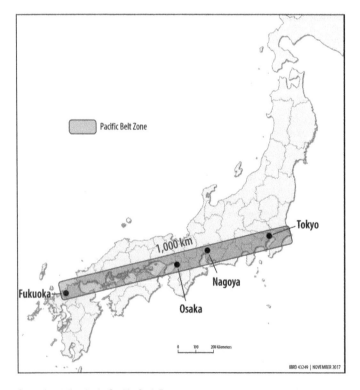

Source: Annotations by the Corridor Study Team.

APPRAISING THE PACIFIC BELT ZONE INITIATIVE: THE ENGINE FOR JAPAN'S INDUSTRIALIZATION

The Pacific Belt Zone served as a driving force for Japan's rapid economic growth in the 1960s. It extends approximately 1,000 kilometers from the district of Kanto in the southwest to the northern part of the district of Kyushu, spanning the cities of Fukuoka, Osaka, Nagoya, and Tokyo (map 5.1). Industrialization, initially in the form of recovery from the devastation of World War II, began advancing in the four major industrial zones in this area in the 1950s.[1] However, concerns spread that excessive centralization and dependence on these major industrial zones could impair further economic growth. To avoid this, the government of Japan sought to link the four major industrial zones to form the Pacific Belt Zone, to treat this zone as a corridor of broader economic activity, and to encourage development in the entire zone.

The Pacific Belt Zone initiative was proposed while Japan was deliberating a plan to double its national income from 1960 to 1970.[2] To achieve this goal, Japan needed to triple its national industrial production. Intensive development of the Pacific Belt Zone was considered essential to achieve high growth within this limited period of 10 years.

At that time, ports and harbors, highways, railroads, and other infrastructure were being developed in large cities across the Pacific Belt Zone. However, the Income-Doubling Plan concluded that the process of industrial location should not widen regional disparities, and should underscore efficiency in industrial distribution. The term "Pacific Belt Zone" did not appear in the final version of the plan, allegedly because of political sensitivities. Some districts located outside the zone objected strongly to prioritizing development of the zone because they were concerned they might remain undeveloped under the initiative.

The need for an integrated development plan covering the entire country was recognized soon after World War II. The Comprehensive National Development Act was established in May 1950. This act aimed to promote social welfare and ensure the comprehensive utilization of national land and proper location of industry. Although the Act stipulated that a comprehensive national development plan, so called long-term spatial plan to show the ideal state of territory, should be drawn up. Though this plan also avoided specific descriptions about regional priorities for industrial location, the Pacific Belt Zone initiative was considered as a background of intensive capital formation to spur rapid economic growth for the nation.

To promote industrialization in the Pacific Belt Zone, large-scale infrastructure projects to develop expressways, high-speed railway systems, power plants, ports and harbors, and other facilities were intensively promoted. Funding this massive investment solely with domestic sources was not possible because Japan's level of savings was insufficient. It was also difficult for private businesses to make massive capital investments by borrowing from financial institutions in Japan. The World Bank became an important catalyst. World Bank loans totaling US$930.4 million covered 31 projects, ranging from expressways, shipyards, and high-speed railway systems (the Shinkansen bullet trains) to electric power, private sector industrial plants and factories, and agricultural development. Virtually the entire amount (96.4 percent) lent was used to promote industrialization in the Pacific Belt Zone. Compared to Japan's annual public investment, which ranged from US$1.514 billion in 1955 to US$8.142 billion in 1965, World Bank lending Japan was not huge. However, the impact was significant. The loans demonstrated the Japanese government's strong commitment to develop large-scale infrastructure projects, while World Bank support signaled the feasibility of these projects and gave the private sector confidence in making long-term investments.

The needs were dire. As the Watkins Report reported in 1956, "The roads of Japan are incredibly bad. No other industrial nation has so completely neglected its highway system."[3] The investments dramatically improved road conditions. The improvement rate (ratio roads with more than 5.5 m width) for national roads went from 38.4 percent (1956) to 77.7 percent (1970), while the

pavement rate for them went from 18.5 percent (1956) to 75.1 percent (1970).[4] The Meishin Expressway and the Tomei Expressway were fully opened in 1965 and 1969, respectively, to connect regional agglomerations in the Pacific Belt Zone. In addition, high-speed railways (Shinkansen, or bullet trains), which enabled high-speed mass passenger transport, were launched between Tokyo and Osaka in 1964, between Osaka and Okayama in 1972, and between Okayama and Hakata (Fukuoka) in 1975.

Along with public investments in infrastructure, capital investment by private enterprises increased. Despite a brief dip in 1965–66 following turmoil in Japan's securities market, capital investments by private enterprises soared. At the same time, the stock of social capital increased rapidly, even on a net basis. The stock of social capital was remarkably concentrated in the Pacific Belt Zone.[5] Alongside an effort to actively introduce foreign technologies, Japan's crude steel production more than quadrupled, from 22.1 million tons in 1960 to 93.3 million tons in 1970. In 1965, Japan surpassed what was then West Germany to become the world's second-biggest crude steel producer after the United States. Japan's oil refining volume increased sixfold from 1960 to 1970. This surge in manufacturing materials strongly supported the manufacture of industrial products, including cars and machinery.

Overall, capital investment by private enterprises far exceeded public investment. This trend was more apparent in the Pacific Belt Zone than any other region in Japan (figure 5.1). The concentration of petrochemical, steel, car manufacturing, and other industries in the Pacific Belt Zone indicated that many private enterprises in these industries considered capital investment in the Pacific Belt Zone to be more economically rational than in other parts of Japan.

The development of infrastructure invigorated economic activities, which in turn increased the volume of freight transportation by truck 6.5 times (from 20.8 billion ton-kilometers in 1960 to 135.9 billion ton-kilometers in 1970); the volume of cargo handling at ports and harbors 4.2 times (from

FIGURE 5.1   Private investment/public investment were higher in the Pacific Belt Zone than in other regions of Japan, 1960–70

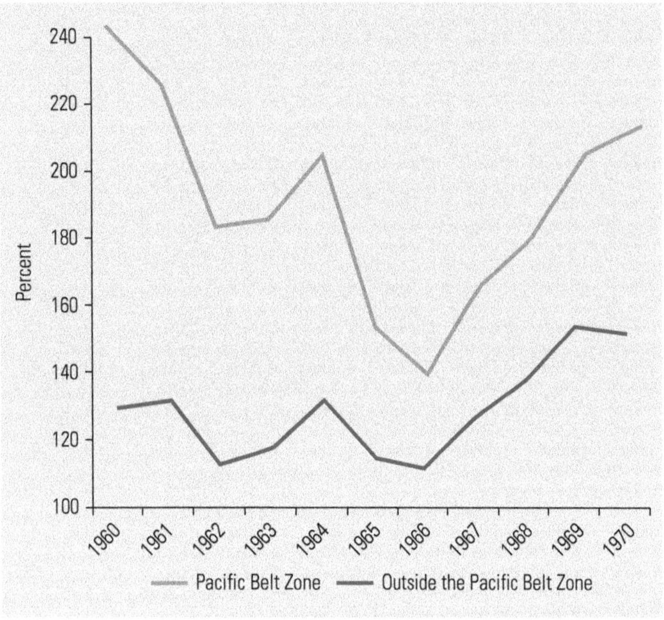

    —— Pacific Belt Zone   —— Outside the Pacific Belt Zone

Source: Calculations by the Corridor Study Team based on Cabinet Office, Government of Japan.
Note: The Pacific Belt Zone consists of 19 prefectures.

> **Remarkably, economic and social disparities between the Pacific Belt Zone and other regions did not widen much. Benefits were widely shared.**

440 million tons in 1960 to 1.852 billion tons in 1970); and the volume of power generation 2.9 times (from 100.1 billion kwh in 1960 to 293.9 billion kwh in 1970).[6]

The total value of shipments of products manufactured or fabricated in the Pacific Belt Zone increased 3.8 times (from JPY24.7 trillion (1960) to JPY94.4 trillion (1970), in 2005 prices). The rates of increase in the traditional centers of Tokyo (291.2 percent), Osaka (327.4 percent), and Fukuoka (251.6 percent) were lower than the average for the entire Pacific Belt Zone. This suggests that industrial activity was dispersed by such measures as regulating factory locations and promoting development projects across the entire zone.

Cases of dynamic private initiative include the construction of a steel plant in Chiba Prefecture by Kawasaki Steel Corporation (now known as JFE Steel Corporation); the expansion of production of four-wheel vehicles by Toyota Motor and Nissan Motor; and the launch of production of four-wheel vehicles by Honda Motor and Suzuki Motor. Both the government and the private sector propelled economic development, sometimes competing for limited financial resources such as World Bank loans and governmental finance, and sometimes cooperating to introduce foreign technologies or promote efforts to develop technology.

High economic growth yielded rapid and huge positive outcomes. While the policy objective had been to double national income within ten years, from 1960 to 1970, this goal was achieved in only seven years. Japan's economy surpassed what was then West Germany in 1968 to become the second-largest economy in the world. This income increase was constantly led by vast demand of private consumption to improve people's standard of living, which was satisfied by enhanced production capacity. A virtuous cycle was established, in which robust private consumption spurred investment, investment improved technologies, technological improvements enhanced the quality of industrial products and lowered their prices, and consumption increased, boosted by an increase in income. By repeating this cycle, Japanese industries increased their export competitiveness, which increased tax revenues and savings in Japan.

Since imports exceeded exports throughout the entire period of high economic growth, the contribution of exports to the increase in income was seemingly limited. However, vigorous domestic private consumption was backed by an increase in imports of raw materials, and the financing for such imports was underpinned by steadily increasing exports. During the 1960s, exports of machinery, steel, and cars expanded greatly. This expansion was sustained by the global economy and trade, which grew strongly and steadily during the 1960s.

Social indicators also improved significantly. For example, Japan's infant mortality rate declined from 30.7 to 13.1 for every 1,000 births from 1960 to 1970.

A growth cycle was established that supported improvements in living standards for most Japanese citizens

Remarkably, during this period of high economic growth, economic and social disparities between the Pacific Belt Zone and other regions did not widen much.[7] While some gaps between the Pacific Belt zone and the other regions persisted because the Pacific Belt Zone had always fared better in terms of indicators such as per capita income and infant mortality, even rapid economic growth in the Zone did not expand such gaps. As both the Pacific Belt Zone and the other regions made rapid improvements, indicators in the other regions reached the same level as the Pacific Belt Zone in several years.

The public also perceived that the income gap was not widening. According to a public opinion poll conducted at the time, the ratio of respondents who considered themselves to be middle class increased from 76.2 percent in 1958 to 89.2 percent in 1967.[8] The penetration rates of consumer goods such as electric washing machines, electric refrigerators, and television sets soared from 21 percent, 5 percent, and 24 percent, respectively, to approximately 90 percent after the economic growth of the 1960s. Then people switched to buying color television sets, air-conditioners, and cars.

Three main factors accounted for such balanced development: the demographic dividend and internal migration; enhancement of agricultural productivity, along with growth in employment opportunities in industries other than agriculture; and government policies to correct regional disparities.

The demographic dividend and internal migration

During the reconstruction period following World War II, the number of births and population growth increased remarkably, peaking in the three-year period from 1947 to 1949. The period of high economic growth period coincided with a demographic dividend when the citizens in this population bulge reached working age. Moreover,

industrialization in the Pacific Belt Zone caused rapid population inflows into this area. As a result, the total population as well as the working-age population in the zone increased greatly. In 1962, 43.7 percent of job-seeking junior high school graduates and 35.2 percent of job-seeking high school graduates in the other regions (235,000 youths) found employment in the Pacific Belt Zone. This population migration increased the number of households in Japan and strengthened consumer demand for durable goods and other goods and services.

Enhancement of agricultural and nonagricultural productivity

In parallel with the nation's industrialization, the ratio of agricultural and forestry output to the total production in all industries declined steadily in both the Pacific Belt Zone and in the other regions. Meanwhile, agricultural productivity improved significantly because of mechanization, the introduction of chemical fertilizers, and other efforts. As a result, agricultural and forestry output increased from 1960 to 1970. In the other regions, nonagricultural earnings increased for two reasons. First, job opportunities in industries other than agriculture increased, especially in the prefectural capitals, where urbanization provided a sales base that boosted consumer spending. Second, the pool of migrant workers employed in agricultural off seasons in the Pacific Belt Zone increased, raising the ranks of part-time farmers. In the other regions, the ratio of full-time farmers decreased from 36.5 percent (1960) of households to 16.9 percent (1970) and to 13.4 percent (1975). With this change, the ratio of part-time farmers whose nonagricultural earnings exceeded 50 percent of their respective total earnings increased from 29.6 percent (1960) to 46.6 percent (1970) and to 58.3 percent (1975). In addition, the maintenance of producer prices for rice under the foodstuff control system stabilized and sustained farmers' incomes. However, enhancement of production technologies and favorable weather conditions greatly increased the rice harvest, especially in 1967 and 1968. The rice surplus became a financial burden at the national level.[9] To deal with the surplus, the national government implemented a rice paddy reduction program and other measures.

Government policies aimed to correct regional disparities and share benefits

The population shift from the rural areas to metropolitan areas is largely related to income and employment disparities. Figure 5.2 shows high correlation between the excess in-migrants ratio in three major metropolitan areas in the Pacific Belt Zone and the disparities in income.

The need to correct regional disparities was emphasized in the first Comprehensive National Development Plan and the concept of "Well-balanced development between regions" continued to be core concept for the

succeeding Comprehensive National Development Plans. Particular attention was paid to government support for the regions where productivity was lower. The government of Japan has sought to develop infrastructures, transfer fiscal resources and redistribute industries to rural areas. As a result, the disparity of household income in regions and excess demographic shift to the three major metropolitan areas have been eased. The almost linear decreasing trend of in-migrants ratio and income disparity can be found for the era of rapid economy growth. As explained, the total investment amount in the Pacific Belt Zone, including capital investments by private enterprises, exceeded investment in the other regions. However, the stock of per capita social capital (on a net basis) in the Pacific Belt Zone and the other regions was similar during the period of high economic growth up to 1970.[10] Then the other

FIGURE 5.2 **Demographic shift to the three major metropolitan areas and the income disparities in the region**

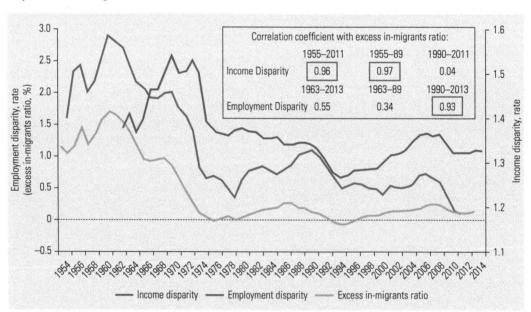

Source: White Paper on Land, Infrastructure, Transport and Tourism in Japan 2015.
Note: The excess in-migrants ratio is calculated as follows: "(in-migrants – out-migrants in three major metropolitan areas) / population of Japanese."
Income disparity is calculated as "the three major metropolitan areas average of the income of one prefectural resident / national average (excluding the three major metropolitan areas)," Employment disparity is calculated as the ratio of active job openings to active job applicants, which is "the three major metropolitan areas average of the ratio of active job openings to active job applicants / national average (excluding the three major metropolitan areas)."
The numbers of the graph are the correlation coefficient of the excess in-migrants ratio for each period and the disparity index.

regions far surpassed the Pacific Belt Zone. This result suggests that policies to prevent widening regional disparities worked.

Allocation of government spending to different regions

Approximately half the revenue for local government depended on the national treasury, including local allocation tax grants, national treasury disbursements, and local government bonds. Local taxes covered only about 30 percent of local budgets. This level was criticized as "30 percent autonomy" by those who favored more self-determination. Nevertheless, significant resources from the national government played an important role in securing a national minimum in the nonprofit sector and in redistributing income among regions. Across all regions in the country, per capita fiscal revenue was almost the same.

New industrial cities

One example of a policy to eliminate regional disparities was a measure to designate 15 new industrial cities. Most of these cities were outside the Pacific Belt Zone (map 5.2). This effort aimed to avoid the excessive concentration of people and industries in preexisting large cities. Under the policy, some existing cities were expanded—such as prefecture capitals like Sendai Bay, Akita Bay, and Tokushima—and some entirely new cities were built—such as Doou, Joban-Koriyama, and Hyuga-Nobeoka—as hubs of industrial siting and regional development. In all, JPY72 trillion was invested to develop infrastructure in the new industrial cities during the 34-year period from 1964 to 1998.[11]

In these new industrial cities, infrastructure developments were followed by the construction of factories, focused mainly on the heavy and chemical industry sector. However, during this period, Japan's industrial structure was undergoing a rapid shift from manufacturing to services. Thus, the launch of new industrial cities was not enough to form regional hubs capable of generating many new job opportunities based on the expansion of manufacturing. The exceptions were the

districts that included prefectural capitals.[12] One conceivable reason for the lack of success to achieve the goal intended by the launch of the new industrial cities was the failure to foresee private enterprises' preference to expand business within areas where they were already located, based on criteria of economic rationality. While the development of the new industrial cities is presumed to have contributed to curbing the expansion of disparities between the Pacific Belt Zone and other regions, there are arguments for and against the value of supporting new industrial cities.

The Comprehensive National Development Plan proposed creating cities as regional development hubs that would implement development policies in their respective districts. Various efforts to enhance the capital of each prefecture were promoted, including efforts to improve urban functions (such as commerce, production, education, and culture) and to

MAP 5.2 **Fifteen new industrial cities were established to spread benefits throughout Japan**

Source: 1962 Law for Promoting Establishment of the New Industrial Cities.

enhance regional development without over-dependence on megacities like Tokyo, Osaka, and Nagoya. Transportation networks were improved, and private enterprises were supported in effort to expand their production sites beyond headquarters in the major cities to other parts of the country. Along with structural shift of manufacturing from material industry such as chemical and metal industry to mechanical and electronic one, industrial location increased in rural areas, for example, along newly developed expressways and production share of conventional coastal industrial areas along the Pacific Belt Zone has relatively decreased. Such efforts and industrial location shift contributed to the expansion of market size and the increase of employment opportunities in the other regions.

Health care

The government also tapped the nonprofit sector to enhance balanced growth across the country. In the area of health and medical care, one of the major goals was universal health insurance coverage. This goal was achieved in 1961. It enabled Japan's health care infrastructure to offer equal opportunities for access to medical care. Other policies with a focus on local areas included efforts to increase and improve public medical institutions and medical personnel; measures to secure medical services in remote districts; and health and hygiene activities carried out through coordination with relevant personnel (such as activities by life improvement instructors to improve nutrition). Water-related infectious diseases were curtailed by increasing the coverage of the piped water supply nationwide, which increased from 53.4 percent (in 1960) to 80.8 percent (in 1970) to 91.5 percent (in 1980). While the industrialization and associated development of infrastructure advanced rapidly in the Pacific Belt Zone and other regions, some improvements in social capital took longer. For example, coverage of sewerage systems increased from at 8 percent in 1965 to 23 percent in 1975 to 36 percent in 1985 to 51 percent in 1995.[13]

Education

Several laws were passed to ensure that equal opportunities in education (especially in compulsory education) would be provided and educational standards would be upheld and improved. These included the Basic Act on Education (1947), the Act on National Government Contribution to Compulsory Education (1952), and the Act on National Government Contribution to Equipment and Facilities of Public Schools (1953). Concrete measures included the allocation of national budget resources to local governments to achieve a specified number of pupils or students and of assigned teachers per class, implementation of unified curricula, and operation of a textbook authorization system. In addition, candidates for principal and assistant principals of elementary schools and junior high schools were required to serve as teachers in remote districts before they could be appointed. Because of these efforts, it makes little difference where one receives compulsory education in Japan. Japanese citizens have broadly supported equal opportunities and uniform quality in compulsory education. This equality and uniformity is considered to have played a major role in facilitating the increase of employment opportunities and the internal migration that accompanied the rapid industrialization of Japan.

The social costs of pollution were not adequately considered during the planning and implementation stages

Rapid industrialization also had a serious negative impact, in the form of environmental deterioration and pollution (map 5.3). Air pollution worsened. Sulfur oxide emissions increased ninefold from 1955 to 1971 in the three major metropolitan areas of Japan, for instance. Sometimes it was difficult to stay outside during daytime hours in these cities. The incidence of bronchial asthma and other diseases reached high levels in many areas in the Pacific Belt Zone.[14] Following outbreaks of several serious diseases caused by water contamination, including Minamata disease and Itai-Itai disease, Japan was recognized worldwide as a "Paradise of Pollution." Rapid urbanization also worsened garbage problems. In 1971, the so-called Tokyo Garbage War broke out. While the City of Koto had been disposing of garbage for 23 special wards of Tokyo solely by using landfills, the Koto City Authority used force to prevent garbage from being deposited from the City of Suginami, which was reluctant to build a new waste treatment plant.[15]

In 1964, a project to develop petroleum industry complexes in the eastern part of Shizuoka Prefecture, located in the Pacific Belt Zone, was canceled because of local residents' opposition to exposure from pollutants. Concerns about pollution and environmental deterioration grew, starting in the mid-1960s. According to a public opinion poll conducted in 1970, the majority of respondents considered economic growth to be negative. The ordinary session of the Diet in 1970 was known as the Pollution Diet because many bills related to the environment were enacted. In the early 1970s, litigation concerning all four major pollution-related diseases was concluded in favor of the plaintiffs.[16] Since then, Japan has made a full-scale effort to pursue pollution control measures.

Effective development of transport corridors requires active and responsible participation by many actors

Japan's high economic growth with a focus on industrialization in the Pacific Belt Zone achieved extremely rapid and significant results in terms of increasing income. This positive impact is attributed to large-scale industrial development by leveraging the dynamism of private enterprises in the transport corridor, the formation of human resources through improvement of education and health and medical services, effective utilization of such human resources through internal migration, and the establishment of a growth cycle supported by improvements in living standards

MAP 5.3 **Health damage related to air pollution soared in the Pacific Belt Zone**

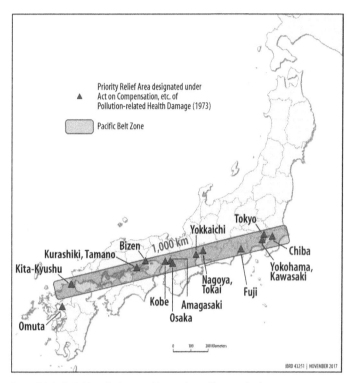

Source: Priority Relief Area, Environmental Restoration and Conservation Agency.
Note: The red triangles indicate Priority Relief Areas designated under 1973 Act on Compensation, etc., of Pollution-Related Health Damage.

for the vast majority of Japanese citizens. No significant disparity between those regions undergoing rapid industrialization and other regions occurred. Figure 5.3 presents a conceptual framework for the cycle that led to Japan's high economic growth.

On the other hand, the social costs of pollution were not adequately considered during the planning and implementation stages. Thus, appropriate preventive measures could not be taken. This oversight offers a lesson for economic development through rapid industrialization. To ensure the effective development of transport corridors, all relevant players must fulfill their respective functions, including the national government (which is responsible for formulating development plans, allocating budget resources, and improving the legal system); local governments (which are responsible

FIGURE 5.3 **Japan's rapid economic growth was supported by a virtuous cycle**

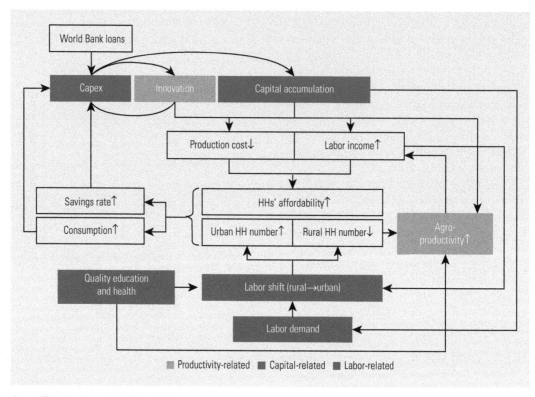

Source: JICA, with reference to Yoshikawa 2012.
Note: capex = capital expenditures; HH = household.

The alignment of the transport corridor is a major determinant of the wider impacts.

for promoting investment by private enterprises, and adequately monitoring enterprises to ensure their compliance with laws, regulations, and standards); enterprises (which pursue entrepreneurship, and meet requirements for compliance, disclosure of information, and the like); citizens; communities; judicial bodies; and the media. Such functions include considering and implementing measures to minimize or avoid negative impacts such as pollution.

The wider economic benefits of rail corridors take at least 10 years to emerge.

UNDERSTANDING THE WIDER ECONOMIC BENEFITS OF EUROPE'S HIGH-SPEED TRAIN PROJECTS

Western Europe has an extensive transport network, with a number of rail corridors designated as components of the Trans-European Network–Transport (TEN-T) (map 5.4). This section analyzes the context, design, implementation, and wider economic benefits (WEB) of three corridors that represent the diversity of rail corridors in Europe:

1. LGV Sud-Est connecting Paris and Lyon in France, a national passenger High Speed Rail (HSR) line.
2. North West Europe High Speed Rail (NWE HSR) connecting Paris, Brussels, Cologne, Amsterdam and London.

MAP 5.4 The Trans-European Transportation Network connects most of Western, Northern, and Southern Europe, the United Kingdom, and Ireland

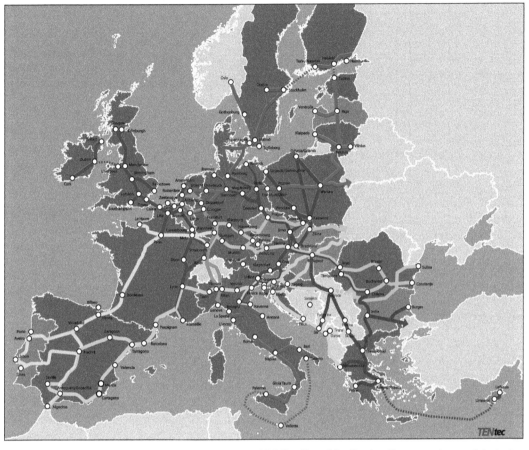

Source: European Commission, 2017, Trans-European Transport Network: TEN-T Core Network Corridors, http://ec.europa.eu/transport/infrastructure/tentec/tentec-portal/site/maps_upload/SchematicA0_EUcorridor_map.pdf.

NWE HSR is a transnational high speed passenger rail network.

3. The Rhine-Alpine Corridor is a north-south multi-modal corridor that runs through the core of western Europe. The focus is on the rail freight component.

The first two examples explore the broader context within which the corridors developed to demonstrate how the economic and political environment was conducive to investment in such large-scale and complex transport infrastructure. The discussion then turns to the rationale and design of the corridors, including key decisions on the alignment of the corridor, which is a major determinant of the wider impacts. Next, the case reviews the implementation of the corridors, emphasizing the type of financing, including the challenges of using private capital for rail infrastructure. Finally, it examines the wider economic benefits, identifying main impacts that can be documented with peer-reviewed literature.

The third example takes a slightly different approach. Many of the core rail sections of the Rhine-Alpine Corridor were developed in the latter half of the twentieth century, although significant replacement, upgrading, and modernization has occurred since then. The WEB of the Rhine-Alpine Corridor have emerged over a longer time line—a fact this study seeks to analyze.

LGV Sud-Est: pioneering high-speed rail in Europe

France was the pioneer of HSR in Europe.[17] LGV Sud-Est was the first line in France's high-speed rail network (LGV, Ligne à Grande Vitesse, high-speed line). The line links the capital city of Paris with France's second-richest city, Lyon, with high-speed TGV (Train à Grande Vitesse, high-speed train) services operated by the national rail operator, SNCF.

LGV Sud-Est is 409 kilometers (km) long and has two intermediate stations between Paris and Lyon, Le Creusot and Mâcon-Loché. Operations began in 1981. The financial success and popularity of LGV Sud-Est reinforced support for high-speed rail in France, though later lines did not achieve the same financial and socioeconomic returns. Over the past 30 years, additional high-speed lines have been built, developing a hub-and-spokes network centered on Paris, with further lines under construction. The total length of the high-speed passenger rail network in France is now over 2,000 km.

High-speed rail is a relatively new mode of transport in Europe. As one of the oldest high-speed rail corridors, the LGV Sud-Est line was chosen as a case study because it is possible to draw upon ex post studies that look at the wider economic benefits over a longer period. This longer time frame reflects a broader issue in assessing the wider economic benefits of rail corridors: the impacts of these investments take a long time to emerge. A good rule of thumb is at least 10 years.

Context

By the 1950s, rail was losing modal share to road, and from the 1960s rail was losing modal share to air in France (Crozet 2013, 13). More broadly, the financial position of the French National Railways (SNCF), like many other public enterprises in France at the time, was deteriorating. The railways were seen to be in terminal decline (Dunn and Perl 1994). The French government commissioned a review of public enterprises, which was released in 1967. This influential report (Nora Report 1967) advocated for public enterprises to adopt a commercial, financially sustainable approach and operate more like private companies. A key recommendation was to differentiate potentially competitive market services from government-subsidized services provided by public enterprises (Albalate and Bel 2012).

For SNCF, this meant that rail services that were not subject to a public service contract would need to compete with other modes. Unsurprisingly, there was considerable reluctance to embrace the report's recommendations, which represented a fundamental cultural change for the railways. However, external factors, including the economic crisis induced by the 1970s oil shocks, reinforced the need to reduce the financial losses of public enterprises (Gilbert and Perl 2012, 43). The development of the TGV therefore occurred within the context of a state-directed policy of commercial viability. The oil shocks also reinforced the need for a transport system that was independent of oil supplies.

The political and institutional environment of France in the 1970s was also conducive to the development of the TGV (Albalate and Bel 2012). Political power was stable, and government authority was highly centralized, with decision making concentrated in Paris. As is discussed later in this section, this power structure allowed the central government to issue a special instrument (a public declaration) for the construction of LGV Sud-Est, which permitted significant expropriation without consultation (Crozet 2013, 13).

Rationale and design

Before LGV Sud-Est was opened, the Paris-Lyon conventional rail line was already the busiest rail corridor in France. This line connected the Île-de-France, the region centered on Paris, with Rhône-Alpes, the region centered on Lyon. These were (and are) the two regions of France with the highest GDP and the largest metropolitan populations. The existing conventional rail line, which traveled through Dijon, faced significant capacity constraints and was losing modal share to air (Gilbert and Perl 2012, 44). This is a key point for this corridor: the high-speed rail link was connecting two prosperous regions of France, with existing levels of traffic reaching capacity constraints on the route.

SNCF sought to develop a long-distance, high-frequency rail service linking Paris and Lyon within two hours, which would make the return trip attractive as a day trip, through the construction of a largely dedicated high-speed rail line (Meunier 2002, 6). SNCF's objective was to make rail the preferred mode of transport for travel between the two cities, competing with air. The alignment avoided intermediate cities, with two purpose-built out-of-town stations to provide access (Le Creusot and Mâcon). Avoiding intermediate cities reduced the rail distance between Paris and Lyon by more than 100 km (Vickerman 2015). Therefore, the TGV was designed to target long-distance travelers—generally, business and leisure travelers—rather than reducing journey times for commuters or other short- to middle-distance travelers (Crozet 2013, 4). Again, this decision aligns with the wider objective for the service to compete with air.

The focus on minimizing end-to-end journey times and the lack of intermediate stations led to concerns in the 1970s that the TGV would result in further urbanization in Paris, at the expense of the underdeveloped countryside. There had long been anxiety about economic concentration in Paris, particularly since Gravier's famous thesis, *Paris and the French Desert* (1947), which argued for regional investment to support the development of a balanced national economy. The concerns extended to Lyon, which, it was feared, could turn into a "low rent suburb" of Paris (Meunier 2002, 6). However, although the project was declared to be in the public interest, there was very limited public consultation and the alignment planning was largely conducted internally at SNCF. Essentially, SNCF made a strategic decision to prioritize maximizing modal share over regional development.

Implementation

The line was developed in two phases. The first phase—the 274-km southern section between Saint-Florentin (174 km south of Paris) and Sathonay (8 km north of Lyon)—opened in 1981, reducing the journey time from Paris to Lyon from 4 hours to 2 hours 40 minutes. The second phase—the 116-km northern section from Combs-La Ville (27 km south of Paris) and Saint-Florentin—opened in 1983, reduced the journey time further to less than 2 hours. The line was implemented as a public project, with the €2 billion infrastructure cost (2005 prices) financed entirely through SNCF borrowing (Vickerman 1997). The rolling stock fleet of 107 TGV-PSE (Train à Grande Vitesse—Paris Sud-Est) sets was manufactured by Alstom, a French multinational company operating in rail markets worldwide. The unit cost for the infrastructure construction of LGV Sud-Est was approximately €5 million per km. LGV Sud-Est had the lowest cost per km for high-speed rail infrastructure construction in a global comparison of high-speed rail development (Campos, de Rus, and Barron 2009). This low cost structure reflects a range of external and design factors. First, the population density of France is relatively low, allowing for a relatively straight alignment. There are no tunnels on LGV Sud-Est. Similarly, the decision to avoid intermediate cities reduced the length of the line, which is significantly shorter than the conventional rail line between Paris and Lyon. The TGV was also designed to be interoperable with the conventional rail network. The existing urban lines in Paris and Lyon are used to reach the terminal stations, further reducing the overall cost.

The lack of public consultation also contributed to the low cost of construction. In 1976 a formal public declaration was issued for the construction of LGV Sud-Est, an action by the French state that diminished the importance of private interests. SNCF then identified a "broad swathe of right-of-way" in the French countryside within which land was acquired through eminent domain, with consultation limited to a public inquiry that was largely a legitimization of the existing design (Meunier 2002, 6).

Economic analysis

In general, LGV Sud-Est was successful in technical, commercial, and economic terms. The line generated traffic volumes and revenues beyond the levels forecasted by SNCF (Melibaeva, Sussman, and Dunn 2011). The estimated financial internal rate of return of LGV Sud-Est was 12 percent, the minimum return for a project to be considered financially viable by SNCF. The expected financial internal rate of return was comfortably exceeded in ex post studies, at 15 percent (Vickerman 1997). A key objective of LGV Sud-Est was to compete with air by providing a high-frequency long-distance service between Paris and Lyon. The ex ante appraisal estimated that the reduction in journey time from high-speed rail would generate a significant modal shift from air transport (Crozet 2013, 19). By 1997, 16 years after the line opened, the TGV had captured 70 percent of the Paris-Lyon market, and air transport had fallen from 31 percent to 6 percent of total passenger traffic on this route (Campos and Gagnepain 2009). In commercial terms, the line also exceeded expectations. LGV Sud-Est was financed by SNCF through borrowing, and the debt was fully repaid 12 years after operations commenced (Vickerman 1997).

An early and often referenced study on the wider impacts of LGV Sud-Est was carried out five years after the service began (Bonnafous 1986). The study highlighted the growth in business travel on the corridor, which increased by 56 percent between 1980 and 1985. Business trips from Lyon to Paris grew at over double the rate of those from Paris to Lyon, suggesting that the improved accessibility increased the market size for Lyon-based firms.

Rail infrastructure alone does not deliver the economic impacts envisioned. Rail infrastructure must form part of a comprehensive package of measures for economic and social development.

However, the growth in business travel was not uniformly distributed across sectors. The TGV has particularly benefited the service sector in Lyon. Expansion was greatest for high-value services in Lyon, including market research, advertising, and consulting firms. Business travel for the sale or purchase of services grew by more than 100 percent. The impact on manufacturing was far more limited. The result from surveys of 10 cities in Rhône-Alpes and Burgundy showed that proximity to TGV services was not a determining factor in the choice of location for industrial companies, but was a factor when industrial companies were choosing between alternative locations that were otherwise similar (Bonnafous 1986).

Specialist businesses, such as public relations, no longer needed to relocate to Paris to expand beyond the local market. Service businesses could maintain relationships within the company and carry out sales activities in Paris while remaining based in Lyon, which offered a higher quality of life. The line introduced a fundamental shift in the way distance was perceived between the two largest population centers in France, from spatial to "temporal distances" (Melibaeva, Sussman, and Dunn 2011). The perception of Lyon as being "two hours away from Paris" influenced the behavior of users, inducing a significant level of business travel, and eventually altered the broader economic and social relationship between the cities (Melibaeva, Sussman, and Dunn 2011).

The differential impact of high-speed passenger rail on services and manufacturing reflects the respective sectors' different needs for mobility. High-speed passenger rail largely benefits companies that rely more on face-to-face contacts (Albalate and Bel 2012). These companies tend to be involved in higher value-added service activities and cluster in larger cities to access agglomeration benefits (Chen and Hall 2012).

Another sector that grew was tourism. Day trips to Lyon increased significantly through TGV tourism packages, as well as conference-related travel. This shift, however, also reduced the volume of overnight stays, which fell from an average of 2.3 days in 1980 to 1.7 days in 1992 (Melibaeva, Sussman, and Dunn 2011). This required a restructuring of the hospitality sector to adapt to new groups of customers.

These findings contradict the earlier fears of the Lyon business community of a centralization of economic activities in Paris. Lyon grew rapidly. Demand for office space around the TGV station, Gare de la Part-Dieu, in particular, increased substantially. Between 1983, when the TGV became operational on the whole line from Paris to Lyon, and 1990, office space around the station increased by 43 percent (Melibaeva, Sussman, and Dunn 2011). Further commercial development in the old city center of Lyon was physically restricted, and the arrival of the TGV supported the creation of the new Part-Dieu business district. A number of Paris-based technology companies moved their back office operations to Lyon to capitalize on the lower cost base.

On balance, the TGV has generated a net economic benefit for both Paris and Lyon, with no strong evidence to suggest Paris has gained at the expense of Lyon (Cheng, Loo, and Vickerman 2015). However, there is some evidence that increased access to Paris redistributed economic activity to Lyon from surrounding subregions, such as Bourgogne and Rhône-Alpes, widening disparities within regions (Vickerman and Ulied 2009). Some areas within Lyon fared better than others. Notably, the traditional downtown area lost significant numbers of companies to the station area (Melibaeva, Sussman, and Dunn 2011).

These shifts highlight the difference between the *interregional* and *intraregional* impacts of high-speed passenger rail corridors. Reducing the journey time between Paris and Lyon to two hours does not appear to have exacerbated interregional disparities between Paris and Lyon. However, there is evidence that Lyon has benefited from a centralization of economic activities, particularly in the services sector, to the detriment of neighboring cities in the region. This aligns with a broader conclusion that high-speed

rail tends to reinforce the position of large regional cities, such as Lyon (Chen and Hall 2012).

A similar pattern of concentration occurred at Mâcon-Loché, one of the two intermediate stops on the line. While employment grew by 13.5 percent in Mâcon from 1999 to 2006—which has been attributed to the TGV—it fell in nearby cities (Melibaeva, Sussman, and Dunn 2011). Mâcon was already a major employment area for the region. The arrival of the TGV helped secure its position at the expense of nearby cities, from which businesses relocated. Also, the pattern of increasing intraregional disparities between Lyon and the Rhône-Alpes region has been replicated at the intermediate city Mâcon and in the Saône-et-Loire region. Interesting, the same pattern did not occur in the second intermediate city, Montchanin-Le Creusot. Despite an 85-minute journey time from Paris, only two new companies had been established around Le Creusot's TGV station six years after its opening, with no discernible local economic impact in terms of jobs or commercial development. It is likely that other factors of Le Creusot's location, such as the isolated station and poor road access, limited its development (Melibaeva, Sussman, and Dunn 2011). Furthermore, the TGV station serves a group of smaller towns rather than a single urban area, which has likely impaired the TGV's consolidating effect around Montchanin-Le Creusot.

North-West Europe high-speed rail: Connecting five major European cities

North-West Europe High Speed Rail (NWE HSR) connects five large European cities, Paris-Brussels-Cologne(Köln)/Frankfurt-Amsterdam-London (PBKAL). It is more accurate to refer to NWE HSR as a *network* rather than as a corridor because there are multiple connections between the cities, rather than a linear route. Nonetheless, this high-speed network connects the metropolitan core of Europe and offers insights into the impacts from cross-border passenger high-speed rail. NWE HSR is 932 km long and has four cross-border links, including the Channel Tunnel. The network is operational, with international services being run by a number of operators, including Eurostar and Thalys. The network is also used for fast intercity services within the five participating countries.

Context
The development of NWE HSR was spurred by the growing congestion of air and road links between the cities in the network, and the need to improve transport between these metropolitan areas (Vickerman 2015). Following the economic crises of the 1970s, European governments cut capital spending on infrastructure significantly. The gap between the level of infrastructure investment and the growth in transport demand widened. By 1990, real spending on infrastructure was only at the levels of the mid-1970s. The infrastructure deficit was growing, and transport needs could not be met (Johnson and Turner 1997, 45). Environmental concerns also drove the shift to rail, as the negative impacts of mass motorization were being felt. There was a consensus among governments to promote a modal shift from air and road to rail (Peters 2005).

The drive for improved transport connectivity came not just from governments. European industry also played an important role in promoting transnational transport networks. An influential lobby group, the European Round Table of Industrialists (ERT), produced a series of reports in the 1980s and early 1990s advocating for the European Union (EU) and national governments to invest in capital-intensive projects to improve transport infrastructure. ERT membership consisted of around 40 chief executive officers (CEOs) of major transnational corporations, including Total, BP, Volkswagen, and Rolls Royce. ERT's landmark report, *Missing Links: Upgrading Europe's Transborder Ground Infrastructure*, published in 1984, argued for a number of core projects, including a tunnel under the English Channel linking the United Kingdom and France and a general network

of high-speed railways in Western Europe (Peters 2005). The project to develop the North-West Europe high-speed rail network was launched in 1989 with an official agreement between France, Belgium, Germany, Netherlands, and the United Kingdom.

Rationale and design
NWE high-speed rail was conceived as a network offering substantial reductions in journey times between the five countries. Figure 5.4 shows the reductions in journey times on the NWE high-speed rail network from 1989, when the network was planned, to 2009, when the whole network was operational. These reductions are between one and three hours, representing a 50 percent time saving for most routes. It is a city-to-city network, largely ignoring intermediate towns, except for a few, including Lille and Calais-Frethun in France and Ashford and Ebbsfleet in England. The impact of high-speed rail passenger connections on these intermediate towns is discussed later in the section.

An underlying rationale for the network was to compete with air, reflecting both the increasing congestion in the aviation market in northwestern Europe at the time, as well as the growing awareness of air transport's environmental impact. The first LGV line between Paris and Lyon, discussed earlier, had demonstrated how high-speed rail could capture air market share. The PBKAL cities are less than 500 km apart, falling within the optimal medium distance range of 400 km to 600 km for competition with air (Chen and Vickerman 2017) (see map 5.5).

At the international level, the development of NWE high-speed rail was one of the Priority Projects of the Trans-European Transport Network, endorsed by the European Commission in 1994, designed to promote accessibility across the European Union and improve the functioning of the single market (map 5.4). Alongside the objectives to enhance the competitiveness of rail transport and improve the wider sustainability of the transport network, it was also envisioned that the PBKAL network would release capacity on existing lines, freeing up tracks for freight traffic, and improving the quality rail freight services.

Implementation

In 1993, operations commenced on the first section of the network, between Paris and the Channel Tunnel (which was still being built), via Lille. This section is also part of the French TGV network, referred to as LGV Nord, and was developed as a public project with significant funding from the European Commission (EC) via the European Investment Bank (EIB). The original route proposed by SNCF avoided the city center of Lille, with a station at the point where the lines diverged to London and Brussels. However, political mobilization by the mayor of Lille at the time (and future French prime minister) Pierre Mauroy led to the route being diverted through Lille city center (Chen and Hall 2012). The impacts of the TGV on Lille are discussed in the following section.

It is worth discussing two components of the NWE high-speed rail network, the Channel Tunnel and Channel Tunnel Rail Link (also known as High Speed 1 in the United Kingdom), in more detail because they illustrate some of the challenges of private sector provision of high-speed rail infrastructure. In both cases, the governmental agreements to develop the projects stipulated the use of private capital for financing.

The most technically challenging section of NWE HSR was the Channel Tunnel. A treaty between the United Kingdom and France for a 50-km twin tunnel for rail was signed in 1986. The Treaty of Canterbury specified how the project would be financed, "without recourse to government funds"; that is, on the basis of project risk. The project was structured as a design-build-finance-maintain (DBFM) private sector concession. The concession was awarded to the private Eurotunnel consortium (Eurotunnel) under a concession agreement with both governments. The concession runs until 2086. Even for a large infrastructure concession, the contractual structure for the Channel Tunnel was unusually complex.

FIGURE 5.4 **The journey time between major stations in northwestern Europe fell by about half on most routes between 1989 and 2009**

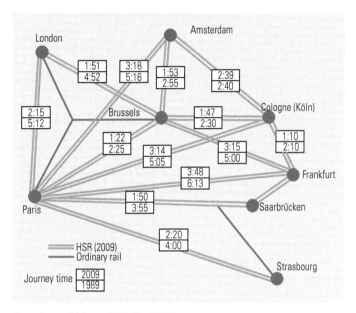

Source: Chen and Vickerman 2017, citing EU 2010.

Eurotunnel was itself a partnership between the UK and French concessionary companies. The contractor TML was also a "joint venture of joint ventures" between UK and French construction companies (Vickerman 1995). The capital structure of the project was 20 percent equity and 80 percent debt. In 1987, around 50 percent of the shares were offered to the general public (which lost much of its investment in the later restructuring). Some 200 banks were involved in the loan syndication. The EC supported the project through substantial financing through the EIB.

The anticipated cost of constructing the Channel Tunnel in 1985—broadly, the time the concession was awarded—was £4.7 billion (2004 prices). The actual cost was about twice that: £9.5 billion (2004 prices). The cost overrun for the Channel Tunnel has often been used as a case study to illustrate the difficulty of controlling costs on megaprojects (see, for example, Priemus, Flyvbjerg, and van Wee 2008). Alongside the escalation of capital costs, the actual traffic volumes fell

MAP 5.5   **High-speed rail connects the core of North-West Europe and the United Kingdom**

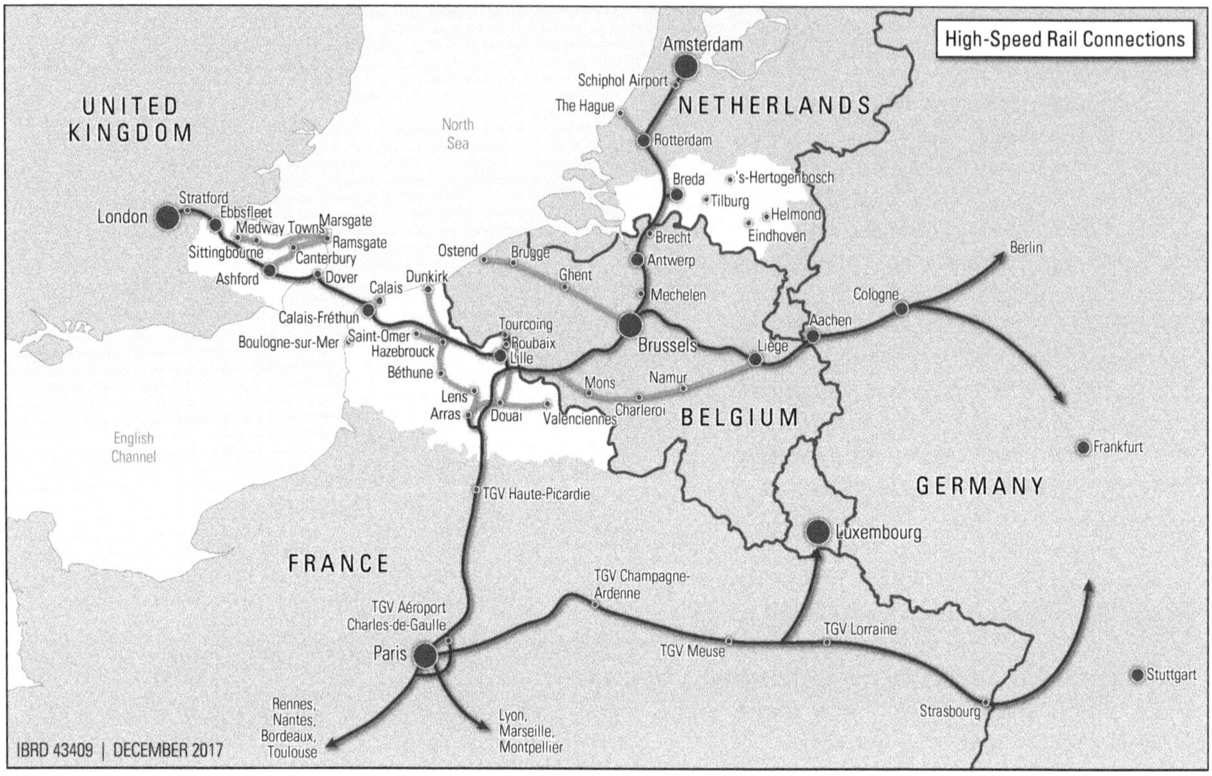

Source: Cheng, Loo, and Vickerman 2015.

well short of the forecasts. Revenues failed to cover debt service and the concessionaire defaulted in one year, requiring a major financial restructuring. In 2007 there was a further restructuring, with debt-for-equity swaps leaving financial institutions as the major shareholders. In 2009, Eurotunnel paid its first dividend, 15 years after commencing operations in 1994.

The section of PBKAL in the United Kingdom, the Channel Tunnel Rail Link (CTRL), was also developed under a project finance structure. In 1996, London Continental Railways (LCR) won the contract from the UK government to develop the rail section between London and the Channel Tunnel under a design-build-finance-maintain concession. LCR was a consortium of banks and construction and transport companies. Construction of the rail link, which became known as High Speed 1 (HS1), commenced in 1988, with phase 1 opening in 2003 and phase 2 in 2007. Upon the opening of phase 2, the journey time from London to Paris was reduced to 2 hours 15 minutes, and London to Brussels to 1 hour 51 minutes. LCR was besieged with financial difficulties stemming from lower-than-expected revenues. As a result, the UK government guaranteed a major bond issuance to restructure LCR's debt. In 2006, LCR was reclassified as a public corporation, as the company effectively had come under the UK government's control. In 2009, LCR was formally renationalized.

These issues are not unique to private infrastructure rail projects. For example, the Betuweroute, a public project to construct a freight railway in the Netherlands that was completed in 2007, experienced similar issues in terms of cost overruns and weak revenues. However, the contractual structures of the Channel Tunnel and High Speed 1 concessions resulted in significant disagreements between the parties involved, which compounded the financial issues.

Services on several sections of the network overlap, and are provided by competing operating companies. Thalys runs services between Paris, Brussels, Cologne, and Amsterdam. These compete with TGV services on the French section, and with Eurostar, which runs between Paris, Brussels, and London. The German state railway, Deutsche Bahn, withdrew from the Thalys consortium and now competes with Thalys between Brussels and Cologne (and travels on to Frankfurt). This plurality of service providers on the same routes makes it more difficult to book train tickets, impairing the goal of being competitive with airlines (Vickerman and Ulied 2009). However, the different operators have taken more steps recently to increase the ease of booking for consumers. Alongside international high-speed rail services, the PBKAL network is also used for regional high-speed services for commuting traffic.

Economic analysis

Before considering the wider economic benefits for the major and intermediate cities, it is worth reiterating how the network was largely developed as a series of national sections. Studies carried out at the national level in the mid-1990s found relatively low levels of economic returns for the sections in the United Kingdom, Belgium, and the Netherlands. The section in France, LGV Nord, was already operational by 1993, and was experiencing traffic volumes that were significantly lower than expected, primarily due to lower international passenger traffic.

A report carried out by the EC Working Group on PBKAL highlighted the need to include cross-border, or "community," benefits, or else risk underestimating their economic returns. For PBKAL, the report estimated that community benefits accounted for more than one-quarter of the overall benefits. Their inclusion allowed the national sections to exceed the hurdle rates for approval (Peters 2005). This in turn led to increased funding from EC sources, particularly the European Investment Bank. By 2003, EIB had provided €2.4 billion in funding for PBKAL (EIB 2003).

Major Cities

A recent study analyzed the wider economic benefits of high-speed rail by comparing employment rates in the PBKAL cities and outlying areas between 1999 and 2008 (Cheng, Loo, and Vickerman 2015). The average employment growth of 10.1 percent in the PBKAL cities was higher than the 8.9 percent in the hinterlands. However, there was significant variation among the cities. Amsterdam presented an interesting case, registering employment growth of 14.1 percent—the second highest among the core cities—even though it was not fully connected to the NWE HSR network until 2009. A key conclusion of the study was that the wider impacts of high-speed rail were dependent on location, and that transport improvements would not necessarily result in local economic development—particularly on cross-border or interregional routes (Cheng, Loo, and Vickerman 2015). Based on this analysis, it was suggested that passenger high-speed rail in northwestern Europe has not had a transformative economic impact, particularly because most sections lack intermediate stations.

Yet the same study also had a more positive conclusion about high-speed services. It suggested a tendency for cities and their hinterlands to converge since high-speed services have been introduced. This convergence seems to be acting in the opposite direction from the pattern of centralization associated with passenger high-speed rail. For already-congested cities that lack space for expansion and where rent and property prices are already high, high-speed passenger rail service can shift growth to the connected towns.

Lille

Lille is often held up as an example of the positive benefits of high-speed rail (see, for example, Greengauge 2006). By the 1980s, the coal, steel, and cotton industries in the city were struggling against cheaper imports, alongside a gradual reduction in the supply of raw materials (Hickman, Bonilla, and Banister 2015, 306). As mentioned, the mayor of Lille lobbied intensively for LGV Nord to stop in the city center, making Lille a major transport hub with direct train connections to London, Paris, and Brussels.

A key aspiration with the arrival of LGV Nord was the development of the knowledge-based economy in Lille. Analysis of employment patterns showed that Lille has had the highest increase in knowledge-intensive employment in the Nord-Pas-de-Calais (NPDC) region, and significantly above the national average (Chen and Hall 2012). Access to Paris within one hour brought Lille within commuting distance, which supported growth in public services within Lille. The same study found that other subregions in the NPDC region that did not have access to TGV services had the lowest knowledge-intensive employment. Chen and Hall (2012) suggest that, more broadly, the arrival of passenger high-speed rail and transport infrastructure has supported the economic restructuring from industry toward high-value services and the knowledge economy.

In Lille, the TGV station was located close to land that was available for commercial development. The Euralille development was a major regeneration project to create a new urban center in Lille, including commercial, residential, leisure, and conference facilities. The first phase was built in parallel with the construction of LGV Nord (Ureña, Phillippe, and Garmendia 2009). Euralille was structured as a joint venture between local authorities and private investors. It included job creation programs, offering training to local unemployed people.

This package illustrates the need for complementary investments alongside infrastructure access in order to generate positive, wider impacts. It is also important to note that while the Euralille development resulted in job creation in Lille, net employment growth is questionable. As was the case for the LGV Sud-Est corridor, there is evidence of centralization of economic activity in the regional hub (Lille) as a result of its increased accessibility, at the expense of smaller cities in the region (Vickerman 2015).

The Rhine-Alpine Corridor: supporting the development of Europe's industrial core

The third case study focuses on the Rhine-Alpine Corridor, one of the nine core network corridors of the Trans-European Transport Network (map 5.6). The Rhine-Alpine Corridor is multimodal, integrating a number of corridors, including Rail Freight Corridor 1 (RFC 1). While this corridor does not have dedicated rail freight lines and passenger trains operate along the route, the underlying rationale for the Rhine-Alpine Corridor clearly emphasizes freight transport. In other words, the basis for designating this route as a core transport corridor in Europe is its importance for the international transporting of goods. For the purposes of this report, this corridor was selected to illustrate how the wider impacts of rail corridors have extended to influencing the spatial structure of national economies.

Description

The Rhine-Alpine Corridor is a north-south corridor extending from the North Sea ports of Rotterdam and Antwerp to the Mediterranean port of Genoa in northern Italy. The corridor is a primary artery for transporting goods in Europe. Over 1 billion tonnes of freight are transported on the corridor annually, of which 370 million is cross-border. The share of rail on the corridor is approximately 12 percent, with 34 percent for road and 54 percent for inland waterways (EC 2015, 11).

The corridor passes through five countries: the Netherlands, Belgium, Germany, Switzerland, and Italy. A significant length of the corridor follows an inland waterway, the River Rhine, a historically significantly transporting route in Europe. Other than the first section of the river in Switzerland (the High Rhine, or Hochrhein), the corridor follows the Rhine from Basel to the Rhine delta on the North Sea. The River Rhine remains an important means of transporting bulk commodities between the North Sea ports and France, Germany, and Switzerland.

The Rhine-Alpine Corridor is a mature corridor, with end-to-end road and rail connections from Rotterdam to Genoa. Electrification is complete along the length of the corridor, and freight speeds of 100 km per hour are possible on over 90 percent of the route. The entry and exit of the corridor are maritime ports, including Antwerp and Rotterdam at the northern end. The Port of Rotterdam is the largest port in Europe, handling 466 million tonnes in 2015, and is the eleventh-largest container terminal globally. There are substantial intermodal nodes along the corridor, including at Duisburg in the Ruhr Valley in Germany. Duisburg Port is the world's largest dry port, with road, rail, and inland water connections. Increasing demand has resulted in the need for significant investments in the corridor, primarily addressing the need for capacity enhancement and interoperability, including 60 rail projects.

Historical development

The history of the corridor can be traced back to the Roman period, when the trade route between Northern and Southern Europe emerged out of the economic asymmetry between these two regions. Lower-value goods such as salt, amber, wool, and wood were being traded in the North, and higher-value goods such as spices, silk, and precious stones in the South (Drewello and Scholl 2016, 2). Key cities on the Rhine emerged during the Roman period—including Cologne, Bonn, and Basel—and a network of land routes, waterways, ports, and warehouses was

MAP 5.6   The Rhine Alpine Rail Freight Corridor: "From sea to sea without barriers"

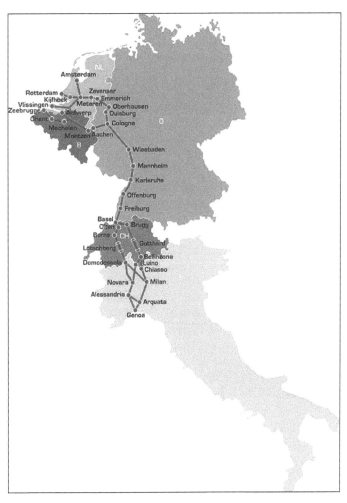

Source: RFC Rhine-Alpine, "From Sea to Sea without Barriers," https://www.corridor-rhine-alpine .eu/home.html.
Note: Map is as of 2017.

developed by the Romans to facilitate trade in what is now the Netherlands. This includes a likely transhipment port at Domburg, located south of Rotterdam, with seafaring vessels traveling to the British Isles and river barges to Cologne (Grazhdankin 2012). Transport was central in the early formation of spatial

> **The development of the Rhine-Alpine transnational rail freight corridor had as much to do with the harmonization of standards as the physical construction of railway infrastructure.**

economic structures along the corridor, with the River Rhine as the central axis.

From the early 1800s, the countries along the corridor were engaged in industrial revolutions, alongside acceleration in the development of natural resources, particularly in the Ruhr and Saar regions (in Germany). In the Ruhr Valley, growth in coal production was followed by the formation of large steel and chemical industries, furthering the growth of agglomerations along the corridor. The population of the Ruhr Valley grew from 400,000 in 1850 to 3.8 million in 1925 (Taylor 2015).

The development of railway networks contributed to the expansion of industry along the corridor, and key sections of the Rhine-Alpine rail corridor were first developed in this period. These included the Mannheim-Karlsruhe-Basel Railway, also known as the Rhine Valley Railway, which was built using German public funds between 1840 and 1855; and the "Iron Rhine," a freight railway connecting the Port of Antwerp (Belgium) to the Rhine Basin in Germany via the Netherlands, which was built between 1868 and 1879. The cross-border section is no longer in use. Passenger and freight international traffic instead currently use the Montzen line, which avoids the Netherlands. However, Belgium is now seeking to reopen the Iron Rhine due to capacity constraints.

An interesting early example of a transnational approach to rail development is the Gotthard line, a primary north-south rail axis in Switzerland, and a key section of the Rhine-Alpine Corridor. A dense rail network had developed in Switzerland by the 1870s. However, there was no line through the Swiss Alps. All north-south traffic traveled east or west around Switzerland. In 1871, the Gotthard Railway Company, a private enterprise, was incorporated to develop and operate a new north-south line and significantly reduce the journey times of transit traffic. This included the construction of the first Gotthard Tunnel, a 15-km rail tunnel under the Swiss Alps, between 1872 and 1881. The Gotthard Tunnel was at the time the longest tunnel in the world (and the same

is currently true for the Gotthard Base Tunnel, a new tunnel that is discussed later in this section).

The sources of finance for the line and tunnel were largely outside Switzerland. Combined, the governments of Italy and Germany contributed two-thirds of the capital for construction, demonstrating that the benefits of the line were recognized by other countries on the corridor (the same approach is institutionalized today through the EU). In return, Italian and German rail operators were offered preferential tariffs for use of the tunnel, and a profit sharing arrangement was put in place. Essentially, for those providing capital for the project, this was a return on equity in the form of dividend payments (Anastasiadou 2011, 33).

International Cooperation
Beyond the physical construction of infrastructure, an international regime to coordinate and facilitate cross-border freight traffic emerged. Germany led an earlier period of development of the rail corridor. The German Railway Union, formed in 1847, had significant influence on railway development across Central and Northern Europe, and promoted cooperation between the various national and regional railway administrations. By 1879, the German Railway Union had 110 railway administrations across Germany, the Netherlands, Luxembourg, and Austria (Austro-Hungary), which collectively administered a network of over 50,000 kilometers.

In parallel, the Swiss government led an initiative to establish agreements between governments that would facilitate international traffic. Starting in 1874, a series of conferences were organized by the Swiss government, which sought to develop a common standard for rail goods transport to facilitate more efficient cross-border traffic in Europe. In 1882, a conference was held to set international standards for rolling stock, resulting in the Technical Unity on Rail Transport (L'Unité Technique, UT), which included parameters such as loading gauge, maximum vehicle length, and the position of couplings. In 1890, the International

Convention Concerning Railway Freight Transport was signed by representatives of 11 European countries, including all countries on the Rhine-Alpine corridor.

The task of harmonization of standards continues to this day. The current focus is on the implementation of the European Rail Traffic Management System, which, alongside enhancing interoperability with the deployment of a common signaling system, has the ability to significantly enhance capacity. The development of the Rhine-Alpine transnational rail freight corridor has had as much to do with the harmonization of standards as the physical construction of railway infrastructure.

Economic analysis

Corridor Level

As discussed, the origin of the Rhine-Alpine corridor was the River Rhine, a natural transportation route from Lake Constance in the Swiss Alps downstream to the Rhine delta in what is now the Netherlands. The River Rhine was a major determinant in shaping the economic geography of a number of major industrialized nations in Western Europe. Later, the globalization of trade, exploitation of natural resources, and the Industrial Revolution spurred railway development, further increasing the density of people and economic activity along the corridor.

In 1989, the area served by the corridor was dubbed the "Blue Banana" by the French geographer Roger Brunet, who originally named it the Dorsale européenne (European backbone). The European backbone refers to an arc of Europe starting in northwestern England in the United Kingdom, and extending through Greater London, the Randstad (Amsterdam, Rotterdam, and the other urban centers in the western Netherlands) and Brussels, down through the Ruhr Valley in Germany, along the Rhine through southern Germany and Switzerland, and finally into the "industrial-triangle" of northwestern Italy (Milan-Turin-Genoa).

This spatial concept captures what may be the largest agglomeration in the Western countries, a discontinuous, 1,500-km urban corridor stretching from Manchester in north-western England down to Milan in Northern Italy. The corridor has a population of over 100 million, and spans major European cities including London, Amsterdam, Brussels, Frankfurt, Zürich, and Milan (the European backbone can be easily identified through empirical analysis of population density). The European backbone has a high number of metropolitan areas with high per capita incomes, high labor force participation in services, and low unemployment relative to the rest of Europe (Heidenreich 1998).

The concept of a single, linear European backbone is highly contested. The concept omits key urban centers such as Paris, as well as the urbanization along the northern Mediterranean coast. Moreover, with the expansion of the European Union, the geographical center of Europe has been moving eastward, with new growth poles in Central and Eastern Europe. Nonetheless, by global standards, there is a dense agglomeration of people and economic activity along this urban corridor, which has survived the transition from industrial to service-based economies.

The transport corridor that is now designated the Rhine-Alpine Corridor has co-evolved with this agglomeration. Originally with the River Rhine, and later with railways and roads, this transport corridor has provided the infrastructure to support the development of Europe's industrial core. It is estimated that the region served by the Rhine-Alpine Corridor currently generates approximately 20 percent of the European Union's GDP.

Gotthard Base Tunnel

Some 135 years after the original Gotthard Tunnel was inaugurated, a second rail tunnel was opened in 2016 to expand capacity for rail freight. The Gotthard Base Tunnel, at 57 km in length, is the longest tunnel in the world. Switzerland has a long history of providing routes for transit traffic through the Alps. Indeed, the country was formed in the Middle Ages around these trade routes.

The primary rationale for the construction of the Gotthard Base Tunnel was the modal shift of transalpine traffic from road to rail. There were growing calls to address the congestion caused by the volume of heavy freight traffic on the roads in the Alps, reduce the level of road accidents, and minimize negative environmental impacts, including air and noise pollution. Despite the absolute growth in rail volumes, the rapid growth of road freight eroded the modal share of rail.

In 1994, under the Swiss system of direct democracy, the Swiss electorate voted to commit Switzerland to transferring freight traffic from road to rail, resulting in a constitutional commitment for a modal shift to rail. In 1998, the public voted for the construction of the tunnel to be publicly funded using the Public Transport Infrastructure Fund (FinöV). The sources of the fund were taxes on heavy vehicles, a tax on gasoline, and the value-added tax (VAT). In 1999, an act came into force setting a target of 650,000 truck journeys per year (against 1.4 million truck journeys in 2000). The tunnel was to be a key instrument in achieving this policy objective. The agency responsible for implementation was AlpTransit Gotthard Ltd, an enterprise established for this purpose and fully owned by Swiss Railways. The total cost of construction of the tunnel was €11 billion (US$12.3 billion).

A key study in 2011 estimated that the two new tunnels (Gotthard Base Tunnel and Lötschberg) would, combined, generate a 20 percent increase in rail traffic, including a 13 percent modal shift from roads. The economic analysis used a 60-year appraisal timeline and a discount rate of 2 percent, assessing the economic, environmental, and social impacts. The cost/benefit ratio was calculated at approximately 1, with a caveat that regional economic and trade benefits were not captured (Ecoplan and Infras 2011, 70). Another study completed before the opening of the tunnel (but after construction commenced) more conservatively estimated that the tunnel would increase rail's modal share by 2.5 percent—an improvement, but far less than

that required to achieve the constitutionally mandated target of a modal shift from road to rail (Metron 2009, 34).

Conclusion

A number of conclusions can be drawn regarding the wider economic benefits of rail corridors in Europe. The first is that none of the passenger high-speed rail lines reviewed in this study have had a transformative economic impact. The LGV Sud-Est line and the PBKAL network connect the most densely populated and prosperous regions in France and northwestern Europe, respectively, and therefore have served to reinforce the existing importance of these regions. However, it can be argued that these high-speed lines have helped maintain economic development, as capacity constraints in the transport system had the potential to limit growth. In other words, while it is not possible to accurately assess the counterfactual, these rail corridors have helped support existing centers of economic activity.

There is some evidence that high-speed rail has widened disparities within regions, further concentrating economic activity in cities served by high-speed services. This has been observed at both the terminal and intermediate cities on the LGV Sud-Est line. However, there is less evidence that high-speed rail has led to an overall centralization in a core-periphery structure.

The two passenger rail corridor case studies also demonstrate how high-speed rail in Europe primarily has affected the services sector, while having little or no impact on manufacturing. Passenger high-speed rail essentially supports face-to-face contact, which is a critical factor in the development of higher-value services and the knowledge economy.

Timing is also critical. The PBKAL network became fully operational around the same time as the global financial crisis. The resulting economic downturn reduced passenger traffic volumes, which in turn curtailed wider impacts. The earlier financial failure of the privately financed sections of the PBKAL, the Channel Tunnel, and High Speed 1 suggest that caution should be applied when forecasting traffic volumes.

The Rhine-Alpine Corridor case study illustrated how a natural transport corridor evolved over centuries to become the core north-south route for the movement of goods in Europe. This corridor helped shape the economic geography of the region it served, including having a role in the formation of states. In the latter half of the twentieth century, the development of railways on the Rhine-Alpine Corridor supported the rapid growth of manufacturing and the development of natural resources, helping to create the industrial core of Western Europe. This case study demonstrates the importance of rail freight in the historical economic development of Europe.

Finally, the study has shown how rail infrastructure alone does not deliver the economic impacts envisioned. To do so, infrastructure must form part of a package of measures, as was the case in Lille, where the arrival of the TGV was accompanied by measures to support urban regeneration.

THAILAND, THE DETROIT OF THE EAST?

The growth of Thailand's automotive production and exports is considered an economic success story. Although Thailand began producing motor vehicles and parts in the 1960s, it catered primarily to the highly protected domestic market through the 1990s. Production for export has been important only since 2000. In 2015, Thailand produced more than 2 million vehicles, making it the world's ninth-largest automotive producer. Roughly half the industry's final output is exported. Employment within Thailand's automotive sector (final assembly plus parts) exceeds 250,000 workers, about 4 percent of Thailand's manufacturing workforce.[18] In light of these achievements, *The Economist*

(2013) dubbed Thailand the "Detroit of the East," harkening to Detroit's glory days as the center of the U.S. auto industry.

Three sets of factors have driven Thailand's success in attracting automotive production. The government sponsored a brand new industrial cluster to address the overconcentration of production around Bangkok, including a new deep-sea port and a petrochemical complex to produce energy for production. It also supported improvements in transport infrastructure and public utilities, while providing incentives to induce investment. Meanwhile, it maintained a flexible policy stance to adjust to changing external conditions such as macroeconomic conditions, access to finance, and inflows of foreign direct investment. The result was a successful public-private collaboration with both domestic and foreign investors that spurred a new direction for heavy industry in Thailand, especially in the automotive industry.

A set of integrated transport infrastructure investments and government policies aided a shift in Thailand's industrial base to heavy manufacturing.

The centerpiece was a proactive set of infrastructure investments, beginning in the late 1980s, centered on the creation of a high-capacity deepwater port to facilitate the importing of raw materials and exporting of finished products. The new port, known as Laem Chabang, is located 75 km southeast of Bangkok. Unlike the historic and highly congested Bangkok port, located upstream from the coast on the Chao Phraya River, Laem Chabang can receive large oceangoing container vessels. The Laem Chabang port is integrated with major investments in roads, electricity, and water supplies adjacent to the port and along the highway connected to it. The port, together with the industrial area immediately adjacent to it, might be considered a hub, but the highway system connected to it, with

The development of an efficient gateway for exports—a deep-water port connecting roads and associated manufacturers—spurred Thailand's automotive industry.

infrastructure investments in electricity and water located along this highway system, created a corridor of broader economic activity consisting of the outskirts of Bangkok and the seven provinces lying in a semicircle to the east and north of Bangkok, all linked to the Laem Chabang port.[19] This transport and infrastructure corridor facilitated the establishment and growth of final automotive assemblers (builders of cars, trucks, and SUVs). Crucially, this development occurred in conjunction with the establishment of manufacturers of parts and components along the corridor. The final assemblers were all foreign owned—mostly, but not entirely, Japanese. The parts and components manufacturers included both foreign firms (mainly Japanese) and numerous smaller Thai firms.

Along with this push for infrastructure, the Thai government introduced a set of policy changes shortly after and partly in response to the disastrous Asian Financial Crisis of 1997–98. These changes for the first time permitted unlimited foreign ownership of both final assemblers and parts and components manufacturers in the automotive sector. They also abolished Thailand's restrictive requirements for the local content of motor vehicles produced within Thailand. Without the foreign exchange shortage that accompanied the Asian Financial Crisis, these policy changes probably would not have been politically feasible.

Another factor for the success in attracting foreign investment was noneconomic and difficult to quantify. For historical and cultural reasons, Thailand is an attractive and welcoming venue for Japanese firms. Japanese executives and their families enjoy living in Thailand, giving it an advantage in attracting Japanese investment relative to most of its East Asian neighbors.

The plan focused on providing infrastructure and incentives to promote heavy manufacturing beyond Bangkok

By the mid-1980s, the Bangkok port could no longer support heavy manufacturing within Thailand. The port upstream on the Chao Phraya River was incapable of handling large, oceangoing container ships and required trans-shipment of cargoes to smaller vessels. Meanwhile, the road connection to industrial areas passed through Bangkok's notoriously congested traffic. Japanese expertise and financial support were important in designing a new port area, 75 km to the southeast of Bangkok. This scheme, the Eastern Seaboard Development Plan (ESDP), centered on the new port of Laem Chabang. It was connected by road to the large Map Ta Phut petrochemical complex planned further to the south at Rayong and also served by a deep-water port. The new port was designed specifically to encourage a shift in Thailand's manufacturing base. As a deep-water port, it could accommodate oceangoing container vessels and thereby support the development of heavy manufacturing within Thailand, rather than the garments, electronics, and other light manufacturing that were already important within the country. The planning documents of the time did not anticipate that the resulting industrial development would take the form of export-oriented automotive production, though it was an obvious potential candidate. The new port was intended to support heavy industry in general.

The Eastern Seaboard Development Plan was implemented from the 1980s through the early 1990s. It created a new industrial cluster in three provinces (Chachoengsao, Chonburi, and Rayong)—the Eastern Seaboard (ESB) area—located 80 to 200 km southeast of Bangkok. The ESDP had four main components: the Map Ta Phut Port and industrial/urban complex; the Laem Chabang Port and industrial estate; railways and roads connecting these areas with Bangkok; and the development of water resources and pipelines (map 5.7).

MAP 5.7 **The four components of the Eastern Seaboard Development Plan acted as an integrated unit**

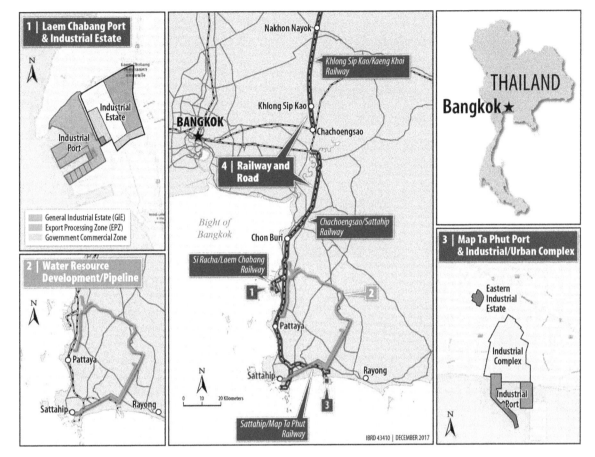

Source: JICA.

The first component, the Map Ta Phut area, was intensively developed to ensure the expansion of the production of heavy chemicals. The port consisted of a multipurpose berth and two berths for liquid cargo. Industrial estates with the necessary infrastructure were developed in a 380.8-hectare (ha) area—later expanded to 804.8 ha by the Industrial Estate Authority of Thailand (IEAT). By 1998, 50 companies were operating there. The natural gas plant in the complex produces ethane, propane, and liquified petroleum gas (LPG) from the natural gas delivered to the port. A plant with an initial production capacity of 3.5 thousand cubic feet (mcf) / day was followed by a second (250 mcf/day) and a third (350 mcf/day)

plant. These plants serve the domestic demands for energy and materials for the heavy chemical industry. Initially, the Thai government identified four industrial sectors for potential national projects (chemical fertilizer, soda ash, reduced iron, and heavy chemicals). The government finally decided to concentrate on heavy chemicals after a comprehensive examination, taking into account the macroeconomic conditions and the business feasibility.

The second component, Laem Chabang, leveraging on its deep-sea port for importing and exporting, became the center of the manufacture and assembly of automotive vehicles and electronics. At that time, Thailand was in desperate need of a

FIGURE 5.5   **Transport, utilities, and investment incentives ranked high in companies' decisions to operate on the Eastern Seaboard**

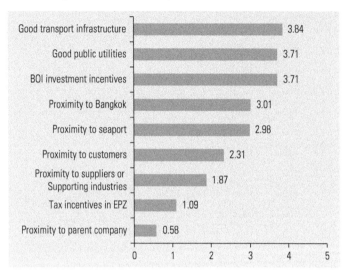

Source: JICA.
Note: Responses were based on a 1-to-5 scale, with 1 = not important and 5 = very important. BOI = Board of Investment; EPZ = export-processing zone.

deep-sea port. The site met that need with a depth (16 m) that was much deeper than Bangkok's port (8.5 m–11 m).

The third component focused on railways and roads to connect these areas with Bangkok. Their development has resulted in closer and tighter connections among these regions. Railways are used for the long-distance bulk shipment of containers from and to Laem Chabang, as well as heavy chemicals from Map Ta Phut. Japan supplied official development assistance (ODA) to finance three of the four sections of rail (Si Racha–Laem Chabang, Sattahip–Map Ta Phut, and Kiong Sip Kao–Kaeng Khol). The Thai government financed the fourth (Chanchoengsao–Sattahip). Japanese ODA also financed the construction of the Chonburi-Pattaya Highway, the Bangkok-Chonburi Highway, and the Outer Bangkok Ring Road.

The fourth component, the water supply system, has been developed to meet industrial demands, as well as the residential demands of the growing population serving the industries. Nong Pla Lao Dam is the main

water source, with pipelines connecting it to Map Ta Phut and Laem Chabang.

Development policy, focusing on providing incentives and relevant infrastructure, played an important role in accelerating industry's development in these regions. In a survey of 113 companies operating on the Eastern Seaboard (figure 5.5), firms stated that the three most important factors in their decision to locate in the region were transport infrastructure; public utilities; and investment incentives, which were more favorable than those in Bangkok. "Proximity to Bangkok" was also important, but the quality of social services and education has yet to be improved to ensure a quality of life as high as that in Bangkok. "Proximity to seaport" as an alternative to Bangkok also ranked high.

The government encouraged development of privately operated and financed industrial estates along the highway system connected to Laem Chabang port. Aside from a small publicly owned industrial estate adjacent to the port, the development of industrial estates was left to the private sector. These industrial estates were not confined to automotive-related production, but also included the full range of Thailand's manufactured exports. Within these estates, the private operators provided electricity connections to the public grid, made industrial land available for sale or lease, and in many cases offered standard factory buildings for lease to foreign or domestic firms.

Although Thailand offered incentives to promote the decentralization of manufacturing, infrastructure was more important

Since the 1960s, Thailand's Board of Investment (BOI) has used a combination of fiscal incentives to engineer the decentralization of manufacturing production away from the immediate vicinity of Bangkok. For the scheme, BOI divided the country into three zones and offered different incentives in each zone, including reductions in import tariffs and temporary exemptions from the corporate income tax and (after 2013) nontax incentives, such as permits for foreigners to buy land or for skilled workers and experts to work in Thailand. Zone 1 included the five provinces immediately adjacent to Bangkok, including Samut Prakan, where Toyota is located. Zone 2 consisted of nine provinces, including Chonburi and Ayuthaya, where Mitsubishi, Ford, Mazda, and Honda are located. Zone 3 included the remaining 62 of Thailand's 76 provinces, all more distant from Bangkok. No automotive producer has ever located in Zone 3. Although a rationale for encouraging firms to locate in Zone 3 could be made based on the lower incomes of the provinces there, poor infrastructure prevented significant manufacturing development from occurring in those provinces. The incentives offered were not sufficient to overcome this drawback. The BOI's decentralization policy did not succeed.

To some extent, the BOI's incentive structure was at variance with the government's infrastructure policy. The Eastern Seaboard scheme was explicitly intended to concentrate scarce infrastructure resources along the southeastern corridor connected to the Laem Chabang port, all within the BOI's Zones 1 and 2. At the same time, the BOI was attempting, unsuccessfully, to encourage manufacturing firms to locate outside this area. The Eastern Seaboard scheme assumed that workers would relocate to where the jobs could be found. The BOI's incentives assumed that industry could be induced to locate wherever workers lived. The latter scheme did not work, and the decentralization objective was abandoned in 2013. The new system is said to be intended to encourage high-technology, skill-intensive investments. It remains to be seen whether this strategy will be important for the future of the automotive industry, but experience does not suggest that the BOI's incentives will have much effect on firms' decisions.

The Thai automotive industry has steadily increased Its production, value added, and exports, thanks to good policies and connectivity

From 1960 to 1997, the automotive industry pursued a program of import substitution, replacing imports with domestic production. During this phase, industrial output fluctuated with domestic demand. During the economic boom from 1987 to 1996, when real GDP grew at almost 10 percent per year (Warr 2005), the automotive industry expanded rapidly, reaching an output of roughly half a million units in 1996. With the collapse of demand during and after the Asian Financial Crisis of 1997–98, output plummeted to just over one-fifth of this level. Over the next 15 years, the policy changes and infrastructure investments described produced a resurgence of output, which reached around 2 million units in 2015 (figure 5.6, panel a).[20] The export share of this output grew from roughly zero in 1997 to over 60 percent in 2015 (figure 5.6, panel b). In the 20 years after 1995, immediately before the crisis, sales to the domestic market grew from 0.5 to 0.8 million units and exports expanded from near zero to 1.2 million units.

In 2014, automotive exports earned US$33.6 billion, 16 percent of total merchandise exports and 19 percent of total manufactured goods exports. Of this total, vehicle exports made up just over half, while parts and components made up the remainder. Automotive imports totaled US$13.5 billion, of which only 15 percent consisted of vehicles, while the remainder was parts and components. Around one-quarter of all vehicle exports were to other ASEAN (Association of Southeast Asian Nations) countries (reflecting the 1992 ASEAN Free Trade Agreement) and another quarter to Australia (reflecting the 2005 Thailand-Australia Free Trade Agreement). Perhaps surprisingly, other ASEAN countries are the largest source for Thailand's vehicle imports, followed by the European Union (EU) and Japan.

FIGURE 5.6   **Thailand's automotive output and exports have soared since the mid-1990s**

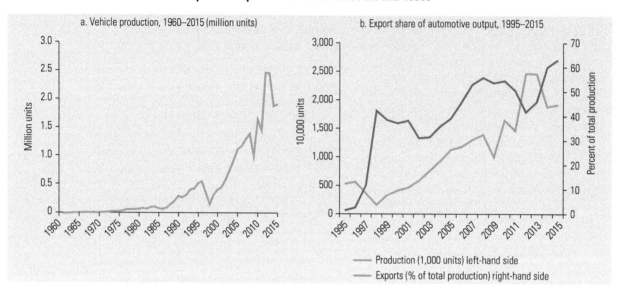

Sources: Thai Automotive Industry Association; Federation of Thai Industries; and Automotive Intelligence Unit, Thailand Automotive Institute, Bangkok.

Other ASEAN countries are the main destination for exports of parts and components exports, followed by Japan and the United States.

From just over 5 percent of manufacturing value added before the Asian Financial Crisis, the value-added share of Thailand's automotive industry had doubled to 10 percent by 2014 (figure 5.7, panel a). The industry's employment share within manufacturing is estimated at roughly 4 percent. The difference between this share and its value-added share reflects the high capital intensity of the automotive sector. Commercial vehicles (primarily 1-ton pickups) represent about 60 percent of Thailand's total vehicle output. This share has declined steadily, from around 70 percent in the early 1990s, replaced by passenger vehicles.

A striking feature of the Thai auto industry is that the import content of vehicles produced in Thailand has declined steadily since the early 1990s (figure 5.7, panel b). This started occurring well before the local content requirements were abolished in 2000. The steep decline continued until around 2005. The moderate increase since then has been due to the high electronics content of vehicles, which require more sophisticated imports. The abolition of local content requirements apparently was attractive to final assemblers. The lesson is that export-oriented manufacturers will attempt to source their parts locally when they can—but they do not want to be compelled to do so.

Comparing Thailand's automotive production and export performance with those of neighboring Malaysia and Indonesia highlights the policy differences between these countries (figure 5.8). Malaysia and Indonesia were both committed to national car policies. Foreign ownership was restricted and local content requirements were enforced, as they were in Thailand before 1997. In 1999, Thailand's vehicle output was only slightly larger than Malaysia's. By 2015, it was more than three times Malaysia's output. The comparison is even more dramatic in the case of exports. Malaysia's automotive exports have grown only marginally compared with Thailand's. Indonesia has performed better than Malaysia in both respects, but still much less well than Thailand.

FIGURE 5.7   **The net value added of Thai automotive exports has increased greatly since the late 1990s**

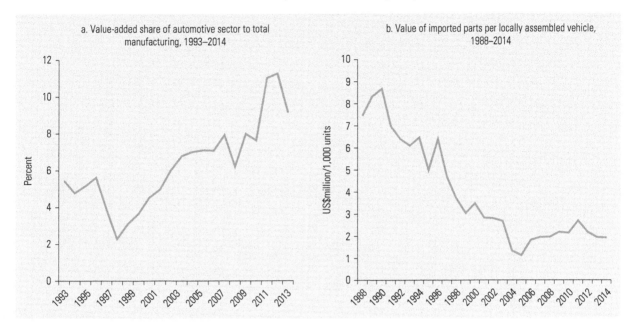

a. Value-added share of automotive sector to total manufacturing, 1993–2014

b. Value of imported parts per locally assembled vehicle, 1988–2014

Sources: Panel a: National Economic and Social Development Board, Bangkok. Panel b. Calculations by Warr and Kohpaiboon (2017), based on official data sources. Data on the import value of parts are drawn from UN Comtrade. Vehicle production data are from the Thai Automotive Industry Association; Federation of Thai Industries; and Automotive Intelligence Unit, Thailand Automotive Institute, Bangkok.

Different kinds of vehicle assembly firms tend to cluster differently along the corridor and have different impacts on employment

An industrial survey of plant-level data for three representative years—1996, 2006, and 2011—reveals that vehicle assembly includes two quite different kinds of firms.[21] Large, multinational car manufacturers engage in significant manufacturing within Thailand and produce within very large plants. Small, Thai-owned assemblers produce for niche markets within Thailand. The latter include firms that assemble buses and certain types of trailer trucks using imported new or used engines. These firms undertake very little actual manufacturing activity within Thailand.

The large, foreign-owned vehicle assemblers are linked to many parts suppliers. These suppliers tend to be small to medium sized and include both foreign- and domestically owned firms. New parts supplier plants tend to locate in the area surrounding car assembly plants. For example, the number of parts supplier plants located in Samut Prakan province increased from 56 (in 1996) to 122 (in 2006) and to 144 (in 2011). These parts suppliers have been crucial to the development of the Thai automotive sector. Domestically owned firms are smaller and more labor intensive, as measured by output per worker. Turnover among firms is higher among the Thai-owned input suppliers. This is indicated by the average age of plants responding to the surveys in the three years covered. In 1996, the average age of Thai-owned plants exceeded the average age of foreign-owned plants, but by 2011 this difference had been reversed. Over the five-year interval between 2006 and 2011, the average age of foreign-owned input suppliers increased by roughly five years, but the average age of Thai-owned suppliers increased by only half as much—even though the number

FIGURE 5.8   **Thailand outperformed Malaysia and Indonesia in number of vehicles produced and their export value, thanks to good policies**

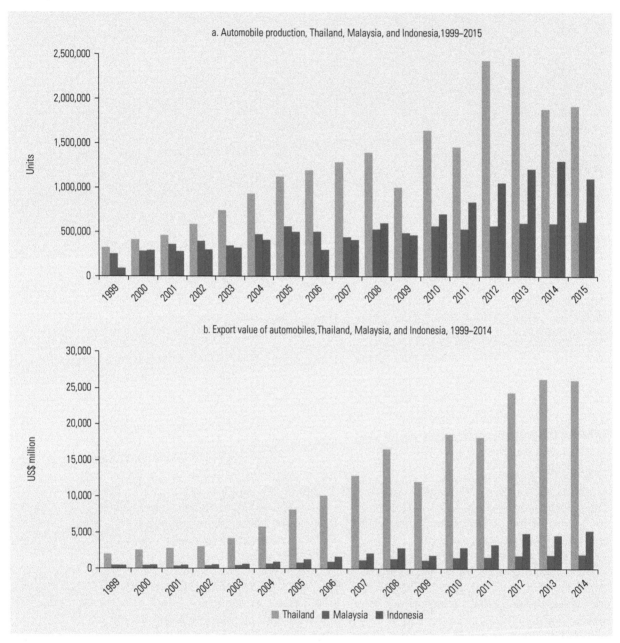

Source: Compilations by Warr and Kohpaiboon (2017) from the UN Comtrade database, using the WITS (World Integrated Trade Solution) website, http://wits.worldbank.org/.

of Thai firms increased only marginally. Many Thai firms had left the industry, to be replaced by others.

The location of the final assembly and auto parts industries changed during the decade between 1996 and 2006. Assemblers and parts suppliers have located along the highway system connected to the Laem Chabang port. Parts suppliers have tended to locate close to the final assemblers.

Econometric analysis suggests that the entry of foreign input suppliers after 1997 did not have positive spillover effects on domestic suppliers (Warr and Kohpaiboon 2017). The differential between the two groups in output per firm, capital intensity, and labor productivity was significant in each case and did not converge over time. Did the long period of local content requirements before 1997 have lasting effects on the productivity of domestic input suppliers, relative to foreign suppliers? The findings from the industrial surveys suggest that the answer is no.

Public infrastructure significantly raised labor productivity among both foreign and domestic final assemblers and parts suppliers

Beginning with the development of the Laem Chabang port, the Thai government invested in infrastructure upgrades in the eight provinces close to the Eastern Seaboard scheme (Bangkok, Samut Prakan, Nonthaburi, Pathum Thani, Ayutthaya, Chon Buri, Rayong, and Chachoengsao). The aim was to improve the investment climate for manufacturing firms—including, but not solely, automotive final assemblers and parts suppliers. These infrastructure upgrades consisted of investments in improved roads, industrial-capacity supplies of electricity and water, and telecommunications. Infrastructure upgrades in the other 68 provinces were significantly less extensive. If successful, the infrastructure investments should have raised labor productivity relative to those areas that did not receive similarly favorable treatment. The Industrial Census data can be used to investigate whether the intended effect was achieved.

This study calculated labor productivity both inside and outside the improved infrastructure regions. This is done for each of the three years of the Industrial Census and for both foreign and local firms. The Industrial Census records no foreign final assemblers outside the region with improved infrastructure (the eight provinces) in 1996 and 2011. Thus, for foreign final assemblers, the "inside/outside" comparison can be made

> **The development of the Thai automotive industry, enabled by a set of transport infrastructure investments, created hundreds of thousands of manufacturing jobs and led to a small but significant reduction in poverty.**

only for 2006. The "inside" mean for that year is more than three times the "outside" mean. For local firms, the "inside" mean is at least twice the "outside" mean in each of the three years. Performing similar calculations for parts suppliers reveals similar results. The means of labor productivity are again higher "inside" than "outside," except for foreign firms in 1996 and 2011, where the "outside" means are higher.

Recalling that the Industrial Census is a sample survey of only selected firms rather than a true census of all firms, it makes sense to ask whether these differences on the sample-based mean estimates of labor productivity are statistically significant. The results of a significance test between the average labor productivity inside and outside the regions with improved infrastructure are presented in figure 5.9.[22] For foreign assemblers and parts suppliers in 2006, labor productivity is significantly higher "Inside" than "Outside." This is also true for local final assemblers and local parts suppliers. However, results for 1996 and 2011 are less conclusive on this significant difference because of some missing data in 1996 and a problematic response rate to the survey in 2011 (as discussed earlier) that are not reported in figure 5.9.

Wider economic effects of infrastructure improvements

During the development period of 1981–95, the ESDP had a positive effect on growth of per capita GDP and population on the Eastern Seaboard. Manufacturing growth propelled the region to produce the second-largest value added of all regions in the country (table 5.1).

Map Ta Phut flourished as a petrochemical center, mainly because of the lack of domestic competition and the growing domestic

FIGURE 5.9   Labor productivity inside and outside the improved infrastructure regions

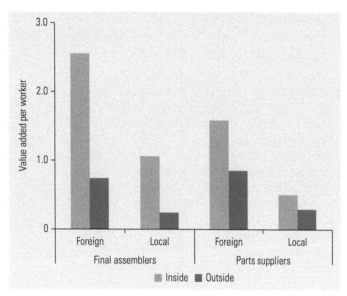

Source: National Statistical Office, Industrial Census 1997, 2007, 2012.
Note: Data are as of 2006.

demand for products. In contrast, Laem Chabang became a center for the automotive electronics industries, deviating from an initial intention of the government to make it a light industry hub. This growth was on the back of inflow of foreign direct investment from Japan, and the shift of production from Bangkok.

The impact was not confined to these two locations. It also extended to the areas between them and Bangkok, through a series of industrial parks, industrial estates, and industrial zones (map 5.8).

The heavy industrialization was accompanied by some negative side effects, including foul smells and water pollution from the heavy chemical plants. A Joint Committee consisting of the Industrial Estate Authority of Thailand, the Office of Environmental Policy and Planning, the Pollution Control Department, and the Department of Industrial Works was established to deal with these

TABLE 5.1   The Eastern Seaboard had the second-best set of macroeconomic indicators among regions of Thailand during its development period of 1981–96

	Nationwide	Bangkok and Vicinity	Eastern (ESB)	Central	Western	Northeastern	Northern	Southern
GDP per capita								
1981	20,278	63,198	26,212 (35,564)	17,845	18,610	7,860	12,402	15,740
1995	49,514	149,592	80,232 (121,376)	48,558	37,295	16,631	23,681	31,735
GDP per capita (% yoy)								
1981–86	3.4	2.2	5.8 (7.6)	2.5	3.5	3.7	3.5	3.0
1986–91	9.3	11.0	8.4 (8.5)	9.5	5.5	6.2	5.3	7.2
1991–95	7.3	6.0	11.5 (12.1)	11.2	6.6	7.0	5.5	5.2
Manufacturing value added (ratio to the whole country)								
1981	100.0	72.2	11.2 (10.6)	3.3	3.1	3.9	3.5	2.7
1995	100.0	63.2	15.8 (14.9)	6.5	3.6	5.0	3.8	2.1
Population growth (% yoy)								
1981–86	1.9	2.9	2.2 (1.5)	1.1	1.6	1.7	1.4	2.5
1986–91	1.5	2.6	2.1 (2.5)	1.3	0.8	1.3	1.1	1.6
1991–96	1.4	0.6	2.3 (1.9)	0.7	1.9	1.4	2.0	1.0

Source: Japan International Cooperation Agency.
Note: ESB = Eastern Seaboard; yoy = year on year.

environmental problems. It identified seven factories for guidance on improvements.

What role did the ESDP play in the wider economic benefits, such as GDP growth? Answering this question is problematic. More rigorous evaluation of the likely impacts of better infrastructure on the automotive sector and economic benefits is needed. To do so, this study drew on an existing general equilibrium model of the Thai economy, known as JamlongThai. Using this model, this study analyzed the effect infrastructure improvements had on reducing the production and distribution costs of automotive firms. The purpose is to ascertain the effect that infrastructure development on the Eastern Seaboard had on automotive output, exports, and employment. This analysis, in turn, can be used to examine the effect that these industry outcomes have had on the substantial reduction of poverty incidence that has occurred in Thailand in recent decades.

The JamlongThai model is a 65-sector general equilibrium model with a highly disaggregated household structure. This disaggregation of households permits the model to produce estimates of the effects that economic events have on poverty incidence within Thailand. The model is documented in Warr (2010).

Based on the interviews with industry participants, this study estimated that infrastructure improvements reduced the costs of export-oriented firms by around 15 percent.[23] The database of the JamlongThai model relates to 2007. Thus, it incorporates the impact of the cost-reducing infrastructure investments that had occurred before then. The simulations estimate the unobserved counterfactual in which these cost reductions did *not* occur. The estimated impact of the cost reductions is thus the difference between the observed value of the variables and the simulated counterfactual value of these variables in which the cost reductions did not happen.

The simulation indicates that in the absence of the productivity gain in the whole automotive sector—including parts as well

MAP 5.8   A network of industrial parks, industrial estates, and industrial zones spread from the Deep-Water Port to Bangkok

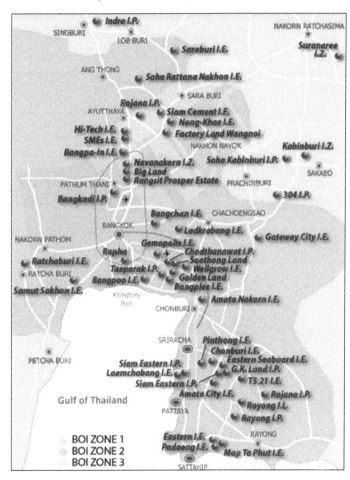

Source: Tokyo Development Consultants (Thailand) Co., Ltd.
Note: BOI = Board of Investment; I.E. = industrial estate; I.P. = industrial zone; I.Z. = industrial zone.

as assembly—real GDP would have been 0.9 percent lower (table 5.2). Put differently, the estimates indicate that the 15 percent productivity gain in the automotive sector raised the level of annual real GDP in Thailand by just under 1 percent. It is important to recognize that this is a permanent increase in the level of GDP per year and not just a temporary one-year increase in the level of GDP. The cost reductions led to an increase in the level of skilled real wages of 1.15 percent and an increase in unskilled real wages of 0.75 percent. The high skill intensity of the automotive sector explains the differential in wage effects.

TABLE 5.2   Simulated macroeconomic effects

Measure	Simulation: Final assembly plus parts
Real GDP	−0.907
Real household consumption	−1.537
GDP price index	−0.428
Consumer price index	−0.667
Wages	−1.147
Paid skilled	−0.749
Paid unskilled	
Unpaid skilled	−5.071
Unpaid unskilled	−1.021
Average capital rental	−1.601
Output of petroleum	−1.254
Government revenue	−0.820
Government expenditures	−0.992
Government budget balance (million baht)	871.308

Source: Warr and Kohpaiboon (2017) calculations, using the JamlongThai model of the Thai economy.
Note: Values are percent change, unless stated).

These wage effects occurred through an increase in the demand for labor resulting from the growth of automotive output. In the absence of productivity gains, output would have been lower, producer and consumer prices would have been higher, exports would have been lower, imports would have been higher, and the domestic consumption of automobiles would have been considerably lower.

The estimated effects on the incidence of poverty are shown in figure 5.10. Without the increases in automotive productivity, poverty incidence would have been higher, especially in urban areas. Relative to the massive reductions in poverty incidence that have occurred in Thailand, these estimated impacts are significant, but small. Holding the real value of the poverty line constant, between 1986 and 2014, poverty incidence in Thailand declined from 67 percent to 11 percent of the total population. This remarkable achievement implies that over 28 years, the incidence of poverty declined by 56 percent of the population, at an average rate of decline of 2 percent of the population per year. The estimates in figure 5.10 mean that the reductions in automotive costs reduced poverty incidence by an estimated 0.2 percent of the population. In a

population of 60 million people, this means that 0.12 million (120,000) people moved from levels of real consumption below the poverty line to levels above it. This number includes both poverty reduction among those directly employed in automotive parts and assembly firms and among those receiving remittances from these workers. Investments in infrastructure that raised productivity enabled the automotive sector to contribute to poverty reduction in Thailand. However, when viewed from within the parameters of the simulation, those infrastructure investments do not appear to have been a major driver of the huge reductions in poverty incidence that have occurred. It is important to note that these calculations do not measure the total poverty-reducing effects of the infrastructure investments described, but only those that operated via the automotive sector. Thus, the full effects would be much larger.

Lessons from the Thai case study

Development of the infrastructure supporting an efficient export gateway (Laem Chabang port and the associated Eastern Seaboard corridor) was a necessary condition to achieve the Thai government's goal to reorient the country to heavy manufacturing in the late 1980s and early 1990s. The policy reorientation built on the choice that major manufacturers around the world were making to relocate production internationally to lower-cost venues. Financial support and intellectual inputs from Japanese sources played an important role in developing the Eastern Seaboard corridor, which paved the way for Thailand to become a new manufacturing center for Japanese automotive companies. Nevertheless, Thailand's infrastructure development was not specific to the automotive industry, and the growth of the automotive sector was not anticipated by the planners concerned.

Thailand's automotive sector has not become the "Detroit of the East" because the industry is largely foreign owned.

FIGURE 5.10   **Simulated effects on the incidence of poverty (headcount measure)**

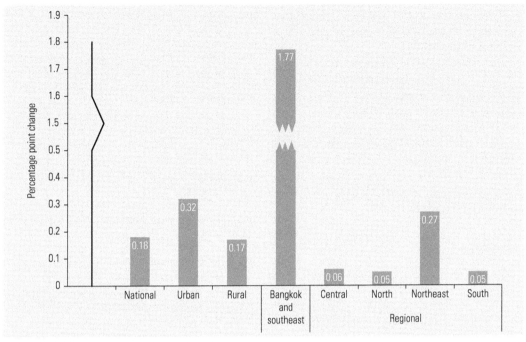

Source: Calculations by Warr and Kohpaiboon (2017), using the JamlongThai model of the Thai economy.
Note: Positive numbers mean increases in the simulated level of poverty incidence. Changes in poverty incidence are reported as the difference between the simulated level of poverty incidence (post-shock) and the initial level (pre-shock), both expressed in percentage form. For example, in 2007 (the year of the model's database) the initial (pre-shock) level of poverty incidence for the total population was 14.36 percent. The reported change in national poverty incidence above is 0.18 percentage point, meaning that the simulated level (post-shock) is 14.36 + 0.18 = 14.54 percent. That is, it is estimated that without the effect of the productivity-enhancing effect that infrastructure investments had on the automotive industry, in 2007 poverty incidence would have been 0.18 percentage point higher, at 14.58 percent of the population.

Nevertheless, the growth of the automotive sector generated hundreds of thousands of manufacturing jobs that would not otherwise have existed. Thailand avoided the failed "national car" policies of some of its neighbors. It permitted full foreign ownership of vehicle manufacturing, but did not eliminate its high rates of protection of final vehicles. These tariffs were largely irrelevant to the development of the export-oriented component of the automotive industry. Thailand's steps to liberalize input supplies by abolishing local content requirements, and to become an export platform, ironically facilitated higher, not lower, local content. Following the relaxation of restrictions on foreign entry of input suppliers (1997), multinational enterprise final assemblers often preferred domestically located but foreign-owned firms that supplied

components directly to them (tier-1 input suppliers). Not many of the existing indigenous input suppliers survived this period, but those that did mainly became tier-2 suppliers, supplying inputs to the tier-1 suppliers.

Thailand's investments in transport and other infrastructure reduced costs for manufacturers and thus contributed greatly to the development of the Thai automotive sector. This development led to a small but significant reduction in poverty.

Summing up and moving to the next chapter

This chapter has conducted a qualitative appraisal of major transport corridors around the world by means of narrative critiques. The three transport corridor projects examined were Japan's Pacific Belt Zone Initiative, Europe's high-speed train projects, and the emergence of Thailand's automotive industry with the help of robust investment in transport infrastructure.

Building on this qualitative assessment, chapter 6 performs a quantitative appraisal of two contemplated transport corridors in the eastern and western parts of South Asia. Using the holistic appraisal methodology developed by the report, it draws on spatial data, econometrics, and simulations to appraise the proposed China-Pakistan Economic Corridor in Pakistan and the Kolkata-Dhaka transport corridor in Bangladesh.

NOTES

1. The four major industrial zones are Keihin Industrial Area, which includes Tokyo; Chukyo Industrial Area, which includes Nagoya; Hanshin Industrial Area, which includes Osaka; and Kita-Kyusyu Industrial Area, which includes Fukuoka.
2. The so-called Income Doubling Plan was proposed by the Industrial Location Subcommittee of the Economic Council established under the then–Ministry of International Trade and Industry. The Cabinet approved the Plan in 1960.
3. *The Report on the Economic and Technical Feasibility of the Proposed Kobe-Nagoya Expressway.*
4. The improvement rate is the ratio of the length of road improved (in conformity with the standards specified in the Road Structure Ordinance) to the total road length. Data from the Government of Japan's Road Statistics Annual Report.
5. Social capital refers to capital related to roads, ports/harbors, rail, airports, subways, public apartment houses, sewage, waste disposal, water supply, urban parks, schools, social education/culture, river control, forestry conservancy, coastal protection, agriculture, forestry, fishery, national forests, industrial water, and postal services.
6. All of these figures are total values on a nationwide basis. Because of limitations of data on transportation and power, they cannot be calculated separately for the Pacific Belt Zone.
7. Because accurate statistical data specific to the Pacific Belt Zone do not exist, data for economic and social statistics by prefecture have been used. Specifically, this analysis uses data for 19 prefectures: Ibaraki, Saitama, Chiba, Tokyo, Kanagawa, Shizuoka, Aichi, Gifu, Mie, Osaka, Hyogo, Wakayama, Okayama, Hiroshima, Yamaguchi, Kagawa, Ehime, Fukuoka, and Oita. These prefectures make up 27.7 percent of Japan's total land area and accounted for 79.3 percent of the value of Japan's total exports of products manufactured or fabricated in 1970.
8. Public Opinion Survey on National Life (Cabinet Office), 1958–70.
9. Japan's Staple Food Control Act required the Government of Japan to purchase rice at the fixed price determined considering labor costs in urban areas. The act was passed in 1942 to secure stable food supplies and stabilize inflation. It was abolished in 1995.
10. The figures are the totals for the following 15 domains: roads, ports and harbors, aviation, public rental housing, sewerage and drainage services, waste treatment, water supply services, urban parks, education and cultural facilities, flood control, soil saving, coast administration, agriculture/forestry/fisheries, national forestry administration, and industrial water management.
11. To put this total in context, the national budget totaled ¥3.3 trillion in 1964, and ¥88.0 trillion in 1998.
12. Analysis by Shimokobe Atsuchi, a former senior bureaucrat who played a central role in drawing up and revising the Comprehensive National Development Plan, cited in Economist Hensyu-bu (1999, 102–16).
13. The figures for sewerage system coverage come from data that cover all of Japan. For areas where a sewerage system was not available, downsized septic tanks for combined treatment were developed to treat miscellaneous wastewater and sewage together. A subsidy program encouraged households across Japan to adapt the septic tanks.
14. In all, 41 districts—all in the Pacific Belt Zone—were designated as areas suffering from severe air pollution and a high incidence of bronchial asthma and other pollution-related diseases under the Compensation System for Pollution-Related Health Damage launched in 1974. The aggregate number of

certified patients as of December 31, 1988, was 108,489 (Ministry of the Environment).

15. A plant was finally built in Suginami in 1982.

16. Japan's four major pollution-related diseases are Minamata disease (Kumamoto Prefecture), Niigata Minamata disease (Niigata Prefecture), Yokkaichi asthma (Mie Prefecture), and Itai-Itai disease (Toyama Prefecture).

17. LGV Sud-Est is often regarded as the first high-speed line in Europe. However, the first high-speed line was actually the "Direttissima" line in Italy connecting Florence and Rome, which opened in 1978. Unlike LGV, the Direttissima was not designed exclusively for high-speed passenger services, which partly explains its relative obscurity.

18. The total employment is based on industry sources. Thailand's manufacturing workforce totals 6.5 million.

19. The eight provinces constituting this corridor are Bangkok, Samut Prakan, Nonthaburi, Pathum Thani, Ayutthaya, Chonburi, Rayong, and Chachoengsao. Within the corridor, industrial clusters link final manufacturers and parts suppliers. For example, a major cluster in Samut Prakan province centers on Toyota, one in Ayutthaya centers on Honda, and another in Rayong centers on a commercial alliance between Ford and Mazda.

20. Output surged temporarily in 2012 and 2013. An initiative of the populist government of Prime Minister Yingluck Shinawatra (2011–14) to provide households with tax rebates for the purchase of new passenger vehicles stimulated domestic demand by more than half a million units a year in the next two years, leading to total output of 2.5 million units. Output contracted correspondingly when a military coup in July 2014 led the policy to be abandoned.

21. The industries of interest in this study are ISIC 3410 (manufacture of motor vehicles) and ISIC 3430 (manufacture of parts and accessories for motor vehicles and their engines). Although the data are intended to cover all producers in these industries, the actual response rate has varied widely across years. This was particularly important in the case of the 2011 census, which was severely disrupted by flooding in central Thailand. Many firms did not respond. For example, the data indicate that the number of large final assembly plants declined substantially from 2006 to 2011. In actuality, no firm left the industry, but many did not respond to the survey. For this reason, the comparison between the 1996 and 2006 surveys is possibly the most instructive.

22. The analysis assumes that the sample is an unbiased random sample from the overall population of relevant firms. The null hypothesis is that true labor productivity for the full population is the same inside and outside the improved infrastructure regions. The alternative hypothesis is that "inside" productivity is higher. Can the null hypothesis be rejected in favor of the alternative hypothesis? This can be tested by calculating the t-statistic for the estimated mean difference and comparing it with the critical values from a one-tail t-test. The t-test is one-tailed because the alternative hypothesis is that labor productivity is higher inside than outside the improved infrastructure region, not just that it is different, which would correspond to a two-tailed test.

23. In June and July 2016, the authors conducted interviews with representatives from major automotive manufacturers, current and former government officials who were closely involved with the development of Thailand's automotive industry, and other experts. Government agencies and officials interviewed included the Ministry of Industry and Industrial Estate Authority of Thailand (IEAT), Bangkok; National Economic and Social Development Board, Bangkok; Siriruj Chulakaratana, chief, Office of Industrial Economics, Ministry of Industry, Bangkok; Sanoh Unakul, TDRI founder, former deputy prime minister, former director-general, NESDB; IEAT, Port Authority of Thailand, and representatives from the automobile industry, Laem Cha Bang Industrial Estate, Chonburi Province. Representatives from manufacturers included Paiboon, Isuzu Sales (Thailand), Bangkok; Suparat Sirisuwanangkura, senior vice president, Toyota Motor Thailand Co., Ltd; Trevor Nugus, CEO, Auto Alliance, Rayong Province; and Asanee Kulakow, Mitsubshi Motors, Chonburi Province. Kanit Sansuprann, Thai Airways, Bangkok, and Ruth Banomyong, Thammasat University Business School, were also interviewed.

REFERENCES

Albalate, D., and G. Bel. 2012. *The Economics and Politics of High-Speed Rail: Lessons from Experiences Abroad*. Lanham, MD: Lexington Books.

Anastasiadou, I. 2011. *Constructing Iron Europe: Transnationalism and Railways in the Interbellum*. Amsterdam: Amsterdam University Press.

Bonnafous, A. 1986. "The Regional Impact of the TGV." *Transportation* 14 (2): 127–37.

Campos, J., G. de Rus, and I. Barron. 2009. "A Review of HSR Experiences around the World." In *Economic Analysis of High Speed Rail in Europe,* edited by G. de Rus, 19–32. *Informes 2009, Economía y Sociedad*. Bilbao, Spain: Fundación BBVA.

Campos, J., and P. Gagnepain. 2009. "Measuring the Intermodal Effects of High Speed Rail." In *Economic Analysis of High Speed Rail in Europe,* edited by G. de Rus, 71–88. *Informes 2009, Economía y Sociedad*. Bilbao, Spain: Fundación BBVA.

Chen, C.-L., and P. Hall. 2012. "The Wider Spatial-Economic Impacts of High-Speed Trains: A Comparative Case Study of Manchester and Lille Sub-regions." *Journal of Transport Geography* 24: 89–110.

Chen, C.-L., and R. Vickerman. 2017. "Can Transport Infrastructure Change Regions' Economic Fortunes? Some Evidence from Europe and China." *Journal of Regional Studies* 51 (1): 144–60.

Cheng, Y.-S., B. P. Y. Loo, and R. W. Vickerman. 2015. "High-Speed Rail Networks, Economic Integration and Regional Specialisation in China and Europe." *Travel Behaviour and Society* 2: 1–14.

Crozet, Y. 2013. "Performance in France: From Appraisal Methodologies to Ex-Post Evaluation." OECD Discussion Paper 2013–26. Prepared for the Roundtable on the Economics of Investment in High Speed Rail, December 18–19, New Delhi.

Drewello, H., and B. Scholl. 2016. *Integrated Spatial and Transport Infrastructure Development*. London: Springer.

Dunn Jr., J. A., and A. Perl. 1994. "Policy Networks and Industrial Revitalization: High-Speed Rail Initiatives in France and Germany." *Journal of Public Policy* 14 (3): 311–43.

EC (European Commission). 2015. "Rhine Alpine: Work Plan of the European Coordinator." http://ec.europa.eu/transport/sites/transport/files/themes/infrastructure/news/doc/2015-05-28-coordinator-work-plans/wp_ra_final.pdf.

Economist. 2013. "Thailand's Booming Car Industry–Detroit of the East." April 4. https://www.economist.com/blogs/schumpeter/2013/04/thailands-booming-car-industry.

Ecoplan and Infras. 2011. "Wirtschaftlichkeitsstudie NEAT 2010–Hauptbericht." https://www.bav.admin.ch/dam/bav/de/dokumente/aktuell-startseite/berichte/wirtschaftlichkeitsstudieneat2010.pdf.download.pdf/wirtschaftlichkeitsstudieneat2010.pdf.

EIB (European Investment Bank). 2003. "EIB £400 Million Loan for Completion of Channel Tunnel Rail Link." http://www.eib.org/infocentre/press/releases/all/2003/2003-050-eur-560-mio-for-completion-of-channel-tunnel-rail-link-ctrl.htm.

ERT (European Round Table of Industrialists). 1984. *Missing Links: Upgrading Europe's Transborder Ground Infrastructure*. Paris: ERT Secretariat.

EU (European Union). 2010. *High Speed Europe: A Sustainable Link between Citizens*. Luxembourg: Publications Office of the European Union.

Gilbert, R., and A. Perl. 2012. *Transport Revolutions: Moving People and Freight without Oil*. New York: Routledge.

Gravier, J.-F. 1947. *Paris and the French Desert*. Paris: Partulan.

Grazhdankin, A. S. 2012. "The Role of the River Rhine in the Formation of the Spatial Structure of the Economy of European Countries (1st Century BC–19th Century AD)." *Baltic Region* 2: 100–08.

Greengauge. 2006. "High Speed Trains and the Development and Regeneration of Cities." http://www.greengauge21.net/wp-content/uploads/hsr-regneration-of-cities.pdf.

Heidenreich, M. 1998. "The Changing System of European Cities and Regions." *Journal of European Planning Studies* 6 (3): 315–32.

Hensyu-bu. 1999. *Kodo Seicho-ki eno Shogen (Jyo) (Ge)* (Testimony to the High Economic Growth Period). Tokyo: Nihon Keizai Hyouronsha Inc.

Hickman, R., D. Bonilla, and D. Banister. 2015. *International Handbook on Transport and Development*. Cheltenham, United Kingdom: Edward Elgar Publishing.

Japan, Cabinet Office, Government of Japan. National Accounts of Japan. Tokyo.

———. *Public Opinion Survey Concerning People's Lifestyle*. Tokyo.

JICA (Japan International Cooperation Agency). 1999. "Eastern Seaboard Development Plan Impact Evaluation." https://www.jica.go.jp /english/our_work/evaluation/oda_loan /post/2000/pdf/01-01.pdf

Johnson, D., and C. Turner. 1997. *Trans-European Networks: The Political Economy of Integrating Europe's Infrastructure*. London: Macmillan.

Melibaeva, S., J. Sussman, and T. Dunn. 2011. "Comparative Study of High-Speed Passenger Rail Deployment in Megaregion Corridors: Current Experiences and Future Opportunities." Paper No. JRC2011-56115, Proceedings of the 2011 Joint Rail Conference, Pueblo, Colorado, March 16–18, 541–61.

Metron. 2009. Effect of the Gotthard Base Tunnel on the Transfer of Freight from Road to Rail. http:// www.alpeninitiative.ch/dms/alpentransitboerse /doc/atb_studien/09-Studie-Metron_en/09%20 Studie%20Metron%20englisch.pdf.

Meunier, J. 2002. *On the Fast Track: French Railway Modernization and the Origins of the TGV*. Westport, CT: Praeger.

Nora Report. 1967. *Rapport sur les Entreprises Publiques*. Paris: La Documentation Française.

Peters, D. 2005. "Networking for Trans-national 'Missing Links': Tracing the Political Success of European High Speed Rail." In *The Network Society: A New Context for Planning*, edited by L. Albrechts and S. Mandelbaoum. New York: Routledge.

Priemus, H., B. Flyvbjerg, and B. van Wee. 2008. *Decision-Making on Mega-Projects: Cost–Benefit Analysis, Planning, and Innovation*. Cheltenham, United Kingdom: Edward Elgar Publishing.

Taylor, R. 2015. *A Review of Industrial Restructuring in the Ruhr Valley and Relevant Points for China*. Institute for Industrial Productivity. http://www.iipnetwork.org /Industrial%20Restructuring%20in%20 the%20Ruhr%20Valley.pdf.

Ureña, J. M, M. Philippe, and M. Garmendia. 2009. "The High-Speed Rail Challenge for Big Intermediate Cities: A National, Regional and Local Perspective." *Cities* 26 (5): 266–79.

Vickerman, R. 1995. "The Channel Tunnel: The Case for Private Sector Provision of Public Infrastructure." In *Transport and Urban Development*, edited by D. Banister. London: Chapman and Hall.

———. 1997. "High-Speed Rail in Europe: Experience and Issues for Future Development." *Annals of Regional Science* 31: 21–38.

———. 2015. "High-Speed Rail and Regional Development: The Case for Intermediate Stations." *Journal of Transport Geography* 42: 157–65.

Vickerman, R., and A. Ulied. 2009. "Indirect and Wider Economic Impacts of High Speed Rail." In *Economic Analysis of High Speed Rail in Europe*, edited by G. de Rus, 89–103. *Informes 2009, Economía y Sociedad*. Bilbao: Fundación BBVA.

Warr, P. 2005. "Boom, Bust, and Beyond." In *Thailand Beyond the Crisis*, edited by P. Warr, 1–65. London: Routledge.

———. 2010. "Thailand." In *Agricultural Price Distortions, Inequality and Poverty*, edited by K. Anderson, J. Cockburn, and W. Martin, 283–99. Washington, DC: World Bank.

Warr, P., and Archanun K. 2017. "Thailand's Automotive Manufacturing Corridor." ADB Economics Working Paper 519, Asian Development Bank. https://www.adb.org /publications/thailand-automotive -manufacturing-corridor.

Yoshikawa, H. 2012. *Kodo Seicho*. Tokyo: Chuokoron-Shinsha.

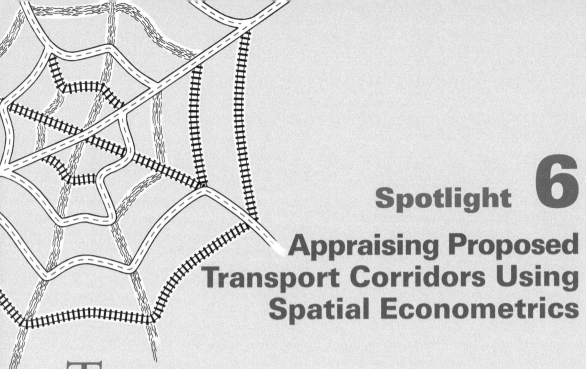

Spotlight 6

Appraising Proposed Transport Corridors Using Spatial Econometrics

This spotlight discusses the relative ability of current econometric approaches to help policy makers appraise the proposed placement and design of corridor intervention packages. Faced with many proposals for transport corridors with uncertain wider economic benefits (WEB) and limited funding, policy makers are calling for more rigorous appraisals of the placement and intervention design for transport corridors. Adding urgency to the task, the tolerable margin for error in appraisals is declining, including because of the high alternative costs (for example, forgone opportunities from not investing more in other areas with social benefits, for example, education). Therefore, the approaches discussed go beyond conventional cost-benefit analyses. Although many of them have been applied in evaluations after the project is completed (ex post), the emphasis here is on rigorous evaluation while the project is being designed (ex ante) (Melecky, forthcoming). This spotlight groups the econometric approaches into three groups: network econometrics; single-equation, reduced form (RF) econometrics; and structural general equilibrium (GE) econometrics.

The focus is not on the theories motivating these applied econometric methods, because more than one theory could motivate the use of a single econometric method. The theory of new economic geography (NEG), for instance, can motivate both the application of RF and GE econometrics using spatial data. Similarly, both the theories of trade gravity and NEG could motivate application of least square regressions.

Several recent studies have summarized and systematized the approaches and findings in the literature on the impacts of transport infrastructure investments. These studies use both more qualitative (Bosker and Garretsen 2010; Straub 2011; Redding and Turner 2014; Berg et al. 2017) and more quantitative (Melo, Graham, and Brage-Ardao 2013)[1] approaches. Although they discuss the comparative advantages of different modeling approaches (Redding and Turner 2014), they do not emphasize the ex ante perspective of project appraisals and the possible range of econometric approaches policy makers could consider as more reliable. For instance, Bakkera, Koopmans, and Nijkamp (2010) take the project appraisal perspective, but focus mainly on cost-benefit analyses (CBA) in the urban context. Laird and Veneables (2017) also take the project appraisal view, proposing disciplining structure for more rigorous CBA. But their useful think piece stops at intermediate development outcomes, apart from employment. This spotlight takes an alternative perspective to fill a possible gap in the literature, inform policy makers, and provide some direction for future research.

This spotlight does not go as far as reviewing the different objectives and preferences that policy makers seek to optimize and that could be empirically derived from data. To that end, Bougna et al. (forthcoming) present a simple policy maker's objective function that considers multiple WEB.

NETWORK ECONOMETRICS

Network econometrics could be a useful approach to estimate how investments in *transport corridors* could trigger positive spillovers to the wider economy, spur broader economic activity, and generate net WEB. The comparative advantage of network econometrics could be in appraising the proposed placements of corridors—rather than the design of interventions to spread the economic surpluses generated by the corridors from the aggregate level across spatial units (such as state districts) and ultimately to people.

In its basic form, network econometrics endorses the revival of historical corridor routes such as the Silk Road and the Grand Truck Road.[2] These proposals are driven by the idea that the historical, rich networks of agents have not completely disappeared and still hold potential. The proposals assume that—despite new borders and other obstacles for movements of trade, capital, and labor—these rich networks have persisted in a restrained form, maintaining ties in terms of culture, business, and trust (Starr 2007). By improving trunk infrastructure and providing modern transport and trade facilitation, these "tried and true" corridors are expected to produce greater surpluses—and perhaps even diffusion effects—than a greenfield project driven by a competing idea.

Optimization of a road network in terms of logistics and engineering is another aspect of network econometrics used in more localized contexts (urban, regional, national), rather than in the context of transnational or transcontinental transport corridors. Within a given budget, this type of network econometrics primarily optimizes the road network, accounting for road costs, typography, and existing traffic flows (Gastner and Newman 2006). The engineering and logistics optimization typically has not linked the transport network optimization to broader development objectives such as trade, income, or environmental quality. But recently, the transport network optimizations that have penetrated economics have begun to examine such development objectives. Consequently, hybrid papers that bridge the disciplines of engineering, logistics, and economics have been emerging.

The idea of optimizing logistics is close to the idea of maximizing market access. It makes sense for a transport corridor to be placed in such a way as to maximize the access to markets for both exporters and importers. In turn, this should create economic opportunities for those agents that become connected to markets for the first time or in better ways. But how can the market access be relevant for higher development objectives, such as household income and consumption, best be measured? One simple way to measure market access has been to divide the sum of the population in all domestic and foreign cities above X million to which tradable goods and services can be transported from a given domestic city by the travel distance from the domestic city to all other domestic and foreign cities. The benefit of connectivity to markets of big cities very far away is thus discounted to zero by the increasing transport distance (cost) (Burgess et al. 2015). For instance, the policy maker's objective when deciding where and how to place a transport corridor could be situating a trunk highway across country borders in a way that maximizes access to markets for all cities with populations of more than X million in the countries cofinancing the venture.

Network econometrics based on simple market access measures could miss important aspects concerning the placement of transport corridors. Two such aspects are the *importance* and *relevance* of potential market access or trade connectivity. Page et al. (1999) highlight importance and relevance as components of *centrality* in the context of Google's system of ranking pages for searches (PageRank). The criterion "importance" considers whether the new (transport) connection from city A is to a city B, which is "well connected" with many other connections that provide indirect connections for city A, or to not-so-well-connected city C, which does not provide these indirect markets with access connections. For instance, Donaldson and Hornbeck (2016) adjust the simple measure of market access for importance.

The relevance of the potential direct and indirect connections that a transport corridor can provide also needs to be considered. The potential of connecting to big but already highly competitive markets may not be as useful for city A in a developing country as connecting to another big city with markets that are less competitive, where country A's exporters can more easily penetrate this new market with old or new products. For instance, Baum-Snow et al. (2016) consider the relevance of market access and adjust for market competition in their market access measure. But relevance could be a much richer concept, including matching demand preferences and the structure of the supplying industries, as well as distinguishing between the relevance of market access for exporters and importers (Duranton et al, 2013). For instance, in calculating market access, a possible new transport connection of a district in country A that exports pork to a city with a large population that observes Jewish kosher or Muslim halal rituals (and thus does not eat pork) in neighboring country B can be viewed as a new potential market. However, this market could be irrelevant for the pork-exporting district and should be heavily discounted, if not discarded.

Existing transport and trade obstacles (prohibitive border crossings, tariff and non-tariff trade barriers) also need to be considered for relevance. The literature on trade connectivity considers such aspects of

relevance, but without the focus on the wider economic benefits for households along transport corridors (Baniya et al. 2017). The probability of these obstacles being removed in the future also affects the relevance of the potential new connections.

As the number of considerations increases, their relevance and importance—and thus centrality—could be summarized by spatial propensity scores that capture the likelihood that exporters and importers in each location, such as a district through which the potential transport corridor will pass—will benefit from the new connectivity and market access. But even such rich and spatially disaggregated propensity scores could fall short of the future reality because of changing global value chains, urbanization, and city development strategies.

In this dynamic context, potential cities to be connected by transport corridors could be thought of as agents with varied decision rules (heterogenous response functions). So, too, can corporations that shape the growth of these cities (for instance, if they decide to reshape their global supply chains as market dynamics change). Suppose that, in the next 20 years, one city wants to become an international financial center, another city wants to attract research-and-development clusters and become the next Silicon Valley, and yet another city wants to become a major manufacturing hub. These three cities would be expected to respond to potential connectivity in different ways. Further, knowing or observing the responses of other cities, a city can reinforce its strategy or change it. Considering such varied decision rules of agents could be important for determining which two cities are the priority to connect through transport corridors and via which mode of transport (road, rails, waterways, airways).[3]

To exploit the full potential of network econometrics and incorporate historical, existing, and forward-looking perspectives, agent-based modeling (ABM) could be helpful. Like GE econometrics and RF regression analysis, ABM could provide greater structure to network econometrics to help identify how a corridor intervention will affect different cities, countries, and continents directly and indirectly through second-round and systemic interactions. But like GE econometrics, ABM needs many assumptions. Its highly nonlinear nature makes it prone to big errors if mis-specified (even partly). Moreover, simpler market access measures could be readily linked to development outcomes such as income growth, at least in an RF manner (Donaldson and Hornbeck 2016; Duranton, Morrow, and Turner 2013). This second step could be prohibitive for more complex network econometric approaches such as ABM.

Given the state of development in network econometrics, a combination of approaches could be useful to help determine the priorities for placing transport corridors. Computations based on the notion of centrality could be the most reliable currently. More research into developing ABM that views cities as heterogeneous agents could be the most promising approach to help determine corridor placements in the future.

REDUCED-FORM ECONOMETRICS

Single-equation, reduced-form (RF) econometrics is the most popular method in the literature to evaluate the ex post impact of transport infrastructure on development outcomes. The most rigorous setups involve difference-in-difference estimation based on a carefully selected control group and instrumental variables (IVs) to address possible biases due to endogenous placements. To further sharpen identification, such a setup is often complemented by a set of conditioning variables, matching techniques, or placebo treatments (see chapter 4 in this volume; and Redding and Turner 2014).[4] With proper IV identification and controls, RF regressions are readily applicable to (ex post) evaluations. Further, their flexible functional form helps in adding terms that interact transport corridor connectivity with

unique characteristics of locales and population groups to study the conditional (heterogenous) effects of a transport corridor and the effects of its complementary polices (see chapter 6). Carefully selecting control groups and finding both a valid and relevant instrument—one that is both exogenous to the dependent variable and able to sufficiently explain the treatment variable—are probably the biggest technical struggles for the RF approach.

The main issue for policy decision making is that RF regressions do not enable structural identification of the transmission mechanisms and the analysis of system-wide (GE) effects—including indirect (second-round) effects and effects beyond the immediate vicinity of the transport corridor. Moreover, the traditional RF setups are constrained to analyzing the corridor effect on one development outcome at a time.

Some of the shortfalls of single-equation, RF econometrics could be remedied by readily available extensions of the approach. For instance, RF regressions with a common factor (a corridor intervention) for a panel of development outcomes can help analyze the impact of transport infrastructure investment on multiple development outcomes (such as income, equity, and environmental quality) together.[5] Likewise, extending single-equation, RF regressions to a system of RF equations such as vector auto- regressions (VARs) can help analyze GE effects in an RF manner. For instance, the New Economic Geography theory could be used to motivate the vector of endogenous variables to be included in the (spatial) VAR without imposing the possibly problematic structural restrictions (functional form, cross-equation coefficient restrictions) implied by the theory. One example of an effort in this direction is the work of Revoltella et al. (2016) on transport connectivity and economic resilience.

To date, RF regressions have typically focused on effects near transport corridors and not those further away. While using macroeconomic data and simulations lacks locational specifics compared to spatial data, it could be a good complement to capture more system-wide (GE) effects when using RF econometrics.

STRUCTURAL (GENERAL EQUILIBRIUM) ECONOMETRICS

Using calibrated or estimated parameters, structural general equilibrium (GE) econometrics is the second most popular type of econometrics for appraising the impact of transport connectivity on development outcomes (Bosker, Deichmann, and Roberts 2015; Burgess and Donaldson 2012). It helps analyze several development outcomes jointly, while identifying clear transmission channels, linking model parameters to behaviors of economic agents founded in microeconomic theory, and considering feedback effects and counterfactuals. These models hold great potential. But the current applications are rather far from exploiting it.

From the current policy-making perspective, the existing applications of structural GE econometrics have some shortfalls. Typically, the structural application considers only a limited number of transmission mechanisms and clearing markets (such as labor mobility only, ignoring land and capital market channels). Neglecting some transmission mechanism can distort the predicted dynamics, including because of possibly omitted variables and the resulting estimation bias when the structural models are estimated without some important markets. Further, the assumed functional forms and cross-equation coefficient restriction (see, for instance appendix A in Bosker Deichmann, and Roberts 2015) could help increase the precision (efficiency) of the model. However, if they are not in line with the process that generated the data in reality, these restrictions could result in low fit to the data (reality) and low predictive ability.[6]

This is not to imply that structural estimations should be viewed as inferior for future policy making and abandoned. To the contrary, structural GE econometrics is probably the most promising tool for appraising the WEB of transport corridor interventions. More effort is needed to develop its potential. These efforts should focus on covering all important markets, heterogeneous impacts, and system estimations that could help improve the data fit of both structural GE and other structural models.[7] The models also need to be back-tested, including simulating moments of the model variables and comparing them to the moments of actual data.

USEFUL DEVELOPMENTS IN THE LITERATURE

A number of papers are trying to bridge the different econometric methods to advance understanding of the effect of large infrastructure projects on socioeconomic development. Several studies have linked measures of market access (network econometrics) with income growth using RF regressions—including estimated equations motivated by a structural model (Donaldson and Hornbeck 2016; Duranton, Morrow, and Turner 2013). This approach, however, suffers from endogeneity and recursive problems between market access and growth. Endogenizing market access (introducing a first-stage regression) or using instrumental variables could help. But, using this approach, the literature links market access only to a single final outcome (income) at a time, but not multiple outcomes. Also, it has not considered GE effects, including the possibility of losers left behind in regions with low connectivity to markets when the majority of the population emigrates to regions that are served by the transport corridor. It also has not taken into account the role of complementary interventions (such as access to finance to scale up the production of local tradable goods and ease emigration).

Some academics and practitioners point to the methodological tension between RF and

GE econometrics. Several recent papers examine this possible tension by comparing these two econometric approaches quantitatively. For instance, Baum-Snow et al. (2016), Rothenberg (2013), and Alder, Roberts, and Tewari (forthcoming) compare the results of RF and GE econometrics applied to the India Golden Quadrilateral (GQ) Highways. While the RF and GE results differ in all studies, only Baum-Snow et al. (2016) reject the results of GE modeling as inferior and possibly misleading.

Even more recently, some papers have attempted to combine network and GE econometrics (Alder 2017; Fajgelbaum and Schaal 2017). Because the task is computationally very intensive, heuristic network rules and algorithms from operational research are used to implement such approaches more easily. Although the two applications do not go as far as modeling cross-border agent networks—for instance, in trade and global value chains—they are quite promising. For instance, Alder (2017) combines a network algorithm for highway placement with GE econometrics to estimate a counterfactual for the Indian policy on the Golden Quadrilateral (GQ) highways system (see chapter 4 and 6) by following China's policy for the National Express Network (see chapter 4). He finds that the GQ construction generated aggregate income surpluses, but they were shared unequally across regions—including because the counterfactual network would have been larger than the GQ, supporting greater sharing with lagging regions, and thus stimulate further aggregate gains. Fajgelbaum and Schaal (2017) combine operations research methods and a neoclassical trade model with mobile labor to estimate the GDP gains from an optimal expansion of current networks in 25 European countries. They find large gains from such an optimal expansion.

Cross-border applications that account for corresponding obstacles and imperfections are still scarce. Also, neglecting the role of and dynamics in the movement of capital and the frictions in land use could lead to incomplete specifications when trying to match the model to the processes generating the actual data. Hence, despite the potential leap in theoretical rigor and precision (efficiency) of this economic synthesis, its reliability in practice is open to question.

CONCLUSION

There are trade-offs in using a single econometric approach to appraise a large transport infrastructure project. The main trade-off could be between efficiency and the reliability of the chosen approach. Econometrics that is more explicit about the economic structure and transmission mechanisms behind economic corridors could produce much more precise and intelligent estimates if correctly and completely specified. But if misspecified (even partly) or incompletely specified, such econometrics can produce misleading results. In contrast, RF econometrics struggles with endogenous placement issues and ignoring indirect effects. This trade-off could apply to estimating both the optimal placement of a transport corridor and the optimal intervention design to diffuse its overall net economic benefits.

Conditional effects and interactions of corridor placement with other local factors—such as market conditions, policies, and institutions—are important but rarely addressed. For RF regressions, the struggle to separate the effects of transport infrastructure from other parallel effects—that is, to achieve clean identification—makes the inclusion of interactive (conditional) effects problematic. Despite possible biases due to issues with reversed causality (endogeneity), these interactive effects need to be applied more (see chapter 6). Because nonlinear structural GE models are commonly log-linearized using only the first-order Taylor series expansion (not a higher order one), interaction terms typically disappear from the structural GE econometrics. But they do not need to.

TABLE S6.1 **There are trade-offs between different econometric approaches to appraise proposed corridors**

Econometrics approach	Current reliability in determining:		Econometric potential in determining:		Further research needed to attain the potential:	
	Placement	WEB	Placement	WEB	Placement	WEB
Network	High	Lowest	High	Low	High	Low
Reduced form	Low	Highest	Low	Medium	Low	Medium
General equilibrium	Low	High	Medium	High	Low	High

Source: Melecky (forthcoming).
Note: WEBs = wider economic benefits.

Hence, GE econometrics has a great potential for credibly researching the conditional effects of transport corridors.

Table S6.1 illustrates the trade-offs between different econometric approaches. It roughly sorts the corridor econometrics discussed in this spotlight by their current ability, econometric potential, and amount of work needed ("distance") to attain this potential in helping policy makers reliably determine corridor placement and the potential of a corridor intervention package for spreading economic benefits. For instance, network econometrics probably has the greatest ability currently to appraise the optimal placement of cross-border transport corridors. However, its ability to appraise the design of corridor intervention package is rather small because it focuses more on immediate and intermediate outcomes than on final development outcomes—the WEB that households receive. Current structural GE econometrics could be efficient in appraising expected WEB, but it is less reliable. Structural GE econometrics has the greatest potential to appraise WEB efficiently and reliably, but considerable research is needed to meet this potential.

Since the process of deciding on the placement and design of transport corridor intervention is dynamic, sequencing more reliable and more efficient econometric methods could be also useful. Prefeasibility studies and assessments could be deployed, using only simpler and more reliable econometrics (network econometrics focused on the concept of centrality, combined with RF regressions). Later, feasibility studies and project appraisals could introduce more efficient methods (network econometrics based on the integration of heterogeneous agents and structural GE econometrics) to think through possibly richer dynamics of interactions, as well as the direct, indirect, and second-round effects of the corridor intervention.

Finally, the appraisal econometrics that is currently available does not estimate the link between the potential for market *access* and the actual *use* of this access by firms (in terms of trade and travel) and people (in terms of travel for jobs, education, health, and the like). The econometrics largely assumes that the link exists and is on average the same in every context. But this assumption can be problematic. For instance, if complementary factors are needed so that firms and people can actually use the market access potential provided by transport connectivity, this link cannot be assumed. It can be broken in many countries, or vary greatly across different economic actors and/or geographic units. The appraisal econometrics for transport corridors and related research should seek to shed more light on the empirical dimensions of this microeconomic mechanism—including by building on existing anecdotal evidence (see spotlights 1 and 2).

NOTES

1. Also see chapter 4 in this book.
2. See https://en.wikipedia.org/wiki/Silk_Road; https://en.wikipedia.org/wiki/Grand_Trunk _Road.

3. Railway and waterways are more suitable for bulk transport, while roads and airways could be more suitable for fragmented supply chains (boutique production, such as Italian shoes) or high-value perishables (for example, Maldivian tuna to Japan).

4. Other empirical, "reduced-form" methods include semiparametric and nonparametric econometrics (Pagan and Ullah 1999; Graham, McCoy, and Stephens 2014).

5. See chapter 4 for application of this idea in the context of a metaregression analysis.

6. For the comparison to the reduce form model to be fair, one must compare the log-linearized version of the nonlinear GE models to the RF models. But in this case, the predicted number of relevant variables by GE models to be included in the econometrics is also typically smaller than the number typically used by RF models. Also, the cross-equation restrictions are binding and increasing the efficiency/robustness trade-offs, especially if the log-linearization were to be done at a higher-order Taylor expansion.

7. See Lall, Wang, and Deichmann (2010) for the three-stage least-squares method; and Fan and Chan-Kang (2008) for the full-information, maximum-likelihood method.

REFERENCES

Alder, S. 2017. "Chinese Roads in India: The Effect of Transport Infrastructure on Economic Development." Working Paper, University of North Carolina, Chapel Hill.

Alder, S., M. Roberts, and M. Tewari. Forthcoming. "The Effect of Transport Infrastructure on India's Urban and Rural Development." Unpublished manuscript. Forthcoming.

Bakker, P., C. Koopmans, and P. Nijkamp. 2010. "Appraisal of Integrated Transport Policies." In *Integrated Transport: From Policy to Practice*, edited by D. Banister, 117–36. Abingdon, UK: Routledge.

Baniya, S., S. Murray, N. Rocha, and M. Ruta. 2017. "The Trade Effects of the New Silk Road." Presentation, World Bank, Washington, June.

Baum-Snow, N. B., J. V. Henderson, M. A. Turner, Q. Zhang, and L. Brandt. 2016. "Highways, Market Access and Urban Growth in China." Working Paper C-89114-CHN-1, International Growth Centre, London.

Berg, C. N., U. Deichmann, Y. Liu, and H. Selod. 2017. "Transport Policies and Development." *Journal of Development Studies* 53 (4): 465–80.

Bosker, E. M., U. Deichmann, and M. Roberts. 2015. "Hukou and Highways: The Impact of China's Spatial Development Policies on Urbanization and Regional Inequality." Policy Research Working Paper 7350, World Bank, Washington, DC.

Bosker, E. M., and H. Garretsen, H., 2010. "Trade Costs in Empirical New Economic Geography." *Papers in Regional Science* 89 (3): 485–511.

Burgess, R., and D. Donaldson. 2012. "Can Openness to Trade Reduce Income Volatility? Evidence from Colonial India's Famine Era." Preliminary draft.

Burgess, R., R. Jedwab, E. Miguel, and A. Morjaria. 2015. "The Value of Democracy: Evidence from Road Building in Kenya." *American Economic Review* 105 (6): 1817–51.

Donaldson, D., and R. Hornbeck. 2016. "Railroads and American Economic Growth: A 'Market Access' Approach." *Quarterly Journal of Economics* 131 (2): 799–858.

Duranton, G., P. M. Morrow, and M. A. Turner. 2013. "Separate Appendices with Supplemental Material for: 'Roads and Trade: Evidence from the US.'" http://real.wharton.upenn.edu/~duranton/Duranton_Papers/Current_Research/Supp_FunTrade.pdf.

Fajgelbaum, P. D., and E. Schaal. 2017. "Optimal Transport Networks in Spatial Equilibrium." Working Paper 23200, National Bureau of Economic Research, Cambridge, MA.

Fan, S., and C. Chan-Kang. 2008. "Regional Road Development, Rural and Urban Poverty: Evidence from China." *Transport Policy* 15 (5): 305–14.

Gastner, M. T., and M. E. Newman. 2006. "Shape and Efficiency in Spatial Distribution Networks." *Journal of Statistical Mechanics: Theory and Experiment* 2006 (1): P01015.

Graham, D. J., E. J. McCoy, and D. A. Stephens, 2014. "Quantifying Causal Effects of Road Network Capacity Expansions on Traffic Volume and Density via a Mixed Model Propensity Score Estimator." *Journal of American Statistical Association* 109 (508): 1440–49.

Laird, J. J., and A. J. Veneables. 2017. "Transport Investment and Economic Performance: A

Framework for Project Appraisal." *Transport Policy* 56 (2017): 1–11.

Lall, S. V., H. G. Wang, and U. Deichmann. 2010. "Infrastructure and City Competitiveness in India." Working Paper 22/2010, WIDER (World Institute for Development Economics Research), United Nations University, Tokyo.

Melecky, Martin. Forthcoming. "Appraisal Econometrics for Transport Corridors: Optimal Placement, Intervention Design, and Wider Economic Benefits." Forthcoming as MPRA Paper, University Library of Munich, Munich.

Melo, P. C., D. J. Graham, and R. Brage-Ardao. 2013. "The Productivity of Transport Infrastructure Investment: A Meta-analysis of Empirical Evidence." *Regional Science and Urban Economics* 43 (5): 695–706.

Pagan, A., and A. Ullah. 1999. *Nonparametric Econometrics (Themes in Modern Econometrics)*. New York: Cambridge University Press.

Page, L., S. Brin, R. Motwani, and T. Winograd. 1999. "The PageRank Citation Ranking: Bringing Order to the Web." Stanford InfoLab, Stanford, CA.

Redding, S. J., and M. A. Turner. 2014. "Transportation Costs and the Spatial Organization of Economic Activity." Working Paper 20235, National Bureau of Economic Research, Cambridge, MA.

Revoltella D., P. Brutscher, A. Tsiotras, and C. Weiss. 2016. "Linking Local Business with Global Growth Opportunities: The Role of Infrastructure." *Oxford Review of Economic Policy* 32 (3): 410–30.

Rothenberg, A. D. 2013. "Transport Infrastructure and Firm Location Choice in Equilibrium: Evidence from Indonesia's Highways." Working paper, under revision.

Starr, S. F., 2007. *The New Silk Roads: Transport and Trade in Greater Central Asia*. Baltimore: Johns Hopkins University Press.

Straub, S. 2011. "Infrastructure and Development: A Critical Appraisal of the Macro-Level Literature." *Journal of Development Studies* 47 (5): 683–708.

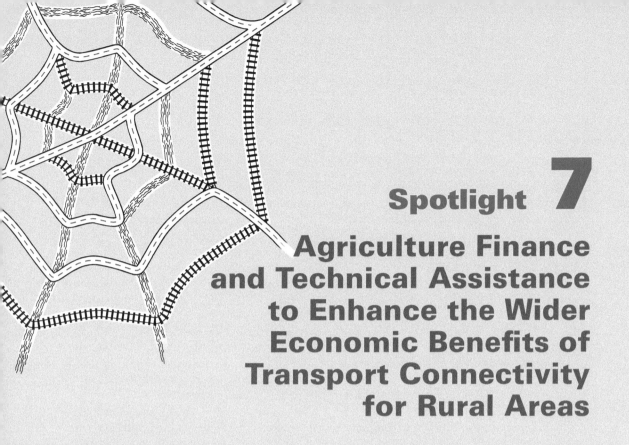

Spotlight 7

Agriculture Finance and Technical Assistance to Enhance the Wider Economic Benefits of Transport Connectivity for Rural Areas

For several decades, Asian, African, and Latin American countries have improved highways, secondary roads, waterways, and railroads, with some impressive results. Farmers and others in rural areas who are close to these corridors have used these newly reliable transport links to get inputs and take their products to market.

For instance, farmers near new corridors in one Nepal district sold more of their products and increased their incomes by 20 percent because they accessed markets more easily and lowered their transport costs, the Asian Development Bank found (ADB 2009). Similarly, 42,000 small farmers in Peru improved their productivity and incomes because of the newly established linkages with processors and traders in the corridors, according to the U.S. Agency for International Development (USAID 2008). In some areas, the benefits have helped reduce poverty. For example, in Bangladesh, after the Jamuna Bridge was built in 1998, the western part of the country was linked to the main consumption centers in the east. With the arrival of the bridge, agricultural techniques improved faster in the west than in the east (Gautam 2016).

To seize the opportunities brought by improved transport connectivity, accessible business services—such as different agricultural finance instruments, insurance, and warehouses—are essential for micro, small, and medium-sized farmers.

Consider the case of Raju, a small farmer in an Indian village, who produced rice for his family and sold his surplus at a local market. When a highway was built that connected his village to the town of Chhindwara, his family income dropped dramatically. New traders and producers moved into his area, which forced small farmers like him to lower their prices or crowded them out altogether. Thus Raju had to find new business opportunities. He learned that producing tomatoes was profitable, now that transport costs were lower and the time to take the crop to market was reduced. But he needed start-up financing to grow the new crop. While his family and friends lent him some funds, the amount was not enough to buy the inputs. He also needed to learn how to market his crop.

For this, he needed some way to access finance and information. Traditionally, when small farmers such as Raju tried to expand their crops or start new farm-related activities, they could not get the credit they needed to buy seeds and fertilizer or cover the costs of harvesting, processing, marketing, and transporting their products. Or they could not provide banks with the information needed to prove they were viable borrowers. Or they did not have the necessary collateral. Thus they turned to informal, local moneylenders, who often charged steep interest rates. With the improved transport links, some government agencies and nongovernmental organizations have moved into previously unserved rural areas, along with private financial institutions.

Organizations such as these remain a better option for rural dwellers like Raju to get credit and other financial and technical services than online banking, which does not provide larger credit amounts and long-term credit. Moreover, online lending often requires credit seekers to apply in person at financial institutions—which are located in cities or towns that are so far away that the potential borrowers do not make the trip.

Improved transport connectivity has brought financial institutions to more remote areas, which can help farmers gain access to credit, increase their productivity, expand their businesses, and add value to their products. In India, for example, once the country invested in roads and markets, some commercial banks moved into rural areas, which in turn provided farmers with the funds they needed to meet their increasing demand for fertilizer, tractors, water pumps, and livestock, and thus improve their output, a World Bank study found (Binswanger, Khandker, and Rosenzweig 1989). Governments also encourage financial institutions to enter areas where commercial finance for agriculture is limited, particularly where transport corridors were improved.

Governments have also sought various ways to promote lending to agriculture. These include using credit guarantees, interest rate subsidies and caps, and warehouse receipts as collateral for loans. They have extended subsidized crop insurance, offered grants that match loans from financial institutions, provided venture capital funds, and set

mandatory lending quotas for certain sectors they see as priorities.

In South Asia, lending quotas are the tools most often used and account for the largest volume of agriculture finance. For example, in India, where farmers were mostly financed by money lenders until 1950, the government introduced a quota scheme 40 years ago. Since then, financial institutions have been required to lend to specific sectors, such as agriculture. The policy seems to have channeled more commercial bank loans to the agriculture sector (Nathan Associates 2013).

India also introduced subsidized crop insurance linked to credit, which increased banks' willingness to make agricultural loans. In addition, the country has a range of financial institutions—state, cooperative, and commercial banks—that can reach different types of farmers and micro, small, and medium-sized enterprises (MSMEs). It also uses wholesale-retail links that allow commercial banks to purchase loan portfolios from local financial institutions to meet their priority lending requirements. However, this is a system unique to India. Its many types of public and private financial institutions and wholesale-retail arrangements would be hard to duplicate elsewhere.

Although lending quotas have expanded farmers' access to loans, they have also had some negative effects. They have increased the costs of lending for banks. The quality of the banks' loan portfolios has dropped because they were required to lend to riskier clients.

In Bangladesh, the use of another tool—interest rate caps on agricultural credit (from commercial banks) (Bangladesh Bank 2017)—may have squeezed banks' profit margins and discouraged them from lending to the sector. Caps may lead banks to exclude more marginal clients, especially those who need smaller loans and/or live in rural areas.

In Sri Lanka, in an attempt to motivate public and private banks to lend to agriculture, the government introduced partial credit guarantees to share the credit risk with lenders. In Mozambique, the Berira Catalayatic Fund (BCR), a $20 million venture capital fund, helps supply goods and services to small farmers located along a particular transport corridor. Managed by AgDevCo and financed by the governments of Norway, the Netherlands, and the United Kingdom, it offers debt and equity loans (from $50,000 to $500,000) and technical assistance to the investor companies. By 2013, BCF had invested more than $3 million in 12 projects that had helped over 10,000 farmers (Gálvez Nogales 2014).

In Tanzania, the government introduced a matching grant scheme, called the Catalytic Trust Fund, to support agribusiness companies that create jobs and income for small farmers. In Sri Lanka, the government also has extended matching grants (linked to the farmers' own funds and loans) to encourage groups of small farmers to invest in agricultural technologies and improve postharvest practices. These improvements leverage the bank loans and increase the likelihood of repayment.

Farmers' ability to get loans can also increase when producers, processors, and traders can use their warehouse inventories (called warehouse receipts) as collateral to secure loans. In India, the government also subsidizes storage infrastructure—specifically, the construction of rural warehouses—which encourages farmers to use the warehouse receipts scheme to obtain credit.

When governments or their agencies have improved the transport links in Southeast Asia, Africa, and Latin America and the Caribbean through economic and transport corridor projects, they have often offered technical assistance on various aspects of production—such as marketing, information technology, management practices, market research, postharvest handling, agroprocessing, and connecting smaller agribusiness to larger firms—which promoted agricultural finance and investment. For example, a USAID project to reduce poverty in Peru focused on developing infrastructure and businesses, which promoted investment

in these areas. This approach has been replicated in other Latin American countries (Gálvez Nogales 2014).

Efforts have also been made to create farmer cooperatives, which can help small farmers achieve a critical mass to obtain loans. The cooperatives can also act as intermediaries between the farmers, public warehouses, agribusinesses, and banks. In India, for example, Frito Lay, a subsidiary of PepsiCo, helped establish cooperatives to contract with the company and provided them with inputs and technical assistance. More than 14,000 potato farmers participated (Dutta, Dutta, and Sengupta 2016). Elsewhere, cooperatives are involved in logistics, such as transporting products to warehouses and silos, and arranging for the credit the producers need to buy inputs, scale up their operations, and improve postharvest marketing.

While some of the approaches work well in some countries, they are not a one-size-fits-all solution. Each country's situation must be examined to determine which of the measures is needed or feasible. Where possible, the private sector should be included, even if its involvement extends the time needed to achieve results. Moreover, where the government offers financial support or subsidies, these efforts should be temporary and be confined to the start-up phase of creating sustainable financial services. Otherwise, they become long-term budget outlays. Finally, the risks of overexposure in a portfolio from expanding targeted loans to a certain sector or geographic area along a transport corridor must be carefully assessed.

REFERENCES

ADB (Asian Development Bank). 2009. "Asian Development Bank's Contribution to Inclusive Development through Assistance for Rural Roads." Evaluation Study. https://www.oecd.org/derec/adb/47166759.pdf.

Bangladesh Bank. 2017. "ACD Circular No. 02: Agricultural & Rural Credit Policy & Program for the FY 2017-18." https://www.bb.org.bd /mediaroom/circulars/circulars.php#

Binswanger, H. P., S. R. Khandker, and M. R. Rosenzweig. 1989. "How Infrastructure and Financial Institutions Affect Agricultural Output and Investment in India." World Bank, Washington, DC.

Dutta, A., A. Dutta, and S. Sengupta. 2016. "A Case Study of Pepsico Contract Farming for Potatoes." *IOSR Journal of Business and Management*. http://www.iosrjournals.org/iosr -jbm/papers/ICSE%20Conference/14.75-85. pdf.

Gálvez Nogales, E. 2014. "Making Economic Corridors Work for the Agricultural Sector."

Agribusiness and Food Industries Series No. 4, Food and Agriculture Organization of the United Nations, Rome.

Gautam, M., and R. Faruqee. 2016. *Dynamics of Rural Growth in Bangladesh: Sustaining Poverty Reduction.* Washington, DC: World Bank.

Nathan Associates. 2013. "Re-Prioritizing Priority Sector Lending in India: Impact of Priority Sector Lending on India's Commercial Banks." Economic Impact Analysis. Nathan Associates, Arlington, VA.

USAID (U.S. Agency for International Development). 2008. "The Peru Poverty Reduction and Alleviation (PRA) Program." http://pdf.usaid.gov/pdf_docs/Pdacn111.pdf.

6

An Illustrative Appraisal of Complementary Interventions to Enhance the Wider Economic Benefits of Transport Corridors

Policy makers are increasingly interested in appraising large transport infrastructure proposals using rigorous methods beyond a simple cost-benefit analysis. They want these appraisals to be comprehensive and cover the "wider economic benefits" (WEB) of these investments—that is, benefits that go beyond savings of travel time and vehicle operating costs. They would like to ensure that such transport infrastructure projects benefit both the big firms involved in foreign trade and the small enterprises that could take advantage of the increased connectivity and market access to pursue new economic opportunities. They are also interested in mitigating the possible negative impact of corridors, whether on environmental quality, income inequality, or gender inclusion. They would like to identify any potential losers the corridor investments might produce and offset those losses to the extent possible.

This chapter develops an illustrative framework to appraise large transport infrastructure projects in South Asia and beyond. As an illustration, it focuses on India's Golden Quadrilateral (GQ) and North-South-East-West (NSEW) highway systems (map 6.1).[1] First, it shows how to estimate the impacts these two systems have on WEB (the overall net spatial impact on development outcomes, such as economic welfare, equity, social inclusion, and environmental quality) by applying the "difference-in-difference" (DiD) method to district-level data from 1994 to 2011. Second, it discusses how to examine the dependence of these impacts on initial conditions in input (capital, labor, land) markets, output (product) markets, and governance by using interaction terms in the DiD regressions. Third, it shows how to use the estimated DiD model to simulate an appraisal of two proposed highway systems in the region: the

MAP 6.1 **Two highways in India are used to illustrate the appraisal framework**

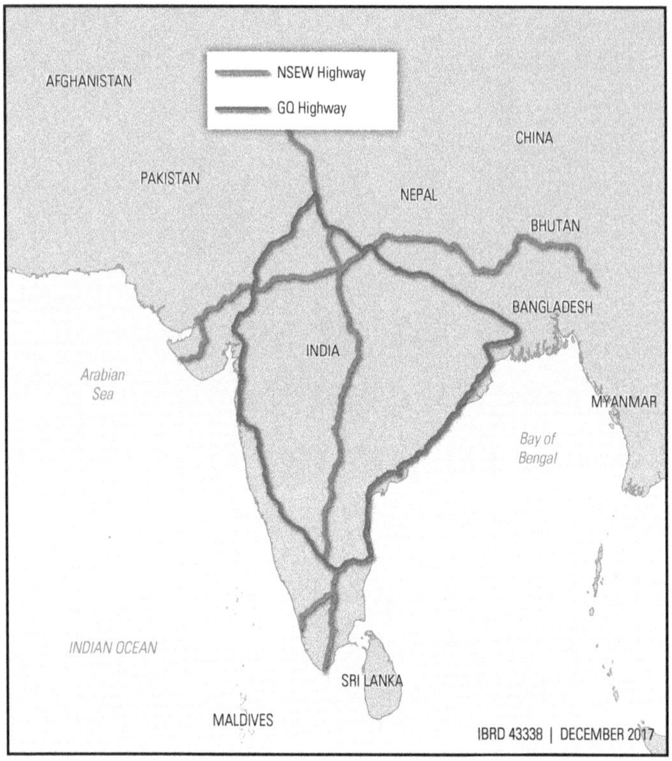

Source: National Highways Authority of India, http://www.nhai.org/gqmain_english.htm.
Disclaimer: This publication follows the World Bank's practice in references to member designations, borders, and maps. The boundaries, colors, denominations and other information shown in any map in this work do not imply any judgment on the part of The World Bank, ADB, JICA or DFID concerning the legal status of any territory or the endorsement or acceptance of such boundaries.

> **The efficiency of land, labor, financial, and product markets and the effectiveness of local policies and institutions can help determine how widely the economic benefits are shared.**

China-Pakistan Economic Corridor (CPEC) in Pakistan, and the Kolkata-Dhaka corridor in Bangladesh (Melecky, Sharma, and Subhash forthcoming).

The WEB include measures of welfare (district-level GDP and household consumption); inequality (district-level poverty); social inclusion (total employment and female employment in regular wage jobs); and environmental quality (thickness of aerosol particles, carbon dioxide emissions, and nitrogen dioxide emissions). In addition, the estimation looks at the structural transformation in employment (the share of farm versus non-farm employment), an intermediate outcome of interest (see chapter 4). The change in connectivity is measured by the distance from the GQ (NSEW) highway and is identified following the method developed by Ghani, Goswami, and Kerr (2016) to estimate the impact of the GQ corridor.[2] Capital market conditions are measured using indicators of household and firm-level access to banking. Labor market conditions are captured with rates of literacy and secondary schooling. Land markets conditions are measured using indicators of land use patterns. Product markets conditions are captured with indicators of industrial composition and private ownership. Governance is measured using a state-level index that looks at infrastructure; social services; fiscal performance; justice, law, and order; and the quality of the legislature.

A MULTI-STEP METHODOLOGY WAS USED TO ESTIMATE THE WIDER ECONOMIC BENEFITS OF HIGHWAYS IN INDIA

The study uses a differences-in-differences methodology to estimate the impact of the highways on the district-level outcomes of interest (figure 6.1). This method compares the change in the outcome of interest after the highway was constructed in districts located close to the new highways (the "treatment districts") to those located far away from them (the "control districts"). The computed differences capture the change in the outcome before and after the highway was built. It controls for the confounding effect of unobserved factors that do not vary over time (that is, factors that are time-invariant). For instance, districts

FIGURE 6.1   The difference-in-difference method is used to estimate the impact of the two existing Indian highways

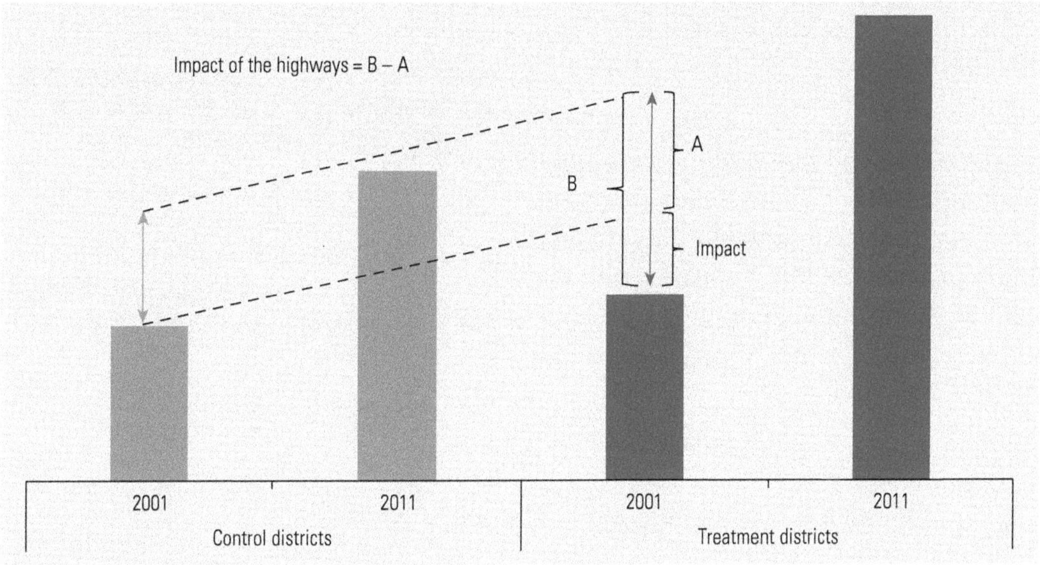

Source: Corridor Study Team.
Note: The difference-in-difference method assumes that the change (without intervention) of control and treatment districts is the same between 2001 and 2011 (the parallel path assumption). Therefore, the average change without intervention (A) is obtained by subtracting the results of 2001 from the results of 2011 for control districts. The change in treatment districts between 2001 and 2011 is B. The impact of the treatment (in this case, building the GQ or NSEW highway system) is obtained by subtracting A from B. GQ = Golden Quadrilateral; NSEW = North-South-East-West.

that are near the highways could have been relatively productive even before the highways were built. The set of second differences compares the change across treatment and control districts. That is, it controls for the confounding effect of unobserved factors common to control and treatment districts that do vary over time (factors that are time-varying). For instance, it is possible that reforms undertaken around the same time as the highway was built caused a general rise in productivity across India. Thus, the identification assumption behind this approach is that unobserved, time-varying factors had the same impact across both control and treatment districts (see box 6.1).[3]

The analysis further assesses the possibility that investments in highways generate wider economic benefits only when certain market conditions are present that allow people to exploit opportunities opened up by the improved access to markets. That is, highway and other large transport investments may need to be complemented with other policy and institutional reforms to support the transport corridor intervention in specific locales. For example, highways could have a bigger impact on firms in areas with better access to finance or to skills, or in areas with better functioning land markets.

The study undertakes this assessment by adding interactive labor, land, and capital market conditions to the regression framework (figure 6.2). The impact of complementary factors is the difference of the impact of highway in districts with low levels of complementary factors and the impact of highway in districts with high levels of complementary factors. The impact of the highway was obtained using the DiD method (see figure 6.1). Taking the

difference of the differences therefore makes the method a triple-difference (DDD) estimation (see box 6.2).

THE WIDER ECONOMIC BENEFITS OF HIGHWAYS ARE ESTIMATED USING DISTRICT-LEVEL DATA

The analysis uses a district-level panel data set to estimate the impact of the highways. Districts are the primary administrative unit of India below the state level. In 2010–11, the last year in the data set, there were about 640 districts in India.

While public investments can increase net economic benefits in the aggregate, sharing those benefits widely across locations and specific population groups is more difficult, and depends on the effectiveness of complementary policies and institutions.

BOX 6.1   Estimating the average impacts of the highways

Formally, the underlying regression specification can be described as follows:

$$Y_{i,t} = \beta \times Highway_i \times Post_t^{Highway} + \phi_i + \varphi_t + \varepsilon_{i,t}. \qquad (6.1.1)$$

This regression is estimated on a district-level panel data set. Here, $Y_{i,t}$ is an outcome of interest in district i and year t. The dummy variable $Post_t^{Highway}$ is equal to 1 in years after the highway has been completed, and 0 in the years before that. The dummy variable $Highway_i$ is equal to 1 in districts close to the new highways (the treatment districts) and 0 otherwise. The variable ϕ_i is a set of district fixed effects that controls for time-invariant district-level factors, and φ_t is a set of year dummies that controls for unobserved time-varying factors common to all districts. The impact of the highways is estimated by β, the coefficient on the treatment term (the interaction $Highway_i \times Post_t^{Highway}$), measuring how the change in the outcome after the highway was built differed across control and treatment districts.

This basic specification is adjusted to account for the fact that the estimation is simultaneously estimating the impacts of *two* highway networks, the GQ and the NSEW. There are two factors to consider in this regard. First, in estimating the impact of either highway network, it is

important to control for the presence of the other one. Second, the two networks could have had different impacts. In other words, there were two sets of treatment districts: those close to the GQ, and those close to the NSEW.

Following Ghani, Goswami, and Kerr (2016), districts were assigned to distance bands based on proximity of the district centroid (the geometric center of each district) to the GQ. The bands are: more than 100 kilometers (km) from the nearest GQ point; 40–100 km from the GQ; 0–40 km from the GQ; and nodal districts.[a] Indicators were then interacted for each district distance band with a variable indicating the years after the completion of the GC. This process was then repeated for the NSEW. Thus, the specification estimated is as follows:

$$Y_{i,t} = \beta^{GQ} \times GQ_i \times Post_t^{GQ} + \beta^{NSEW} \times NSEW_i \times Post_t^{NSEW} + \phi_i + \varphi_t + \varepsilon_{i,t}. \qquad (6.1.2)$$

Here, GQ_i (or $NSEW_i$) is a vector of dummies indicating the distance band from the GQ (or NSEW) to the centroid of district i, while $Post_t^{GQ}$ (or $Post_t^{NSEW}$) is a dummy equal to one in the years after the GQ (or NSEW) is completed. The

(box continued next page)

BOX 6.1   Estimating the average impacts of the highways (continued)

---

omitted distance band dummy corresponds to districts more than 100 km from the highway (GQ or NSEW). The variable ϕ_i is a set of district fixed effects, and φ_t is a set of year dummies (or state-year dummies).

Depending on the outcome, the panel dataset covers either four of the data spells (1994–95, 2000–01, 2004–05, and 2010–11) or just two spells (2000–01 and 2010–11). Since the GQ network was largely complete by 2005, the indicator $Post_t^{GQ}$ is set equal to 1 in the years 2004–05 and 2010–11, and 0 otherwise. Work on NSEW started after 2005. Thus $Post_t^{NSEW}$ is set equal to 1 only in 2010–11.[b]

The impact of the GQ is measured by the β^{GQ}, corresponding to the 0–40 distance band from the GQ, which is denoted by $\beta^{GQ,0-40}$ hereafter. Since the

estimation is controlling for $NSEW_i \times Post_t^{NSEW}$, $\beta^{GQ,0-40}$ in effect measures how the post-GQ change in the outcome differed between districts 0–40 km from the GQ highway (the GQ treatment group) and districts more than 100 km from both highways (the control group). Similarly, the impact of NSEW is measured by the β^{NSEW}, corresponding to the 0–40 distance band from the NSEW, denoted by $\beta^{NSEW,0-40}$. The main results tables thus report these two βs.

The preferred specification replaces the year fixed effects with more flexible state-year fixed effects. This controls for unobserved state-level differences in growth patterns, which is important, given the documented divergence in economic growth across Indian states.

---

a. As in Ghani, Goswami, and Kerr (2016), the estimation assigns nodal districts to a separate category, and does not treat them as treated districts. Nodal districts correspond to major metropolitan areas and their peripheries, and thus are distinct from the average Indian district.

b. Certain segments for the NSEW were not complete by 2011. The analysis takes this into account when assigning districts to distance bands around the NSEW.

The main source for the district-level data is the South Asia Spatial Database, which is being developed by the World Bank's Office of the Chief Economist for South Asia.[4] This database is intended to bring together data on India (and other South Asian economies) from a range of sources—such as official censuses, administrative records, surveys, satellite imagery, and official maps—into a single source of spatial platform data. It covers two points in time (2000–01 and 2010–11) and has four administrative levels (ranging in spatial detail from state or province, district, and town or village to hundreds of thousands of gridded cells, or "tiles").

This study selected those district-level variables from this database that measure specific WEB outcomes of interest and initial market conditions that could have interacted with the highways to generate varied impacts.

The analysis supplemented the spatial database variables with additional district-level measures of welfare and labor market conditions derived for this study from various rounds of India's National Sample Survey (NSS) of Employment and Unemployment. The NSS labor force data are available for 1994–95, 1999–2000, 2004–05, and 2010–11. Thus, the panel data set covers four years if the outcome variable is derived from the NSS data, and two years otherwise.

Table 6A.1 in online annex 6A lists the main outcome variables used in the study and their primary data sources. Measures are broken down by district. The outcome

> **The use of detailed spatial data and econometric analysis can add more rigor and depth to the appraisal of transport corridors.**

FIGURE 6.2   The triple difference-in-difference method is used to estimate how the impact of the highway depends on complementary factors

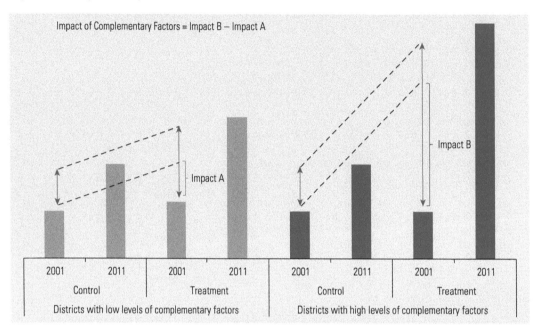

Source: Corridor Study Team.

BOX 6.2   Estimating conditional impacts: Do highway impacts depend on market conditions?

A further estimation also tests the hypotheses that the impact of the highways depended on conditions in factor and product markets. This estimation exploits variation in initial market conditions across districts, and adopts a triple-difference (DDD) approach by interacting the treatment $(Highway_i \times Post_t^{Highway})$ with variables capturing initial conditions in districts. The exact specification for the conditional impacts is as follows:

$$
\begin{aligned}
Y_{i,t} =\ & \beta^{GQ} \times GQ_i \times Post_t^{GQ} \\
& + \beta^{NSEW} \times NSEW_i \times Post_t^{NSEW} \\
& + \delta^{GQ} \times GQ_i \times Post_t^{GQ} \times Z_i \\
& + \delta^{NSEW} \times NSEW_i \times Post_t^{NSEW} \times Z_i \\
& + \gamma_1 Post_t^{GQ} \times Z_i + \gamma_2 Post_t^{NSEW} \times Z_i \\
& + \phi_i + \varphi_t + \varepsilon_{i,t}.
\end{aligned}
\qquad (6.2.1)
$$

Here, Z_i is a vector of initial conditions of interest in district i. The effect of initial conditions on the impact of the highways is estimated by the δs, the coefficients on the triple interaction term between $Highway_i \times Post_t^{Highway}$ and the vector of initial conditions Z_i.

For illustration, suppose that the Z_i in question is a variable measuring the efficiency of land markets, with higher values indicating more efficiency. The corresponding δ^{GQ} (or δ^{NSEW}) coefficient measures how the impact of the GQ (or the NSEW) depends on the efficiency of land markets. A positive estimate of this δ^{GQ} would imply that the impact of the GQ on the outcomes of interest was more positive in districts with more efficient land markets.

Many potential Z_i variables are available for each factor and product market. The estimation of interaction effects is also complicated by the fact that potential Z_i variables could be correlated.

(box continued next page)

BOX 6.2   Estimating conditional impacts: Do highway impacts depend on market conditions? *(continued)*

This makes it important to check if an estimated interaction term is robust to controlling for interactions with other potential Z_i variables. Hence, a practical issue arises of choosing a sparse regression specification while not ignoring the importance of controlling for correlated Z_i variables. The estimation addresses this issue by employing a simple iterative algorithm that starts with the full set of interaction variables and progressively drops interaction terms with low p-values, until only a small set of interaction terms is left. As a result of this procedure, the set of Z_i variables in the final specification varies across outcome variables. The procedure ensures that the results being shown are robust when controlling for other interaction terms.

---

variables correspond to four WEB categories: conomic welfare, inequality, social inclusion, and environmental quality. The measures of economic welfare are the GDP per capita and mean household per capita expenditures for each district, while inequality is measured using rural and urban poverty headcount rates. The measures of social inclusion are the percentage of the working-age population that is working and the percentage of regular-wage ("good") jobs to total employment, both disaggregated by gender (map 6.2). The second measure is the preferred measure of social inclusion. The measures of environmental quality include measures of particulate matter (smog) in the air, as well as measures of air pollution (carbon dioxide and nitrogen dioxide levels). A measure of deforestation was discarded because data were not sufficiently varied between districts near the highways (the "treated" districts) and those further away (the "control" districts). In addition to these final outcome variables, the analysis also estimates impacts on the breakdown of total employment by farm and nonfarm jobs, which is an intermediate outcome of interest.

Annex table 6A.2 lists the main interaction (initial market condition) variables and their sources. They are categorized by type of market: labor, land, capital, and product. The main labor market variables are measures of human capital as of 2001: the literacy rate and the percentage of those with a secondary school or higher educational qualification. The land market variables measure the extent of land that is suitable/available for agriculture, as well as the capacity of the district for mineral production. Thus, they are measures of the nature of land endowments in districts. The capital market variables measure household access to bank services (that is, to formal bank accounts), and firms' access to bank loans, as of 2001. The product market variables include a measure of product diversification, as well as a measure of the share of private firms in industrial establishments; both are intended to proxy for competition in the product market. A third measure is the share of agroprocessing in manufacturing. This variable proxies for the initial level of opportunity for factory work available to low-skilled workers, who constitute the majority of the workforce, particularly in

The design of corridor investments and their complementary policies should be based on a better understanding of the underling mechanisms that generate development outcomes.

MAP 6.2 **The data set includes a range of measures of wider economic benefits**

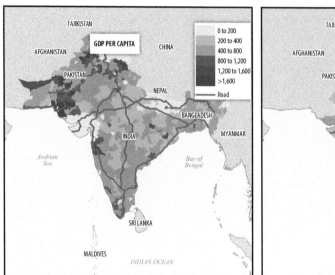
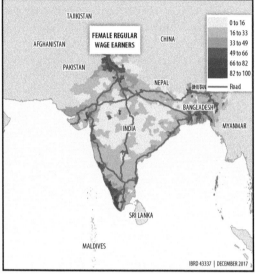

Sources: GDP per capita: India: Directorate of Economics and Statistics, Planning Commission, Government of India 2011; Bangladesh: Bangladesh Bureau of Statistics 2011; Pakistan: World Bank 2017a. The GDP per capita estimation is based on calculations based on the World Development Indicators and the South Asia Spatial Database (Li et al. 2015). Female regular wage employment: India: Census of India–Primary Census Abstract (PHC–PCA), Office of the Registrar General and Census Commissioner, India; Bangladesh: Labor Force Survey 2005; Pakistan: Social and Living Standard Measurement Survey 2012–2013.

Disclaimer: This publication follows the World Bank's practice in references to member designations, borders, and maps. The boundaries, colors, denominations and other information shown in any map in this work do not imply any judgment on the part of The World Bank, ADB, JICA or DFID concerning the legal status of any territory or the endorsement or acceptance of such boundaries.

rural areas. The hypothesis is that a large agroprocessing sector also signals better supply chain infrastructure (such as warehouses, cold chains, and other logistical facilities) in rural areas.

The state-level measure of governance is drawn from a recent study (Mundle, Chowdhury, and Sikdar 2016) that scores the 19 largest Indian states along five dimensions: infrastructure; social services; fiscal performance; justice, law, and order; and the quality of the legislature. The scores are based largely on "output" measures, such as proportion of trials completed in fewer than three years (one of the indicators for the justice, law, and order dimension) and development expenditures as a share of total expenditures (one of the indicators for the fiscal performance dimension). The overall "Governance Performance Index" (GPI) combines the score on these five dimensions. The 2001 value of

the GPI is used as an initial interaction condition in the estimations.[5] This is shown in annex table 6A.3.

A major challenge in putting together the final district database was the matching and harmonization of districts across time. Many new districts have been created over time, leading to changes in district boundaries and names. Currently, there is a total of 707 districts in India, compared to 640 in the 2011 Census of India and 593 recorded in the 2001 Census of India (for a list of sources, see annex table 6A.4). The analysis addressed this issue by mapping newly created districts back to their unique parent district in 1999.[6] For instance, if district X in 1999 was split into districts Y and Z by 2010, the 2010 data for Y and Z were combined to recreate the parent district X in 2010. In addition to aggregating new districts up to their 1999 parent district, districts in the remote areas of Jammu and Kashmir and northeastern states of India have been dropped. This is standard practice in district-level studies on India, including previous studies of the impact of the GQ highway. After these steps, the data set consists of around 425 districts per year.

Finally, the geocoded data on the location of GQ and NSEW were merged into the district database.[7] This information was used to calculate the distances of the district centroid from the nearest points on the GQ and NSEW networks. The districts were then grouped into four distance bands from each highway: nodal district; 0–40 km from the highway; 40–100 km from the highway; and more than 100 km from the highway (map 6.3).[8] Thus, there are eight distance bands in total. Annex table 6A.5 lists the joint distribution of the sample according to these distance bands.

As explained in the methodology section, the study uses these distance bands to identify the "treatment" and "control" districts in the differences-in-differences estimation. Specifically, the 0–40 km distance band from the GQ (or the NSEW) identifies the GQ (or NSEW) treatment districts, while the control districts are those more than 100 km away from either highway. Figure 6.3 shows that the sample contains about 70 GQ treatment districts and about 40 NSEW treatment districts. There are about 200 districts in the common control group.

One concern about the analysis is that districts close to the GQ could also be close to the NSEW, which would make it hard to distinguish the impacts of each highway system. However, annex table 6A.5 shows that there is little overlap across districts in terms of nearness to these highways. Most of the districts that are close to the GQ highway (0–40 km from the GQ network) are more than 100 km from the NSEW network, and vice versa. This increases our

MAP 6.3   Distance of districts in India from the GQ and NSEW highways is measured from the district's centroid

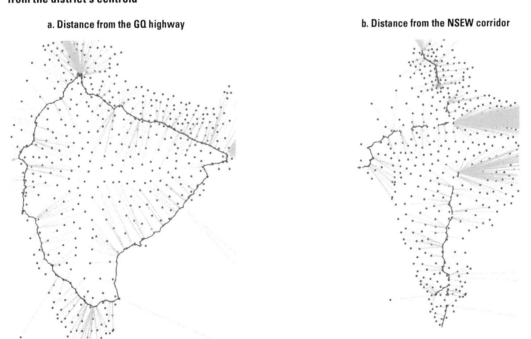

Source: World Bank's Spatial Database for South Asia (SARCE), https://spatialdatabase-southasia.herokuapp.com/.
Note: The red line GQ/NSEW highway systems, the blue dots signify district centroids, and the green lines signify the linear distance from highways to the district centroids.

confidence in being able to distinguish between the impacts of the GQ and NSEW highways.

ESTIMATION RESULTS FOR THE TWO EXISTING HIGHWAYS IN INDIA

Average impacts of the highways

Annex table 6A.6, panels a through d, shows the results of estimating equation 6.1.2 by ordinary least squares (OLS). This is the baseline differences-in-differences specification measuring the average impact of the highways. The panels report estimates from regressions that include a full set of state-year fixed effects. This is the preferred specification because it controls for unobserved state-level variables that could have been changing significantly during the study period. The impact of the GQ is given by $\beta^{GQ,0-40}$, the coefficient on the GQ treatment term $GQ_i^{0-40} \times Post_t^{GQ}$, which measures how the change in outcomes varied across treatment districts (those 0–40

km from the GQ network) and control districts (those more than 100 km away). Likewise, the impact of NSEW is given by $\beta^{NSEW,0-40}$, the coefficient on the NSEW treatment term $NSEW_i^{0-40} \times Post_t^{NSEW}$.

The first result of note is the impact of the highways on the movement of labor from farm to nonfarm work: that is, on structural transformation (figure 6.4). This happened during a period in which the share of non-farm employment in total employment was generally increasing in India; specifically, the share of nonfarm employment rose by 2.5 percentage points in the baseline (the control districts), following the construction of the GQ. According to the point estimate of $\beta^{GQ,0-40}$, which is statistically significant at the 1 percent level, the GQ highway increased the share of nonfarm employment by an additional 1.6 percentage points. Thus, the impact was large. The GQ also increased the share of nonfarm employment among females by 2.4 percentage points. The estimate of $\beta^{NSEW,0-40}$ is also positive and

FIGURE 6.3 **One in four districts was "treated"**

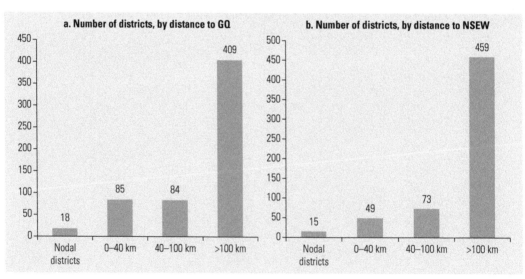

Source: Corridor Study Team.
Note: GQ = Golden Quadrilateral; NSEW = North-South-East-West.

statistically significant. Overall, the NSEW highway appears to have raised the share of nonfarm employment by about 2.5 percentage points in the general population as well as among females.

The positive impacts of the highway construction on the farm to nonfarm transition suggests that limited access to markets is a reason for India's slow structural transformation. The lack of market access has reduced employment opportunities beyond the farm, while keeping workers trapped in low-productivity agriculture by shielding the sector from competition. This hypothesis, however, does not imply that highways should lead to a movement away from farm work in *every* district. In districts with a strong inherent comparative advantage in agriculture, it could theoretically lead to a movement into the agricultural sector. The results only suggest that the former direction of movement is the case for the *average* treatment district.

Moving to final outcomes of interest, the regressions suggest that the GQ highway had a statistically significant positive impact on district output per capita (figure 6.5). Looking at the results for the GDP per capita (in logs) variable, the point estimate of $\beta^{GQ,0-40}$ implies that the highway increased GDP per capita growth over 2001–11 by 4 percentage points. This is of significant magnitude, given the baseline increase of 27 percent. However, the corresponding estimated impact of the NSEW corridor is statistically insignificant.

The regressions do not find statistically significant impacts of either highway on other measures of welfare, such as mean household per capita consumption expenditures. Nor do the regressions detect significant impacts on inequality (poverty headcount rates) and the main measure of labor market inclusion, the share of regular-wage ("good") jobs.[9]

These results are somewhat unexpected, given the positive impact on GDP per capita, and the prior finding that the GQ had a significant impact on output, productivity, and wages in formal manufacturing

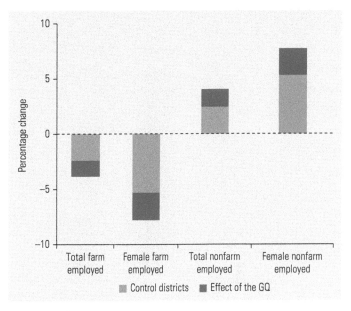

FIGURE 6.4 **The economic restructuring induced by the highways shifted employment from the farm to the nonfarm sector**

Source: Corridor Study Team.
Note: GQ = Golden Quadrilateral.

(Ghani, Goswami, and Kerr 2016). The formal manufacturing sector still constitutes only a small share of output, and an even smaller share of employment, in most Indian districts. It is possible that increased market access from the highways mainly benefited formal manufacturing and the relatively small number of skilled workers employed in that sector. This was enough to cause a significant increase in total (and per capita) district GDP. But because the growth in formal manufacturing started from such a small base, it did not lead to a detectable increase in the total number of regular-wage jobs or in the incomes of low-skilled individuals. The results thus suggest that the economic benefits of the highways were not widely shared.

Interestingly, the results also suggest that the structural change caused by the highways was not in itself enough to lead to a significant increase in "good" (that is, regular-wage) jobs. Nor was it enough to reduce poverty significantly. The opening up of market access drove workers off the farm,

FIGURE 6.5   **While the average income grew, the other benefits were not widely shared, and environmental quality deteriorated**

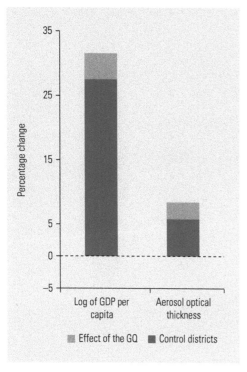

Source: Corridor Study Team.
Note: GDP = gross domestic product; GQ = Golden Quadrilateral.

but not necessarily into better-paying jobs. It could be that because most farm workers are uneducated, they could not shift into well-paying jobs in other sectors. Other labor market frictions, such as barriers to rural-urban migration or restrictive labor regulation of formal jobs, could also be at play here.

Another potential explanation for these results is the possibility of migration between the districts in response to the highways. That is, the highways did increase the demand for nonfarm labor significantly, but immigration into the treated districts was sizable enough to wipe out any equilibrium wage increase. This explanation is at odds with the well-established facts that India's rates of domestic migration are low by international standards and that most

domestic migration in India is within a district (Kone et al. 2016). But it bears further investigation, possibly with district-level migration data.

Finally, the regressions examine the highways' impacts on measures of environmental quality. While they do not detect a significant impact on carbon dioxide and nitrogen dioxide levels in the air, it appears that the GQ highway led to an increase in air pollution (smog) related to particulate matter. Specifically, the GQ is estimated to have increased particulate pollution (as measured by "aerosol optical thickness") by 0.02 point relative to a baseline increase of 0.06 point. This signals a significant trade-off between economic benefits and pollution.

How the impacts could have depended on product and factor market conditions: estimates of interaction effects

This section presents estimates of the DDD specification spelled out in equation 6.2.1. The main results, which look at interactions with product and factor market conditions, are shown in annex table 6A.7, panels a through d. The panels are arranged by outcome categories: welfare outcomes in panel a, distributional outcomes (inequality) in panel b, labor market outcomes (inclusion and structural change) in panel c, and environmental quality outcomes in panel d.

As noted, a simple iterative procedure was used to reduce the number of extraneous interaction variables. Thus, the set of interaction variables in the final specification varies across outcomes. These regressions include state-year dummies to control for state-level shocks.

Panel e shows the interaction results when a measure of state-level governance performance was included among the interaction terms. These regressions use year dummies instead of state-year dummies because the governance variable does not vary within states.

The broad hypothesis is that gaining the full benefits of market access could have depended on certain factor endowments, such as skills (which are immobile in the short to medium terms), and on the efficiency of product and factor markets. If this hypothesis is correct, then low average levels of factor endowments or market efficiency could explain why the *average* district did not experience widespread benefits of the highway construction. Identifying such complementary factors can point to how the construction of highways could be combined with complementary public investments or policy reforms to maximize their benefits.

Capital markets: households' access to bank accounts and firms' access to loans

The results for capital markets are intriguing, and hint at a complex relationship between market access and access to formal banking (figure 6.6). Consider the impact of the GQ on mean household consumption expenditures per capita. The estimated coefficient on the interaction between the GQ treatment and a measure of households' access to bank accounts is negative and significant (annex table 6A.7, panel a).[10] This implies that the impact of the GQ on household expenditures was less positive in districts where households had better access to formal savings accounts. Given that the main use of these formal accounts is to save, one potential explanation is that even though the highways increased household earnings, a larger fraction of that additional income was saved in locations where households had better access to formal channels of saving. This could reflect an unmet demand among households for channels to diversify assets to build resilience to shocks ("save for a rainy day").

Another potential explanation is that highways help bring capital to unbanked locations; this would explain why the highways have less impact on some outcomes in areas where the access to finance was better initially. There is some support for this hypothesis in recent research on the impact of connective infrastructure in China (Banerjee, Duflo, and Qian 2012). However, the results of this study do not support this hypothesis. Firms' access to finance enhanced the impacts of the NSEW (figure 6.6). When looking at the share of nonfarm jobs among females, the regressions find that the estimated coefficient on the interaction between the NSEW treatment and a measure of firms' access to formal financing is positive and significant (annex table 6A.7, panel c). The estimated interaction effect of firms' access to formal financing and the NSEW on the share of female farm employment is consistently negative (annex table 6A.7, panel c).[11] This suggests that firms' access to formal loans could have enhanced the impact of the highways on structural transformation.

Labor markets: skills

The results indicate a complementarity between highways and skills. Regarding the impact on the share of nonfarm employment, the coefficient on the triple interaction between a measure of secondary schooling (the initial percentage of 15+-year-olds with secondary school education) and $GQ_i \times Post_t^{GQ}$ is positive and statistically significant at the 1 percent level (annex table 6A.7, panel c; figure 6.7). This implies that the GQ had a significantly more positive impact on nonfarm employment in districts with more secondary education. The point estimate of the δ^{GQ} implies that relative to a district at the 10th percentile of the secondary schooling measure, the impact of the GQ on the share of nonfarm employment was 7 percentage points higher in a district at the 90th percentile. Similarly, the interaction of the secondary school variable with $NSEW_i \times Post_t^{NSEW}$ is positive and statistically significant.[12] The same pattern is also observed with regard to the impact on the share of nonfarm employment among females.

FIGURE 6.6 **Access to finance for firms and households had different impacts on spreading WEB**

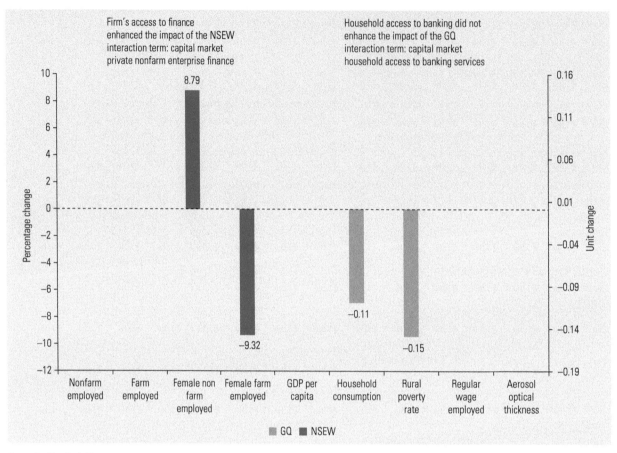

Source: Corridor Study Team.
Note: The figure shows only those results that are significant at 1 percent. Household consumption and GDP per capita are in log terms. GDP = gross domestic product; GQ = Golden Quadrilateral; NSEW = North-South-East-West; WEB = wider economic benefits.

Education also seems to have enhanced the impact of the NSEW on regular-wage jobs—although in this case, it is basic literacy that seems to have mattered. The estimated coefficient on the interaction between the literacy rate and $NSEW_i \times Post_t^{NSEW}$ is positive and significant when the outcome being examined is the share of regular-wage jobs in total employment (annex table 6A.7, panel c). It implies that in moving from the 10th percentile of the literacy measure to the 90th percentile, the impact of the NSEW on the share of regular-wage jobs would increase by 12 percentage points.

Results for GDP per capita as an outcome also hint at a complementarity between connectivity and skills. While the results for the GQ are not statistically significant, in the case of the NSEW, the coefficient on the triple interaction between basic education (the initial literacy rate among 7+-year-olds) and $NSEW_i \times Post_t^{NSEW}$ is positive and statistically significant at the 5 percent level (annex table 6A.7, panel b). The implied complementarity is large in magnitude; moving from the 10th percentile of the literacy measure to its 90th percentile, the impact of NSEW on per capita

FIGURE 6.7   Education boosted the impact of the two highways

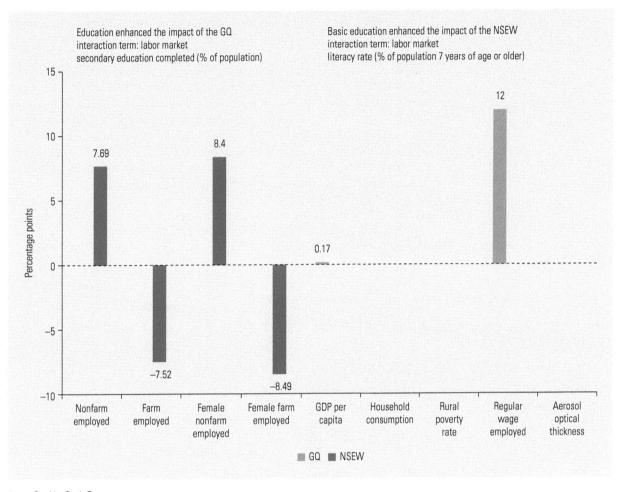

Source: Corridor Study Team.
Note: The figure shows only those results that are significant at 1 percent. Household consumption and GDP per capita are in log terms. GDP = gross domestic product; GQ = Golden Quadrilateral; NSEW = North-South-East-West.

GDP would increase by additional 17 percentage points. This increase is large, even compared to the 27 percent increase in baseline growth in GDP per capita during 2001–11.

Consistent with these patterns, the estimated coefficient on the interaction between the literacy rate and $NSEW_i \times Post_t^{NSEW}$ is positive, although marginally insignificant, for two other economic welfare outcomes: mean household consumption expenditures per capita, and the reduction in urban poverty headcount (annex table 6A.7).

As shown in annex table 6A.7, panel d, the negative impact of highways (the GQ) on particulate matter air pollution (aerosol optical radius) is mitigated by having a better-educated population (as measured by the share of the population that has completed secondary schooling). This could be because more educated individuals buy higher-quality, environmentally cleaner vehicles as their incomes rise. Another possible explanation for this interaction is that the way in which economic activity changes after the highway is built is more environmentally friendly in more educated districts. Notably, districts with higher levels of secondary schooling experience a greater impact of the GQ on the shift from farm to nonfarm jobs. This reduced pollution from the burning of straw on farms, which is a major contributor to particulate pollution in India.

Land markets

The results suggest that the impact of the highways also depended significantly on the share of cropland in a district's total land area (figure 6.8). This interaction variable can be seen as a proxy for a district's comparative advantage in agriculture. A higher share of cropland also signals a bigger constraint on the availability of land for industrial purposes.

As for the impact of the GQ on the share of nonfarm jobs among females, and on the share of regular-wage jobs among both males and females, the coefficients on the interaction of the GQ treatment with the cropland measure are negative and statistically significant (annex table 6A.7, panel c). For example, the estimates of the interaction term imply that moving from the 10th to the 90th percentiles of cropland share would reduce the impact of the GQ on nonfarm employment among females by 5 percentage points, and the share of regular wage jobs by 0.1 percentage point. This is consistent with the hypothesis that the extent to which improved market access shifted people out of farm jobs was negatively related to comparative

FIGURE 6.8   **Land market conditions had mixed impacts on spreading WEB**

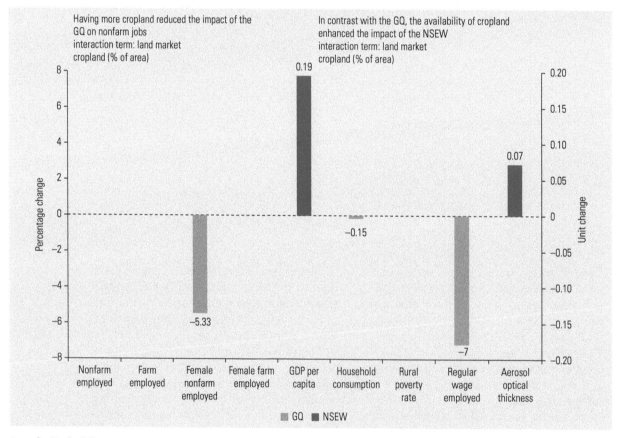

Source: Corridor Study Team.
Note: The figure shows only those results that are significant at 1 percent. Household consumption and GDP per capita are in log terms. GDP = gross domestic product; GQ = Golden Quadrilateral; NSEW = North-South-East-West; WEB = wider economic benefits.

advantage in agriculture (or depended positively on the availability of industrial land). The impacts on household consumption per capita are also consistent with this hypothesis. Namely, the coefficient on the interaction of the GQ treatment with the cropland measure is negative and statistically significant (annex table 6A.7, panel a). The GQ districts gained less from market access if they had less land available for nonfarm usage.

The results also suggest that the nature of the interaction with land conditions differed across districts near the GQ and the NSEW. First, more cropland is not significantly associated with a lower positive effect of the NSEW on nonfarm jobs, which suggests that unlike the case of the GQ, a larger share of cropland did not impede the structural change caused by the NSEW (table 6A.7, panel c). Second, looking at GDP per capita, the coefficient on the interaction of the NSEW treatment with the cropland measure is positive and statistically significant: having more cropland seems to have enhanced the impact of the NSEW highway on per capita output (annex table 6A.7, panel a). A potential explanation for these results is that some districts in the areas connected by the NSEW began to specialize in high-value, tradable farm products and agroprocessing. Among these districts, having more cropland increased the gains from market access, while not necessarily impeding the creation of non-farm jobs in agro-related industries.

Product markets

The regressions also tested the hypothesis that the gains from highways depend on efficiency and competition in product markets. This part of the analysis relies on proxies for product market competition at the district level, such as the share of the private sector in formal manufacturing. No statistically significant and consistent interaction was observed between these measures and the impact of the highways; perhaps it reflects the crude quality of the available measures.

There is, however, a positive and statistically significant interaction between the share of agroprocessing in local industry and the impact of the GQ in reducing rural poverty (annex table 6A.7, panel b). There could be two reasons for this complementarity. First, as discussed, for the structural change wrought by the GQ to have translated into widespread benefits, the availability of suitable jobs for the vast reserves of low-skilled workers leaving the farm could have been critical. Agroprocessing could be an important source of suitable jobs for rural workers. Second, the size of the agroprocessing sector could be acting a proxy measure for the quality of "soft infrastructure" (such as warehouses and cold chains) in rural areas. This is indicative of a complementarity between "hard" infrastructure like the highway and soft connective infrastructure.

Governance

In addition to specific conditions in factor and product markets, the impact of connectivity could also depend on crosscutting institutional factors such as the quality of governance. Better-governed areas, for instance, might have been better at enacting complementary policies in locations affected by the new highways. The regressions test this idea by including a measure of state-level governance performance in 2001 as an additional interaction term. As noted, state-year fixed effects cannot be included. Hence, the results with governance interactions should be interpreted with the caveat that they may not be robust to controlling for unobserved state-level shocks. Accordingly, these results are presented separately in annex table 6A.7, panel e, and are not included in the main results shown in annex table 6A.7, panels a through d.

The statistical significance levels and signs of the product and labor market interaction effects shown in annex table 6A.7, panels a through d, survive the replacement of state-year fixed effects with year fixed effects, and the addition of a governance interaction term. Thus, the estimated interaction effects of product and labor market conditions remain unchanged in this alternative specification. Second, the newly included governance and highways interaction terms are not statistically significant for most outcomes, with the important exception of labor market inclusion measures. These results are shown in annex table 6A.7, panel e.[13] Regarding the share of regular wage jobs in total employment—the preferred measure of the creation of "good" jobs—the interaction of governance with the GQ is positive and significant. The same effect is observed in the case of regular-wage jobs share among females. These findings suggest that better governance enabled a wider sharing of the impacts of highways in creating more numerous, more inclusive, and better-quality jobs.

THE SIMULATED IMPACTS OF TWO PROPOSED CORRIDORS: THE CHINA-PAKISTAN ECONOMIC CORRIDOR AND THE KOLKATA-DHAKA CORRIDOR

The simulation method

This section simulates and discusses the expected impacts of two corridors that have not yet been built: the China-Pakistan Economic Corridor (CPEC) in Pakistan, and the Kolkata-Dhaka corridor in Bangladesh. These simulations are based on the estimated regressions describing the impacts of the GQ in India, and are intended to illustrate how micro data and econometric modeling can be used to better assess the varied impacts of proposed transport investments.

The simulation uses estimates of the GQ instead of the NSEW, for two reasons. First, we are more confident about the estimates of GQ because they are based on data for a longer span of time after the highway was built. Second, there are similarities in the market access effects of the GQ and the simulated corridors; like the GQ, both the CPEC and Kolkata-Dhaka corridor will connect places along their paths to major external markets, ports, and/or metropolitan areas.

The estimated regression model for India assumes that the impact of the GQ depends on a set of initial conditions in input and output markets in the places located along the corridor. If the GQ were to be replicated in a different location, such as the proposed paths of the CPEC or the Kolkata-Dhaka corridor, it would have a different impact because the initial market conditions in those locations were different (see box 6.3).

Of the three proposed arteries for the CPEC, the easternmost one was chosen because it resembles the GQ the most, passing through well-populated areas and several cities and towns, and connecting major metropolitan nodes and ports (international gateways).

The simulation exercise focused on assessing the *spatial variation* in the expected impacts of the proposed corridors along their prospective paths, and not on assessing their average impact. The simulated corridors are only roughly comparable to the GQ, and their average impact could differ from that of GQ for several reasons. However, if the mechanism of impact is the same, the way in which it depends on initial conditions is expected to be similar.

The simulation for the CPEC and the Kolkata-Dhaka corridor used district-level data from Pakistan and Bangladesh on the distance to the proposed corridor and relevant market conditions. The exercise measured the distance of district centroids to the nearest point on the proposed highway, and identified districts within 40 km of the proposed highway. Following the estimated model for India, these districts were considered the "treatment" districts; that is, the districts that would be affected by the proposed corridor. The impacts were simulated for only these districts.[14] Also, following the Indian estimation, major metropolitan districts that lie on the proposed corridor path, like Dhaka in Bangladesh and Karachi in Pakistan, were treated as "nodal" districts and excluded from the simulation.

Data on market conditions were estimated from household- or firm-level surveys, or sourced from satellite data. Because the highways have not yet been built, the exercise used the most recent values of the variables to simulate "initial" market conditions. As much

BOX 6.3   Simulating the effects of a transport corridor in another country

Based on the estimated regression model for GQ, the expected impact of a proposed corridor in country c is simulated using data on initial market conditions of districts d that lie along the path of that corridor:

$$\Delta Y_{d,c} = \beta^Y + \delta^Y (Z_{d,c} - Z_{India}), \qquad (6.3.1)$$

where $\Delta Y_{d,c}$ is the expected impact of the corridor on outcome Y in location d of country c. β^Y is the estimate of the average impact of GQ on outcome Y in India. The vector δ^Y consists of estimates of how

the impact of GQ on Y depends on initial market conditions Z in a district with upgraded connectivity. The vector $Z_{d,c} - Z_{India}$ measures how initial conditions in location d in country c differ from their average values in locations in India along the GQ.

This formula expresses the basic idea behind the simulation: the impact of a GQ-like corridor on location d in country c will differ from the average impact of the GQ because initial market conditions in location d are different from their averages along the path of the GQ.

---

as available data allow, the simulations used sources and definitions of indicators equivalent to those used in India. For example, the share of cropland in land area was based on MODIS satellite data, the same source as in India. In some cases, it was not possible to avoid minor differences in the source type or variable definition. For example, variables on educational attainment were based on census data for India and Bangladesh, and household survey data for Pakistan. Annex tables 6B.1, 6B.2, and 6B.3 in annex 6B present the summary statistics and data sources for Pakistan, while annex tables 6C.1, 6C.2, and 6C.3 in annex 6C present corresponding information for Bangladesh.

Because comparable measures of subnational governance for Pakistan and Bangladesh are unavailable, the exercise excluded the effects of governance from the simulations. Hence, the simulations are based on the baseline estimations for India that did not include the governance variable as an interaction term (the estimation results presented in annex table 6A.7, panels a through d).

The simulation results

Annex table 6B.4 in annex 6B presents the simulated impacts of the CPEC on WEB, while annex table 6C.4 in annex 6C presents

results for the Kolkata-Dhaka corridor. The focus is on the spatial variation in impacts, and not the mean impact. This discussion is therefore limited to those outcomes for which there were statistically significant interaction effects with one or more initial market conditions in the case of the GQ. Thus, even though output per capita is an important outcome variable, it is not discussed here because the simulations could not estimate how the impact depends on market conditions with sufficient precision. We can predict that the proposed corridors will have a positive impact on output per capita, but not how it will vary spatially.[15]

Map 6.4 depicts the simulated impact on per capita consumption expenditures of households (in logs) through "heat maps." The district-level predicted impact was normalized by its mean value across all the treatment districts, thus showing its relative value across districts.

The average impact of the GQ on household expenditures was measured imprecisely (that is, it is statistically insignificant). However, its dependence on land and output market conditions was statistically significant—namely, the dependence on the share of cropland in total area, and the percentage of firms that are privately owned. The positive impact on household expenditures

MAP 6.4 **The simulated relative impact on mean per capita household consumption expenditures shows disparities along the Kolkata-Dhaka Transport Corridor (Bangladesh segment)**

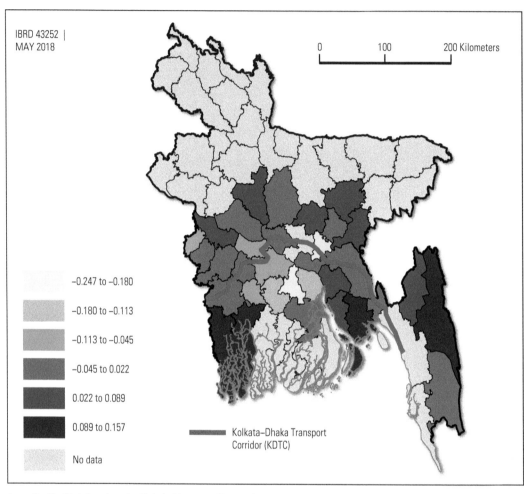

IBRD 43252 |
MAY 2018

0   100   200 Kilometers

−0.247 to −0.180

−0.180 to −0.113

−0.113 to −0.045

−0.045 to 0.022

0.022 to 0.089

0.089 to 0.157

No data

Kolkata–Dhaka Transport Corridor (KDTC)

Source: Corridor Study Team based on Melecky, Sharma, and Subhash (forthcoming).
Note: Units refer to average per capita household consumption expenditure, in logs. The red line indicates the highway.

could be expected to be smaller in districts with a larger share of cropland. As discussed, one explanation is that districts with more land devoted to farming could find it harder to reallocate land to industrial uses and the service sector, limiting their ability to benefit from improved market access. In contrast to cropland, greater private ownership of firms is expected to enhance the positive impact of corridors on household expenditures—most likely because of greater market contestability in those districts.

The spatial variation in the share of cropland in Pakistan and Bangladesh is greater

than in the share of private ownership. Moreover, the predicted impact on household expenditures is more sensitive to the share of cropland, based on the estimated model for India. The simulation therefore suggests that, for both proposed corridors, the spatial variation in impacts on household expenditures will be mostly influenced by variation in the share of cropland—that is, by the variation in land market constraints. For example, districts close to Karachi (for CPEC) and Chittagong (for the Kolkata-Dhaka corridor) could experience the biggest impacts on household expenditures because they have more land available for industrial uses. Because the Kolkata-Dhaka corridor passes through areas with more diverse shares of cropland, the variation in the simulated household expenditures will be greater for this corridor.

Map 6.5 presents simulated impacts on the reduction in the headcount measure of poverty. A more positive effect on this indicator implies a wider sharing of economic benefits. Although the *average* impact on poverty reduction was not estimated precisely for the GQ, it was significantly bigger in areas with a larger share of agroprocessing firms in the total number of manufacturing firms.

The hypothesis is that in such locations, a relatively large share of low-skilled individuals was already employed in the agroprocessing industry, a sector expected to benefit of increased market access. Such workers could be better predisposed to share benefits of better market access, moving up the value chain to better jobs without having to acquire new skills or move to new jobs. Even poor workers in agriculture could possibly benefit from the growth of the local agro-industry.

Along the proposed path for the Kolkata-Dhaka corridor, high variation in the share of agroprocessing in the manufacturing sector

MAP 6.5 **The simulated relative impact on the reduction in poverty (headcount measure) varied along the Kolkata-Dhaka Corridor (Bangladesh segment)**

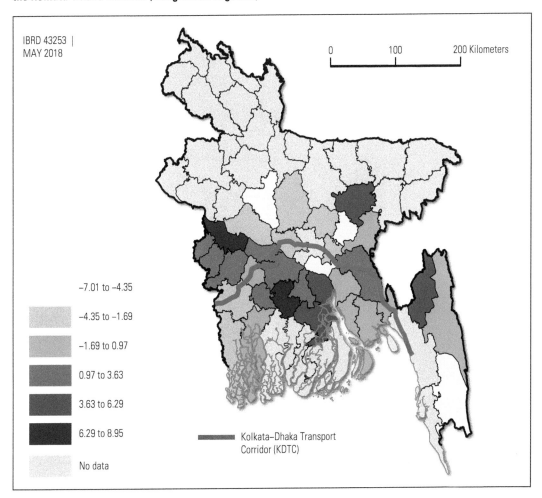

IBRD 43253 |
MAY 2018

0   100   200 Kilometers

−7.01 to −4.35

−4.35 to −1.69

−1.69 to 0.97

0.97 to 3.63

3.63 to 6.29

6.29 to 8.95

No data

Kolkata–Dhaka Transport Corridor (KDTC)

Source: Corridor Study Team.
Note: The red line indicates the highway.

could result in significant variation in the corridor's impacts on poverty reduction across the connected districts. The range of expected impacts is nearly 15 percentage points. For the CPEC, district-level estimates of the share of agroprocessing were not available. Instead, the analysis relied on province-level data. Hence, the simulated impacts show no variation within provinces. Even the variation across provinces is relatively small; much of the eastern arm of the CPEC passes through provinces with similar levels of agro-industry, such as Sindh and Punjab.

The simulated impacts on the share of regular-wage jobs in female employment—a measure of women's inclusion in the labor market—also vary significantly. The variation depends on the share of cropland in the total land area (map 6.6). Land constraints could restrict women's ability to benefit proportionately from improved market access. The effect of land constraints on the variation in the expected impact on women's inclusion is even more pronounced for Bangladesh. The range in simulated impacts is on the order of 7 percentage points for the

MAP 6.6 **The simulated relative impact on the share of regular wage jobs in women's employment shows major disparities along the Kolkata-Dhaka Transport Corridor (Bangladesh segment)**

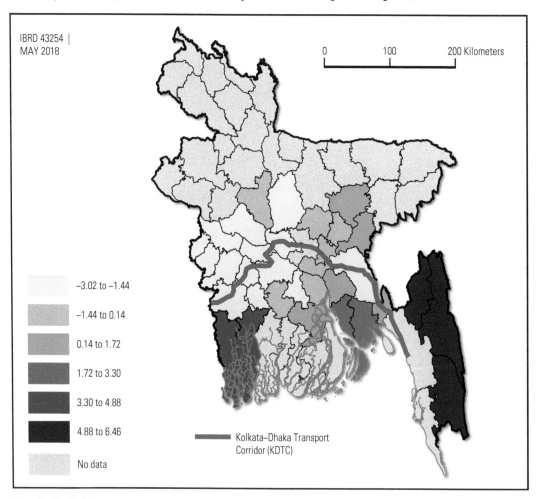

Source: Corridor Study Team.
Note: The red line indicates the highway.

CPEC and 9.5 percentage points for the Kolkata-Dhaka corridor. Several districts near the central leg of the Kolkata-Dhaka corridor could miss out on the benefits of increased female labor market inclusion because of severe land constraints. Along the CPEC, the land market constraint could dampen benefits in districts nearer to the northern leg of the corridor.

On average, the simulated impact of corridors on air pollution (as measured by the aerosol optical thickness indicator) is negative, but spatial variation is substantial across districts in Pakistan and Bangladesh (map 6.7). The spatial variation is driven by differing levels of higher education; districts with higher rates of secondary school completion could see a smaller rise in air pollution. Two explanations are possible. First, while the advent of highways should increase road traffic in every treatment district, those with highly educated populations might tend to switch to cleaner vehicles, even if they are relatively more expensive. Second, as the GQ estimates implied, areas with more secondary schooling experience a larger structural transformation toward nonfarm jobs. In those

MAP 6.7 The simulated relative impact on air pollution (aerosol optical thickness) should alert policy makers about needed action in some districts along the Kolkata-Dhaka Transport Corridor (Bangladesh segment)

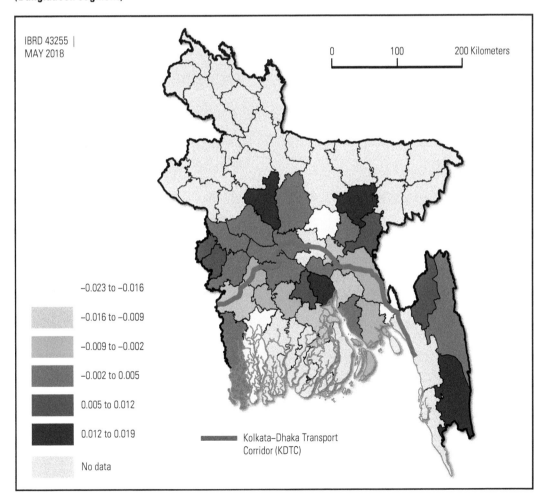

Source: Corridor Study Team.
Note: The red line indicates the highway.

districts experiencing greater structural change, farms might burn less straw—a major contributor to air pollution in South Asia.

CONCLUSION

This chapter has illustrated how the use of detailed spatial data and econometric analysis can bring more rigor and depth to the appraisal of transport corridors. The estimations found that the improved connectivity generated by the GQ and NSEW highway networks contributed significantly to structural transformation of the districts. The shift from farm to nonfarm employment was statistically significant in both cases. Each network had a significant positive impact on district-level per capita GDP. However, this impact was not widely shared. The estimation did not find similar positive effects for household consumption, poverty, and employment, including those of females. Moreover, the analysis found evidence of significant trade-offs in the impacts on WEB, estimating that while GDP increased significantly, air quality decreased significantly.

Initial conditions

With respect to initial conditions, the analysis found that initial local market conditions are important in determining the outcomes of highway upgrades and the ways and extent to which WEB are shared across geographic units. The central mechanism through which highways affect development is increased trade across connected locations. This expansion was accompanied by a reallocation of resources to more productive firms and to sectors of comparative advantage. Conditions in labor, land, capital, and product markets could matter because they affect this process of reallocation.[16] For example, in districts with a comparative advantage in manufacturing, limited availability of land for nonfarm uses could lessen the gains from a highway by constraining the reallocation of land toward manufacturing. In a district with a comparative advantage in agricultural products, limited availability of

farmland could constrain the potential to gain from a highway.

Access to financial services. The results suggest that access to credit by nonfarm enterprises amplified the shift of women to better (regular-wage) jobs induced by the NSEW, while reducing farm employment of women in districts connected to the NSEW by nearly an equal amount. Thus, firms' access to credit seems to enable and amplify the wider economic benefits of highways. In contrast, the impact of the GQ on household expenditures was less positive in districts where households already had better access to formal savings accounts.[17]

Labor market conditions. Labor market conditions, as measured by the literacy level, amplified the positive impact of the NSEW on the per capita GDP of connected districts. Higher levels of literacy and secondary education also seem to have lessened the negative environmental impacts of the highways. Similarly, a higher level of secondary education was associated with a more positive impact of the GQ on regular-wage employment, particularly for women, and a more negative impact on farm employment. Overall, the estimated interactions suggest that the low average level of schooling in India may have prevented the benefits of connectivity from being shared more widely.

Land market conditions. A greater area of cropland constrained local firms and households from pursuing the higher-value nonagricultural opportunities opened up by greater market access stemming from the construction of the GQ. Nonfarm employment for women was also constrained. In contrast, in NSEW districts where more cropland was available, GDP increased more. One explanation is that some areas located near the NSEW have rich potential in tradable farm products and agroprocessing. Their gains from market access were thus boosted by the availability of cropland.

Product market conditions. The initial industrial composition or other product market conditions could be important factors in ensuring that transport corridors help reduce poverty. The estimations found that a higher share of agroprocessing in manufacturing significantly improved the impacts of the GQ on reducing poverty. A strong base in agro-processing seems to have helped unskilled rural workers moving off the farm find a job. Districts with more agroprocessing are also likely to have a better quality of "soft infrastructure" (such as warehouses and cold chains) in rural areas. The result indicates a complementarity between hard infrastructure, like the highway, and soft connective infrastructure.

Governance. Regular-wage employment increased more in states with better governance. One explanation is that better-governed areas were better at foreseeing and implementing policies that enhanced the highways' impact on job creation. These results should be interpreted with caution. The governance measure is at the state level and could be reflecting other unobserved differences across states.

Complementary policies and institutions

The illustrative case study of highways in India thus suggests that public investments in transport corridors can yield net economic benefits in the aggregate. However, widely sharing these benefits across districts and populations can be more difficult, and depends on the effectiveness of complementary policies and institutions. India's GQ highway, for example, increased net output and manufacturing sector activity, but a clear significant effect on reducing poverty and boosting access to better (regular-wage) jobs cannot be confirmed. This wider sharing of economic benefits could depend on conditions in land, labor, financial, and product markets. For the GQ, the estimations suggest that the highway did reduce poverty significantly in areas (districts) with a sufficiently large agroprocessing base (while in the average district near the highway, poverty did not drop). Wage employment among females increased in districts where land was available for nonfarm uses. For the NSEW, the impact on wage employment was enhanced by higher levels of education.

The results are largely consistent with the idea that transport corridors lead to wider economic benefits by increasing market access and trade across connected locations. This process requires a reallocation of land, labor, and capital to sectors of comparative advantage. The GQ, for example, led to a significant reallocation of workers from the farm to the nonfarm sector. The benefits of transport corridors—and how widely they are shared—therefore depend on how quickly and efficiently land, labor, and capital can move to new sectors of promising activity. This could be the key reason why the impacts of highways like the GQ depend on initial market conditions.

To further illustrate this complementarity, the analysis used the GQ impact estimates to simulate the expected impacts of two proposed corridors: the CPEC in Pakistan and the Kolkata-Dhaka corridor in Bangladesh. The corridor impacts that were found to be dependent on initial conditions in the appraisal of the GQ were used to appraise the expected variation of WEB across newly connected districts in the two countries. This simulation assumed that the impact mechanics for the proposed projects match those of the GQ. The simulation aimed to illustrate how project appraisers could screen for significant variations from district to district (spatial variations) in the expected impacts of a corridor project, and identify the complementary reforms that are most needed.

The simulations suggest that the proposed corridors could have significantly varied impacts on household expenditures, poverty, the inclusion of women in the labor market, and air pollution. The variation would be driven by spatial differences in levels of higher

> **Policy makers should focus on identifying the underlying constraints in the local context of prospective corridors—whether these are policies and institutions constraining the use of key factors of production (land, labor, capital, or product markets) or other factors, such as low skills in the local labor market or poor governance.**

education, land market constraints, and industrial composition along the paths of the proposed corridors. For example, in districts located in the central leg of the proposed Kolkata-Dhaka corridor and in the northern end of the CPEC, the impact on women's employment in regular-wage jobs should be lower because of constraints on land use, which limit women's shift from farm to non-farm jobs.

The simulation exercise highlights an element largely missing in the media and policy forum discussions on these proposed highways: the fact that their wider economic impacts could vary greatly across locations because of differences in existing market conditions. Significant reductions in poverty, for example, are likely to occur only in places where a sizable number of low-skilled workers are already working in the agroprocessing sector—an industry expected to benefit from improved market access.

The results also illustrated the potential environmental trade-offs from transport corridors. The estimates suggest that the GQ increased particulate air pollution. While not surprising, given the increase in traffic, this potential negative impact is largely absent from policy decisions.

The main message for the design of corridors is that the efficiency of markets and the effectiveness of local policies and institutions could complement investments in transport corridors and steer their overall spatial impact on development outcomes—that is, the net wider economic benefits. Investing in human capital and better governance is also important, as are policies that could mitigate the potential negative effect on environmental quality. The design of corridor investments and their complementary policies should be based on a better understanding of the underlying mechanisms through which the corridor in question could affect development outcomes. Thus, more analysis is needed than a simple extrapolation of the patterns observed in the case study. For example, for the GQ, the availability of land for nonfarm uses and the level of secondary education seem to have been the main constraints preventing socioeconomic benefits from being shared more widely. But this does not imply that agriculture-intensive locations or areas with low education and skill levels are not suitable for the placement of corridors. Instead, the lesson to draw is that policy makers should focus on identifying the underlying constraints in the local context of prospective corridors—whether these are policies and institutions behind the constrained use of land or the factors behind low skills in the local labor market.

NOTES

1. The Golden Quadrilateral (GQ) highway, together with the NSEW corridor and port connectivity highways, connect many of India's major manufacturing, commercial, and cultural centers. Both roadways are four-lane highways.

2. Datta (2012) uses a similar methodology, although not with district-level data.

3. Researchers develop "identification assumptions" or "identification techniques" to clearly isolate the effect of the intervention (treatment)—in this case, the highway that was built—from the confounding effects of other factors on the outcome of interest.

4. As of writing this draft, the database was still being tested and was not available to the public. The authors were able to download data upon special request. The intention is to make the data set public.

5. The analysis could not use alternative, better-known state-level measures of governance dimensions, such as the World Bank's state-level Ease of Doing Business indicator, because to our knowledge none of the other measures are available for the initial period of our study.

6. The reference year of 1999 was chosen because a wave of new states were created between 1999 and 2001, leading to a sharp rise in the number of districts and significant renaming of districts over the course of a few years. Mapping districts to their 1999 definitions is therefore the more conservative approach to harmonizing districts.

7. The authors are grateful to Ejaz Ghani and coauthors (Ghani, Goswami, and Kerr 2016) for sharing these data, which they compiled

using official highway maps. The merger of the GQ data was relatively straightforward because the network was largely complete by 2005. This study used the final GQ network map to calculate distances of district centroids to the highway. The NSEW distance calculation was more complicated because some sections of the network, particularly in its eastern leg, had not been completed by 2010. The analysis ignored those incomplete sections of the NSEW when calculate district distances to the NSEW.

8. For comparability, these distance bands were chosen to correspond to those used in the study by Ghani, Goswami, and Kerr (2016) of GQ. The distance cutoffs are not the same because they calculate distance to the highway from the district's nearest edge, while this study does so from the district's centroid.

9. Night lights intensity, a commonly used proxy for economic activity, also was not affected significantly.

10. Moreover, the estimated coefficient on the interaction between the GQ treatment and the banking access measure is negative and significant when the outcome being examined is the reduction in the poverty headcount. Since the headcount measure is derived from the consumption expenditures measure, these interaction results are consistent with each other.

11. Regarding the impact on the share of regular-wage jobs in female employment, the interaction between firms' access to finance and the NSEW is negative. This is in apparent contrast to the positive interaction impact of firms' access to finance and NSEW on nonfarm jobs. However, it reflects a positive interaction impact of firms' access to finance and the NSEW on total female employment, which is the denominator for estimating the share of regular-wage jobs in female employment. Overall, the interaction between firms' access to finance and the NSEW increased female nonfarm employment more than it decreased female farm employment. There was no significant interaction impact on the absolute number of regular-wage jobs among females, but since the interaction impact on total female employment was positive, the interaction impact on the ratio of regular-wage jobs to total jobs was negative.

12. The interaction term on $GQ_i \times Post_t^{GQ}$ and a measure of literacy, however, is negative and statistically significant. This is puzzling, given that, in general, the coefficients on the interaction with educational measures go in the positive direction. However, the regression also controls for the interaction between secondary schooling and $GQ_i \times Post_t^{GQ}$, so this result could be an artifact of the correlation between these two educational measures. This puzzling pattern did not emerge for the NSEW.

13. Panel e corresponds to the same set of outcomes as panel c, replacing state-year dummies with year dummies and adding governance interactions. Notably, the significance and signs of the other interaction terms are similar in these two panels.

14. The treatment group also includes all districts through which the proposed corridor would pass, regardless of how close it would come to the district centroid. Overall, the exercise identified 41 districts for the CPEC in Pakistan and 33 treatment districts for the Kolkata-Dhaka corridor in Bangladesh.

15. Recall that the impact estimate for the GQ is +4 percent.

16. For a recent literature review of how connective infrastructure affects development and the mechanisms behind those impacts, see Bougna et al. (forthcoming), a companion background paper for this report.

17. This conditional impact could still be desirable if the access to formal payment and savings methods encourages people to save and accumulate assets to protect against shocks ("save for a rainy day"). However, the lack of household asset data prevents this study from testing this hypothesis.

REFERENCES

Banerjee, Abhijit, Esther Duflo, and Nancy Qian. 2012. "On the Road: Transportation and Infrastructure Growth in China." Working Paper 17897, National Bureau of Economic Research, Cambridge, MA.

Bougna, Theophile, Martin Melecky, Mark Roberts, and Yan Xu. Forthcoming. "Transport Corridors and Their Wider Economic Benefits: A Critical Review of the Literature." Policy Research Paper, World Bank, Washington, DC.

Datta, Saugato. 2012. "The Impact of Improved Highways on Indian Firms." *Journal of Development Economics* 99 (1): 46–57.

Ghani, Ejaz, Arti Grover Goswami, and William R. Kerr. 2016. "Highway to Success: The Impact of the Golden Quadrilateral Project for the Location and Performance of Indian Manufacturing." *Economic Journal* (Royal Economic Society) 126 (591): 317–57.

Kone, Z. L., M. Y. Liu, A. Mattoo., C. Ozden, and S. Sharma. Forthcoming. "Internal Borders and Migration in India. *Journal of Economic Geography.*

Melecky, Martin, Siddharth Sharma, and Hari Subhash. Forthcoming. "Wider Economic Benefits of Investments in Transport Corridors and the Role of Complementary Policies." Policy Research Paper, World Bank, Washington, DC.

Mundle, Sudipto, Samik Chowdhury, and Satadru Sikdar, 2016. "Governance Performance of Indian States: 2001–02 and 2011–12." Working Paper 164, National Institute of Public Finance and Policy, New Delhi.

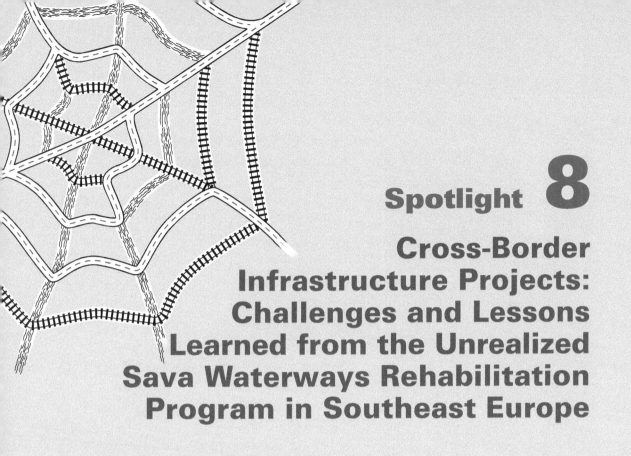

Cross-Border Infrastructure Projects: Challenges and Lessons Learned from the Unrealized Sava Waterways Rehabilitation Program in Southeast Europe

This spotlight reviews the preparation of a regional project, the Sava Waterways Rehabilitation Program, in Southeast Europe. The project was not implemented, and the World Bank investment was eventually withdrawn because of challenges that could not be resolved. Still, the experience is instructive as it illustrates the problems faced by regional bodies, national governments, subnational entities, and international organizations regarding cross-border infrastructure projects.

PRELIMINARY ATTEMPTS TO RESTORE THE REGIONAL WATERWAY

Before 1990, the Sava River had an important role in regional transport in the former Yugoslavia, from where it meets the Danube River at Belgrade, extending through what became four separate countries (Serbia, Bosnia and Herzegovina, Croatia, and Slovenia). Navigation was possible for much of the year from Belgrade all the way to Rugvica, near Zagreb, in what is now Croatia, along 683 river kilometers. Some 5.2 million tons of freight was transported each year, composed of bulk inputs and outputs to and from the heavy industry located along the way. The conflict from 1991 to 1995 was particularly hard on the Sava River and nearby areas because these were often the front line. Maritime infrastructure and ports were destroyed, the riverbanks and surrounding areas were heavily mined, and the towns and industry were devastated.

After the Dayton Peace Accord (DPA) was signed in Bosnia and Herzegovina, the Sava River crossed four sovereign countries, traversing Slovenia and Croatia, then forming the border between Croatia and Bosnia and Herzegovina, becoming the border between Bosnia and Herzegovina and Serbia, and finally crossing Serbian territory to join the Danube in Belgrade (map S8.1). Within Bosnia and Herzegovina, the river crossed the two entities created by the Dayton Peace Accord—the Federation of Bosnia and Herzegovina (FBH) and the Republika Srpska (RS)—as well as the Brčko Administrative District (BAD).[1] Given the issues the new countries faced after the war, the Sava River was neglected, with little maintenance or reconstruction in the ports or industry after the war. By 2004, volumes carried on the

MAP S8.1   The SAVA Waterway Rehabilitation Project Traversed Several Former Yugoslav Republics

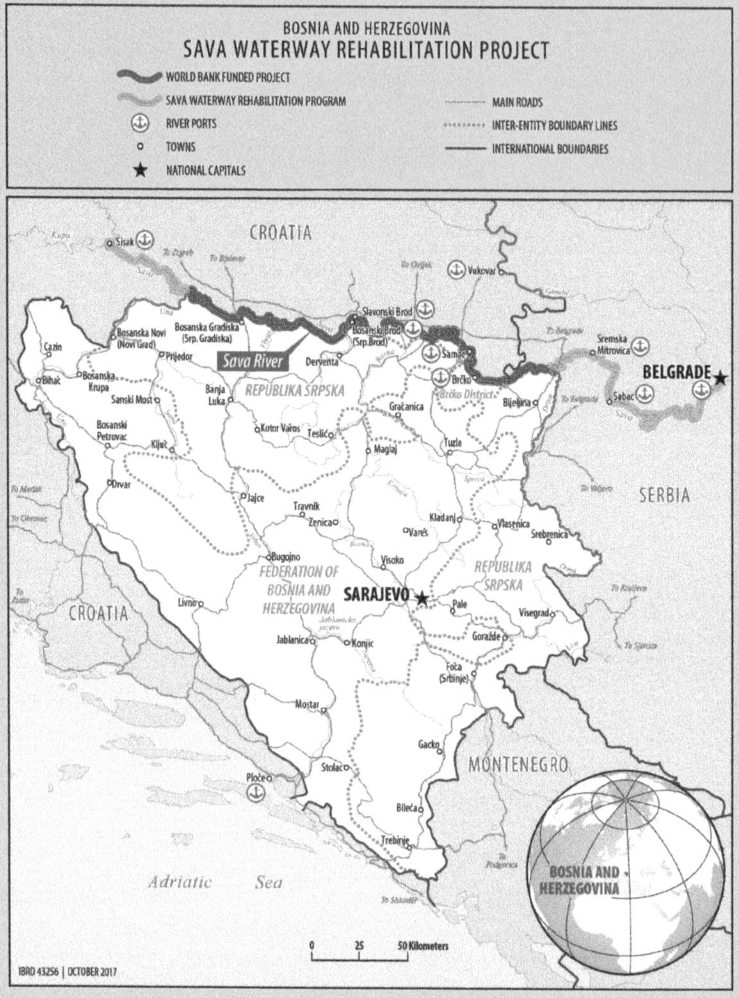

entire waterway had dwindled to less than 400,000 tons a year, reflecting limitations on navigability, draft, a lack of navigational markings to indicate the channels for safe passage, and the danger from unexploded ordnance and unmarked wrecks. In some of the river's upper sections, navigation was possible for only 100 days a year or less because of draft restrictions. The dangers were so large that the owners of vessels could not obtain insurance to operate on the waterway.

By the early 2000s, these countries realized that the status quo was unsustainable, so they created a Framework Agreement on the Sava River Basin (FASRB), with the support of the Stability Pact for Southeastern Europe (SPSEE), the Office of the High Representative (OHR) in Bosnia and Herzegovina, and the European Union (EU). The Framework Agreement was signed in Kranjska Gora (Slovenia) in December 2002 by Slovenia, Croatia, Bosnia and Herzegovina, and the former Federal Republic of Yugoslavia (as Serbia and Montenegro were known at that time). The Framework Agreement came into force on December 29, 2004. It sought to create an international navigation regime on the Sava River and its tributaries; a regimen for sustainable water management; and various measures to prevent or restrict the risks and eliminate the hazards to navigation.

The Framework Agreement also created the International Sava River Basin Commission (ISRBC), based in Zagreb, an efficient, capable organization that was to design/implement a program to carry out these tasks and liase with the Danube River Basin Commission.[2] The Sava River was designated an International Waterway, along with the three ports of Belgrade (Serbia), Brčko (in Bosnia and Herzegovina), and Sisak (Croatia). The commission's operating costs were to be covered by the participating countries, which would also provide more funds for further agreed-upon activities. The ISRBC commissioned a prefeasibility and feasibility study and the necessary environmental impact assessment (EIA), which were finalized at the end of October 2008. They recommended that the Sava River rehabilitation should occur in two phases: from Belgrade to Brčko, achieving Class Va status; and from Brčko to Sisak, achieving Class IV status.[3]

The program was considered regional because it involved a shared public good (the Sava River), the different parties showed ownership, and there were clear regional spillover benefits and a mechanism for coordination among the national governments. Moreover, it was supported by the European Union, the Stability Pact for South Eastern Europe, the Office of the High Representative, and the World Bank. The private sector was interested in investing in vessels, port structures, and the river's operations/maintenance if it was safe and reliable, and the parties agreed on the goals. What could possibly go wrong? Unfortunately, a great deal.

INSTITUTIONAL CHALLENGES TO WORKING ACROSS BORDERS

While the three national governments supported the proposed program, the level of support differed, sometimes markedly, reflecting the asymmetric distribution of costs and benefits, the countries' domestic priorities, and the resources available to each. The estimated cost to raise the

height of the bridges to allow safe passage for larger vessels underneath, dredge and protect the river, introduce electronic marking/vessel identification and tracking systems, and remove sunken wrecks was €87 million.[4] However, based on the river length or border in each national territory, costs were to be split between the three main countries—Croatia (61 percent), Serbia (20 percent), and Bosnia and Herzegovina (19 percent)—while the main beneficiaries (Serbia, and Bosnia and Herzegovina) were responsible for the smallest shares, reflecting the part of the river within their boundaries. Serbia, despite the modest amount of investment it would need, saw the Danube River and Tiso River as its main priorities, reflecting the traffic carried on those systems.

Another problem was in Bosnia and Herzegovina: Under the Dayton Peace Accords, transport and related infrastructure were the responsibility of the two entities, the Federation of Bosnia and Herzegovina (FBH) and the Republika Srpska (RS) and their ministries, but international transport agreements were the responsibility of Bosnia and Herzegovina's State Ministry of Transport, which believed it was responsible for these transport links. The Republika Srpska did not accept this. Although it supported the project, it did not recognize the authority of the state government of Bosnia and Herzegovina. Since the government had no authority to borrow money and no income to repay debt, World Bank funds had to be provided to or through the entities. This was a formidable obstacle.

Similarly, the Dayton Peace Accords placed responsibility for air transport and regulations between the entities at the state level: the Federation of Bosnia and Herzegovina and the Republika Srpska.[5] The accord's Annex 9 implied that the state was responsible for international and interentity water infrastructure, such as river traffic—which the Republika Srpska also disputed. To confirm the mandate, a state-level law on inland water transport would be needed. Although one was drafted, it was never adopted, because of the opposition from the RS representatives in the State Assembly, who believed that the Federation of Bosnia and Herzegovina and the Republika Srpska, along with BAD, were responsible for all intra-entity river traffic, along with all aspects of waterway management/operations/infrastructure for the Sava River sections within their borders.

The laws to regulate vessels on the Sava River in Bosnia and Herzegovina were also unclear. On the sections where it crossed Serbia, traffic would be regulated according to its Law on Internal Navigation.[6] Where it crossed Bosnia and Herzegovina, traffic would be regulated by Bosnia and Herzegovina's Law on Internal and Maritime Navigation.[7] While there was some symmetry between the laws, it was unclear which one regulated traffic on sections shared either with Croatia or Serbia, or which law regulated traffic on the short section of river within BAD boundaries. This issue could have been resolved, but again there was no political consensus. While the international organizations proactively helped with the drafting and signing of the Framework Agreement and created the International Sava River Basin Commission, preparations continued against a backdrop of waning international influence in the domestic affairs of Bosnia and Herzegovina. Without this international support, obtaining the consensus of key subnational stakeholders (primarily the entities) was impossible, and ultimately derailed the whole process.

Another problem involved which agency would maintain the river in Bosnia and Herzegovina. If the entities were responsible for the infrastructure, then their respective ministries of transport would ensure it was navigable and safe. But the management and maintenance of the river appeared to be the responsibility of the two entity's ministries of environment and water, and the two line agencies for managing water resources in the basin. Again, the situation was confused but could have been resolved with a political consensus. Details about the role of the private sector were not even discussed because

the countries could not find common ground on the larger issues.

PRACTICAL CHALLENGES TO CROSS-BORDER IMPLEMENTATION

The next stage of preparation required the engineering designs (for river protection, dredging, and channel enhancements), including the hydraulic modeling of water flow given rainfall and runoff predictions, and safeguards for the whole length of the river. The World Bank team originally proposed that Bosnia and Herzegovina apply for a Project Preparation Advance (PPA)—which could equal up to 20 percent of the credit/loan amount—to fund the work for the Bosnian and Serbian sections. Croatia, as an EU candidate country, could have sought an EU grant to cover its preparations. The World Bank proposed that Bosnia and Herzegovina use a PPA to pay for the limited design work for the Serbian section because most of the design work was on the section in Bosnia and Herzegovina, and Bosnia and Herzegovina would also receive a disproportionate share of the benefits when implemented. However, The Republika Srpska's Ministry of Finance ruled against this, noting that a PPA would require the same approvals as any loan or credit agreement. Given the lack of political consensus in the three parliaments in Bosnia and Herzegovina over ownership, responsibilities, and operations, it was unlikely to be achieved.

The International Sava River Basin Commission then brokered an agreement between the three national governments. At that level, it was agreed that Croatia would be responsible for developing the design on the section from Brčko to Sisak, using financial assets from the available Instrument for Pre-Accession Grant (IPA) funds and EU grants. The EU was willing for the grants it gave to one country to be used to benefit another, as long as the design of the downstream section was progressing. The tripartite agreement followed the same suggestion for the downstream section as earlier: that consultants procured by Bosnia and Herzegovina would be responsible for preparing the design from the river mouth in Belgrade to Brčko. To this end, Bosnia and Herzegovina's Ministry of Transport applied for EU grant money under a different window than Croatia had used to fund the design/work to remove the embedded mines in Bosnia and Herzegovina and Serbia—which was needed before the design/dredging/construction phases could begin.[8] Unfortunately, Bosnia and Herzegovina's parliament challenged this before the grant agreement was signed between the EU and Bosnia and Herzegovina because it believed the grant money allocated to Bosnia and Herzegovina would be spent to benefit Serbia, without a clear quid pro quo from Serbia.

Even without these problems, the timeline for approving the grant was long, and it depended on the World Bank confirming that its funds would be available. However, the Bank's finances depended on preparations moving forward in the countries, including funds being approved to de-mine the river—something to which the EU would not agree until the World Bank committed to its proposed investment. This Catch-22 was difficult to overcome.

Implementation arrangements were also problematic. Croatia would use its line ministry as its implementing agency, while continuing to coordinate through the International Sava River Basin Commission. Serbia would use Plovput, the public agency with management and maintenance responsibilities on the Danube and Tiso rivers within its boundaries. In Bosnia and Herzegovina, the most efficient option would have been to establish a small coordinating unit at the state level, reflecting the status of the river and the need for international cooperation with the other two countries and the ISRBC, with maintenance contracted out to a suitable body. However, this was not acceptable to Republika Srpska, even if Plovput was the contracted party, as it did not recognize the authority of the State Ministry of Transport in Bosnia and Herzegovina in this area.

Financing for construction was equally problematic. Croatia and Serbia were both members of the World Bank Group's International Bank for Reconstruction and Development (IBRD); Bosnia and Herzegovina was a member of the World Bank's International Development Association (IDA), and thus eligible for financing at favorable (concessional) terms; and Slovenia, at that time, had graduated from the World Bank, and thus was not eligible for World Bank financing. The Bank committed to provide IDA financing for Bosnia and Herzegovina's share of the regional program, while the parallel project in Croatia was to be financed entirely with EU grants. Thus, while Bosnia and Herzegovina was willing to use nonconcessional funding provided by a multilateral development bank to rehabilitate the ports, river, and access infrastructure, Croatia and Serbia wanted to use EU grant money under different windows, each with a different timeline regarding availability and the likelihood of being provided, reflecting their respective status as candidate and preaccession countries.

The contracting/tendering strategies were also challenging because the river formed the border between two of the countries along much of its length. The design consultant needed to prepare an implementation/contracting strategy to launch works from the river mouth at Belgrade to Brčko (234 kilometers). It would have to show that the works were needed in three countries, two entities, and BAD, sometimes on different sides of the river and within the river in the same spot, using funds from three different sources, and with up to five implementing units. The practical challenges to designing such a contract in an efficient manner proved extremely difficult.

THE CURRENT SITUATION

The World Bank, after a preparation period of over four years, decided insufficient progress had been made and withdrew its potential support. This led the EU to withdraw its grants for the preparations and de-mining.

Even today, communities along the river and the vessels that operate on it must contend with challenges similar to the ones they faced in 1995.

MAIN MESSAGES

Strong regional leadership and coordination were and are needed at the national level and with key stakeholders at all levels, which did not happen. Agreements must involve technical decisions, as well as delineating financing and institutional responsibilities for preparing, implementing, and operating all the program's phases. While the international organizations proactively helped with the drafting and signing of the Framework Agreement and created the International Sava River Basin Commission, preparations overlapped at a time when international influence in the domestic affairs of Bosnia and Herzegovina was waning. Without it, obtaining the consensus of key subnational stakeholders (primarily the three entities) was impossible. While this is an exceptional case, the lesson is that international organizations must ensure a consistent level of support to the stakeholders throughout the process.

While this program was never implemented, progress was made in creating the Framework Agreement and the International Sava River Basin Commission, improving the sustainability of management in the river basin, and identifying the major challenges to introducing a navigation system. These actions would not have occurred without the initial financing, and more important, technical support from the international organizations working in the region. However, even if the program had progressed, financing the preparation and subsequent work would still have been a major obstacle, given the cross-border nature of the preparatory work and subsequent physical works interventions, both of which, if implemented in the most efficient manner, required the contractor to work across national borders. A pooled trust fund, administered by the World Bank, for preparing/implementing works and maintenance, would have helped resolve these obstacles, and also would have enhanced the World Bank's convening power.

NOTES

1. The Brčko Administrative District (BAD) was created by the Dayton Peace Accords, since the competing claims of the two entities, the Federation of Bosnia and Herzegovina (FBH) and the Republika Srpska (RS), were impossible to overcome, given that their territories overlapped in the Brčko District. The BAD is self-governing, and at that time was internationally supervised. The DPA was later amended and the BAD received the same status as the other two entities.
2. The International Commission for the Protection of the Danube River—based in Vienna—was created to ensure the sustainable, equitable use of water and freshwater resources in the Danube River Basin.
3. Class IV European inland waterways of international importance require a draft of 2.5 meters and allow vessels of 1,000 to 1,500 tons, while Class Va waterways require a draft of 2.5–2.8 meters and allow vessels weighing 1,500–3,000 tons.
4. The cost of removing the unexploded ordnance was to be funded by EU grants.
5. Dayton Peace Accords (1995), Annex 4.
6. Official Gazette of RS, November 14, 2001, no. 58.
7. Official Gazette of FBH, December 28, 2005, no. 73, year XII.
8. After the war in the western Balkans (from 1992 to 1995), many areas contained mines on both sides of the front lines. Despite extensive efforts to remove them, by the end of 2008, there were still 220,000 land mines and unexploded ordnance in over 13,077 locations, which were killing and injuring more than 30 people each year at the time the project was being prepared. A total of 1,755 square kilometers (3.4 percent of the countries' territory) was still considered hazardous. The Sava River's south bank was considered particularly dangerous because the river was the front line for much of its length.

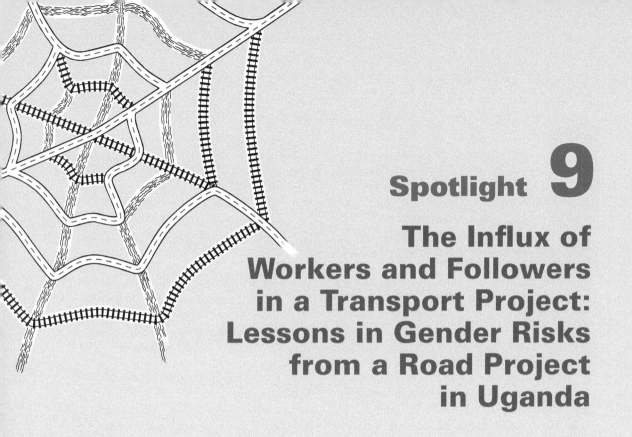

Spotlight 9

The Influx of Workers and Followers in a Transport Project: Lessons in Gender Risks from a Road Project in Uganda

Bank-financed projects often involve civil works on road corridors that require workers and goods/services to be supplied from outside the local area because local labor is not available or lacks the necessary skills. In many cases, the influx of workers and service providers is compounded by others who follow the workers to sell them goods/services or to find jobs and business opportunities. This rapid in-migration to the project area is called a *labor influx*. Under certain conditions, it can negatively affect the host communities (World Bank 2016a).

LABOR INFLUX AND GENDER RISKS

An influx of labor and service providers can pose various risks. Appraisers, project sponsors, and other stakeholders may fail to recognize the issues and their effect on the project, especially when problematic social behavior is culturally tolerated or even accepted, nationally or locally. The risks are varied.

Risk of social conflict. Conflicts can flare up between local communities and construction workers that may be related to religious, cultural, or ethnic differences, or based on competition for local resources, and put pressure on already-overstretched social services. Tensions can also occur or be sparked among different groups in the labor force, and preexisting conflicts in the local community may be exacerbated. Ethnic and regional conflicts may be aggravated if workers from one group move into the territory of another. Some workers coming from outside the region may have higher incomes than the local workers, which can cause resentment, particularly when the newcomers have relationships, with married women and girls.

Increased risk of illicit behavior and crime. The newcomers may increase feelings of insecurity in the local community. Criminal activities may increase, including theft, physical assaults, substance abuse, prostitution, and human trafficking both by locals and newcomers drawn to the area by the project. Local law enforcement agencies may not be equipped to deal with the temporary increase in population.

Influx of additional population (followers). Especially in projects with large footprints and/or a longer time frame, others may

257

migrate to the project areas, exacerbating problems of the labor influx. These people may look for jobs with the project. The followers could also include worker's family members, as well as other traders, suppliers, and service providers (including sex workers). The influx is induced by the heightened economic opportunities surrounding the road construction investment.

Impacts on community dynamics. Depending on the number of newcomers and their engagement with the host community, the composition of the local community and social dynamics can change significantly, and preexisting social conflict may intensify.

Increased burden on and competition for public services. The presence of workers and service providers (and sometimes their families) means more demand for public services such as water, electricity, medical care, transport, and education. This is particularly the case when the influx is not accompanied by extra or separate supply systems.

Increased risk of communicable diseases and burden on local health services. The influx can introduce communicable diseases, including sexually transmitted diseases (STDs), or incoming workers may be exposed to diseases to which they have low resistance. Both situations strain local health resources. Workers with health concerns—such as substance abuse, mental issues, or STDs—may not wish to visit the project's medical facility and instead may go to local medical providers, further straining local resources. Health and rescue facilities may be overwhelmed and/or ill equipped to address the industrial accidents that occur on large construction sites.

Gender-based violence (GBV). Construction workers are mainly younger males who are away from home, are separated from their families, and are unknown in the local areas. They may believe that they can behave in ways they normally would not, without fear of repercussion. This typically leads to fraternization—close social relations considered inappropriate with those who are unrelated to one another, typically with local females. It also leads to unacceptable and/or illicit practices, such as unwanted aggressive advances and sexual harassment of women/girls/minors and exploitative sexual relations.[1] In addition, it may lead to an increase in human trafficking, where women and girls are forced into sex work. In rural settings, where law enforcement is limited, the risk of sexual harassment, especially of younger females, is apt to be high. It can become dangerous for them to walk on roads to and from schools, markets, jobs, and water collection points. They often face rude stares or derogatory comments, taunting, hounding, groping, or rape. Women are especially afraid to walk alone in poorly lit or isolated areas.

Sex work. The high influx of outside workers can spark or lead to more sex work. The concentration of male workers who earn relatively higher incomes, can draw in young girls and women, exacerbating the risks of gender-based violence and STDs.

Child labor and school dropouts. Increased opportunities for the host community to sell goods/services can lead to children being asked to produce and deliver them, which, in turn, means they must drop out of school. Young women, in particular, may drop out because of early marriages or pregnancies.

Local inflation of prices. A significant increase in the demand for goods/services can lead to price hikes and/or crowding out of local consumers.

Increased pressure on rental accommodations. Depending on workers' income and their accommodations, demand for housing may increase, which can also cause price hikes and crowd out local residents.

Increases in traffic and related accidents. Transport of supplies and workers can increase traffic, accidents, and the burden on local facilities. Some drivers with the project may speed on the construction roads, causing accidents and injuries.

These effects are usually worsened by the low capacity (at the local level) to manage and absorb the incoming labor force, especially when civil works are in or near vulnerable communities and other high-risk situations.

THE NEGATIVE IMPACTS OF A LABOR INFLUX RELATED TO A ROAD PROJECT IN UGANDA

In a road project in Uganda—the Uganda Transport Sector Development Project (TSDP) and Additional Financing—supported by the World Bank, the negative outcomes of the labor influx were profound. The project aimed to improve the links and efficiency of Uganda's transport system by upgrading its national road network and improving the management of the roads, road safety, and transport. It was launched by the Uganda National Roads Authority (UNRA). Work on the 66-kilometer stretch from Kamwenge to Fort Portal Road begun in August 2013 and was expected to be completed by January 2016. But the road project had a number of negative environmental and social impacts, such as exacerbating existing GBV and Violence Against Children (VAC) that overwhelmed the project and led the World Bank to suspend and subsequently cancel it in December 2015 because the government failed to conform to certain environmental and social standards/practices. The project offers several important lessons in understanding the types of gender risks that can arise and how they must be managed.

The project was the subject of a World Bank Inspection Panel investigation. The panel's request for inspection, registered on September 28, 2015, addressed complaints from communities along the Kamwenge-to-Fort-Portal road alleging a variety of negative environmental and social impacts, in addition to those identified by the project's Environmental and Social Impact Assessment (ESIA). The GBV impacts included the road workers' sexual relations with minor girls, as well as sexual harassment of female employees.

Confirming the facts in the allegations was extremely difficult (World Bank 2015)—partly because many community members and officials were reluctant to discuss the issues. However, over time, the World Bank's missions gained more insight into the complaints, particularly when the Bank hired social consultants in April 2015. The Bank also worked closely with the civil society organization Joy for Children Uganda (JFCU), which supported the community in lodging the complaint during a mission in May 2015. As a result, the Bank concluded that there was credible evidence that some road workers had engaged in sexual misconduct with minors. This demonstrated to the Bank yet another side of the serious nature of the GBV risks associated with the labor influx that needed to be mitigated.

Lessons learned

The World Bank prepared a detailed report describing the issues and the Bank's response at the corporate and project levels (World Bank 2016b). Three major lessons stand out from the experience in this report.

Lesson 1. It is necessary to create a clear institutional architecture and understand/address capacity constraints. This involves defining the roles/responsibilities of different parties to address gender-based risks so they can collaborate to mitigate them. Responsibilities need to be legally and contractually binding. All parties must ensure compliance with national laws, standards, and regulations related to occupational health and safety, labor welfare/conditions, the environment—including management of quarries, social issues (specifically gender issues), and road safety. These parties include the implementing agency (usually the road agency/authority acting as the employer on the road contract); road works contractor (including subcontractors); the supervising engineer; districts or local governments where the roads cross local communities; central government ministries responsible for gender, education, and health; local community service organizations that work on these issues (for prevention and response); and the police. These parties need a joint mechanism for working together to address gender-related risks. Financial resources and arrangements also need to be clear to avoid turf wars. Further, it is critical to appraise the different parties' capacities to carry out their responsibilities. If weaknesses are observed, the project needs to develop an action plan to overcome them before it is too late.

Lesson 2. It is important to understand the social and environmental context of the project. More must be invested initially to understand the environment where the project will be implemented. This social context is essential to identify the broad risks to poor rural communities, among others, caused by large influxes of local and foreign construction workers, and then create measures to reduce them. Further, social/tribal norms, behavior, and culture must be examined to address gender-based risks. There should be stakeholder focus groups, interviews, and meetings. An upstream assessment is also needed to identify social and environmental issues in projects, focusing on the country context, as well as the local context.

Lesson 3. It is important to prepare/launch measures to address emerging gender risks. The main recommendations from the Environmental and Social Impact Assessments (ESIAs) and stakeholder focus groups, interviews, and meetings must be translated into actions in the project's environmental and social management plans and supervised regularly. A fundamental change is needed to ensure that systemic social risks are addressed in a timely manner in the ESIAs and Environmental and Social Management Plans (ESMPs) of infrastructure investments; appropriate mitigation measures are identified to deal with them; enforceable construction-related mitigation measures are included in the contract; the capacity of implementing entities to manage the contract and enforce the measures is carefully appraised; and the World Bank's supervision of the measures' implementation become a focus of Bank support. The ESMP and mitigation measures should be an integral, enforceable part of construction contracts. The site-specific ESMP should be approved in a defined period after construction begins. These activities, and the cost of the measures, should be explicit in the bidding documents and final contracts to ensure they are implemented. Best practice measures include the following:

- Ensure that the borrower is committed to addressing these issues.
- Address child protection risks before the project begins and throughout the project cycle.
- Incorporate social and environmental mitigation measures into the civil works contracts.
- Incorporate strong environmental and social oversight responsibilities and staffing needs in the supervising engineer's contract. It is critical that an independent third party oversee issues related to GBV.
- Improve the quality of the ESMPs and ensure that labor influx concerns are included.
- Ensure that local authorities are actively engaged.
- Ensure that the contractor and supervising engineer implement their mandates on these issues.
- Ensure that adequate community-engagement and grievance-management committees are created to receive, channel, and refer or respond to complaints or issues.
- Provide adequate resources for this work.
- Agree on identification and reporting protocols for GBV and violence against children when these occur and ensure that information flows from households to the responsible parties (police, referral service providers, institutions' management) for timely action.
- Develop and implement a zero-tolerance sexual harassment policy.
- Implement a workers' code of conduct that is included in their contracts and is enforced.
- Launch awareness campaigns for workers and communities through education and communications materials (such as posters), as well as through the local media, with radio and TV talk shows, advertisements, or programs.
- Encourage the participation of all stakeholders including men to prevent GBV within

the community and worker-led efforts on the employee's side to prevent GBV.

- Encourage the local recruitment of workers.
- Empower women and girls with job opportunities through affirmative action measures during the recruitment process.
- Provide gender-segregated sanitation facilities at all project sites.
- Ensure safe walking paths for women, children, and the disabled by maintaining easy access, introducing traffic management controls, and conducting safe infrastructure and road safety campaigns.
- Ensure that sufficient background checks are made on the workers and obtain information about them—including their names, places of origin, next of kin, and reference letters from previous employers or authorities from the previous places they lived. Issue identity cards so the public can easily identify them.
- Identify workers who will address these issues and place them throughout the workforce to act as the eyes and ears on the ground.
- Ensure that worker accommodations do not create opportunities for committing sexual offenses by restricting housing to certain areas and collaborating with local authorities and landlords to monitor and report on behavior that violates the code of conduct or the country's laws.
- Ensure strict fleet control arrangements, especially so drivers do not commit crimes or drive recklessly.
- Hire an HIV/AIDS service provider to develop awareness, counseling, testing, treatment and support for workers and community members, including highly vulnerable groups like sex workers.
- Ensure a partnership with a civil society organization(s) throughout the project if risks are great.
- Build the host communities' resilience using empowerment models for children and youth, such as BRAC International's Empowerment and Livelihoods Assistance (ELA) model for adolescent girls.[2]
- Ensure that those in power do not retaliate against people who identify risks related to the project. Provide opportunities for anonymous reporting through hotlines and coordination with the police.
- Collaborate with police authorities to ensure that workers' criminal behavior is punished and thus deters such future behavior.
- Ensure that response measures are created, including a minimum package for survivors of gender-based violence (referral paths for health, psychosocial support, legal redress, reintegration into schools, livelihood assistance and training programs, fighting stigma, and protection of the identities and dignity of survivors).

NOTES

1. The term "minor" is defined on the basis of a country's legal framework. In many countries, the age of consent (which determines who is no longer a minor) is 18 years. The World Bank, in line with UN Secretary-General's Bulletin guidance of 2016, takes the cutoff age to be 18 years (World Bank 2016a).
2. See http://www.brac.net/search/item/723 -empowerment-and-livelihood-for-adolescents.

REFERENCES

World Bank. 2015. "Management Response to Request for Inspection Panel Review of the Uganda Transport Sector Development Project – Additional Financing (P121097)." World Bank, Washington, DC.

———. 2016a. "Managing the Risks of Adverse Impacts on Communities from Temporary Project-Induced Labor Influx." Note, Operations Policy and Country Services and Environmental and Social Safeguards Advisory Team, World Bank, Washington, DC.

———. 2016b. "Uganda Transport Sector Development Project—Additional Financing: Lessons Learned and Agenda for Action." World Bank, Washington, DC.